Autobiography
of
Dr. Karl Ernst von Baer

Dr. Karl Ernst von Baer

Autobiography
of
Dr. Karl Ernst von Baer

Edited and with a Preface by
Jane M. Oppenheimer

Science History Publications
U.S.A.

Originally published as *Nachrichten über Leben und Schriften des Herrn Geheimraths Dr. Karl Ernst von Baer, mitgetheilt von ihm selbst* by Vieweg, Braunschweig, 1886 (second edition)

Published in the United States of America
by Science History Publications/U.S.A.
a division of
Watson Publishing International
P.O. Box 493, Canton, MA 02021
© Watson Publishing International 1986

The present study is one of a series of *Resources in Medical History*, selected in collaboration with the American Association for the History of Medicine, and funded under the Special Foreign Currency Program of the International Programs Branch, National Library of Medicine, Bethesda, Maryland

Translator: H. Schneider, Israel Program for Scientific Translations
Scientific Editor: Jane M. Oppenheimer
Literary Editor: William R. Stewart
Indexer: Maria Coughlin

Library of Congress Cataloging in Publication Data

Baer, Karl Ernst von, 1792–1876.
  Autobiography of Dr. Karl Ernst von Baer.

  (Resources in medical history)
  Translation of Nachrichten über Leben und Schriften des Herrn
Geheimraths Dr. Karl Ernst von Baer.
  Reprint. Originally published: 2nd ed. Braunschweig: Vieweg, 1886.
  Includes index.
  1. Baer, Karl Ernst von, 1792–1876. 2. Biologists—Estonia—Biography.
I. Title. II. Series.
QH31.B15A3413 1986   574'.092'4 [B]   86–1924
ISBN 0-88135-079-6

Printed in India by Amerind Publishing Co. Pvt. Ltd., New Delhi

Preface to the English Edition

In 1853 Thomas Henry Huxley published an admirable translation, covering 63 pages, of selections from two of Karl Ernst von Baer's works: from an 1826 article on "The Relations of Affinity among the Lower Forms of Animals," and from the Fifth Scholion of von Baer's embryological treatise, the title of which Huxley translated as "On the Development of Animals, with Observations and Reflections." In a judgment that has often been quoted, Huxley said that von Baer's works "embody the deepest and soundest philosophy of zoology, and indeed of biology generally, which has yet been given to the world." When it was published the book containing this translation no doubt found its way into most good libraries of biology, but it is a rarity today. To the best of my knowledge this is the only extensive translation into English of any of von Baer's general works, and it is not very extensive at that.

In 1956 a translation, by C. D. O'Malley, of the short *On the Genesis of the Ovum of Animals and Man* appeared in *ISIS*, and the same year a translation, by A. W. Meyer, of von Baer's equally short *Commentary* on this treatise appeared in a somewhat flawed monograph. Von Baer is generally acknowledged to have been a thinker of paramount importance in the development of embryology, and he is well known for his broad views of nature, but readers of English not fluent in German, his native language, have had little opportunity to read his own words. Thus an English translation of his *Autobiography*, to the year 1864 (born in 1792, he died in 1876) is very welcome indeed.

The *Autobiography* is largely a treatment of von Baer's professional life. Slightly over two pages at the very end deal with what he called his "inner life." Here he wrote that he never knew how to plan a book: beginning is easy, but finishing is hard, he said. Indeed this book does not read as though planned at all. It rambles, it repeats itself. Sometimes the footnotes far exceed in length the passages they are designed to illuminate, as do some of the annotations to the list of writings at the end. For instance a "bibliographical" note to a reference to a short newspaper article von Baer had published on the fortunes and misfortunes of Reguly, a Hungarian philologist, covers eight fascinating pages of fine print in the list of *Writings* included in the *Autobiography*.

More than once in the volume von Baer advised his scientific audience to omit reading the first seven chapters and to begin at Chapter 8, which discusses his studying with Ignaz Döllinger and the beginning of his life as a mature scientist. It is true that the first seven chapters are devoted largely to von Baer's educational experiences in Estonia, where he was born, and to his theories of education. But not only pedagogical experts will find these chapters of interest; they were far-seeing, written at a time when professional science was just beginning to come into its own, and when a place had to be made for it in a classical curriculum centuries old.

On the strictly scientific side, biologists will find an exposition of his embryological ideas particularly interesting. Von Baer abstracted thoughts expressed in his technical works at greater length that may be new to some who emphasize only his importance as a proponent of the new epigenesis. He saw some value in competing ideas, also. "The conclusion which I had come to during my work with the chick . . . held that all apparently new formations were in fact, during their development, transformation." Caspar Friedrich Wolff went too far in his emphasis on principles of epigenesis, he wrote further on. "It is true that neither head, nor limbs, nor any other parts are already present, but they become. Yet they do not come into existence by truly new formation, but by a transformation of something already existing."

The *Autobiography* also contains much of interest relating to personal aspects of his professional life. He was petulant over what he believed to be tardy recognition of the importance of his discovery of the mammalian egg, and over his problems with his publishers over the incompletely published second volume of the *Embryology of Animals*; these derived in part from his moving from Königsberg to Saint Petersburg in 1834. He sometimes wrote polemically, in the fashion of his day. He gave some reasons for his move to Saint Petersburg and his near-abandonment there of embryology in favor of earth sciences and anthropology, but his explanations are not thoroughly convincing. A constellation of factors was no doubt at play in the mind and emotions of this complex man that is beyond satisfactory analysis. His predecessors Caspar Friedrich Wolff and Christian Pander had before him moved from Germany to the Imperial Academy of Sciences in Saint Petersburg, and once there had all but abandoned embryology; Von Baer did not even mention this. But his health, and his love of the outdoor life, were important components of von Baer's decision, and these he discussed frankly. In this light, but also for their own sake, readers will be fascinated by his vivid descriptions of the hardships he endured during some of his geographical explorations, and by his consummate physical courage.

His intellectual courage was no less considerable. Perhaps the most outstanding attribute of his personality that imbues his writing throughout is his complete and utter honesty. Just as the single idea of development permeated all his writing and united the most diverse threads of his thought, a single trait, *integrity*, underlies all aspects of his person as they are illuminated by his wonderful *Autobiography*.

Jane M. Oppenheimer, Ph.D.

TECHNICAL NOTE TO THE READERS

The number of orthographic inconsistencies found throughout this book in its original languages seems unbounded. (The word *languages* is plural because from time to time German becomes Latin on a more than word-by-word basis.) Generic names are set sometimes in Italic, sometimes in Roman type. Specific names are sometimes capitalized, sometimes not. Many variations are found in the titles given to one periodical or another, whether full or abbreviated. One particular Russian surname, that of one of von Baer's travelling companions, contains a letter that is transliterated as *v* most of the times that it is used, but occasionally it suddenly becomes *w*. We are reminded of what T.E. Lawrence replied to the printer of *Revolt in the Desert* in response to a list of queries regarding inconsistencies in his spelling of Arabic proper nouns: "There are some 'scientific systems' of transliteration . . . . I spell my names anyhow to show what rot the systems are." Lawrence at least wrote always in sentences; von Baer even provides us with a partial sentence that deliberately stops in the middle and lacks punctuation at its non-end. He didn't get around to finishing it.

Von Baer's inconsistencies are part of his charm; by them he indicates to us what he measures as inconsequential. In this edition, we have tried to retain most of them to preserve the character of his style, but we have eliminated others for the sake of comprehensibility. The addition of *sic*s where appropriate would have left the text too polka-dotted to be readable, so we have almost always omitted them—a practice that we believe von Baer would have approved.

J.M.O.

Preface by the Order of the Knights of Estonia

The Order of the Knights of Estonia have requested their honored member, Doctor of Medicine and Philosophy Karl Ernst von Baer, Honorary Member of the Academy of Sciences of St. Petersburg and Corresponding or Full Member of most foreign academies, to provide them with an authentic account of his life, particularly the history of his education and his printed works. He has been so gracious as to let the Order have the account which follows.

Convinced that this story will be of interest not only to the narrow circle of our body, but also to the scientific world at large, and as a token of the very special esteem in which its famous member is held, the Order of Knights has resolved to print this account with the appended bibliographical list of his works on the occasion of his forthcoming Jubilee on the twenty-ninth of August of this year, as an expression of its sincere congratulations.

In the name of the Order of the Knights of Estonia:

1864

Baron A. von der Pahlen
Knight Commander

Remarks of the Author Concerning the New Edition of 1866

In that this autobiography is now being entrusted to the general book trade, a preface appears to be necessary on my part also.

As may be learned from the preceding public announcement by the Knights of Estonia, this body has requested me to compile an authentic account of the course of my life, as well as a complete list of my works, which they intended to have printed on the occasion of the then imminent celebration of my doctoral jubilee. I acceded to this honorable request, and the Order prepared an elegant edition of four hundred copies of this autobiography and list of my works with the provision that, except for the copies to be distributed in Estonia proper, the larger libraries in this country (Russia) and abroad, those scientific societies which also deal with the natural sciences, and some prominent experts, were to receive copies. As it turned out, however, demands for the book could not be satisfied, even in Estonia. Consequently, Mr. Röttger, proprietor of the local branch of H. Schmitzdorf's Imperial bookstore, obtained permission from the Knights to prepare a new edition which is intended for the general public.

Under these circumstances it appears necessary to stress the fact that, in its first third, this biography was written by me as a report *en famille*, which enabled me to voice my opinions concerning the educational system, with particular reference to my (Estonian) fatherland. Still, from the second third on, I had before my eyes the natural history public at large. If the book had been originally destined for publication in its entirety, I would have taken this attitude from the very beginning and would not have allowed the early period to occupy so much space. Also, in listing my works, I had access to our country's meticulously accurate bibliographical authors' index*. Not only would I be loath to revise the whole, but such a step would hardly appear expedient as the contents of a number of additional copies the Baltic provinces are to receive ought to be identical with those of the copies distributed earlier. Be that as it may, my advice to scientists wanting to cast a glance at this work is to disregard the first seven chapters and to start with the eighth, whence, in Würzburg, I myself started to become a scientist.

*See introduction [to section on *Writings*].

Altogether, this work was projected by me as no more than a report to the Order of the Knights of Estonia.

May, 1866   Dr. v. Baer

Table of Contents

ACCOUNT

OF THE

LIFE AND WORKS

OF

Dr. KARL ERNST VON BAER

PRIVY COUNCILLOR

AS TOLD BY HIMSELF

PUBLISHED ON THE OCCASION

OF THE

FIFTIETH ANNIVERSARY OF HIS DOCTORAL DEGREE

ON AUGUST 29, 1864

BY THE

ORDER OF THE KNIGHTS OF ESTONIA

SECOND EDITION

BRAUNSCHWEIG

FRIEDRICH VIEWEG AND SON

1886

NACHRICHTEN

ÜBER

LEBEN UND SCHRIFTEN

DES

HERRN GEHEIMRATHS

Dr. KARL ERNST von BAER,

MITGETHEILT VON IHM SELBST.

VERÖFFENTLICHT BEI GELEGENHEIT

SEINES

FÜNFZIGJÄHRIGEN DOCTOR-JUBILÄUMS

AM 29. AUGUST 1864

VON DER

RITTERSCHAFT EHSTLANDS.

ZWEITE AUSGABE.

BRAUNSCHWEIG,

VERLAG VON FRIEDRICH VIEWEG UND SOHN.

1886.

Introduction

Having been invited to prepare an authentic account of my works and life, I believed that if I were to comply with the latter part of this request, I had to concentrate primarily on the history of my education. As is usually the case with a scientific career, my life has proceeded without any particularly remarkable occurrences. If I were to attempt to write "interestingly," I would have to amplify and embroider some minor travel adventures. But even these, however important they may appear to him who experienced them, usually leave everybody else quite unmoved, unless, of course, one perishes in them, a contingency which, with me, has not yet materialized. For my part, therefore, I have always regarded an autobiographical undertaking as superfluous to the extreme and have never responded to whatever invitations of this sort I might have received. In any case, the year of my death not being known to me, my biography could never lay claim to being complete.

However, as the country appears to be interested in a comparison between past and present, and as I am able to go back far enough to contribute to such an enterprise, I readily consent at this point. Thus my endeavor will be focused more on the impressions I gathered and my philosophy of life as based on these, but primarily on the course of my education, rather than on a chronologically complete description of the course of my life with respect to country and family. Such an undertaking, it appears to me, would serve nobody. On the other hand, the time granted to me permitting, I should like to discuss in greater detail views which I have come to hold concerning educational affairs. Not that I think that I have much to say that is new to professional educators or, if they be of different opinions, that I could convert them to mine. I harbor too much genuine respect for these gentlemen not to know that they are not only *tenaces propositi*, but also tenacious in their opinions. I simply want to reserve the right to express my opinions—not preconceived, but evolved by experience—on other points of view as well. This experience might indeed be one-sided; it can do no harm, however, if one more voice makes itself heard. Now and then such a voice might fall on fertile ground.

As far as concerns the works published by me, these are listed in the "General Author Index of the Provinces of Livonia, Estonia, and Courland" (*Allgemeinen Schriftsteller—Lexicon der Provinzen Livland, Ehstland und Kurland*) by Recke and Napiersky (four volumes in 8°, 1827–1832), and, particularly, in "Addenda and Continuations (including supplements)" [*Nachträgen und Fortsetzungen (nebst Ergänzungen)*] by Napiersky and Beise (two volumes,

3

1859–1861) with a completeness which astounded me, as I myself had contributed nothing to this end. When this reference work was prepared, I was indeed invited to indicate my printed works of which, at the time, there were only a few. Although I did so, I was advised after some weeks that nothing had arrived. Whether the material reached them at a later date I do not know. The information concerning the date of my birth, etc., which in previous bibliographical works was frequently all wrong, is quite correct here. However, these data could have been extracted from the *Curriculum vitae* which I had to prepare for the authorities on occasion of my graduation. However diligently the scrupulous authors of "Addenda and Continuations" (*Nachträge und Fortsetzungen*) might have leafed through the literature of Russia, they were bound to miss some of the works published in Königsberg. On the other hand, they attributed a "Contribution to the History of Syphilis" (*Beitrag zur Geschichte der Syphilis*) (Oken's *Isis*, 1826, p. 728) to me in which I had no part. The author of this article writes under the signature of S. J. Beer, general practitioner, Würzburg. He defends the Jews against the allegation that syphilis was prevalent among them at an earlier date than among other people. The Hebrew text to which this allegation refers supposedly indicates the opposite. This is entirely foreign to me.

The list appended to this work is, therefore, the most comprehensive possible and I am not ashamed to admit that there were several items that had faded from my memory, which have been brought back to me only through the labors of Messrs. Napiersky and Beise. The meticulous completeness at which their author index aims has served me as a guiding principle—with one exception. The *Schriftsteller-Lexicon* went so far as to also include occasional poems and has even mentioned authors who were delivered of such opuscula only once. Now this, if not overpedantic, is at least overpatriotic. Who has not at least once produced a *pièce d'occasion*, and who, once the occasion has passed, still wishes to take responsibility for it?

Many of my still living fellow students from Dorpat will remember that as a student I was quite handy with rhymes. I think I may also say that they were mostly accepted with applause, but only because at those merry student meetings one is more inclined to honor good ideas than good verses or even profound thoughts. As far as I know, nothing of this was ever printed. However, in order not to foster the idea that something was lost by not mentioning these rhymed expectorations, even those for which printer's ink was misused, I hasten to confess that there was indeed a time when, encouraged by my facility at versification, I had the notion that there might be a poet hidden in my breast. However, an attempt at verification turned out to indicate quite unmistakably that Apollo was not among those who sat beside my cradle. When I tried to avoid jesting, the ridiculous managed to sneak in importunately in the form of hollow pathos or keening elegy.

In the same vein, it seems to me that some newspaper articles are in no need of special mention, in which, on occasion of publicly exhibited curiosities of nature, animals, malformations, etc., I served as the public's cicerone and thus became "Patron of Guides" in Königsberg. In any case, I would now be quite unable to prepare a complete list. There might have been two dozen or more of these articles.

Life

1. Birth

I came into the world on the seventeenth of February, 1792, according to the old-style calendar. Therefore, during my stay in German lands, I took pride in the fact that I was entitled to celebrate my birthday on the intercalary days and that I could expect fate to be obliged to grant me an almost fourfold life span if it wanted to permit me even a moderate number of birthday celebrations. As no joy in life is perfect, however, my claim to be an intercalary-day child according to the Gregorian calendar could not hold water despite the year 1792 having been a leap year. Disregarding the fact that the intercalary day proper is introduced after the twenty-third of February, it is the twenty-ninth which, for all practical purposes, is regarded as such, since it appears only once every four years. Yet in the eighteenth century, the difference between the Julian and the Gregorian calendar was only eleven days and, therefore, the seventeenth of February of the Julian calendar in the eighteenth century was, according to the Gregorian calendar, not the twenty-ninth, but the twenty-eighth of February.

I was born on the Estate of Piep in Jerwen County in the Province of Estonia.

My father, Magnus von Baer, later Knight Commander and *Landrat*, a sort of county executive, was the owner of this estate. My mother, Julie, was not only of the same family, but indeed my father's first cousin, as they both were the children of two brothers. Their union was blessed with ten children. We children cannot be taken as a proof of the opinion now frequently being debated, especially in Paris, that the off-spring of close relatives are often feeble, both physically and mentally, and in particular tend to be deaf-mutes. None of us children have lacked the gift of speech or were ever hard of hearing, either in our youth or in old age. Neither did any other mental or physical defects make themselves felt. It is true that three of us died in our younger years, but of common children's diseases, and a mortality of three out of ten prior to puberty is not extreme. The surviving seven generally enjoyed good health. My oldest sister died at the age of seventy-six, and the three of us who are still alive intend to travel at least that far.

2. Childhood up to My School Years

Notwithstanding the fact that I was ushered into this world on the Piep estate, my first conscious memories are not of there, but of another estate, Lassila in Wierland.

The owner of this estate, an older brother of my father whose first name was Karl, had already been married for some time to a Baroness Kanne of Coburg, but had remained childless. So, as the blessings of matrimony had begun to descend upon my father's house in a veritable outpouring, the end of which was not at all in sight, and as, on the other hand, both my uncle and my aunt enjoyed lively children, my uncle suggested that my father permit him a brotherly share in this abundance. As a result of this agreement, as soon as I was weaned, my slightly older brother Friedrich and I were taken to Lassila, where we were to be brought up as my uncle's children. My brother died very soon after this move; whatever I know of him is based on tradition. I was now guarded all the more carefully by my good-natured and kind aunt who was so fond of children that every child's face pleased her, and the face of a happy child could draw tears of joy from her. She was thus delighted by my high spirits and, as far as possible, tried to protect me from the consequences of my mischief. I must have sensed this since, as I still remember, I always became more talkative in her presence. My uncle was of a more serious cast; to him my prattle sometimes seemed too profuse and he used to scare me, saying that if I went on chattering so much, my lips would be used up to such a degree that, later, they would no longer cover my teeth. This gave me the first moments of anxiety in my life. However, from then on I looked carefully at every stranger entering our house to see whether one of them had used-up lips, and as I did not find even one, I was soon convinced that the danger could not possibly be that serious. I should also mention that the main axiom of my uncle's educational creed was that children had to "obey." According to tradition, this principle was enforced much more strongly in the past, and education was often measured by the amount of corporal punishment administered. Whether the teachings of Jean Jacques Rousseau had already affected us I cannot tell, but a great change seemed to have made itself felt in the method of education. Moreover, my uncle had also particular reasons not to make me timid. He was rather skilled, mechanically, drew and painted very charming water colors and, during the winter days, undertook all sorts of common mechanical jobs. No glazier was ever permitted to set foot on the estate; all glazier's work, without exception, was done by himself. He also liked to do joiner's work. I remember that once he made his wife a pair of elegant shoes and, another time, he painted a shawl for her, in the border of which a palm tree in a tropical landscape paraded, which excited my imagination. When he was engaged in this kind of work, especially in mechanical jobs, he liked me to be present to give him whatever small help I could. Once, in my fifth or sixth year, a plane cut deep into the little finger of my right hand, leaving a scar which I carry to this day and showing that, even if not uncut, I am by no means uncouth.

Altogether, my uncle had some peculiarities which made him almost an eccentric. After finishing whatever schooling the seventies of the previous century could offer, he and my father were sent to Germany to Erlangen University and the Court at Bayreuth. While my father devoted himself to the study of law, his older brother, in deference to the formerly almost universal vocation of local nobility, intended to dedicate himself to service in the army. Being used to independence due to the early death of his father, however, he could never take the decisive step to start soldiering in earnest, and thus he became all the more preoccupied with the minutiae of the art of war. He built entire tent camps in neat cardboard miniatures, with all the foraging and powder carts, kettles, and cannons made of wood and metal. The entire camp, including all its appurtenances, was carefully packed away in the drawers of a pretty cabinet and brought to the estate in Estonia, where it was shown to me now and then on select days of grace, with the provision of *noli me tangere*. At one of the smaller German courts, he had bought himself a major's commission and acquired such paraphernalia as a saber, pistols, and a uniform which, although never used, nonetheless were treated as valuable objects. A tent was also there which was put up from time to time and was used as a summer place, and a drum, to be beaten occasionally for my enjoyment, or else, maybe, to arouse warlike feelings in me. As the two brothers had divided their patrimony equally on their return from Germany, my uncle was able to set up his own army of which he was general, major, and the only soldier at the same time. It was obviously the cavalry to which he had aspired, as he never inspected his holdings except on horse, wearing large top boots, frequently even leather breeches. Just as it had been with regard to army service, so it became for other things as well for my uncle as his age advanced. Long at his preparations and pedantically occupied with trifling details, he often failed to carry out more substantial plans. He had always wanted to visit Germany again, and long after I had left the house even bought a large coach and made other preparations, but the journey itself never took place.

The Lassila estate, among the smaller estates of the country, was pleasantly located, with more charming diversity in its surroundings than is usual in our flat country. A small, L-shaped residence which contained only narrow rooms, it seemed designed to drive people out into the open air, weather permitting, and the steps to the entrance, adorned with two beautiful trees

—a magnificent maple and a younger elm—immediately took those going out into their shade. This was the place where my uncle liked to sit in the summer when he had nothing to do; here, too, he gave audience to his overseers when they came to report to him. A sloping, flower-dotted courtyard enclosing two ponds surrounded by solitary willows beckoned one on, and led into a heavily shaded poultry yard where each brooding hen, duck, goose, and turkey had its nesting box in the shape of little red-roofed houses, or small tents made of wood. When visited during the hatching season, the entire place exuded an uncommonly homey and peaceful atmosphere of which I still have a vivid memory. After hatching season, however, this colorful mixture of fowl and their happily produced offspring crowded the yard and the ponds and afforded the boy the opportunity to engage the strident turkeys in his first heroic deeds, and to practice his steadfastness on the mother geese hissing with their heads thrust forward. Cattle were never permitted on the carefully tended courtyard, and horses only if led.

By today's standards, the garden bordering on another face of the residence could by no means be called pretty, although my uncle was a diligent gardener who planted every tree and tied up every flower himself, at which activity I had the honor to be his faithful famulus. He had his whims however; he had an artificial "Parnassus" piled up, surrounded by a deep moat, and he shaped lilac bushes into a labyrinth or a helix, and fruit hedges into a serpentine path or a maze. I cannot claim that these curiosities were in any way beautiful, but they stirred a boy's imagination, which was also occupied by a delicate, colorful bee house. It was not, perish the thought, a crude bee hive, but rather had all sorts of pavilions, bowers, and similar items. Altogether, this garden could be said to represent an earlier taste which was about to disappear. It is true that the period in which even trees were given artificial shapes had already passed; I saw such things preserved in some places only as curiosities. Thus, the trees were permitted to grow as they could and would, provided their trunks presented a picture of order, i.e., they were aligned in rows. Ornamental and fruit shrubbery were not tolerated, even less so, flowers in groups or clumps. Pathways that were not dead straight were really unthinkable as far as gardens were concerned. On the whole, nature in a garden was not permitted more liberties than absolutely necessary to obtain fruit and flowers. My uncle had sternly decided that the courtyard and its surroundings belonged to nature, the garden to art. There, every blade of grass and every flower was to be protected; here, every grass blade not serving as trimming, every "wild flower" was considered an outrage, and when walking in the garden, he was usually armed with a hoe in order to nip any voluntary activity on the part of nature in the bud. Not only the pathways, but also the spaces for the fruit trees, were covered with a heavy layer of gravel, to keep a tighter rein on their vegetative force. This garden could pride itself on its excellent fruit. Its plums, in particular, were considered the best in the country.

The wider surroundings had nothing of the formal stiffness of the garden, but were pleasant and uncommonly variegated. Behind the poultry yard there was a moist valley floor and high-reaching black alders bordering a meadow adorned with magnificent oaks and other large trees and, at least in some spots, ending in flower-covered slopes.

The not very extensive fields were abundantly covered with flat limestone fragments which, though it was never found, made one believe that the solid limestone stratum could not be far below. Perhaps these limestone outcroppings had only been pushed together by geological processes in earlier times for here and there gravel hills rose up, which we used to call mountains. One of the more remote of these hills, which was embellished on top by a windmill, was a high mountain to me. The fields themselves were surrounded by birch saplings which, in the meantime, have grown into a birch wood. But as if to moderate monotony here also, a dark pine grove on a sandy hillock abruptly joined the birch trees.

Thus it was in these lovely surroundings that I romped about in the first years of my life. Not that these years can be said to have contributed much to my understanding of nature. There was nobody to enlighten me. My uncle, as I mentioned earlier, tried to become a "cavalier" by studying the art of war. Horticulture and agriculture, on the other hand, he learned from experience. In his limited library there was only one book in which the natural sciences must have had some share, since it contained a number of illustrations of animals of which I remember only one pair: the picture of a horned hare and that of a rhinoceros with one horn on the nose and another on its back*.

*My colleague in Königsberg, the witty astronomer Bessel, used to claim that memory had a predilection for the nonsensical and, as proof, he recited such nonsense verses from his childhood primer:

Ein toller Wolf aus Polen frass
Den Tischler und sein Winkelmaass.
   [A mad wolf, Polish, ate for fare
   The joiner and his measure—square].
or
Gebratne Hasen sind nicht bös,
Der Hammer gibt gar harte Stöss.
   [Roast rabbit's good, everyone knows,
   A hammer gives quite heavy blows].

which he was unable to rid his memory of, while he had long forgotten the more sensible verses. The deeper imprint made by the nonsense verses is probably due to the fact that early on they arouse contradiction even in children. The horned hare of that book may have stuck in my memory because I knew already of unhorned ones and, therefore, may have had my doubts. However, against the horn on the rhinoceros' back I could raise no objection. As far as I was concerned, it could have been located on the root of its tail; I would not have minded. How is it then that I definitely remember this picture, while

(Contd.)

Later on I was very glad to find the original of this illustration in C. Gessner's *Historia animalium*. Gessner, in turn, took it from Albrecht Dürer who, though never having seen a rhinoceros himself, had heard of one which had been brought to Lisbon, and painted it so**. As the same moderately-sized octavo volume also contained illustrations pertaining to heraldry, it must have had a really encyclopedic scope. Accordingly, whenever I brought home a snail's shell or a fossil that had become detached from its matrix at the lime kiln, my uncle tried to look it up in this one and only source of knowledge at his disposal, and it failed. My collected nature curiosities were regarded as family property and stowed away in a drawer so that I would not lose them, and for that very reason turned up lost, of course, which I much regretted, mainly because of a steeply-spiraled fossil snail that I did not see in a collection of snails from the Silurian limestone, and that I still remember distinctly.

I do believe, however, that the environs of Lassila did indeed awaken a certain sense or feeling for nature and its objects. At least, later on, I could never see cowslips without remembering how abundant they were in the courtyard of Lassila in the spring, or the delicate lady's slipper (*Cypripedium calceolus*), but remember the first ones which I saw on that estate. The earliest vivid impression that I can remember also came from an object of nature. My uncle and my aunt had to make a formal visit to a neighboring estate (Jömper) to welcome a newly married couple, or something of that sort. My presence was completely superfluous as there were no children there, but nobody dared to leave the madcap without supervision, and so they took him along. Once there, however, the order was: "Stay outside, we shall go in, and come out again soon to drive back home." Nobody, however, told me how close to the carriage I was expected to stay. Therefore I cheerfully started to reconnoiter

having no recollection at all of the others? When I later rediscovered this picture in Gessner's book, I was already a lecturer at the university. Since I then knew that the two horns of the rhinoceros were located on its head and since I realized from the book itself that that illustration was not at all drawn from nature but from the imagination, the fact suddenly emerged from my memory that I had seen the same picture in my early childhood. Other pictures, too, would probably have resurfaced if associated with similar contradictions. Without such, they were lost.

**The fact that C. Gessner included in his book a picture of which he must have known that its painter had never seen a rhinoceros, and the fact that he boastfully stated that it was done by a great master, has always served me as a proof of the slowness with which the idea developed that an object from the realm of the natural sciences must also be drawn from nature. Originally, these illustrations were only pictures of the conceptions in the minds of people, not of objects really seen. Thus there were also pictures of all the legendary animals mentioned in Albertus Magnus, in Olaus Magnus, etc. although no man had ever seen them. Nevertheless, these illustrations were reprinted time and again. C. Gessner was more critical and dropped most of them. Among the mammals, however, he let the rhinoceros pass, a horned hare's head, and some others, while a great many products of the imagination also stayed on in his volume on fish.

the new terrain, drifting from one courtyard into another, and suddenly, to my amazement and rapture, I perceived a peacock who, sitting on a fence, had spread his tail. This magnificence, this splendor, caused me to fall into an insensible stupor. The peacock too did not move, as if he enjoyed my admiration. How long I stood thus struck I do not know but, as I was soon to realize, it must have been rather long. That is to say, I did not wake up until somebody took my arm rather forcefully, and my foster mother stood in front of me, her face very flushed: "For heaven's sake! Where have you been? We were looking for you, we called, nobody answered; we searched for you in the pond to see whether you had drowned!" Still speechless, I could only use my nongrasped left arm to point to the peacock's tail, although I still did not know whether it was real or a delusion. Only then was I properly enlightened. The explanation, however, that the peacock is a bird just like our turkeys and, like the turkey, spreads its tail, satisfied me but little. The impression which this startling sight had made upon me was so lasting that even in my later manhood, after I had frequently seen stuffed peacocks in this pose, I often longed to see once again a tail spread by a living bird of this kind. As no opportunity of this sort seemed to offer itself for a long time, I conceived the fancy that soon after I did see such a sight again, I would have to die. Eventually, in my sixty-third year, as unexpectedly as in my childhood, I again saw a peacock with its tail spread, at a fisherman's place in the Astrakhan steppe. But how very different was the sight and its effect! With the exception of the arc of the brilliant ocellate spots, the rest of the fan seemed rather shabby and translucent as compared with the magnificence perceived earlier. Was it the meager nourishment of the steppe that did not permit the lateral barbs of the long tail coverts to develop fully? Had my imagination grown more experienced and thus more sterile, my sensibility dulled? All three factors probably acted together. As it was, I found the sight rather mediocre and altogether not worth giving up one's life for. Had I died soon after, my fancy would have been a higher presentiment; as it was, so it remained—a fancy.

It would be improper if I were to relate from the memories of my early childhood more than the fact that I really do not know much more of my activities during the long winters. I have more recollections of the beautiful summertime which I spent in the open air until driven back into the house by need for food and sleep. Then I was usually so tired that I went to bed immediately after supper; not infrequently, I fell asleep during the meal and had to be carried to my bed. This was not at all to my foster father's liking. He had acquired the habit of doing such mechanical work as did not require daylight in the late evening hours, and he carried on with it until midnight; on the other hand, he arose very late in the morning, when the rest of the household was already long in motion. The others, by way of compensation, went to bed early and left him solitary. Then—it must have been when I was six or seven years old—when once on a very starlit evening I saw a rather striking shooting star, the brilliant path of which I was able to follow almost down to the horizon, and as a result of this observation, burst into the room to spread the news that a star had just now dropped from the sky, my uncle used the opportunity to try to induce me to stay up later. My report elicited laughter, and my protestations to the effect that I had seen the star fall quite clearly were countered by the assertion that stars could not fall and what I had observed was a meteor. This statement, of course, was less than satisfying and only aroused my desire for more definite conceptions. At this point my uncle declared that if I would be present at eleven o'clock that night, when he was doing his glazier's work, he would give me full explanations about the stars and their doings; right now there was no time for it. To stay awake that long seemed impossible, therefore I asked the servants to wake me up at ten o'clock, so that at eleven o'clock I appeared, quite sprightly and wide awake. I cannot remember the explanations given me concerning the meteors. In any case, they were completely eclipsed by the information that the stars were all very large bodies, freely floating in the sky and much farther away from us and from each other than the nearest country manor. I thought my head would burst trying to digest these revelations. That night, my excited imagination did not let me fall asleep for a long time.

If it was the intention of my foster father to teach me that to satisfy my curiosity or thirst for knowledge (both cravings are originally probably identical, only directed at different objects) I had to learn to make sacrifices, he had achieved his aim. That which had been garnered by sacrifice was all the more valuable to me. There now followed—especially during the long winter months—many such nocturnal enlightenments, some of which I still remember. The affair with the stars led of necessity to other questions, such as the spherical shape of the earth, which I found quite unobjectionable. However, my credibility balked at the assertion that people on the other side "could not fall down." But there were quite different subjects, too, that were dealt with, such as elephants and other huge beasts, Lapps and Samoyeds, the deeds of Alexander the Great, etc. The latter belonged to the subjects that impressed me most deeply, so that I retained several details for the verification of which I later searched in the sources in vain. Altogether it is quite possible that unconsciously I imbibed a fair amount of "information" which really belonged to the realm of myths and which my preceptor himself had picked up somewhere as the truth and handed on as such. Thus I remember that certain large animals are supposed to sleep while leaning against trees, and that one cuts down these trees to catch the animals as they cannot get up again, once they are on the ground. Stories like this are repeated time and again in writings from the Middle Ages on into modern times.

These occasional and quite irregular lectures or discourses notwithstanding, I can by no means boast of early studies. As long as I was in Lassila I did not receive any regular schooling, and thus it came about that I was already in my eighth year without knowing one letter from another. As it was, my uncle thought more highly of physical than of mental training, and he had not the slightest doubt that I would join the army. Neither he nor my aunt had any inclination toward a planned course of instruction, and later it was said that I was to receive my schooling at my parental home. It appears that I was originally accepted in place of a son, and I also regarded them as my real parents, and addressed them accordingly. My only playmate at that time was a dog. As the attitude of this faithful animal toward turkey cocks and geese was the same as mine, it is a matter of doubt as to who imitated whom. In one respect, however, I must claim priority: the dog learned how to unlatch the back door only after I had mastered the art, so that I believe he took his ways of doing things from me. A further token of his acceptance of my superiority was the fact that he willingly served me as a riding horse. Later on, three more children were added to the household, one boy and two girls, the von Dannensterns, children of my father's sister, a widow who had lost most of the remnants of her small property by fire, but who had remained rich in children. All three of the new wards were younger than myself.

It was only then that I was told that I had other, real, parents who came to visit Lassila together with my brothers and sisters, and I was told I would be returned to Piep to enjoy the schooling which a governess had been dispensing to my brothers and sisters for two years now.

3. First Schooling at Home
(1799-1803)

In the summer of 1799, my foster parents brought me to Piep, where my foster mother tearfully said goodbye, while I walked in with a joyful heart to find an older brother, a still older sister, and a younger brother and sister, as well as a cousin, a girl slightly older than myself.

I came to consider the fact that I had not been burdened by regular schooling at too early an age as one of the most propitious circumstances of my life. Now that my powers had ripened, I had even begun to feel slightly ashamed of the fact that I could not yet read. I had the strongest desire to learn and, altogether, to emulate my older brother and sister whom I considered very learned—especially my sister, four and a half years my senior, who had early developed a certain good breeding combined with good sense, and who soon assumed the image of a wise priestess in my eyes, before whom I stood in awe. Later I learned to pity all children who could say of themselves, in the words of Chamisso:

> "Das Lesen war ein Hauptverdruss!
> Ach, wers nicht kann und dennoch muss,
> Der lebt ein schweres Leben!"
> [My reading was with vexation rife,
> But he who can't and yet still must
> He leads a most impeded life!]

In my more mature years, I was never able to read the story of the schooling of the precocious Karl Witte, as told by his own father, without a feeling of indignation. Whether the future professor was grateful to his father for having cut short his merry days of youth, I do not know; however, I doubt it. Such an extreme case of foolishness is fortunately rare, but parents, considering the mass of knowledge to be ingested, often fear of losing time, disregarding the fact that the desire to learn is infinitely more productive than irksome coercion and that where desire is lacking, very little is achieved; and whatever is accomplished is soon lost again.

I was given a simple A B C book, of genuine Reval print and cut. On the first page were the single letters in large print, then single syllables followed by several passages from the catechism, and on the last page a large rooster and some small chicks, all in the simplest of line-drawings, below which there was printed this admonition:

"Der Hahn reizt auf zur Munterkeit,
Auf, Schüler! geh zur Schul' bei Zeit!"
    [The roosters crow; the clocks, they chime:
    Up, pupil! get to schoo! on time!]

Also there were all kinds of short headings in the same continuous print, not broken up into syllables. The single letters of the first pages were spelled out for me by the governess, which took up several days. The next step was simple spelling according to the old mode, since the aged lady did not take kindly to new methods, even assuming that she had heard of them. However, I was most enticed by the rooster and his wise advice. Altogether, I held the book in high esteem as my first bound treasure and the foundation of a future library, no one before having ever trusted me with a book. Instead of picture books, I had received—and even then only sporadically—so-called "gold papers," these being sheets colored in red or blue with Adam and Eve in the center, complete with serpent and tree, and surrounded by diverse animals, all printed in pure gold. Now thoroughly despising these I often held this real book in my hands, after school hours too, and had my brothers and sisters read the complete lines to me. As I was blessed with a good memory, I retained the content of these lines and as I frequently looked at these headings and the separate syllables, I soon found, to my own surprise, that I could read without knowing how it had happened. The separate reading lesson continued for no more than two, at most three weeks after which the governess saw it superfluous to carry on this way; apart from this there were still the other scholastic arts to be pursued with me alone. I was to acquire further competence in reading together with the older pupils. But things were not quite prepared for it. Although my father had procured some good children's books, none were available in more than one copy. Yet we were four at school. How was that problem to be solved? The governess found a way. We were all seated around a narrow desk, my older brother and sister on one side, close to the corner, my cousin at the end and I opposite my brother and sister. Now, one after the other, we were each to read one sentence aloud. When my turn came, the governess turned the book around and held it in front of me. However, to keep our minds on the subject and off all sorts of pranks, we were supposed to follow the sentence just being read with our eyes, which in any case was necessary in order to be able to locate one's starting point at once. As my brothers and sisters were also rather keen on learning, everybody, including myself, was eager to start with his sentence the moment his predecessor had finished his. To this end, I had to get accustomed to follow the text while the book was still turned the other way. Thus, without anyone intending it, I learned to read inverted print. As soon as I had mastered this art, I looked for my sentence while the others were still reading theirs aloud and occasionally recited it before the governess had managed to turn the book toward me. Since she was annoyed at what she regarded as forwardness on my part, but suppressed her annoyance except for a slight growl through her respectable nose, I felt an urge to repeat this feat frequently. As far as I remember, this was the only trick I ever played on the worthy old lady. The skill I had thus acquired served me later for entertainment: I used to read some lines from an inverted book which I held in such a way that others had a proper view of it; there would always be one or another who promptly claimed that I must have known the paragraph by heart. I later put this accomplishment to a more serious use when unfolded, uncut book sheets were sent to me for approval: I was able to read the inverted pages without having to right the sheet every time.

It seems quite obvious that, in our hurried eagerness to chime in with our own little pieces, none of us really paid much attention to the text and context of what we were reading. The book thus maltreated was a volume of Weisse's *Kinderfreund* (The Children's Friend), a book which, for my age at least, was too broad and ponderous, although it might have been very suitable for an older child. But there was also Campe's *Kinderbibliothek* (The Children's Library), which was the right nourishment for my appetite during this and the next year. The verses easily stuck to my memory, where part of them are still to be found*.

Together with reading we naturally began writing also, which did not proceed half so fast with me as I felt the laborious drawing of the letters to be a very boring task. I found Bible history more entertaining; it made a ready impression as my reading skills had soon progressed to a point where I could read Hübner's *Biblischer Historie* by myself, and as I felt attracted by those strange characters depicted in woodcuts. Neither did reckoning, that is, numbering and the first four rules of arithmetic, present any difficulties.

As my private library was enriched by a colored picture book toward autumn, this circumstance was put to use to teach me the first rudiments of the French language. Going over the pictures, the governess told me the French, along with the German terms, for the various objects and their component parts. As far as I was concerned, this seems to have been a rather suitable method, as I remember that several words in my vocabulary have their origin in certain pictures. I was almost totally spared grammar, as far as I remember, so much did I hear my brothers and sisters recite the rules. Concerning geog-

---

*My memory must have been sticky indeed, as I know for certain that I had retained several fragments of the reading exercises of my older brother and sister from the *Magasin des Enfants* by their sound only, as at that time I knew not a single word of French, being preoccupied with memorizing the multiplication table. The pieces in question were those that were exclaimed with particular energy, e.g., the speech in which Tomyris addresses the head of Cyrus, which she had dipped in blood, and the reproaches of Jacob when shown the bloodied shirt of Joseph. It is true, though, that these reproaches were in verses, which always stick easily.

raphy lessons, I can only say that they were rather insipid and that I did not derive any benefit from them. Instead of being given separately a general survey of countries, rivers, or capital cities, let us say, I was to study the subject together with the other pupils. When I joined them, they were bogged down in the middle of France, an endless number of cities being mentioned and looked up in the maps in Homann's Atlas, and thus it continued with an entirely useless compilation of town names. I had so little understanding of the thing as a whole that, as Russia appeared on the map of Europe in green color, and as I found that Russian grass and trees are green, I believed for quite a while that other countries, too, must be the color—that is, yellow or red—in which they were represented on the map.

Altogether, it seems to me in retrospect that the governess was quite suitable for imparting the first elements of instruction, but less so for its more advanced stages. Thus, it was my luck that she was removed after the first year.

There now came into the house a middle-aged theology candidate by the name of Steingrüber, a foreigner who had had the courage to come to Russia to work as a teacher and, at the same time, to learn the Estonian language, in the hope of eventually obtaining a church living. This hope was realized in the end, though rather late, maybe because local people enjoyed more support or because his Estonian, however perfect, sounded somewhat foreign. For us, however, the main point was that not only was he thorough and, in particular, a proficient mathematician, but took pains to find the best methods, and altogether proved to be an eager and experienced teacher. Our entire instruction was now taken in hand seriously. In some subjects I was paired off with my cousin, for instance in French; in others I had to be tutored all alone. Together with my brother who was three years older, I took a course in elementary arithmetic, geometry, stereometry, plane trigonometry, and the first elements of algebra. This course, in particular, was excellent. Since Herr Steingrüber, being an accomplished mathematician, had completely mastered the subject, his instruction excelled in clarity. Otherwise I could hardly have followed it, since I was only slightly more than eight years old when the course began. Right at the beginning of the arithmetic course I was immensely impressed by the fact that, having been shown by the governess how to add, subtract, multiply, and divide, in which activities I had become passably proficient, I was now being made to understand the true nature of addition, multiplication, etc. In later years I was sometimes told of teachers who tried to teach small children the essence of these operations from the first moment, before the children had actually performed them, and then complained about the children's obtuseness. This I cannot but consider the wrong way to go about it. It appears to me that some practice in conceiving numerical quantities is required before these admittedly simple operations can be completely understood. To return to our mathematic studies, we fared equally well with geometry and, following that, with stereometry, but then Herr Steingrüber knew how to explain everything most graphically. Not only did he possess a nice collection of mathematical solids made of boxwood, but he let us prepare such bodies from cardboard or himself cut them anew from rutabaga, in order to prove, for example, that the volume of a cone was one-third of that of a cylinder of equal height and base. The theory of logarithms, which was given as part of the course in trigonometry, I also had no difficulty in understanding; at least I solved the set problems to the full satisfaction of everybody concerned, although later, due to lack of practice over several years, much became unclear again or was entirely forgotten. I was ten years old at the start of the course in plane trigonometry*. Should some conclude from this that I was gifted with an early acumen or a special talent for mathematics, I would be hard put to locate in my memory any other proof for such an assumption**. It appears that it was the lucid, slow, methodically progressing explanation that made it possible for me to understand it fully. Herr Steingrüber had such a predilection for the mathematical aspects of the various subjects, and such fluency in his discourse of them, that he also summoned the two girls of his school to a course in mathematical geography; so far as I know, they did not fail to understand it, although my cousin did not excel in studiousness and apprehension. The above branch of science, which is so thoroughly interwoven with life and holds the explanation for the most common phenomena is, so I believe, quite unjustly neglected in the education of girls or, at most, only briefly touched upon by mentioning the rotation of

---

*This is indeed not much if compared with the child prodigy Karl Witte who, at the age of twelve, wrote a treatise in Latin on higher mathematics. I wanted only to furnish some standard of comparison for common aptitudes and common education.

**On the other hand, I well remember a small incident which would indicate quite the opposite and which often amused me much later after I had grasped the importance of the book presented to me. I must have been about nine years old (since I was still taking reading lessons), when I had a visit from a boy from the neighborhood. He liked my reader so much that he asked me to let him take it home with him for eight days, and I was foolish enough to give it to him. The next day, at the appointed hour, I appeared without my book and reported what had happened. To the question as to what I was now going to read, I answered quite matter-of-factly, pointing at the small library of the teacher which, naturally, to me seemed rather large: "You have quite a lot of books. I could read another one." "Can you read everything?" asked the teacher, who was very dissatisfied with my impudence, the tone of his question already assuming a negative answer. However, I felt hurt by this tone and answered hopefully, "Yes, I can." The teacher went with large strides to his library, pulled out an octavo volume, and ordered me to read the title. I read aloud: *"Critique of Pure Reason* by Immanuel Kant" and looked at the teacher as if to say: why should this be difficult? Angrily, the teacher took the book, opened it in the middle and said, "Now read this page." That page, too, I rattled off briskly, and again looked at him as if to ask: "Didn't I read well?" "Have you also understood?" Understood! Understanding had never been stressed, only reading. I never thought of understanding, and only then realized that I had understood simple books without a special effort of will.

the earth about its axis and the explanation of longitude and latitude in descriptive geography. We boys had to prepare surveys, using a surveyor's table and ranging rods and, in my twelfth year, I had the great joy of presenting my father with a map, prepared by geodetic survey, of the farm and its immediate surroundings, including houses, etc., in which only the trees were drawn by the teacher, as my own attempts were not quite successful. From the above it can be seen that Herr Steingrüber always tried to make the mathematical sciences more interesting by their practical application. In order that we might become used to concise mathematical expression, after each lesson we had to copy the corresponding paragraphs from notebooks which he had prepared for the entire course.

Equally practical were the geography lessons which, based on Gaspari's "Textbook and School Atlas (Without Names of Towns)", started anew from the very beginning. We did not, as is now often the practice, copy the maps freehand, but were taught to trace them completely, using paper made transparent with linseed oil. This method may indeed seem more mechanical, but it takes much less time and since the outline of the countries had to be transferred again onto white paper with the aid of pin pricks which then had to be connected by lines that were subsequently colored, the eye rested on the boundaries of countries and provinces long enough for the memory to retain them, not being exposed to wrong shapes which, to a greater or lesser degree, always prevail with freehand drawings. Each of us boys prepared a complete school atlas and as this kind of work was to our liking we hit upon the idea of inventing a special game. We drew the separate countries to a scale in which they would fit sizable playing cards, taking the shapes of countries from maps of continents whenever the size of a country was too large, and glued the drawings onto thin cardboard rectangles of equal size, which we then used as playing cards in various games. The value of the countries, according to which they would trump one another, was their area as given by Gaspari, which one had thus to know in order to know the value of one's cards.

Only the new method of topography, which took elevation into account, was missing from our lessons. Since mountain ranges and river courses were duly considered, however, the difference, strictly speaking, consisted in the fact that no proper distinction was made between highlands and lowlands, as was the general case prior to Ritter. Provided the shape of countries and states including the course of mountain ranges and rivers is firmly committed to memory—and it is precisely in childhood years that so much of this can be done—the conception of elevation relationships is, I think, most easily established, as will be discovered by anyone whose geography studies predate Ritter. This conception is no doubt essential and necessary for everyone desiring to form a graphic picture of the shape of the surface of continents. But I believe that to consider this approach as the exclusive basis for the study of geography, as was done for some period at least, was wrong indeed.

It is difficult for the child to conceive the elevation relationships of larger land masses and to become familiar with this conception without having continual recourse to relief maps, while the conception of area is quite automatically conveyed by the common type of map. In the end, it is the boundaries of states which, for everyday life and thus for the needs of the pupil, are the most important and also the most referred to. I did not want to suppress these digressions because, at this opportunity, the memory comes back to me of a pupil who, during my stay at Königsberg, was referred to me for tutoring. His teacher in public school was so enthused by the newly-learned Ritter method that he intended to ban all common names of countries and states. When I asked the boy where Lvov or Turin were located, all he could say was: "In the north-Carpathian country" or "In the south-Alpine country." This boy, who was destined to return to the interior of Russia, has profited little from these relief pictures which would have been very suitable for the surface of the moon because it does not really concern us. On Earth, however, where people continually refer to countries and states, these concepts must be given a firm basis as soon as possible because every word heard can then build on this basis. What a pity that every true progress in a science—which this allowing for elevation in geography certainly constitutes, as it is the terrain that determines the migration of peoples and the routes of commerce—must be pursued *ad absurdum*!

It would be futile if I were to try to discuss in detail all the subjects I studied during those early years of my schooling. All I can say is that, as far as I remember the circumstances, our schooling was careful, that I started to study the French language very early and later pursued it together with my cousin, that I started with Latin—of which my brother was the only student— only much later, shortly before the departure of Herr Steingrüber, although, given my good memory, the acquisition of the grammatical forms and of some words would not have been too hard for me. Whether the teacher had some pedagogical reasons for this delay, whether his predilection for the mathematical sciences moved him, or whether there simply was not enough time, I do not know. It is true, though, that considering our differences with regard to age and sex, his duties were manifold indeed since music was also to be practiced, namely singing for my sister and piano-playing for me. The musical part of our schooling was the least fruitful as it turned out that we all had a poor ear for music.

A few words though about our history lessons. The first task all pupils had to carry out was to copy and learn by heart two chronological tables which were designed by Herr Steingrüber himself and which, in not too great detail, listed the main moments of history. Time in these lists was represented and visualized by corresponding distances between the written lines. Any explanations required were given, and it seems that the entire project must have been very useful and practical, as I understood everything and as I know that many dates still retained in my memory originated in those tables; their exact location in the tables still is remembered. Other dates that I later tried to memorize on my own have fared much less well. The following history lessons proper, after the tables were mastered I cannot, however, consider as particularly practical, at least as far as I was concerned. This was a short course in the entire history of the world, which was given to my brother and myself. It was no doubt designed more for my brother, and there was probably no time to instruct me separately. Explanations as well as questions were directed only to my brother and all that was required of me was to sit still and listen carefully. This I hope I did most dutifully, having had an early training in "obedience." But only ancient history, particularly in its more mythical aspects, succeeded in rousing my interest, especially as it contained some names which were also mentioned in other school or children's books that we had leafed through out of duty or curiosity. Medieval and modern history, on the other hand, left me quite cold and must have failed to produce in me any definite ideas, as the only trace they left in my memory is a wonderment at the variety of names. I have thus experienced personally what educators have later explained to me as a general result of their experience, namely, that children indeed show interest in prominent personalities, but are completely indifferent to the movement of peoples and, indeed, masses, and to political developments. In Prussia, history lessons in the lower classes were limited to ancient history, while medieval and modern history were reserved for the upper two classes. I now believe that even at that age, the teaching of history cannot yield the type of fruit one would expect from a knowledge of history, a fruit which is of such an importance to the state. Even the grammar-school pupil of the uppermost class will only in the rarest of cases fully comprehend the motives that move the destinies of peoples or the development of social relations. In Bavaria, at the time of my first stay in that country (1815–1816), a regulation was in force obliging every student, whatever his course of studies, to attend lectures in history. The dissatisfaction with this compulsory measure, which I heard voiced by students of medicine, seemed to indicate that the governmental intention had not really been grasped. I think it also doubtful whether, at the time of their academic studies, most students indeed possess the required maturity and are able to muster the necessary interest to pursue a thorough study of the history of states. A more vigorous interest is usually later in coming, at a time when the maturing man is himself already assuming a position in the state, particularly where affairs of state are discussed publicly. Such study indeed seems desirable for all who are worthy of holding an influential position of any kind, not only for the individual person, but for the whole. If such were the case, I believe that the realization would be far more widespread that social relations cannot be formed according to a preconceived unspecific ideal, at least not overnight, and that any given future can develop only from one specific past. Differences of opinion as to the most desirable type of social organization would, no doubt, exist even then, but wholly unhistorical utopias would arise far less frequently. As long as no special institutes are established for a thorough and mature study of modern history, at least those persons who are to occupy positions affording them influence over the administration and organization of a state should be required to furnish proof that they have prepared themselves by private study of more than elementary historical texts. The English at least study their own history with great vigor. Whether universities are able to provide more than a foundation for this study should be most clearly discernible there. However, in England, even the college boy is already a party man and his interest is therefore aroused much earlier.

But let us return to our original task!

Glancing through the report on the time under Herr Steingrüber, one might come away with the impression that the work given to us was rather serious and strenuous, at least for us boys. Yet we did not feel overburdened. The number of class hours was not too large for our age, being limited to the morning hours of nine to twelve, and in the afternoons, for me, at first from two to four, later to five, except Wednesdays and Saturdays. These standard hours were strictly adhered to, no exceptions being made for birthdays and other festivities. Vacations, too, were very short. But then, very little work was asked of us outside of school hours. Copying, etc., reduced to a minimum, was mostly done during school hours. In summer, most of our free time was spent in the open air, much of it doing garden work we had chosen ourselves. My father had fenced in a section of the farm of about 600 square *Faden* (about 1800 square meters—a little less than half an acre) to serve us boys as a garden or, rather, to be turned by us into a garden. Nobody was allowed to help us except a Russian boy who was to keep us company so that we might learn the Russian language, *ex usu*. As the teacher, a lover of flowers, had a larger garden adjacent to ours, and my father was a keen gardener too, there was no dearth of models. The fact was that we wanted to squeeze everything into our miniature garden: flower beds a few feet long, walks a few yards long, fruit-bearing shrubs, turf seats on which nobody ever rested, moss patches even more dubious, as they served as refuge for all kinds of crawling creatures and, finally, a "Thing," an object meant to represent the Tower of Babel, being closely modeled after an illustration of the same in Hübner's Bible history, without the spiraling ramp however, but consisting of superimposed cylinders of diminishing diameters which were neatly faced with turf, the terraces offering an opportunity for laying out the Hanging Gardens of Semiramis, all of this clearly making our *soi-disant* garden into a quodlibet—all this was proof that full play was allowed to our young minds, without trying to dominate them. This freedom had the result that we remained ever enthusiastic and learned to drive ourselves of our own accord. As it was, the work in the garden was rather pressing in spring and many a wheelbarrow filled with turf had to be pushed along in the early morning from quite a distance, as we were not allowed to cut the turf in the close vicinity, and part of the work had to be carried out before school hours. It is true that at times the wheelbarrow became rather heavy, and I had to rest frequently, but as the instructions for the garden came mostly from my brother and seemed to me like my own, there was no occasion for grumbling. However, my *amour propre* will not permit me to conceal the fact that the Tower of Babel was in its entirety my very own invention. It had to be watered very often to prevent the flowers on the terraces from drying up. Semiramis probably found this less of a problem, as her terraces were wider and the watering was done by slaves.

In summer and fall, work was less hectic. There were flowers to look over and fruit to be picked, as we had about half a dozen fruit-bearing shrubs, the fruits from which naturally seemed to us superior to those of the big garden, which were also at our disposal.

Although there is less activity in the open air in winter than in summer, children in the country, unless they are definitely coddled by their parents, are much less cooped up than town children. There was no lack of the usual sledding and skating parties, sometimes providing an opportunity for the boys to demonstrate their gallantry to the girls. In the long winter evenings we boys were kept busy with cardboard work and map drawing, both under the supervision of the teacher at whose lodgings we stayed on such evenings, or there were games and other activities in the main building together with the girls.

All that was fine, except for a less favorable, extraneous circumstance. The neighborhood boys soon dropped out of sight. When I came to Piep, the nearest estate, Sitz, was almost overfilled with boys and young men, most admittedly older than myself, but some also of my age. All these, belonging to three related families, disappeared very soon, with the exception of one Baron Wrede who later on became the owner of the Sitz estate and who was considerably older than we. These disappearances were due to the then rather common custom of joining the army at a very early age, or being sent to military prep schools. The earlier that young people destined for military service were sent there, the better—that was the general opinion then prevailing. These departures were less felt in the beginning, as our own home was still full, but when it, too, began to empty, I felt my isolation all the more. But that belongs to a somewhat later period.

My father did not believe in early military service*. He favored first a

---

*That is, he did not believe in neglecting schooling for military service. However, once one had started on the latter, it was to be taken seriously. My younger brother had chosen a military career, yet he would not have been sent to the corps when he was ready for the topmost class at school had not there been portents on the horizon of the imminence of a major war. As it was, he joined the corps but had to leave at the end of one year, to take part in the campaign of 1812, then being only sixteen years old.

good schooling which, however, should not begin too early. He himself had already been chained to the school bench at the age of five. Parents always try hard to avoid for their children the errors committed in their own education, as soon as they have recognized them as such. It is to Father, no doubt, that we owe the avoidance of overload, as well as the garden work which called us into the open air, although it appeared that the initiative was always that of the teacher who was responsible for us. Father left the choice of our way in life entirely to ourselves, while stressing that, as far as our future was concerned, we would have to fend for ourselves. As long as he lived he would take care of our education; beyond that, he could do nothing. As he was no friend of long speeches, least of all of admonitions, we had no choice but to take these declarations at their face value, however disinclined children might be to think of the future seriously.

My father, whom many people in this country are certain to remember, was very different from his older brother and in some respects even his opposite. If his brother had engaged in a lifelong flirtation with the military without ever finally deciding, he himself was absolutely sure of his judgment of any situation, whether it affected him directly or not. He was also rapid in making decisions, and resolute in carrying them out. Most active, he liked to get up at four in the morning, brew his own coffee while everybody in the house was still sleeping, and then turn to his various activities which were of the mechanical kind only when absolutely necessary. Otherwise they dealt with practical life, first of all agriculture, to which he was very much devoted, and horticulture, or intellectual activity. The need for mental activity made him an avid reader of books, so much so that he got into the habit of continuously reading on trips and in the carriage, and even when brewing his coffee, a book had to be at hand. His reading matter only very rarely included novels, and only such as were much talked about, like the novels of Walter Scott in their day. His interest centered more on the enlightening and instructive type of literature, not according to any particular direction or purpose as with serious study, but rather as offered by chance, and more in order not to idle away his time than to commit a particular subject to memory. Thus, when I was already a doctor, I found him to my amazement, reading the fifth edition of the Popular Encyclopedia which, with interruptions, he had started to read through from cover to cover! Such a jumble would have confused a man of lesser sense and practical inclination, but for him it was only a means to avoid idleness, unbearable to him when he was alone. Given his practical sense and due to the fact that he had rather seriously studied law, he had successively passed through various so-called official positions, and as people trusted him because of his good sense, his honesty and his fairmindedness, he was frequently appointed guardian to widows and unmarried people, and as adviser in cases of troubled pecuniary circumstances. As all such activities were carried out in an honorary capacity, that is, without payment, my father now and then justifiably prided himself on the fact that, as he put it, his wards were spread over half of Estonia. Even in my old age I had the satisfaction of being told by a number of people that it was only through my father's intervention that their family's property problems had been settled. In his social relations he was cheerful and I can fully subscribe to the opinion I once heard of him, namely that "his character was a happy mixture of gravity and geniality." With his children, as long as they were small, he could act most playfully and he loved to have them stand on his upturned palm, thereby frightening their mother and, even more so, any stranger who happened to be present. With the bigger children he was more serious, not strict if he could help it, although not always able to control his temper, but never morose.

As regards social conditions, he was a man of progress, but at the same time also decidedly in favor of retaining acquired rights and only gradually changing conditions which had become historical, as befits a man who during the best years of his life was able to follow the entire course of the French Revolution. With a kind of fervent enthusiasm he used to speak of the conditions of the German peasants and, to the great astonishment of the neighbors, he often declared that he wished he could conclude his old age as a German peasant. He had in mind the peasants of Bayreuth, whom he had had the opportunity of getting to know during three years' observation. I do not know this particular region, but in the vicinity, in the area around Würzburg, I found a peasantry which, by their prosperity, their portliness, and their independence, could well offer an attractive picture to a northerner.

It was thus one of his aims to raise the level of the rather down-at-heel peasantry of Piep. Not only was our father one of the first in our province to introduce on his estate the growing of clover and the cutting of peat (1801–1802), using peat for the major part of the heating material on the farm in order to preserve the forest, but he also introduced potato growing in the villages*, not without having had need for recourse to force because of the

---

*I do not know whether an attempt was ever made to collect to some degree of completeness reports on the various efforts to turn our earlier, stagnating agriculture into a more dynamic one. On my father's estate I found a copy of a lecture given somewhere by the poet Kotzebue. In this text, by what authority I do not know, the nutritive value of potatoes was set too high, as compared with more recent analysis. Be that as it may, the paper must have attracted some attention, as it was copied. My earliest recollections from Lassila include the ridicule to which Count Rehbinder of Mönnikorb was held up because of his having introduced on his estate the breeding of pedigreed sheep, as well as his peers' gloating over the fact that this had caused him considerable losses. Had the neighbors introduced sheep breeding themselves instead of scoffing, seeing that the climate was no obstacle, the experiments would have shown better results. As it was, Count Rehbinder, being the only producer, lacked a market and he had to process the wool himself, which could not be done profitably. One generation later, merino breeding began to spread and before half a century was over, it was generally accepted and considered

(Contd.)

resistance of the peasants. They were given seed potatoes, but had to deliver the same quantity to the farm stores each year, to have it returned again next spring. In case of nondelivery, punishment was certain. When I later learned how forcibly Frederick II had introduced potato growing in Silesia and how, when the rebellious peasants declared, "We do not eat roots," he had answered: "The King does not at all ask you to eat potatoes; he only orders you to grow them. He himself will eat them and others will do likewise," it seemed to me that my father had taken him for an example. This is as it should be since, during the time that he was a student in Erlangen, he became quite well-known at the court of Markgravine Friederike of Bayreuth, and left with an abiding veneration for this famous sister of Frederick the Great.

In order to provide also for the landless peasants, the so-called migrants, the garden was enlarged and work found not according to the needs of the farm, but for everyone reporting for it. Wages were paid in the form of flour or grain however, never in cash. Only real invalids were fed without having to work.

While resolutely and promptly acting against any resistance, my father would gladly and most sincerely accept every legitimate improvement in the conditions of the peasantry. I still very vividly remember the day when, under Emperor Alexander I, the first humane directives moderating the rules of serfdom, the so-called *Igga üks* were proclaimed in a solemn assembly of the peasantry, after which the first peasant-judges were installed.

My father frequently expressed his sincere appreciation of the impartiality and circumspection with which this body of judges—there were three of them, with the first judge being particularly outstanding—succeeded in dispensing justice. It was quite obvious to me that this institution did much to elevate the self-esteem of the peasantry and I definitely belong to those who regret that, when serfdom was abolished, at which time I was abroad, too much of this institution of 1804 was abolished, too. A great many later difficulties could have been avoided, had this not happened. After my return I even heard doubts that a peasants' court of law had existed at that time. Not only had it existed, but it was salutarily effective wherever autocracy could and would accommodate itself to some slight limitation of its powers.

I have not hesitated to mention these circumstances in order to say that I have been brought up on liberal principles, but that, already as a child, I had seen how difficult it is to improve degenerated social conditions. I will say no more about the peasants' resistance. More painful is another recollection. The first judge of our region, whom I mentioned earlier, was at the same time

very profitable. A detailed description of the progress of agriculture in our province would also show how long the local estates stuck to the traditional three-field system and everything associated with it, and would put the peasantry's rigid clinging to tradition into its proper perspective.

its wealthiest peasant, a sensible and active man whom my father always treated with a certain respect. As a result of his judicial function, however, he became suddenly a poor man: a barn in which he kept his supplies as well as his money was burned down one night by a vengeful litigant, after which he urgently asked to be relieved of his post. Incidentally, the fact that there now exist saving banks which are used by the peasants is to be considered a welcome piece of progress.

Although I have seen my father take action for improvement, I never heard him make liberal speeches. I myself was carried away in the liberal direction—probably beyond the true center—by the speeches of my second teacher, but was later compelled to wheel about, not by historical studies or accumulating administrative experience, but due to my preoccupation with the embryology of living things on the one hand, and the urge that I felt, as a grown man, to take part in the political process, on the other. As a consequence I became deeply convinced that social developments could not proceed differently from organic ones; that is, gradually, and that the outcome of such developments could be healthy only if conditions were completely ripe and had existed for some time. Any excessive haste in progress was comparable, I felt, to an overheating of my incubator, bringing only destruction; and any prolonged stoppage, to a dying down of the fire, causing, if not sudden death, then a slow ebbing away of life.

I am quite aware that the aforesaid is of little avail in teaching anybody the Golden Mean, because just as it is a physical necessity for every man to be at the center of his physical horizon, thus is it a mental inevitability for every man to regard his own opinion as the true center of his mental horizon, since the latter is just as inseparable from his own person as is his physical horizon. Still, it seems to me that men who want to move forward—to want to move backward is altogether against nature—would do well to accustom their thoughts to the observation of organic development.

As I probably will not return to this subject again, I do not wish to leave out that, being satisfied by slow progress (whether I am too easily satisfied I cannot tell, for reasons just mentioned), I am glad to have discerned some progress this year, not large, but quite decisive, in the circumstances of our peasantry.

Because of her character—a tranquil, home-loving, quietly level-headed woman and tender mother who loved her children undemonstratively and without fuss—there is much less to tell of my mother than of others.

4. Further Schooling at Home
(1803-1807)

Conditions changed in 1803. My oldest sister married very early and thus had left school; my cousin, too, was taken home by her parents. On the other hand, a younger brother and a younger sister started their schooling. At the same time, teachers changed as well. Herr Steingrüber left us after three and a half years, and a younger man, Herr Glanström, came in his place. Herr Glanström was a local man who had started to study medicine, but had been interrupted in his study when Emperor Paul suddenly recalled all Russian subjects who were staying in foreign countries in 1798. He was a man of many talents who had already pursued several scientific subjects at the university, and now after the interruption was diversifying himself even more. He had a peculiar liking for modern languages, in the acquisition of which he was very gifted, but he was less partial to ancient languages. Mathematics appeared to have escaped him, at least so it seemed, as he completely refrained from teaching the subject, with the exception of the basic operations, which he taught to our younger brother and sister. He played the piano but, for relaxation, preferred the violin or the harp. But such crafts as pasteboard-work, paper coloring, or map drawing, which we had learned from Steingrüber, were completely foreign to him; nor was he a gardener. Actually, he had no pedagogical training and had become a private teacher only because his chosen career had been interrupted. Although his cheerful and sympathetic character caused us to like him better than his rather bilious predecessor, we could not but feel—having grown more perceptive in the meantime—that he took his duties somewhat less seriously.

Studies in the French language, already begun, were continued, as was Latin, myself and my brother studying it. The two of us also started to grapple eagerly with the English language and, for a short period, we had some Italian. The facility of giving clear expression to one's thoughts was exercised in German compositions, but we had no trace of mathematics, Greek, or history. In their place, in our free time, our teacher now and then read to us a drama or a ballad, or gave us such things to read. Gradually it happened that, when we older boys were busily translating, to which end we had to first locate the words in the dictionary, Herr Glanström found something different to do in the adjacent room. This practice possibly had its origin in my piano-playing which was to be continued after all. Probably convinced that nothing would ever come of it, the teacher soon stopped listening altogether, nor did he give me new material to practice. Instead, he let me rattle off one and the same sonata so many times that I myself soon ceased to pay attention and, at times, was astonished to find myself at the end without having turned more than the first page. Finally, after I had acquired some digital facility as well as an insight into the secrets of reading music, it was decided to make an end of it. This inattention on the part of the teacher, however, increased to such a degree that a sort of self-government and independent study evolved in our school. Moreover, I was appointed geography teacher to my sister, five years younger than myself. I accepted this appointment with such alacrity that I myself composed a textbook in duodecimo format, the main virtue of which was its brevity. I do not know where I got the idea to combine this with historical notes or, as I saw it, a historical survey of the states concerned. The material for this I could hardly have found elsewhere but in Galetti's brief outline of world history. This first evidence of my itch to teach, in a stiff cover painted red by myself, must have been written in 1804. It was also at this time that our independent study began to become valuable in a way which has not remained without effect on my future life. It was probably one day in the year 1804 that I found Herr Glanström with a book in one hand and a couple of plants in the other. When I asked him what he was doing, he said that he was looking up the names of these plants. As I could not understand how he could find in the book the names of plants just now picked, he explained the matter to me. I was now eager to use the book myself, but it was only a borrowed one and, therefore, could not be passed on to me. I did not rest, however, until the owner of this book, a teacher by the name of Mickwitz, at Weissenstein, to whom I owe eternal gratitude, agreed to lend it to me for some months until my father could obtain another copy for me. This book was written for independent study and was the botanical handbook of Koch who was not, however, the later famous botanist W. D. J. Koch, professor at Erlangen, but an earlier one who, if I am not mistaken, was a clergyman at Magdeburg*. Together with my older brother, I now started to eagerly pursue the study of botany, quite without guidance, since it soon turned out that botany, too, was one of the subjects that our teacher wanted only to nibble at. Although the book was generally well-conceived and arranged in several subdivisions according to Lamarck's system, positive identification was at first very hard. I do not believe that during the first summer we were able to name positively more than fifty plants. This is no wonder, as all the difficulties, and even the shortcomings of the book had to be found out in use. How little do those who have their betters to turn to know about the difficulties of isolated independent study! Who, for instance, would guess that a primrose, which has a pronounced calyx, should not be looked up under the category "calyx," but only under "involucrum." This was a fault in the book's format,

---

*As the book is not at my disposal at this time, I am unable to give its exact title.

not a difficulty of nature. However, as the book also included an alphabetical list of the common garden plants, giving their generic names, its faulty arrangement could thus also be recognized. Other difficulties were indeed presented by nature herself, e.g., in the plain grass flowers. Yet overcoming difficulties has its own rewards. We became so fond of botany that, in the following year, we could hardly await the coming of spring and, wading through patches of remaining snow on muddy roads, we walked to a nearby mountain to find *Hepatica triloba*, at that time *Anemone hepatica*, which we knew by sight, but could not name. It was not yet flowering. On the other hand, some catkins and the female flowers of hazelnut trees were already opened. Altogether we pursued botany studies this year more eagerly and with more success, and each of us, using Koch as a guide, built a herbarium. True, our miniature garden ran slightly to seed, and my Tower of Babel dried up completely, but in their place the large garden of nature was opened to us. In 1805, my brother was transferred to Hamburg where he continued his botanical studies and whence he brought back a more elegant herbarium, housing the snow drop (*Galanthus nivalis*) for which, as a very early harbinger of spring, we had searched eagerly but unsuccessfully.

In the meantime I had pursued these studies with even greater zeal at home and had earned the nickname "the botanist." My younger brother, who was still with us, had to take part, and even a sister still younger than my geography pupil, who did not yet go to school nor know how to read, succeeded in picking up some of the Latin plant names which I bandied about.

It was before my departure for Reval, that is in 1806 or, at the latest, in the first half of the summer of 1807, that a *Landrat* by the name of von Ungern-Sternberg (of Noistfer), who had also plunged into botany, spent several days with us. I had the honor of showing him my herbarium and giving him some plants he did not yet know. The region of Piep, while less varied and pleasant than that of Lassila, had a peculiarity in its rather high and narrow hill ridge, long and interrupted at several points and consisting of debris and gravel (similar to the Swedish Åsar). This ridge passed through our estate, and on it were found many plants which even later, I have never seen again in our province, e.g. *Dracocephalum Ruyschianum*. I had found other rarities at other locations. Baron Ungern would not agree with some of my names, but then I also doubted some of his, so that I felt completely his equal. He suggested to my father that he procure for me the *Botanisches Handbuch für Liv-, Cur- und Ehstland* (*Botanical Handbook for Livonia, Courland and Estonia*) by Grindel (1803) in order to spare me the bother of searching for plants that did not exist at all in our region. The faults of this book, however, soon became obvious. It was clearly made up of mere lists, which Grinder had obtained from various places, and to which he tried to fit diagnoses copied from botanical works. Thus, *Erica buccans*, a plant from the Cape, is mentioned as indigenous to Livonia, no doubt because some good man had confused our berry-bearing *Empetrum nigrum* with *Erica*, a heather. I wish the *Landrat* had rather recommended a Latin work—for instance, Roth's *Tentamen florae Germanicae* or the handbook by Schkuhr, which I later found in his library!

Botany was also supposed to become useful. I had discovered large quantities of the medicinal *Valeriana* quite nearby, and even larger quantities of sweet flag in the neighborhood. They were collected for the family medicine chest, as were other herbs less frequently used, some only for baths, or by the peasants. In the meantime I had become a doctor's assistant and, occasionally, even a doctor proper. It turned out that Herr Glanström, with his quiet avocations, had resumed his medical studies. By and by he became doctor on the estate and in the neighborhood, answering a crying need in the country. Since I was of the opinion that a little systematic botany was already half of medicine, I began to toy with the idea of studying medicine itself; thus it was quite natural for me to become his amanuensis. I visited the sick in the villages, reported on their condition and, gradually, I also became the unpaid vaccinator of the neighborhood.

That schooling became more and more irregular under these circumstances can well be imagined. This process, on the other hand, benefited our inclination and ability to improve ourselves by independent study. Thus I got hold of the second and third volumes of Remer's *Handbuch der Geschichte* (*Handbook of History*), the source of which I no longer remember and whose first volume, comprising ancient history, was missing. This concise, yet circumspectly conceived world history attracted me. In order to memorize it better, I started to prepare a rather complete summary in the form of chronological tables in folio size. This grew into a rather imposing stack of sheets which I bound in a stiff, red cover, as I had done with the textbook in geography mentioned earlier. Both *specimina eruditionis* were lost through devastation wrought by female vandals. Before I left for Germany, I stowed them away in a storeroom visited by women only, and very infrequently at that. However, I did not reckon with the fact that members of the female sex, out of utilitarian passion, will strive to employ used paper, which is obviously useless for further writing, to put underneath cakes and bread, as well as using it for bonnet and other sewing patterns, or similar indispensable items. When I returned, having already had some works printed, I wanted to collect these unpublished works as well. They had disappeared without a trace and will remain lost, unless a second older brother discovers some fragments of them some time in the future.

More than these rather early attempts at independent study, it was probably my feeling that after my older brother's departure I was rather alone, which imparted a certain melancholic tint to my mind and which found its external expression in a touch of unsociability. My brothers and sisters who were still with me were so much younger than I that a mutual exchange of

36

ideas and feelings was quite impossible. All of the grown boys from the neighboring estates had disappeared years ago, having been replaced by small children. The only pair of boys of our acquaintance left, both considerably younger than I, lived on a distant estate and, because of the great distance, we saw each other only on rare occasions. I was thus reduced all the more to my botanical excursions, which were flavored by the collection and preservation in spirits of snakes, lizards, and the like. For the study of these objects there was nothing in the house but Esper's summary of the Linnaean system which, having found it in Father's library, I had duly appropriated, but it did not contain anything special apart from a survey of the system.

Whether my father had now finally realized that something was amiss with me, or whether the increasing irregularity of our schooling had him worried, the decision was suddenly made that my younger brother and I were to go to a public school, and my sisters would be sent elsewhere. As a last endeavor we undertook some Horace—what I had read earlier I do not remember— and, at the very end, the Greek alphabet, but nothing beyond reading. On my own initiative, I added the ὸ, ἡ, τὸ; τὶς, τινὸς and similar basic fundamentals, and also had a look at the conjugations which, however, appeared too powerful to be taken by assault.

Thus, at the beginning of August 1807, I was to move to Reval, to study at the Knights' and Cathedral School of which I could form no definite impression. I was rightly worried that I was not really properly prepared. I could rely on my French; that I knew well, better than now. In English, too, I was fluent and I enjoyed reading English literature. But nobody would inquire about these, even less so about my botany, in which I knew very well I would be given no opportunity to show off. As far as Latin was concerned, I thought I would do passably well, but I was greatly worried about my woefully neglected Greek, as I was frequently told that, without a knowledge of Greek, one could not study at all. The first question I had to answer in the presence of my father, when the principal interviewed me to determine into which class I would fit, was: what had I read so far in Latin? As I was able to answer, "most recently, some odes by Horace," he seemed to be inclined towards the Prima*. Next he gave me something to translate, which I did at least without gross distortions of the sense. The further proceedings I remember well, because it showed me how much depends on pure chance in a short test. To test my knowledge of history, I was asked what I knew about the Mongols. Now, in my excerpts from Remer, I had been particularly interested in this people, probably because of their invasion of Russia. Not only could I name all the Mongolian great khans starting from Genghis Khan up to the disintegration of their empire, but I was also able to mention all their conquests,

---

*[Ed. note: Prima, Secunda, Tertia—in German usage, the names of higher school classes in descending order, starting from the uppermost class.]

quite often complete with dates. The principal was very pleased and, as it seemed, astonished; the pointer stood decidedly at the Prima. However, it started wobbling again when I was asked what I knew about the Ptolemies. Whatever luck I had had with the first question, on medieval history, I had that much less with the second. If the subject of the question had been some prominent personality from ancient history I would have known a few things about it from various publications and stories written for young people. As it was, I only knew that the Ptolemies were Greeks and ruled over Egypt, but had no idea about any chronological sequence. Cleopatra I remembered from the aforementioned publications (and how could I have failed to read, in the various *Magasins des enfants* (*Children's Magazines*) and similar works, the story of the pearl?). But nobody ever told me that she was a Ptolemy, nor did I know anything about the dynasty as such. As I then explained that my knowledge of medieval and modern history was acquired by independent study of Remer's handbook, but that I did not have the first volume comprising ancient history, this proof of independent study made the pointer again veer toward the Prima. The test in the mathematical disciplines, given by their teacher, started with trigonometry and ended with the teacher stating that, although much had vanished from my memory, it was clear that it was once there, and as he was going through the whole of mathematics anyway, he, too, would vote for the Prima. I thus became a student of the Prima generally with the provision that I was to take the Tertia for Greek, where that language started. Later, I advanced from the Tertia to the Secunda in this subject, at the same time always remaining in the Prima.

5. The Knights' and Cathedral School in Reval (1807-1810)

My stay at the Knights' and Cathedral School in Reval has always been among my fondest memories. Now that I have several reasons to reflect on the course of my life, with recollections from different periods conjuring up lifelike images before my mind's eye, there can be no doubt that I felt happiest in this period of my life and that, even as seen from this later point in time, I have every reason to feel satisfied with, or grateful for these years. The reasons lay partly in myself, as it was most beneficial for me to again be in close and sustained contact with young people of my age. To this must be added the happy circumstance that the young people with whom I shared the school bench were all to my liking, and their friendship was well worth seeking. Thus there existed no contradiction between my outward behavior and my inner feelings, as just such a contradiction was to trouble me later at the university. But the main reason was to be found in the school itself which, also according to my present opinion, was a very good one, and the prevailing spirit which, at least in the Prima, was excellent.

When, several years ago, most regrettable experiences were had at this same school, and voices had already been heard calling for its complete dissolution, the then Marshal of the Nobility or, as we call it here, the Knight Commander, Count Keyserling, applied to me very urgently for information about the spirit of the school at my time. I was able to assure him that, at least in the upper classes, the spirit was very good and in the Prima, the very best I had ever encountered or heard of. I felt I could trust my judgment that much, even if I was never an educator myself. However, in Prussia, I had had close contacts with several educators, and had also taken an active part in public discussions of educational problems. While I take it as a moral obligation on my part to fully explain my statement to Count Keyserling, this will make it necessary for me to deal also with some extraneous factors.

The spiritual climate prevailing at a school is not independent of outside conditions, cannot be enforced or, once satisfactorily attained, maintained at will; it more or less depends on individual personalities who are not permanent and cannot always be replaced. I am also quite aware of the complaints that, from time to time, were heatedly voiced. This kind of passing tempest is probably experienced by every public institution now and then. Why these complaints became so particularly vocal in our case I believe I am able to explain further below. All one really can do, I think, is to strive after the right kind of atmosphere and hope that, in good time, it will develop.

Let us first be introduced to the ancient history of this institution and its transformation into its present shape, by a former principal, Dr. Alex. Plate*.

As indicated by its name, the Cathedral School is a very ancient institution which, however, has undergone many changes. As everybody knows, the northern part of the province of Estonia was first conquered by the Danish kings and passed into the hands of the Teutonic Order only later. Already during Danish rule, a decree was issued in 1319 to erect, next to the Marien-kirche (Church of the Virgin Mary) or cathedral of Reval, a Hauptschule**, a higher school, as befits any diocese. The unlicensed schools were to stop, and all children were to attend the new Hauptschule or be charged a ten-mark fine. There is no doubt that it was the priests who were obliged to do the teaching. Although there is no clear evidence on this point, general ecclesiastical usage in the German Middle Ages would certainly indicate so. Only gradually were paid laymen employed for teaching. The highest authority, however, always rested with the bishop. The subsequent fate of the school is unknown; it is clear, however, that it managed to weather the changes in sovereignty which passed on to the Teutonic Order and then to the Swedish Crown. Yet it was no longer the only school in Reval since, in 1424, the town was given permission to build its own school in the lower town because it was allegedly too difficult, and even dangerous, for the children to climb Cathedral Hill, especially in winter, and because the town was in any case populous enough for two schools. After many years of devastation, Estonia came under Swedish rule, with the Church and school system in complete ruins. The first years of Swedish sovereignty did not bring any relief in this respect, as a report which Gustavus Adolphus had prepared by a visiting bishop in 1627 mentions the most deplorable conditions. The Cathedral School, for instance, consisted of an old wooden building, twenty-two feet long and twenty feet wide. The deputation which prepared this report also drew up some new laws dealing with education and schooling, and issued a series of admonitory instructions to the clergy. According to available information, the school seemed to have maintained a fairly high level, but declined entirely toward the end of the seventeenth century. This was partly the result of a fire which destroyed most of the buildings on Cathedral Hill, including the school building, but also partly of the fact that the school's finances were very shaky, being based mainly on contributions solicited throughout the country. These never came in at a constant rate, and in hard times, were very sparse indeed. The Great Northern War could only have aggravated these conditions. Immediately after the subjugation of Estonia under the Russian Scepter (1709),

*Plate: *Beitrage zur Geschichte der Ehstlandischen Ritter- und Domschule*. Reval 1840. (Schulprogramm.)

**[Ed. note: Such a higher school contained the upper four classes of an 8-grade primary school.

a most devastating plague broke out in the country. In the higher school founded in 1637 by the Swedish Government and housed in a former monastery in the lower town, only one teacher, Professor Brehm, survived. The Cathedral School lost all its lecturers and simply ceased to exist. The school building itself was used as a barracks for soldiers. There was no dearth, however, of children needing schooling. A former Swedish soldier therefore was appointed schoolmaster. This was the wretched state in which the school was found in 1724 by Rector Mickwitz who had been called to the Cathedral Church. A pupil of the famous Franke of Halle, he had inherited his master's faith and fervor, and used both in his efforts to rehabilitate the school. The Estonian Knights pledged him one hundred talers annually for the rector's salary, but demanded to be consulted with regard to the appointment of the rector, and imposed their will upon the consistory. Mickwitz knew how to collect all the old claims of the school, as well as where to find new sources of assistance, and made himself superintendent of education and of the faculty, which held enthusiastic weekly conferences. It happened that once the school revived, the number of pupils from all classes of the population increased rapidly, so that the number of teachers also had to be enlarged considerably. The Order of Knights soon doubled its contribution and later quadrupled it. Beyond this they also supplied wood for heating and took care of the buildings. In addition, generous gifts and bequests flowed in from individual members of the Order. The school's curriculum extended from reading up to preparation for the university.

With the death of Rector Mickwitz, the irregular sources which only he in his zeal knew how to tap dried up, and the school again found itself in financial straits while, at the same time, the need for proper schooling had become even more pressing. It was at this point in 1765, that is about one hundred years ago, that those conditions finally obtained in which the school was to find itself not only at the time of my stay there, but essentially to this very day. Already under Gustavus Adolphus, the Estonian Knights had wanted to maintain a school at their own cost and for their own needs. For this purpose they had asked for use of the Michaelis Monastery which had been emptied by the Reformation. As the king demanded supervisory rights as well as the city's participation, however, negotiations had broken down. Since the time when Mickwitz had asked for and obtained their yearly contributions, the nobles had gotten used to considering the Cathedral School as their own. When in 1765, Rector Harpe had stressed the need for improved schooling and, to this end, asked a grant of greater means for the Cathedral School in his sermon before the Diet, he was immediately asked to prepare specific proposals, following which the school was granted, in addition to the then current sum of four hundred rubles, another 1,500 rubles annually. It was also decided, however, to appoint a board from among the members of the Order of Knights to supervise the school. This board replaced the previous rector, now an old man, with a younger man, Göbel, then principal of the St. Petersburg Petri School, to serve in the capacity of a principal. They conferred with him concerning the new organization of the school, hired new teachers, and presented the plan worked out by Göbel to the 1768 Diet. The new organization also included the setting up of boarding facilities for twenty children of the less wealthy nobility who could not or would not keep their own private teachers. To this end, the yearly grants had to be raised considerably. As a sort of reward, the school was to be known from then on as the "Academic Knights' School" or "Knights' Academy." It was to prepare its pupils for all walks of life and to be open to all classes. Teachers of the higher grades were to hold the title of professor, the others, that of colleague. The new name of the institute does not seem to have ever received official sanction and, later on, the name of Knights' and Cathedral School became current. The rector, who was originally the school's headmaster, gradually lost whatever influence his position had commanded, since the board of nobles was decisively active.

At first, to satisfy all demands, the curriculum was very extensive. Except for elementary schooling, which was not provided, the curriculum included the French, Russian, Latin, Greek, and Hebrew languages, religion, the arts of writing and arithmetic, mathematics, physics, geography, the history of the world, natural history, philosophy, mythology and antiquities, along with jurisprudence and *belles lettres* (German language and literature). From among all these subjects, the pupil could choose whatever was required for his future calling. Also promised were private lessons in the English and Italian languages, as well as in music, drawing, fencing, and dancing. In order that no pupil should be prevented by weakness in one subject from advancing in another, every pupil could study different subjects in different classes, according to the state of his knowledge. It is obvious that this arrangement went far beyond the usual scope of school curricula and that the school could rightly claim an academic title. As it turned out, however, the school soon felt compelled to restrict this plan for reasons not specified in the aforementioned history by Director Plate. One may assume, though, that it was impossible to find properly qualified teachers for the different subjects, since, given the original plan of free choice, overworking the pupils could not be the reason. Philosophy, mythology, and antiquities were dropped quite early. Lectures in jurisprudence and Hebrew, too, had ceased long before I entered the school.

The general organizational framework with respect to the Board was still in existence and so was the boarding house accommodating twenty boarders who had to pay only a small fee, if any at all. The boarding house included two floors, a so-called upper, and a lower dormitory. The upper dormitory had a superintendent who, at my time, was also the school's principal; the lower one had a man of inferior rank with the title of second inspector. I was brought to the upper dormitory. Vacancies at the boarding school were so much in demand that, to be accepted, one had to enroll several years earlier. The boarding house was exclusively for the children of the nobility. My impressions of the boarding house I shall postpone to a later occasion.

The school served young people from all social classes, the commoners constituting a majority, particularly in the Prima. The arrangement whereby every pupil could sit for different subjects in different classes was still in force in my time and benefited me inasmuch as, in the beginning, I was permitted to participate in the Greek lessons of the Tertia, where they had Greek grammar although, at the insistence of the teacher himself, I also took the Greek language lessons in the Prima. But considering the absence of proper preparation, the Tertia was indeed far more suitable for me. I still know by heart several pieces from the reader by Heinzelmann that was used there. Of later authors, I retain only some verses by Homer which could not be forgotten because they were repeated time and again, as well as some poems by Anacreon, which I read for myself. Other pupils were almost half in Prima and half in Secunda, or in Secunda and Tertia. In the lower classes, there were two boys from Archangel who, until they joined the school, had spoken only Russian, and they had come to Reval to study the German language in which all lessons were given. Why should they have to advance in the Russian language at the same slow pace as in the other subjects? I regretted it very much, therefore, when this arrangement was abolished later. Pedagogues were quick to point out that such an arrangement was difficult to carry through in practice, and it was easier to form a clear opinion about a pupil when the latter studied in one class only. But, after all, is not advancement of the pupil the aim of a school rather than convenience of the teacher? To introduce such an arrangement, where it did not exist before, is likely to be a difficult matter. However, where such a scheme was in existence for more than fifty years, it should certainly not be too hard to maintain. The second argument, I confess, is quite incomprehensible to me. After all, the comprehensive opinion about a pupil is derived from the sum total of the opinions of the different teachers, regardless of whether they teach in the same class or not.

When I entered the Cathedral School in 1807, I found a most worthy staff of teachers there. The two masters of the upper classes, the philologist Johann Conrad Wehrmann, a student of Heyne, and the mathematician Blasche, were most competent in their subjects and had an excellent reputation in the country. Both were most devoted to their duties, especially Wehrmann who exhibited a zeal and stamina the like of which I have never again encountered. Of rather advanced age, and so consumptive that a persistent cough interrupted him repeatedly during every lesson, he had become principal of the entire school about half a year before. In addition, he was principal of the boarding home and, in particular, inspector of the upper floor which housed ten young people. It was his duty not only to supervise their behavior, but also, nearly always upon request of the parents, to guide their studies. This he did every evening by inviting one or another boy into his room, not infrequently two at a time, sometimes even three boys. They then had to show him their work, to report on the lessons and the like, at the same time collecting an admonition or two. These invitations went out quite irregularly, so that every pupil had to be prepared. I was the only Prima pupil in the dormitory; my visits with him were more in the nature of talks. Now and then, however, he gave me private lessons. Thus, he gave me a historical survey of Greek philosophy, which I had to write down after each of these half-hour talks, and show to him the following day.

Yet, despite his manifold duties, Wehrmann never showed any signs of fatigue during his lessons the number of which, it is true, was only moderate for him, about twelve hours per week. For his age, he had an altogether impressive agility, and even rapidity in his movements.

As concerns translation from the Latin (in the Prima), everybody had to be prepared and could be called on quite unexpectedly. Should it turn out that a pupil was not properly prepared (which was rare, but still happened now and then), there were no words of reproach or admonition, only a scathing look and the calling up of another pupil. Both had a rather humiliating effect. When a certain portion had been finished, Herr Wehrmann went over it again cursorily, added some archeological explanations if required, emphasized some uncommon expressions or salient phrases which are easily memorized or had already turned into proverbs—but whatever he did was done briefly, so that there never was a feeling of pedantry or boredom. Lessons in Greek took a similar course, only there he did not tire of repeating many words that were not quite common; that is, he always tried to adapt the proceedings to the pupil's needs. History and geography in the Prima were also his lot. In history, he moved from one European state to the next, starting from their earliest days and, going into reasonable detail, he finished the cycle in three years. Ancient history was missing here, too, being reserved for the lower classes. Geography, however, was regarded only as a filler and dealt only with Russia, being given in the form of an examination or repetition. That is to say, whenever a given portion of history had been done with and there was still some time left, questions were asked about some aspects of Russian geography, streams that are tributaries to main rivers and the like, and the entire class answered in unison and in certain well-established cadences, a custom not usually common in the upper class, but which was obviously aimed at drumming those patriotic names so deep into our memories that they would stick there forever. In this connection, too, I must acknowledge the loyalty and devotion of Wehrmann. Foreigners, of which Wehrmann was one, almost always used to pronounce Russian names with an accent and stress that differed from the proper one and were quite insensitive to this difference. I could mention names of men who for many years had been working under Uvárov, had frequently met him socially, yet still called him Úvarov. Wehrmann, on the other hand, must have made an effort to pronounce correctly which, to be sure, was all the more necessary as the geography and history teachers in the lower classes were all locally-born Germans, who had learned the proper pronunciation from their childhood on. One name only escaped him, that of the generally less known river Khoper which, as any good German would, he pronounced Khóper, whereas not only should the stress be put on the second syllable, but the e of that syllable should be pronounced with a German ö and a mixture of the German i. When, on my travels, I first came upon the Khopièr, I was astonished to recognize the Khóper, so frequently rattled off at school.

Professor Blasche, the mathematician, made a quite different impression from Wehrmann. His walk was grave, without, however, being affected, his speech slow rather than hurried, his manner of expressing himself, as would befit a mathematician, very precise and measured, his delivery, just because of that, uncommonly lucid. We regarded him as a second Laplace, or the latter as a second Blasche, a question which we left undecided. It was his habit to begin his mathematics classes each year from the very beginning reviewing the first elements of geometry and algebra cursorily and going into details only at a later point. In the first two years, this suited me fine. However, as I was staying for three years, I would have preferred, in the third year, to have some differential calculus which appeared to me particularly interesting and valuable when, at the behest of Herr Blasche, we had to copy a paper on differential and integral calculus which he had written and wanted to submit somewhere, but as each of us was given only one chapter to copy, none of us could make head or tail of it. This wish was never fulfilled. Instead, Herr Blasche offered us a series of lectures on astronomy, to be given outside of school hours, where, as he put it, he could go into greater detail than during the physics lessons. Quite a number of pupils volunteered, most of whom did not live nearby and thus had to walk a considerable distance in the early morning. This may serve as an indication of how we felt toward our Laplace, and vice versa. But then, he always knew how to arouse interest. Thus, he declared at the end of this course that the times of sunrise and sunset, given for years now in the Reval calendar for every ten days, had been simply reprinted from year to year, without taking into account the fact that the exact instants of these events were subject to gradual change and it was high time that they were recalculated. Would we be prepared for such an undertaking to be carried out during our vacation? If so, our results would be incorporated in the calendar. This suggestion was accepted with good cheer, since it goes without saynig that in his lectures on the methods of calculation, insofar as they did not go beyond spherical trigonometry, these were explained and practiced. These lectures contrasted with the later work of Humboldt, in which much information is given about the cosmos, but one is never told about the calculations those data were based on. It may be assumed that Herr Blasche did the calculations himself, not relying entirely on his pupils. It turned out that, for the tenth of December, I had miscalculated by several minutes. That I have not forgotten the date of this lapse from grace just goes to show how deeply I was affected by the reproof.

The physics course took several years, as only two days per week were devoted to this science. A pity indeed, since many pupils could not stay in the Prima for several years, and it was the only school which they had to rely on for their life's preparation in physics. Apart from those who went to Dorpat, where they could study physics to a greater depth, many pupils left school without going to the university.

It would be excessive if I were to report on the other teachers, Carlberg, Hirschhausen, at equal length. They were all quite competent in their subjects, also enjoyed general respect, but attracted us much less than the aforementioned. Real enthusiasm spread, however, when in 1809 Pastor Holtz, who had recently been appointed second preacher in the Cathedral Church, took over some classes in the Prima. If I am not mistaken, these classes went under the name of Aesthetics. However, he interpreted the subject rather freely and treated it more as a mental exercise. He let us discuss and recite, and he talked about the development of literature and, indeed, education, which led him to the history of religion. Until then, religious instruction in the Prima consisted of two weekly classes, in which a textbook on Christian morals was presented in a manner not calculated to arouse lively interest. Holtz, a man of great erudition, who talked well and with warmth and dignity, traced the course and meaning of Christianity primarily from the point of view of the history of civilization. His lectures had an academic, widely roaming character, which made them most attractive to us. Unfortunately, Pastor Holtz died after one year because, as we all agreed, in his zeal he had taken upon himself too much at once, trying to be active and helpful everywhere.

It seems superfluous to describe the scope of education in greater detail, as it may be stated that the school tried to uphold the character of a good grammar school. Although since it was an institute associated with the nobility, it had to put greater stress on mathematics than did the Reval grammar school, its achievements in the ancient languages were no less, provided one did not remain in the Prima for too short a period. Upon passing from Secunda into Prima it is possible that the pupil of the Reval gymnasium (a higher school) had a slight edge over the Cathedral pupil, but any imbalance disappeared quickly, thanks to the excellent work of Wehrmann, as well as that of his nephew, Johann Ernst Wehrmann, a competent philologist and later principal himself, who had had his only pre-academic training at the Cathedral School. Thus, what counted was not to leave the institute too soon. Its graduates were accepted by Dorpat University without prior examination as completely prepared, provided they could bring proof that they had stayed in the Prima for more than one year, and this in spite of the fact that, at that time, as far as I know, the Cathedral School had not at all aspired to the right to issue certificates of fitness for university work.

Comparing our school at that time with the two gymnasiums which I got to know in Königsberg, I cannot doubt that a person could get a more comprehensive knowledge of the ancient languages and of ancient history there. However, this is hardly so as regards mathematical knowledge, and most certainly not with respect to interest in scientific training which, after all, is the seedbed of the future. When, at his public comprehensive examination, a pupil of one of the Königsberg gymnasiums did not know how many times Sulla and Marius had held the position of consul, he was pilloried. The Greek language, too, was studied there more thoroughly and more universally than at the Cathedral School, where at any one time there were only a few pupils who acquired this language fully, whereas in my time, Sophocles was not read, and translating into Greek was not practiced at all*. When I ask myself why it was that the zest for learning at our school seemed to be greater, generally speaking, than there, the only answer that comes to my mind is that we did not feel overburdened. In the Prima there was no problem in coping with one's schoolwork. This I know from my own experience: there was always time enough for other things as well, following one's own inclinations. In summer, Sunday afternoons were still reserved for botany. I also liked to read English books whenever I could lay my hands on them. I felt particular empathy with the philosophy of life as I found it in the *Spectator* and in other old journals. There was also time for me to get better acquainted with

---

*At this point I should like to address a question to educators and particularly to philologists. I have the impression that the more eager ones among them tend to move as soon as possible to the more difficult authors. Now I am certainly aware of the benefits of the mental effort involved in finding one's way in an unfamiliar syntax, and I intend to return to this subject later. But does not the abundance of words which the pupil is, after all, supposed to acquire, suffer, and is not his fluency in expressing himself in the ancient languages impaired, when all he is permitted is to plough deeply and strenuously in the classical soil without ever, by cursory reading and roaming, being able to enjoy the flowers in wider fields? The latter deficiency, I might be answered, is easily remedied. This is quite true for the philologist who continues in this discipline. But my question refers to the others, who are the majority, and was inspired by my recollections of a student in Königsberg of whom I was very fond. He came from the gymnasium which was known for the particular stress it put on philological education, and the principal of which was credited with declaring that, according to his belief, whoever was not a qualified philologist had absolutely no right to enjoy the sun under God's sky. This student, then, came from this school with a report card declaring him a special Primus, a leader of the class. Since he had devoted himself to the natural sciences I had much contact with him. Reading Latin diagnoses, he was frequently puzzled, not, naturally by the syntax which, with these diagnoses, is simple enough, if not always entirely correct. But he often asked for the meaning of this or that word. Since he was a Primus of Primuses this surprised me to such a degree that I exclaimed several times, "How is it possible that you don't know this word!"

German literature, for which the city offered incomparably better opportunities than a stay in the country. But the other classes, too, were anything but overburdened. None of the other boarders, ranging from Secunda to Quinta, seemed anxious; none complained that he could not cope; there were none among the younger ones who could not go to bed at ten if they so desired. I was the one who stayed up longest, but only because I followed my own interests, and I was duly warned by old Wehrmann that staying up that long would cause me insomnia in my old age. How different did I find conditions in Petersburg later with my own children! One of them had to stay up until midnight to finish his daily homework. There were, for example, pages upon pages of Latin conjugations he had to write down, apart from many other tasks. What purpose is achieved by letting a child write that much, I have never understood. The child will keep thinking of finishing his work rather than of the conjugations and will early get used to writing hastily. As the body was still quite undeveloped physically, I expressly forbade him to stay up that late. The work must have been very pressing indeed, however, as he secretly asked the servants to wake him up very early. In Königsberg, too, complaints of parents about the overburdening of their children with homework were rather common. If that was the price for their familiarity with the consulships of Sulla, it was a somewhat high one; one must believe that at such times Sulla was not a mere consul, but a dictator. When I had the opportunity to visit several universities in Germany, I was astonished to hear so many complaints by the students concerning the excessive demands of the state with respect to scientific training. These were strains my ears were not quite used to hearing. I was reminded of them again frequently enough when I later read reviews of publications complaining of overwork at schools and its consequences in literary journals. It seems that, at least at that time, this state of affairs did not prevail in any of the schools of the Baltic provinces, as I do not remember having heard any grievances to that effect from students at Dorpat. Moreover, several of the professors who had come to Dorpat from elsewhere had enjoyed the receptivity and scientific zeal of the students, and at least some of them commented on this publicly, such as Burdach in his autobiography. The reason for this scientific receptivity may be found partly in the fact that the number of students at Dorpat who had to worry about making a living as soon as possible, used to be smaller than at most German universities, but partly also in the fact that they were never overtaxed.

If I am to characterize the spirit of the school, I cannot say in retrospect anything but that, according to my present judgment, it was excellent, at least in the upper class. In the lower classes there was naturally more mischief and even rudeness. Laziness and ineptitude, too, made themselves more felt there, but altogether the atmosphere was a good one. After all, I should know, as I always had nine fellow boarders in my room and at the table even nineteen, from all classes. During my time, neither were there any scandalous incidents, of which we would surely have heard. Not that such things could not happen here; in fact, a short time before I joined the school there had been such an incident. It was treated with extraordinary understanding and this sensible treatment, so it seems, had a beneficial effect.

I think I may state that we of the Prima were very industrious, at least the front benchers were. On the very last benches there were, indeed, some who did not seem to appear very regularly and who, as second rankers, were held in little regard by us. This diligence was not maintained by any external stimulants. There was no distribution of prizes in the school, no public examinations, only an ongoing testing within the class throughout the entire course of the lessons, being called to the blackboard, or being asked to translate, or having to answer single questions. It is true that in the lower classes pupils were placed more to the front ("moved up") or to the rear ("moved down") according to whether their answers were good or bad. But this was no longer the practice in the Prima and would have hurt our finer ambitions. We chose our seats according to our mutual esteem and respect, and retained them until the front benchers left school, when we moved up.

What magic, then, kept us working hard? I believe it was the excellence of the head teachers, the respect we felt for them, their knowledge, their character, and their assiduity. Already, I think, the boy has a feeling for his teacher's devotion; with the adolescent, this feeling becomes a fuller awareness. His motives will bless his own future, which is still at an indeterminate distance, but rather recognition and approval by such a teacher and also by his own fellow students. To this must be added the manner in which we were treated, especially by Wehrmann, whom I regard not only as a born pedagogue but, by virtue of his zeal and experience also as a seasoned educator. I have already mentioned that when someone had not properly prepared himself for translation of the relevant portion in the class for classical languages, he simply interrupted him with a reproachful look, but without saying a word, and called someone else. Now there were indeed cases, especially with those living with their families and not boarding, when real obstacles arose, such as an unexpected visitor who stayed long, family celebrations, and the like. To advance such reasons for not being prepared was so disturbing and so unacceptable that most pupils preferred to stay up part of the night. Wehrmann proceeded in a similar manner with Latin exercises. He went over them carefully, correcting every expression which could be replaced by a more elegant one, writing it above in red ink, while a red line of moderate heaviness on the notebook margin marked an expression that sinned against the spirit of the Latin language. A heavy red line on the margin indicated a serious grammatical error*. The former were called half errors, the latter,

*I was very much astonished to learn that at the local grammar schools in Königsberg, which put such a stress on the classical languages, the teacher fully corrected only a few of the exercises. The pupils then had to correct the rest of the exercises themselves according to the corrected ones.

full errors. Public reckoning was on Saturdays, for each exercise separately, but quite briefly. Only the errors were mentioned, the full errors in a tone of disapprobation, the half ones in a tone of instruction. Everything else was left to the careful eye of the pupil, as the exercises had to be rewritten, with all corrections properly made. Wehrmann never rebuked a pupil in public, nor did I ever hear him issue admonishments in public, although he might have done so in the privacy of his room. Nevertheless, the effect of the red lines was as acute as if they had been written in one's own blood.

As I see it, what happened was that a healthy and entirely appropriate ambition was developed. I believe that the absence of external recognition in the form of public examinations, etc., had the effect of making the pupils value only the recognition and approval of their teacher as well as of their own fellow pupils. Another effect was the absence of occasion for envy and ill will. No one could claim that a pupil had obtained undeserved recognition in public by chance, or believe that some pupil was favored with a prize or even with the convenient formulation of a question out of partiality. I have heard such complaints in Dorpat from graduates of the Reval Gymnasium. They suspected the completely impecunious to have been favored with the distribution of prizes, as these consisted of still usable textbooks.

I will not claim, however, that this exclusion of everything public did not have its drawbacks. It seems to me unwise to rob young people of this age of the opportunity to speak before larger assemblies. In St. Petersburg I have often admired and indeed welcomed the self-assurance with which pupils, also of young age, are able to appear in public. Not being used to such conditions, we would have cut very poor figures in their place. On the other hand, of course, we could never have entertained the idea that anyone would try to mislead the public by staging a carefully rehearsed examination. The respect we had for our teachers would have evaporated in no time through such an experience.

No class distinctions and class prejudices were ever permitted to make themselves felt or heard. Not only the teachers, but also the members of the board took the position that pupils were just pupils and rated them according to their knowledge and ability. From the direction our ambition had taken it is quite obvious that we heartily concurred with this attitude and would acknowledge only a ranking based on merit. During the whole of my stay in Reval, I only once heard of a discordant note in this respect, and that was soon rectified. Three sons of a very prominent family from the country had joined the Secunda, and right away, they demanded places which nobody was prepared to grant them, upon which one of them said, "They might be higher in knowledge, but we are higher in rank." This effusion was greeted by such laughter that no utterances of this sort were ever heard again. In the boarding house, too, this pretension was regarded as decidedly stupid.

The school thus was on a proper and well-run track designed not only to lead to a rapprochement between the social classes, but also to convince the young gentlemen of the nobility that prominence could be achieved only by their own efforts. How, then, did it happen, that a few years later such discord and dissension prevailed in this respect? Complaints were uttered to the effect that the board itself had demanded different treatment for the sons of the nobility than for the sons of commoners. At that time, I was too far removed from the scene to be able to form an opinion about these events, but it seems to me that demands such as those ascribed to the board of that time are the surest means to inculcate, early and permanently, the particular principles of "Junkerdom." These times are long past. But I wonder if they did not leave us a legacy. I now hear that the number of commoners in the school today is not large. This is to be regretted and is all the more surprising as today school fees are the same for all social classes, while previously the nobility asked higher fees from those not belonging to the Body of Knights than from its own sons.

But how were morals? I believe that in this respect I can bear witness for the Prima and will try to bring some specific proof. I had only been at school a few days, when I was told of some of the practical jokes that had been played on old Wehrmann in the past. Such heroic feats remain long in the memory of a school and soon assume a mythical form. Also, because of Wehrmann's extreme myopia, it was not exactly difficult to take him in. Upon hearing these stories, the front benchers declared that whatsoever was intentionally annoying old Wehrmann (that is what we always called him), would first find himself up against them. Indeed, during my time, nothing of this sort ever happened. While this attitude may seem quite natural in the Prima, it still shows the emphatic disapproval of the front-bench boys of such churlishness, as well as the tendency of the occupants of less prominent benches to strive after the recognition of the front-benchers. More characteristic, I believe, is the following. After a pair of Primuses who seemed to have been woefully neglected in their early adolescence, had left the school in the first year of my presence there, no trace of smutty talk or the like was ever heard during the subsequent two years whenever boys of the Prima had occasion to meet. This is likely to be a rather rare state of affairs at an age at which sexuality comes to the fore so pressingly. Credit for this is due chiefly to Assmuth, a future provost but then still a pupil in the Prima. Whenever one of these two black sheep opened his mangy mouth, Assmuth involuntarily uttered an expression of most strongly felt revulsion which, at that moment, was of course of little avail. But it had the effect that once these two had left, no similar talk was heard anymore. Had Assmuth set himself up as a moralizer, he probably would not have achieved these results. One does not like to be disciplined by one's peers, but one wants to be respected by those one respects.

As regards morals, I cannot so highly praise the boarding house.

Overflowing with praise in grateful recognition of the time of my stay at the Knight's and Cathedral School, I am afraid I am rapidly achieving the reputation of a hired *Laudator temporis peracti* (praiser of bygone days). I shall, therefore, most carefully enumerate the flaws, failings, and shortcomings that, according to my opinion, could also be found. But first I must beg permission to report on some quite personal matters which I cannot really include under the heading of flaws.

Two circumstances acted clearly in my favor: first, that at school and in town I found more literary facilities than could be the case in the country, but especially that there I found a circle of young people with whom I could establish close friendships, whence began the poetic period of my life.

Toward the end of my stay at my father's home, the more leisure we were permitted by our irregular schooling, the more pressing became the need for wider reading. The literature for adolescents, of which there was quite a stock, no longer satisfied after reading through Campe's travel stories, the discovery of America, and all number of "The Children's Friend" which we received in instalments. Herr Glandström's library contained primarily scientific books on a variety of subjects. On the other hand, I was looking for "belles lettres," my acquaintance with which was limited almost exclusively to Schiller's poetry, to which was occasionally added a drama by the same author. Cheap, complete editions of the more modern German writers were not yet available and the expensive, earlier editions were not to be found at home, nor were they accessible among our neighbors, because of the absence of young people. My father's library was carefully gone through; the *Corpus juris* and Knight's and Common Law, available at the time only in handwriting, were respectfully skipped; several agricultural publications, the "Heedful Homemaker," "Veterinary Surgeon," and the like ignored, and the rest checked in detail; but in addition to some Latin and English chrestomathies and dictionaries, there was little literature in German, and that rather outdated. Gellert, whose fables I had long known, turned out to be not to my liking in his other works; still less did I like Hagedorn and similar writers. Whatever was more to my taste, of which there was not much, was read and reread most often. Thus, there was a small German chrestomathy which included the second book of the travestied *Aeneid* by Blumauer. I read this several times, and soon knew it almost completely by heart.

This hunger for German literature was far more easily stilled at school. Most pupils owned some of it and, put together, there was quite a lot. The small stock of books that I had brought along was to increase rapidly, and my bibliomaniacal strain to burst forth violently. I was hardly two months at the Cathedral School, when the library of Herr Tideböhl, a former principal, was auctioned off. A book auction is always an event in a town removed from the centers of the book trade and feeling a need for books. During the first days, the auction room was so full that an unassuming pupil was quite unable to even see the books. On the third day, however, the auction room had emptied to such a degree that I dared to join the battle with the rest of the combatants. Soon Hederich's *Lexicon manuale Latino-Germanicum* was put on the block. I asked to be given the book for inspection and as I immediately saw on the title page that it included also middle and modern Latin, I did not let go until the book was mine. I was always astonished at the almost universal popularity of Scheller's dictionary for everyday use, as it is restricted to classical Latin only. Yet, a great many Latin words from later periods, particularly the technical terms used in philosophy, medicine, chemistry, and astronomy, still exist and we meet them and want to know their meaning. All this is packed into Hederich, always citing the authority, so that good Latin can be properly distinguished. Etymologies are given as well. I was extremely happy with this acquisition. While I was still feasting my eyes by leafing through the book, a book in Arabic was being offered. Now, I had not even seen an Arabic book yet, but I wanted it, and promptly got it. Next on the block was a large, unbound work the language (or rather languages) of which the auctioneer could not specify. It was passed around, but nobody recognized the language. I felt an even greater urge to own this book, and own it I did, presently. It turned out that this work comprised several volumes of the Icelandic *Sagas,* in the Icelandic-Danish edition. Having by now worked myself into a frenzy, I went on buying Wolff's fundamentals of mathematics, four volumes, Mead's *Monita et praecepta medica*—I was, after all, a future doctor—and many other books which I do not remember any longer.

Even then I should have had the good sense to know that books that are needed are a treasure indeed, while those that are not needed are nothing but a bother. This insight, however, came to me rather late, if at all, at least as far as its practical implications are concerned. Returning home with my riches, I was particularly happy with my Hederich which has remained a most faithful vademecum throughout my life and has accompanied me wherever I set up housekeeping. I think it unjustified to regard this book as obsolete unless and until one has a better one to replace it. For nonphilologists who do not have access to du Chesne (du Cange), it may serve for a first try to obtaining information concerning the reliable meaning of a later Latin word. It is true that Hederich lacks the many quotations found in those major works relating to middle and modern Latin and in particular cases one will have to refer to them, but for a first attempt the dictionary by Hederich will be found to be a rich source which has made comprehensive use of the pertinent literature up to 1738.

The book in Arabic, on the other hand, I did not know what to do with, after I had feasted my eyes on the curly characters. I brought it to old Wehrmann who completely refunded me the kopeks I had paid. The *Sagas* were used for the drying and pressing of plants, in which service they perished in the course of time. The book by Mead is still with me, although in seventy-five years I have not yet managed to read it.

The enrichment of my library had a disproportionately debilitating effect on my cash box. At that time, the boarding pupils had only very modest means at their disposal—obviously a very proper educational principle of old Wehrmann—for even the young pupils had to show him their cash receipts. Yet despite their meager size, these cash boxes were also meant to improve our daily fare. For lunch and supper, which were nothing less than splendid, yet still must have been sufficient to appease our hunger, we were hardly allowed to add anything special, but for breakfast each of us was given only a dry "Timpfwecken,"—that four-horned bun which is becoming a rarity in Reval today and which will constitute an object of antiquarian research in the next century, to supplement which we were permitted to buy ourselves as much milk as we wanted. The same arrangement was in force for tea, after classes. I am inclined to think that this institution, too, was a pedagogical finesse of the old man. He intended to restrain the sweet teeth among the boarders, since it was the excessive love of dainties that, in the past, had been at the bottom of a very nasty affair. But this restraint he intended to be brought about by our own decision. Now, if one of the boys—I am thinking more of the smaller ones—had wasted any sizable part of his pocket money on sweets or even on simple fruit, he had to make do with dry "Timpfwecken" for a corresponding period of days or weeks, which gave him enough leisure to contemplate the virtues of thriftiness. This method of education was indeed not bad at all, because such a demonstration before one's eyes, or should I rather say one's stomach, was far more effective than admonitions. I had partaken in unseeming quantities if not of physical, then of intellectual dainties and, without much need for calculation, had to face the fact that as far as this semester was concerned, there was to be no more milk for me. Not that I regarded that as much of an affliction since fortunately, as far as food was concerned, I had early learned to restrain myself. My foster mother was a perfect cook, especially with respect to all manner of sweet dishes, to which she knew to impart the most enticing form and which she had wanted me to enjoy with all her heart. Not so, however, my uncle, who had intended to bring me up a hero. He always talked contemptuously of these dishes and did not eat them himself. One should eat meat, the rarer the better, if one wanted to grow into something worthwhile. What would he have said of trichinosis? Yet children always want to be grown up, so he succeeded in making me, too, talk disparagingly of the sweet dishes and frequently refuse them of my own free will, which I sometimes did back home at Piep, too, after I had come upon some advice concerning self-conquest in Campe's books, for instance. When now in Reval, in 1807, the dry "Timpfwecken" were poured rumbling onto the table, all I had to do was to weigh one of the two pigskin-bound volumes of Hederich in my hand, to be able to think with gratification: "You have chosen the better part." One always loves best something one has made sacrifices for. This was also the case with Hederich, and might have been the reason I did not apply for replenishment of my cash box, which would have been only natural.

A far deeper need than that for broader literary facilities found its full satisfaction in Reval, a need which, at home, I was not even fully aware of: the need for intimate contact with young people of my own age. I soon learned to respect and cherish my fellow pupils in the Prima. A particularly affectionate and close friendship, however, developed between me and the aforementioned Assmuth, who was my immediate neighbor on the school bench. Soon a sort of a circle was formed by four of us, not in name perhaps, but in deed. We read to each other short Latin compositions, translated some chapters from a Latin author—Livius, if I remember rightly, was one of them—proof that we were fond of our schoolwork also outside of school, and then moved on to a German writer. These sessions were concluded by having tea. The idea of imitating the life of students was completely foreign to us at that time. To round off the idyllic character of these meetings, they were sometimes followed by a dance with the ladies of the houses where we met (of Councilor Hofmann and Alderman Hippius). The friendships soon assumed slightly romantic overtones; in Dorpat, too, I lived at first with Assmuth. I need hardly mention the fact that besides these friendships other emotions of the heart also developed that were quite lively. But, with all candor, these shall remain locked up in the holy shrine of discretion even in my old age.

Tearing myself away from my poetic period, I shall, in keeping with my promise, move over as speedily as possible to the highly prosaic business of enumerating the flaws, failings, and shortcomings that, according to my opinion, could be found at the school in my time. The most obvious defect, and perhaps the only one in the school proper, was the lack of a competent teacher for the Russian language. The man who had been taken on for this job, a former translator with the government, knew the Russian language quite well, but had only little education and for this reason was less respected by us than the other teachers. The results were not slow in coming. Before my time, selections from Karamzin* had been read, which was probably quite proper, in order that the pupils might be introduced to this literature at its most praiseworthy. But then, some well-meaning senator passed through town, and he did not approve of the reading of Karamzin. He thought that the main thing was to improve the boys' moral fiber. To this end, he suggested a chrestomathy which comprised various stories, mostly of antiquity, told for consideration and emulation. This book was just being introduced when I joined the school. It failed, however, to earn our respect as the stories were already known from their original source or via other pathways. We also realized very well that a collection of translations was quite unsuitable for our institute and

*[Ed. note: Karamzin, Nikolai Mikhailovich, 1766–1826, Russian historian, journalist, essayist and poet.]

for an age where one reads only the classics in other languages. How would old Wehrmann have reacted to a suggestion to select such a book for Latin studies! When now, during translation of a piece in which L. Cinna was mentioned, one of the pupils was impudent enough to ask what the letter L stood for, was it perchance Ludwig? The good teacher had no answer and declared that this was quite unimportant; we then knew for sure that he was not familiar with these abbreviations of Roman names, whereupon two conjectures split the class, one for Ludwig, the other for Leopold. The teacher must have realized that his leg was being pulled, but was quite helpless. Similar incidents recurred, as other pupils, too, wanted to demonstrate their wit. I mention these pranks just because they bear out the importance of a passable education even for the teacher whose subject does not immediately depend on it. With the other teachers, we were meek as lambs; only with this teacher did many of us succumb to our hidden capacity for mischief. Later, I regretted very much that we did not take the lessons in Russian more seriously. It was claimed though, that there were no better teachers in the country—but that would mean setting the borders at the Narova. Beyond that river I am sure they could be found, possibly not as cheap, but then, the purpose was not a trivial one either. Neither was there any opposition, at least not from the board. I am rather inclined to assume that it was the teachers themselves who thought that any larger sacrifice in money or time was superfluous. The fact that this subject is better taken care of today is very gratifying.

While I am unfortunately unable to praise the boarding house to the same extent as I did the school proper, I am far from trying to imply that at that time it was all bad, certainly not its upper floor. There, old Wehrmann, as first inspector and superintendent, kept a watchful eye, and I have already related how, by repeated and unexpected checking, he made sure of the pupils' continued application and devotion to studies. There was probably more teasing and mischief, as well as minor pranks, than really necessary, but these are also found in private education at home. Furthermore, supervision was not incessant, so there was no trace to be found of that feeling of oppression, nor that obsequious submission which so easily slips into hypocritical dissembling and, upon cessation of the pressure, finds it all the more difficult to move along under its own responsibility. These consequences of overstrict supervision are very much harder on the pupils than is some moderate amount of mischief against the teacher. When the noise exceeded a reasonable level, Wehrmann had his own wordless method of treatment. He simply opened his door (he had one leading into his study and another one leading into his bedroom) and swung it several times to and fro—that was almost always enough to restore quiet. If the effect was not immediate, all he had to do was to step out of his room into the corridor.

On the lower floor, conditions were worse because the second inspectors were not educators, nor did they have enough education themselves to supervise the pupils' work. I encountered two of these inspectors in succession. Neither was able to impose his authority, and the second one was involved in a scandalous affair which I do not even care to mention in print.

Food and the entire upkeep were very simple, but as the two inspectors shared our meals, we could not really complain, although there was some covert grumbling. The lack of female supervision, however, was a real drawback. There was only a manservant who made the beds and cleaned the tables, to keep our innate untidiness in bounds.

Moreover, as the praiseworthy state of the upper floor was almost entirely due to the personality of Wehrmann, and as it appears difficult to find competent educators willing to take upon themselves the laborious business of supervising boys brought together from various places, some of whom had possibly been neglected at home, I am not at all surprised that some time after it had been enlarged by the addition of a second building, the boarding house was altogether abolished.

As regards my stay at the Cathedral School and the entire period associated with it, I think I have treated it exhaustively enough, and possibly even too much so. This was not done unintentionally, however. I feel compelled to unearth the causes of the periodic fluctuations of this institute during which major changes are introduced or the continued existence of the school is called in question altogether. In discussing this problem, I have so far attempted to present material from my own experience at the time of my stay there. Before proceeding to discuss the question as to the degree to which these fluctuations of the institution might have been due to its organization, however, I should like to express my conviction, and indicate my reasons for holding it, that the Knights' and Cathedral School already much earlier, indeed from the time that it became an institute of the nobility, exercised a most beneficial effect on that body.

By comparing today's standard of education with that prevailing a century ago, the very considerable progress made here is most conspicuous. During the long, devastating wars which Sweden, Poland, and Russia fought over the Baltic provinces, the German inhabitants started to go to seed, as the saying goes. A more correct diagnosis would be to say that the Germans of the Baltic provinces lagged behind in that progress in education which, as a result of the great impetus provided by the Reformation, could be observed among those Germans in the Holy Roman Empire, and also among those in East and West Prussia, as well as among other people who had become Protestant. The institutes founded here to promote education, just as the schools and university under Gustavus Adolphus, were soon destroyed by war, before the seed they had begun to sow had had time to ripen.

This cultural deprivation, or lack of progress, appeared to permeate all social layers, as is borne out by the fact that Dorpat University, founded in 1632, could find almost no local professors and had to employ Swedish and

German immigrants*. Similar conclusions must be drawn from the periodic reports prepared by commissions sent by the Swedish government to check up on the state of the churches and schools. These reports present a sad picture of our country.

The long-lasting Northern War did nothing to improve these conditions and the Great Plague of 1710 aggravated them, as its most devastating effects were reserved for the cities and their centers of learning. After the Northern War, in fact already during it, from 1710 on, life seemed to settle down and, with this relative quiet, the thirst for education awoke. It appears that in this aspiration the nobility lagged behind the third estate, possibly because most of its members saw their natural destiny or advantage in joining the Russian Army as early as possible, or because of other reasons. My earliest childhood memories seem to bear this out, but they also recall the strong impetus given to the cause of education by Rector Harpe's sermon before the Diet. The enthusiasm and readiness for sacrifices with which his pleadings were accepted and immediately translated into reality are certainly a token of the great urgency with which the mid-eighteenth century nobility must have felt the need for progress.

Looking back to the days of my childhood, I now feel that the generation of the nobility which was then in its best years, and which had started its education in about 1770 or somewhat later, did not betray any discernible lack in general education, whereas the oldest persons I met, whose schooling had begun at about the middle of the eighteenth century, were frequently unable to write down their thoughts in an orderly manner and with any semblance of a regular orthography, and often used the German language very incorrectly. This latter circumstance was possibly due to the fact that, still earlier, at the beginning of the century, the Low German dialect was in rather general colloquial use, although documents from this period, at least those that I happened to see, clearly show that High German was taught at school.

I cannot but believe, therefore, that with the new prospering of the Cathedral School, or very soon after that, a significant change must have occurred in the state of general education of the nobility, and I must adhere to my conviction despite the fact that many of my acquaintances, and in particular my father and his brother, had still not had their education at this school. No doubt, the promotion of the Cathedral School increased the number of men capable of teaching, and, most important of all, the esteem in which the nobles held schooling and education was bound to rise after they

*Among the large number of professors employed by the first university at Dorpat (1632-1656) and the second university at Dorpat and Pernau (1690–1710), I could find only three local men: Nicolaus Bergius of Reval, Jacob Wilde of Bauske in Courland, and Arvid Moller from the vicinity of Dorpat who, without being a professor, did give some lectures in this capacity as Rector of the school at Dorpat. Müll. Samml. R. Geschichte, Vol. IX.

themselves had founded a school with great sacrifices, and after a board constituted of their members—presumably the most educated ones—and of trusted representatives of the public was in constant contact with dedicated educators. Therefore, I assess the importance of the Cathedral School for the nobility not merely by the number of pupils recruited from that class, but rather by the general influence it was able to exert, which, already quite soon after they took over the school, seems to me to have been considerable. Although Reval had another institute for better schooling for over a century, namely the gymnasium, it is a fact that the nobility, whether rightly or wrongly I cannot say, made almost no use of it. Their alternative, however, of taking all sorts of adventurous tutors into their homes sometimes had rather deplorable results, of which I could mention some examples*. The frequency of military service was decreasing, though only gradually, but the poorer sections of the nobility still regarded it as a means of permitting their young people, after they had received what was considered sufficient schooling, to see the world and gather experience under some control and supervision, even if for a few years only, so as not to tie them to their native soil forever. Thus, there were in my youth a great many men who, in the service of Mars, had attained the rank of lieutenant or captain or, if they served longer, even major. This type of education was, in any case, better than another, which was quite frequently chosen by the richer nobility, who sent their sons to Paris with the exhortation to acquire the habits and manners of a cavalier at court and in other good society, but not to refuse a duel if the opportunity should present itself. The acquaintance of actors and actresses was easily made and needed

---

*Among them, one from my immediate surroundings, others, by reputation. One of these tutors found his way into my grandfather's home. Some of his school reports, which he was supposed to have produced at weekly intervals, were long kept in the family. In these reports, which I have before me, appear the following comments regarding a female student: "otherwise makes an effort to reed (!) obediently and spels (!), but, unexpectly surprised, changed a quite ordinary letter, a D, once into a W and once into a V." The other reports about the rest of the children are of the same triviality and curious orthography, for example: "Has difficulty with the Lord's Prayer. The rest can be taken for passable." The pièce de résistance of this small collection, however, was a petition involving two rubles. To energetically support his petition, the man thought he had to squeeze in as many high-sounding phrases as the paper would permit. Under his quill, this bombast turned into the purest of nonsense. Thus, he mentioned a "Lutheran-Kalmuck religion." This was too much for my grandfather about whose educational level I unfortunately know very little, but who considered schooling to be of great importance. The man, naturally, was given his two rubles but, soon and equally naturally, also his notice. Other tutors, I have been told, held the belief that the virtue of Christian love could be impressed upon the pupils only by beatings. That, as late as fifty years ago, there were still people who had learned nothing beyond reading and writing, and thought that this qualified them to become tutors, I learned from my own experience when I was given the task of looking for a teacher in Dorpat. But I also learned that these types could not find a position anywhere.

no exhortations. I could relate rather sad examples of this way of life. The best solution was probably to send the young people to a German university or a German court. Sometimes but not often, it appears, they also chose foreign service. The local university and the ease with which one may now see half the world have wrought great changes in this type of "post-school education," but that is an altogether different story.

Here it was my aim to show that the transformation of the Cathedral School appeared to have had a remarkably beneficial effect on our small province very early, and on its numerous nobles in particular. This is probably due to the fact that the nobles considered the institute as their own and were ready to make sacrifices, and that a group of them had steady contact with selected faculty members and with the dedicated Rector Harpe. Also, they had to represent publicly the interests of schooling and education in the Diets, so that these were more talked about in public and, therefore, gained more general recognition. An indirect effect of all this was to make it more difficult for adventurous tutors to obtain places with the families, while it eased the way for good teachers. The direct contribution of the institute, however, though only taking effect at a later time, consisted in its graduates, who played an essential part in the dissemination of scientific education among all social classes, especially among the nobility. This was particularly true if these graduates took along with them, as indeed most of them did in my time, their love for scientific work. I regret not to have before me a more comprehensive list of the pupils of our institute who finished the entire course of studies up to, and including, the Prima. I believe it would show that a large proportion of the members of our highest authority, the Regional Court of Appeals, had obtained their education at this institute. The Cathedral School, being the Knights' own school, is also the mightiest tool with which they can even further improve the education of future generations, as well as guide such education along lines adapted to their needs.

To provide for a complete education of their children from their own means is possible only for the richest, that is, a very small number of families. Only the community as such is able to ensure a good and complete education for the largest number. That, however, the thorough education of a good number of the nobility is a high, indeed in their highest common interest, if they wish to maintain their political significance and all that goes with it, above all to continue to prosper, will certainly not be denied.

Proceeding now to the constitution of the Knights' and Cathedral School, one of the difficulties and causes of friction may be seen in the circumstance that the management and administration of the school is in the hands of an elected group of nobles, the board, which in turn is responsible to the Diet and is obliged to safeguard the general interests of the entire body of nobles. On the other hand, this board is faced by a body of teachers consisting of pedagogues who not only have gone through their general scholastic training, but have been, and still are, trying to pursue their particular main subjects even further. The more devoted a teacher is to his calling, the more will he see his true reward in raising real scholars; these are his pride. Yet the nobility must satisfy those of its members who have children in need of schooling, by providing suitable opportunities for it, with a view to such pursuits as most young people choose according to their respective social position which, in turn, can only develop from the past. This point of view must not be ignored by the board. Equally incumbent upon the board, however, is for it to look toward the future, as every social institution should, and to be fully aware of the fact that it has been entrusted with the care of the educational progress of the nobility as a whole, a mission which is indeed awesome.

It cannot be denied that the organizational structure of the institute has its difficulties, which can hardly be avoided, as the nobility cannot be expected to bear the not inconsiderable costs of the institute's upkeep without making sure, by continual supervision, that it indeed serves its interests. One of these difficulties is that every untoward incident in the school is talked about by all the families throughout the country, which may too easily give rise among some people to the idea of giving up the school altogether, inasmuch as among those who pay are not a few who either have no children to educate, or who are able to take care of them otherwise. Thus, they pay only for the interests of the Order. On such occasions, people suddenly seem to remember earlier occurrences which, in part, have already passed into the realm of myth. When an incident of this type occurs in a government-supported institute, everybody tries hard to prevent knowledge of the matter from spreading beyond those immediately concerned*.

Of much more serious consequences are differences of opinion which may arise between the board and the teaching staff. My only advice for avoiding conflicts of this kind is to save neither efforts nor, as far as possible, money, in looking for competent and devoted teachers and, having found such, to trust their good sense and experience. Thus, it follows that the personal composition of the board should be changed as little as possible, because frequent changes in that group—that is, in the opinions of the management—have a paralyzing effect on teachers. Nevertheless if changes in the curriculum are

*How long such legends, having once spread to the country are kept alive, may be judged from the fact that, in my time, some very respectable grandmothers and great-aunts suffered agonies worrying that their descendants in the Cathedral School were certain to go to seed, because of the fights with the gymnasium boys. Now such quarrels occurred at that time in the most rudimentary and naive forms among a very few pupils of the lowest class, who were thirsting for glory and heroic exploits. If there were tussles of a larger scale they must have occurred at a much earlier period, as nobody at school seemed to have a recollection of any events of this kind. What recollections still existed, appeared to continue in the country. There is no doubt that tales of such Falstaffian adventures reached the ears of family circles, thereby causing the aforementioned grandmotherly concern.

strongly desired by the country, the teachers' committee should agree readily and with the best of intentions, unless such changes should be found completely unfeasible.

During my stay at the Knights' and Cathedral School, I believe that conditions were favorable in all these respects, which is precisely the reason why the institute was prospering just then. The most important teachers, Messrs. Wehrmann and Blasche, were greatly respected in the country, and they, as well as their opinions, were held in high esteem by the board. Nevertheless, certain differences of opinion became apparent even then. It was common knowledge in the country that Wehrmann was a dedicated philologist and made every effort to advance this aspect of education, while there was no lack of voices clamoring for greater stress on subjects which were more closely related to the future calling of a large section of the nobility, namely jurisprudence and the science of war. Such demands, which were probably also voiced in the Diet, could not be completely ignored by the board. Although I have never seen the minutes of the school meetings, I presume that Herr Wehrmann pointed out that teaching the ancient languages is of abiding value only if it leads to a fluent understanding of authors. At least, that is what the results would suggest: his philology hours were not curtailed. Neither was Prof. Blasche able to reduce his hours, if he wanted to retain his method of cursorily repeating at the beginning of each year the material of previous years. Still less was it possible to limit other subjects which in any case were given a few hours only. Therefore, it was decided to introduce extraordinary hours, partly for basic concepts in jurisprudence and partly for fortifications and artillery; pupils in the Prima and Secunda were free to take advantage of them. I decided to take both, and I found the jurisprudence lessons particularly interesting. There was a former jurist among the teachers, Herr Heuser, whom we had thus far not met in the Prima. He took it upon himself to give us a survey of all the (legal) institutions, and as he rejoiced in returning to his former studies, his lectures were most stimulating. I was quite interested in the subtle, sometimes one could even say ingenious distinctions characteristic of the juridical sphere. In any case, these considerations were quite new to us and, as far as later life is concerned, I think that these lessons can by no means be considered a loss; at the least, they widened the mental horizon. The lectures on fortifications and artillery, I, and as it appeared others as well, found less satisfactory, although they were given by the well-liked Blasche. He himself did not seem to enjoy the subject to any degree. Although it was quite agreeable, and by no means superfluous, to get to know the names and purposes of different fortifications and their parts, as well as pieces of ordnance and their parts—and as in Reval the fortifications were still completely intact, we could inspect these things at once on the spot. Yet it seemed that we could have picked up these secrets just as well were an informed lieutenant to take us through the fortifications for, say, two mornings as had happened with me before. Also, the fact could not be denied that we would hardly learn any-thing about the art of utilization of the terrain while sitting on the school bench. Nor did Prof. Blasche ever touch on this particular subject. He used the lesson periods to have us calculate such quantities as the cubic content of walls and bastions, the number of cannon balls in the different piles in an artillery park, etc. To the different recipes for preparing gun powder and rocket starts, and similar practical matters, we paid little attention, as we thought that the old man could not possibly have any experience of his own in these matters. Appreciation of a teacher's competence in his subject appears to be quite essential as far as his students' interest in his lessons is concerned.

These extraordinary lectures were only held during one year of my stay at the school.

Today it is no longer expected that someone will demand lessons in juris-prudence at the school, as one cannot only take a complete course in Dorpat in Roman Law, but also receive explanations of the prevailing national and provincial statutes on the law books.

Differences of opinion will spring up also in the future, however, and more so as each side adheres more obstinately to its position. I consider myself as impartial, standing in the middle between the two camps. Coming from the nobility, I have, however, spent my entire life in the educational sphere. The first circumstance has brought the needs of the nobility closer to my under-standing, the other has caused me to keep thinking about education in science, its meaning and its value. To what degree this has brought my opinions nearer to the truth I am, of course, unable to judge by myself. But I believe that this double relationship gives me a certain right, I am almost tempted to say, an obligation, to speak my mind without restraint, even if this entails the risk of being disapproved of by both sides. What, as a pedagogue, I lack in experience in the narrowest sense of the word, is possibly at least in part made up for by the impartiality of my position. I have also taken a vigorous part in Königsberg in the struggles that were known as "battles" between humanism and realism (in the pedagogical sense). Philanthropinism* was no longer an issue, but there were two gymnasiums in Königsberg, both organized accord-ing to the humanistic pattern, of which the one, having for its principal a man with a many-sided education who was not only a philologist but also a com-petent mathematician, stressed and also furthered mathematical subjects; the other school, the principal of which was almost exclusively dedicated to phi-lology, put value almost exclusively on this subject only. Now the citizens of this town also wanted an institute of an entirely different type, of which much had been heard already—a "Real-gymnasium"** and even managed, through great sacrifice, to collect the funds required. No school could be founded

*[Ed. note: The educational philosophy of Basedow.]
**[Ed. note: Secondary school with an emphasis on the exact and historical sciences.]

without the permission and supervision of the state, however. Whereupon the authorities started to pressure the Magistrate and did not let up, until this institute, too, began to resemble the other two schools and a principal was appointed who, with a fine flourish of rhetoric, made quite clear in his inaugural speech, that everything humane was concentrated in the Ancients and that all humaneness was to be drawn from them.

I found this very unjust. The only real difficulty in the way of realization of the wishes of the Königsberg citizenry appeared to be finding competent teachers, a particularly hard task in this town. But a beginning should have been made in any case. Even if it was impossible to create a full-blown polytechnic school all at once (this, in fact, was what the citizenry had in mind), such an institute might have been achieved in the course of time. There was a definite need for another school besides the two gymnasiums and the important thing was to provide as thorough a schooling there as they did*. Neither did I like the introductory speech, although it was given by a friend of mine. Instead of convincing me, it drew my opposition. Is there not too much human among the Ancients? In fact, their entire Olympus is somewhat too human for us or, considered from a moral point of view, actually subhuman, however superhuman their physical accomplishments. Progressive civilization has indeed placed our ideal of the humane on a higher level, and if someone perceives too much fantasy in the word ideal, I am quite ready to express myself in down-to-earth terms as an educator; what sensible father would wish his sons and daughters to resemble the gods and goddesses of ancient Greece? However much raw material they have provided, and will yet provide for poetry, they can hardly be said to provide models for the education of human beings. "But," one could conceivably object, "the brilliant classics of later times do certainly have an educational effect right down to our own time; who will want to apply the stricter yardstick of our own time to the naive visions from the early childhood of peoples?" I have never denied the Greek source of our culture, but the stricter yardstick of our time certainly has its great value and justification. For what other reason do we withhold certain authors from young people altogether or let them read them only after careful editing? It is just this yardstick which may well serve as proof that humanity has made progress and need not be redrawn time and again from the Greek wellspring.

*Among the artisans of Königsberg were some who, by common school standards, must have been very well-educated. Thus, when in the Physics-Economic Society of Königsberg I spoke of the zoologist Conrad Gessner, I was asked by some from the audience whether this was the same Gessner that had compiled the Latin dictionary? The questioner was a coppersmith. If an artisan wanted to have his son learn something proper, he could get only a mathematical or a philological education. Yet it was these very men who felt they lacked the means to follow the progress in their respective trades. Their request (for a suitable school) was, therefore, quite justified. However, as Königsberg was the home ground of Prof. Löbeck, the famous philologist, the town could be considered a philological hothouse.

What is more, this source would not necessarily have its stimulating effect, had it not long ago and everywhere borne fruit in all European literatures. However, far be it from me to denigrate the value of philological studies in the schools; I only wish that this value not be sought specifically in the humane and, furthermore, I take exception to the use of well-worn stock phrases as evidence, while, as a matter of fact, they do not prove anything. Were the humane attainable only through study of the works of antiquity, and that in their original language only, we would have to despair of the European female sex, of which only an infinitesimal minority has direct access to these sources. Yet no one will doubt the fact that an educated lady owes a large part of her education to the classic peoples of antiquity, since, if this were not so, apart from the sacred songs, she could hardly enjoy any poetry and, apart from church art, few other paintings.

I do not believe I could have found a shorter way to make it clear, that in countless ways, the knowledge of the ancients has had and still has an effect on us through all languages and literatures, and in fact may be said to envelop us. That in this process its original nudity has become somewhat veiled, is a demand of progressing time, which surely nobody can find fault with. And has not every man who today reads Homer or Virgil in the original already absorbed a large part of these works at a much earlier date? To make up the missing part, is it really worthwhile to go the time-consuming route of learning the languages? To my mind, the value of studying the ancient languages is to be sought not in the subject matter of the classics, but elsewhere.

As I mentioned before, I participated very actively in the discussions in Königsberg on schools and school education, which arose on the aforementioned occasion*. What I tried to make clear, primarily to myself, was what

*This participation applied more to private circles than to public occasions. However, once at a rather large meeting, a public dialogue developed between the principal of the philological gymnasium and myself, which deserves to be mentioned here because of its characteristic nature. A popular science society had invited me to lecture on the importance of knowing one's own country. The principal just mentioned was present and although my lecture had nothing to do with philological studies one of my remarks, something to the effect that one should not only regard as worth knowing that which is remote in time and space, must have appeared to him as a challenge. At the end of the lecture he approached me and said, "You were talking of the importance of knowing one's own country—but let us take for once our own Prussia; what does it have that is worth knowing? What, for instance, has happened in Mohringen? In the vicinity of Athens, on the other hand, something worth knowing has occurred in every village." It was his bad luck to have chosen Mohringen, of all places. "In Mohringen," I replied at once, "was born one of the greatest Germans, Herder." Although it is quite common, and somehow also natural, for the immigrant to evince more interest in the new country and its affairs than many a native, my interlocutor seemed rather peevish at having been hoisted with his own petard. Therefore, he continued the dialogue saying, among other things, "In each newspaper issue there is something of Homer." "Just because of that," I retorted, "it seems

(Contd.)

the most general aim of school education ought to be, and to find out, I had to ask exactly where the general benefit bestowed by European school education was to be found. This question thus led me to reflect on the past and the gradual development of education in general, and of scientific education in particular, reflections which I am unable to pursue here. I shall however attempt to summarize their result.

However decidedly we now consider it one of the faculties of our intellectual being to distinguish between our reasoning capacity on the one hand, and our imagination, our emotions, and our desires on the other, it cannot be denied that in "rude" man, that is, man as molded by nature only, these functions mutually replace and displace one another. Peoples in the youth of their development would not have produced such a multitude of often very intricate stories concerning gods and creation, had they been able to distinguish clearly between figments of the imagination and structures of knowledge. When their desire awoke for understanding the world that surrounded them and the course of events, it found satisfaction in these fruits of fantasy, and the richer the imagination of a people, the more diversified were the popular expressions of their fantasies. Selfishness, too, is unconsciously intermingled: each people wishes to obtain preferential treatment from its gods, who thus become more or less national gods.

I have delved deep into the past only because at that period of time the inability to distinguish between the functions of cogitation and of imagination and the suggestions of desires was particularly glaring. There is no need, however, to go back so far to find persons who harbor beliefs of which they do not know whether they are based on logical reasoning, unchecked tradition, or self-centered wishfulness; nor to find, as well, other persons who know exactly the antecedents of their beliefs and are able to erect the edifice of their knowledge from its foundations up. If we call the capability of forming a sound judgment by the name of critical faculty, then the former of the foregoing groups of persons lacks this critical faculty, whereas the latter group possesses it. The general task of a good school now seems to be the development of this critical faculty in us by reducing each subject to its basis and showing how certain theories are logically derived from such teachings; by not only teaching, for example, that the Earth is a spherical body freely floating in space, but also by bringing proof for this claim, as is probably done in all good schools. Formerly, the belief was held that to attain correct thinking habits it was absolutely necessary to be aware of the laws of reasoning, as formulated in logic. Experience, however, has shown that properly exercising the faculty of correct thinking gives better results than knowing the laws of logic,

superfluous now to read Homer in the original." This is even now my considered opinion. Whatever of the Ancients still survives in our culture we encounter at many a turn.

just as exercise is more effective in helping one become a strong and persevering hiker, than knowing the structure of the organs of locomotion and the laws of mechanics. The practice of critical thinking, namely the consciousness of what our convictions are based on, is doubtless also the fruit which the European School system has borne in the course of time. This is also the reason why the sciences have developed in Europe, but not in Asia, and why in Europe well-schooled persons have sounder judgment than unschooled or poorly-schooled persons. Comparing schooled Europeans, even if they are not devoted to a particular scientific discipline, with Asians, it will be found that the latter are not aware of how they came by their beliefs and convictions, whether through tradition from others, or through their own observations and ordered reasoning, or whether they are based on fantasy. Not knowing the origin of their beliefs, they are totally incapable of telling someone else why they hold a certain view. At least, this is my impression of the West Asians with whom I had various contacts for several years. I regret that particular and concrete proof of this cannot be brought without excessive detail*. Yet

*Since citing individual cases is always more convincing than relating generalized results, I will nevertheless give an account of a few cases which can be told briefly.

Once I made a trip across the Caspian Sea in the company of a Bukharan merchant, an Asian quite innocent of European schooling. In his own way, he was quite a sensible person and we became very friendly, as he spoke Russian rather fluently. I liked to sit near him on the deck when he drank tea, and I had him tell me some stories. Once he told me that formerly the Syr Darya used to flow into the Amu Darya, at which time it was possible to travel by boat from Bukhara to Kokand. As this story sounded improbable to the highest degree, I wanted to know how he thought this possible: whether the southern arm of the Syr, the Yan Darya, had been larger at that time and Lake Aral smaller, or whether he had heard of the legend that once upon a time the Amu Darya had flowed into the Caspian Sea and maybe there was some confusion involved. Although he seemed to understand my questions he answered them rather unwillingly and unclearly. But when I asked him on what he based his claim, whether he had somewhere read about the former course of the river, whether this story was based on a legend or the like, he refused to answer and from that moment on he avoided being in my company and looked at me nervously, as if he suspected me of spying. The fact that I wanted to know the source of his belief was too much for him.

The following experience is still more characteristic. Russian military posts on the shores of the Caspian Sea, whether manned by marine or land forces, often employ Armenians as interpreters because, like the Jews, these people study several languages from childhood on. Such a man was also stationed at Fort Novo-Alexandrovsk on the eastern shore of the Caspian Sea. Since I was told that he had been in Khiva on behalf of Herr Karelin to view the much talked about dam closing off one arm of the Amu, I wanted to speak to him. This seemed to please the commander who expressed the hope that I would be able to do something for the Armenian. He expressed this hope to the Armenian, who did not fail to visit me next day with much pleasure. He readily told me about what he had seen of the dam, which was about the same that could have been learned already at the time of Peter I. After concluding his report, which had begun to bore me somewhat toward the end, he added to my great surprise: "But the way the Amu just drops into

(Contd.)

I would like to state that the often heard remark to the effect that Asians and, even more so, the savages proper, were liars and could not be relied upon, appears to me incorrect. It is true that when they intend to deceive they lie as well as Europeans; but, according to my experience, they are altogether unable to distinguish between fact and fiction. For instance, before Europeans penetrated into the interior of Africa, Negroes from the interior had often been questioned about the country, and their statements were later branded as lies. But the men questioned very often had no reason for lying. Yet it is enough to ask an unschooled person whether he had ever seen a certain snow-covered mountain range or an inland lake, which one then proceeds to describe vividly in order to confuse him to the point where he no longer knows whether he has had this knowledge before or whether it was imparted to him just now. However, concerning legends and stories that have taken root in the popular mind, in these he believes implicitly, without asking himself whence they came, and he cannot tell them from his own observations.

the abyss—that is horrifying!" "What?" I gave a start, "how was that?" For the benefit of those readers who are not familiar with the geography of Western Asia, I should add that for several centuries a confused legend has been abroad according to which the Amu Darya sinks into the ground and reappears only at a great distance. Some describe its entrance into the ground as a violent plunge. As no European had seen this phenomenon, and the whole thing seems altogether unbelievable if not impossible, because at Khiva the Amu is already very low, the critical European mind has often discussed the question as to the origins of this legend. The European wants to know, for instance, whether along its upper, not sufficiently well-known course, the river formed a cataract, the description of which had possibly placed it lower down along its course. Chancellor, the first European to come to Khiva, in 1558, already mentions this alleged drop into the ground. It is quite possible in fact that he was the man who created or spread this misunderstanding. I thus started up in expectant surprise, as it seemed that I was about to hear the solution to the puzzle from an eyewitness. My sudden and excited question, however, caused the Armenian to become startled and troubled. Sensing this, I asked him very quietly only to tell me whether he had observed this disappearance himself and what, in fact, he had seen of it? He did not say a word in reply, but the expression of his face changed from reflection to confusion, to shame. He then reached for the door, tore it open, and disappeared, never to show himself again. My only explanation for this curious behavior is that the good man did not at all distinguish between what he had read or heard and what he himself had seen, and it was only my question that had made him conscious of the discrepancy between what he had just told me and what in actual fact he had seen. He could not have had the slightest motive to tell me an intentional lie.

Among the Arab authors whom I occasionally had to leaf through for geographical information, it seems to me that as a rule the oldest are the most reliable ones. They simply report what they have seen. Later authors often want to be more detailed, and accept all sorts of information uncritically, sometimes even erroneous reports concerning objects that they have almost immediately before their eyes. Thus I remember an author living in Persia who included in his descriptions of the southern shore of the Caspian Sea, some totally false information which he accepted lock, stock, and barrel from Greek authors, that is, unless it should turn out to be the perpetuated wisdom of some learned copyist from a later period.

Seeing the schools' true task in the training and practicing of consistent and critical reasoning, and expressing the opinion that European schools have early followed this tendency and thereby helped to raise the scientific knowledge of this continent in particular far beyond that of the others, I believe I have made it abundantly clear that I am not a disciple of philanthropinism or of the theory which holds the true task of schooling to be the cramming into the child's mind, with a slight cerebral effort, the largest possible amount of multifarious information. In his time, Basedow was probably right in finding fault with schools that invested all their energy in the knowledge of antiquity and its languages, carrying children and youths off into worlds long past, while the present world that surrounded them remained totally alien. Today we have periodicals for young people, as well as popular books on the most varied subjects, on camels and coconut trees, volcanoes and cloud formation, astronomy and geography, peoples of the present and of the past, all in such profusion that every boy or man can absorb as much as his interest demands in his leisure hours or during reading exercises. The problem is one of selection, and a good teacher should indeed endeavor to somehow acquaint himself with this immense literature so as to be able to give advice where advice is wanted. All this, however, is no substitute for real mental work. It is this work, let us call it mental gymnastics, which is the true task of the gymnasiums* and related schools. Mental gymnastics is also an effect much harder to achieve by study on one's own than is the enrichment of the imagination through assimilation of all kinds of images of the most different objects. If it is correct that the critical faculty is generally not innate in man, but must be acquired and exercised, then it is obvious why persons who have had no regular school education, while possibly possessing a diligently acquired knowledge of facts, are still often unclear and confused and are by no means equal to those who are used to consistent and ordered thinking; the latter having acquired such factual knowledge, are able to utilize it to much better effect. The claims of pedagogues, that thorough study at a gymnasium also constitutes preparation for subjects not actually taught there, seem to me by no means unjustified.

It remains now to be determined which are the means suitable for exercising the mind. Obviously it is not the volume of knowledge absorbed that leads to this end, but the critical treatment of every subject taught, that is, the

*[Ed. note: Gymnasium—German usage for grammar or secondary school, usually with a classical bias.] The term gymnasium was originally used by the Greeks for establishments in which training was given in wrestling, boxing and exercise and athletics in general. Since these physical exercises were performed in the nude, and since the Greek word for nude is γυμνὸς (gymnos), these localities became known as gymnasiums, nude rooms, so to speak. Later, the term was also extended to places in which mental exercises were performed, or philosophy taught. The Greeks already called exercises of the mind by the same name as exercises of the body—γυμνάζειν. The expression "mental gymnastics" which we used above is, thus, a very natural one.

laying bare of the fundamentals on which the entire edifice of knowledge rests. Mathematics and the classical languages have long been regarded by higher schools as excellent means for this purpose. As far as mathematics is concerned, this choice is quite obvious, as it is particularly suitable for following a critical and consistent method, enabling progress from the most simple, self-evident principles to more and more complex conclusions. Such a systematic consistency, however, is not applicable to the classical languages since there the point is not to erect a whole structure of knowledge on simple principles but to translate foreign thoughts into our language and mode of expression. It is precisely this aspect which constitutes a great exercise of the mind. The entire structure of the classical languages differs from that of more modern languages, in particular from that of our own German, so that it is by no means sufficient to know the meaning of the individual words. We must in fact be able to think a sentence clearly in the spirit of the ancient language in order to express it in the words, and according to the spirit, of our language. As far as the classical languages are concerned, what we call "translating" in fact always consists of this double exercise of the mind, and the slow progression through grammar in the classroom is nothing but the method, empirically arrived at, that leads to a complete understanding. The more modern languages differ far less in structure from our language than do the classical languages. There are, therefore, that many fewer mental gymnastics needed in translating from them than in translating from the classical languages, however useful the modern languages may be in practical life. Their grammar is much simpler and, in some languages, so simple—worn smooth, as the philologists would have it—that, provided one knows the meaning of the words, one is able to translate with only a very slight mental effort.

Once it is agreed that translation from a classical language into our mother tongue constitutes a continuous mental exercise, one must also agree that the complaint heard, not only here, but everywhere, that "I have forgotten all my Latin and Greek; what a pity the time was lost at school !" has no basis. The profit consisted in the intellectual training even if one did not go beyond some simple authors; the more one has managed to read, the higher the profit. But even if one stopped after the first approaches—grammar and a small vocabulary—there should be no need to complain of wasted time, especially here, since our lawyers like nothing better than to intersperse even their most trivial notices with a few crumbs of Latin, no doubt to cover up the lack of gracefulness in their German style. Also, some knowledge of the Latin language has become the mark of a better education to such a degree that sins against the basic rules of Latin grammar are forgiven only if committed by a beautiful mouth.

Thus I fully concur with philologists and pedagogues in their conviction that acquisition of the classical languages has a greater effect on the mind than study of the more modern languages, because the former involve a more intensive training of the intellect. Yet I cannot endorse all of their extravagant utterances precisely because they appear to me extravagant. First of all, I cannot approve of an attitude that considers any comparison of other subjects with the classical languages, or any expression of interest in the former, as an assault on the Holy of Holies. Such overtones are also evident here and there in Plate's history of the Knights' and Cathedral School which I mentioned earlier, and it was, in fact, these that provided me with the first motive for a discussion of this subject. But has the Cathedral School any reason at all to complain about a slighting of the value of the classical languages? Between 1777 and 1799, its board included a man, *Landrat* von Cursell, who, according to his own claim, found his foremost pleasure in the pursuit of the classics. On the bookcase which housed his classics he had placed an inscription, saying *"Deliciis meis"* (for my pleasures) and he bequeathed it to the school. I hope that this inscription, to which old Wehrmann used to draw our attention, has been left intact. Also, since 1799, the board has not been lacking in men who knew enough to respect the classical languages. If despite all this, classical languages could not or would not be granted a position of monopoly, arguments must have been produced which could not be flatly dismissed. Against such arguments must be weighed other considerations, including my preceding attempt at an exact determination of the value of the ancient languages. Such a value, however, must not be postulated under the assumption that the priority of these languages has been manifested for all eternity, and that any comparison with other subjects, therefore, becomes an act of sacrilege.

I also feel rather pained when I hear that conventional platitude, "The school must not merely 'drill' " used as an argument against demands that the school should take into account the future careers of its pupil. The use of stock phrases always gives rise to the suspicion that its user is either unable or unwilling to take the trouble to explain his opinion as consistently built upon basic principles, and prefers to hide behind the authority of old sayings. Preparation for life is certainly a task for the school. The important point is to find the proper proportion between the general sharpening of wits by mental gymnastics, and the provision of material directly useful in later life. Coming back to that somewhat less than noble concept of drilling, the reader must concede that having earlier accorded priority to mental gymnastics as the main task of schools, I will not speak in favor of such "training" and even less for an overly one-sided allowance for future careers. In the other provinces of the Russian Empire, education was excessively fragmented until recently, in specialized schools preparing pupils for the various occupations. The insufficiency of this system has been generally recognized by now, and today the trend is toward more generalized institutions which means, or at least should mean, schools in which the stress is put on mental gymnastics. After many years in which graduates of the cadet corps, the medical academy, etc., have

been switching over to quite different occupations, in which they often excelled, the fact has finally been brought home that people cannot be treated as
so much amorphous dough expected to assume the shape of the dough-press
nozzle through which it is forced. It is now generally understood that people
have latent aptitudes that need only care and nourishing to develop, as the
bud develops into the flower, the shape of which is dormant in the bud. The
different aptitudes, however, can be made to develop only by care which is
sufficiently general. It would amount to a gross anachronism, therefore, if I
were to advise our school to concentrate on future occupations at the expense
of mind training, especially in the lower classes. Boys sitting on those benches
are buds still so tightly closed that even the most experienced teacher cannot
tell into what they may develop. It is my intention, however, to try to also
vindicate those who want to make allowance for the future occupation of these
boys, to which end I must once again return to that unpleasant term "drilling."
When we acquire domestic animals to serve us, such as dogs and horses, we
expect them to be properly broken in, so that they may serve us well, and we
are dissatisfied if they are not so trained. The same holds true for servants
whom we take on, or for officials and estate agents, only that in this case we
do not talk about their being "drilled" but about their being well-informed
in the field in which we want to make use of them. Yet does this not apply
equally to us? For our life's work we need ourselves. Won't we be more
satisfied with ourselves if we find we are properly prepared for this work, and
do we not have reason for gratitude toward a school when we come to realize
that it has qualified us for it? The pedagogues say that the only task of the
school is to prepare the mind, unless they go even further and claim that
children first have to be shaped into human beings*, and that preparation for
the particular future career is a later task in which the trained intellect has a
greater chance to succeed.

I have repeatedly and emphatically declared that I fully concur with the
first half of this theory. As concerns the second half, it is equally evident that
the skills of agriculture, administration, and military service—the most common occupations of the local nobility—must be acquired through direct activity in these occupations. To try to teach elements of these skills in school

---

*This is one more of the slogans that really exasperate me. When I returned with my
family from Germany to Russia, I had four sons, three of whom were of school age.
They were staying in Reval for half a year and it seemed urgently necessary to me to start
them off as early as possible on the first elements of the Russian language, beginning with
the letters of the alphabet. Trying to find a suitable arrangement, I met a teacher who,
with great vigor, tried to make me understand that the children had to be turned into
human beings, a task that he was ready to see to; only then would the time be ripe for
other things. He must have thought me very stupid for failing to be captivated by his
banalities. While inwardly returning the compliment, I declared dryly that these children
were already human beings, and all I wanted was that these small human beings learn
some Russian.

would appear so ridiculous, that I shall waste no further words on it. I also readily believe that a schooled mind will acquire these skills and this elementary knowledge much easier, and master them much more thoroughly than an unschooled one. However, if it must be conceded on the one hand that pursuit of the ancient languages is an excellent vehicle for gymnastics of the intellect, it cannot be denied on the other that the subject matter of these mental exercises has very little, if any, relation to the careers commonly chosen by the nobility. An exception is perhaps the study of law which, if pursued seriously, requires a familiarity with the Latin language.

Yet, is it not conceivable that other types of mental gymnastics exist which, by virtue of their subject matter, are at the same time also of direct benefit to these careers? Have not several branches of the natural sciences already elevated themselves to a consequent methodology which precludes their pursuit without mental gymnastics and logical thinking? I am referring here to those sciences which may be called exact, because they deal with measurement and quantities, and can be expressed in numbers, in other words physics, including mechanics, and chemistry. Pursuing these sciences is certain to sharpen one's wits, while at the same time they find daily application in agriculture. If these sciences are to be utilized by the school to train the mental faculties of the pupils, they must be treated with that thoroughness of which they not only deserve, but which is inherent in them. Concerning the applicability of scientific knowledge to agriculture, I dare not mention to the informed reader more than the simple truth that the whole of agriculture is actually one great endeavor to apply the laws of nature to the best advantage of the farmer. Even if agriculture can be mastered in the field only, and not on the school bench, an insight into its theoretical foundations is certain to promote the learning process and help prevent gross mistakes. To mention an example very much before our eyes: not only do we have a large amount of natural marshland in Estonia but there are many areas which are known to have been forest or good meadow land in the past, which now produce nothing but peat and peat vegetation. Knowing the situation well, I must ascribe this deterioration to the blocking off of rivers by mill dams. In most places, however, this damming up seems to have been carried out in excess of the needs of the mill and given the slight gradient of our rivers, this has had far-reaching effects. If landowners were more knowledgeable and had more experience in the science of mechanics, I believe they would use less water power to greater effect, and would not leave the design and construction of water wheels to the millers who have no interest at all in preserving the land upstream of the mill dam.

Everybody now realizes the value of knowledge in chemistry. Yet, how much sounder would be the judgment of a man who has had the opportunity to acquaint himself methodically with the elements of chemistry and to perform chemical tests himself, even if only very simple ones, rather than trying to learn the subject by independent study from books in later years.

This should not be understood as a suggestion for a change in the present curriculum. If I were called upon to take part in the shaping of the school, I would hesitate to abandon the path well-proven by long experience, as I would not be certain that a new path would compensate for the loss of the old one on which—most importantly—there are to be found the best and most competent pedagogues. It would be very difficult to find teachers of similar qualities for the aforementioned natural sciences. But their number is bound to increase and, in any event, it seemed worthwhile to me to point out the fact that the mind-sharpening element in the classical languages can also be replaced by the natural sciences, that is by the quantitative branches of the natural sciences. The other descriptive branches prove by the very fact of their nonquantitative nature that they have not yet penetrated to basic principles. They are more suitable for the lower and intermediate classes. All images and values from antiquity which we consider essential for the education of mind and heart are obtainable in ways other than via the ancient languages. The search for images and ideas by way of the classical languages is undertaken, even today, only by those who devote their entire lives to their study. Thus, it must be left to them to continuously renew and restore these images. If this were not so, we would all have to study the Hebrew language to read our catechism.

However, if steps should one day be taken to introduce changes in the school, should not serious consideration be given to the possibility of introducing a more extensive course in the exact sciences, to be given either concurrently with, or subsequently to the usual course of studies? Let us consider these two alternatives.

First the concurrent alternative. In my time, physics was taught only in the Prima, and only twice a week. This is very little indeed; in no chapter does it permit detailed treatment, nor even the completion of a general survey in a year's time. Chemistry today seems no less necessary. Without some knowledge of chemistry it is quite impossible to understand not only a contemporary book on agriculture but also a host of other works which are written for the educated classes but remain impenetrable, including publications on the maintenance of health. An elementary knowledge of chemistry is thus a quite general need today. It would hardly be practicable, but seems to me also quite unnecessary, to go into great detail, because the field is too wide. I believe, however, that the slow and systematic assimilation of the fundamentals of the science is bound to make it much easier to continue to study on one's own. The same applies also to mechanics, where it will be equally impossible to go into a depth that would enable one to construct some contrivance or other. The basic concepts acquired, however, should constitute the key with which to unlock works of a more specialized nature for continued study without outside help. These basic concepts are also the means for an understanding of mechanical devices.

Whether such a course could be intercalated into the existing time table, or whether it should be optional and given in extra hours or, finally, whether so-called subsidiary classes would be required—are questions which can be answered only by a person thoroughly familiar with present arrangements, which, admittedly, I am not. I should like to stress this point in order to remove any possible suspicion that these remarks of mine were in any way meant to criticize or improve existing conditions. All I intended was to offer as a subject for consideration opinions relating to local circumstances which, after many years of experience, I have come to hold.

The other alternative about which I have been thinking for some time now without giving it expression, is to offer serious study of the exact sciences following the completed school course for those intending to devote themselves to agriculture. I should like to do that now.

When discussions were initiated concerning radical transformation or even abolition of the Knights' and Cathedral School several years ago, one of the proposals brought up on that occasion appealed to me very much—providing it were to be supplemented by another. According to the proposal, the lower classes were to be abolished altogether as the landed nobility only rarely sent their sons into the lower classes of public schools, preferring to have their first schooling given at home. Town dwellers, on the other hand, easily find opportunities for good schooling for their younger children if they do not also send them to the country, a step I very much favor. It was hoped that abolishing the lowermost classes would release a number of teachers, with the result that several small educational establishments could be opened in the country. This plan appealed to me for several reasons. First of all, I think it is a decided advantage for children to have their first schooling in the country at an age when physical development is so easily stunted and when movement in the open air is so essential for strengthening the physique, and also because a stay in the country offers impressions and experiences to the child which life in town does not offer. What is more, a teacher dealing with a few children is bound to help these children advance far more rapidly than is likely in a situation in which a boy, still so little master of his mental powers, especially of his attentive powers, is expected to use for himself that which is being told to a wide circle. In a smaller, more homelike circle, mental and emotional traits are better observed, and morals more closely supervised than in an open school where it is quite impossible to hold the principal, or even the class teacher, responsible for morals. At most, they can take care to see that no immorality occurs in their presence; that is, they can do police duty, momentarily. In the upper classes, the teacher's intellectual influence will be more effective, while in the lower classes this influence will be displaced by the influence of home life and the pupils' effect upon each other. Pedagogues object to the late enrollment of pupils, saying that their levels of preparedness vary excessively. I have even heard the claim that the best pupils were those who started from the bottom and passed through the entire succession of classes. Supposing this last claim to be well-founded, which appears to me very doubtful, it is to be regretted that progress in public schools has to be paid for more heavily than in private instruction. The school teacher, unable to hold the pupil's attention as easily as in private instruction, feels the need to give him more homework. Thus, the boy not only spends many hours a day on the school bench, only half occupied, but has to spend many hours afterward fully occupied, and that at an age when, in addition to physical activities, an alternation of periods of mental effort and carefree rambling is so natural and salutary. I believe, therefore, that children who are schooled in the country harbor such feelings of overburdening much less often. As for the aforementioned differences in the levels of preparedness, this is easily taken care of. For instance, only the Quinta and Quarta could be abolished and a publication could be circulated in the country specifying the type and extent of preparation required of boys wanting to enter the Tertia. Perhaps even the Tertia could be abolished; I would not recommend such a step without full knowledge of the present situation however. On the other hand, I have not the slightest doubt that to abolish the entire school would be a veritable calamity for the whole country. Higher education needs not only competent experts, that is, people versed in and devoted to the various subjects, but also real pedagogues who have given thought to the educational system and are informed of and trained in the best teaching methods. People of this sort are still very rare among us. The best teachers I have ever known: Steingrüber, Wehrmann and Blasche, were all foreigners. To be sure, this is strictly an individual experience, my own, but I am inclined to think that it was, and probably still is, of general validity. During my stay in Dorpat I saw a great many young people who finished their studies and accepted positions as private teachers, relying on their own schooling. But I never heard of one of them who had made a special study of education and the educational system. I doubt not for a moment that now, after all kinds of small educational establishments and boarding schools have been opened in Dorpat, there are also better qualified pedagogues among the graduates. At the same time, the number of vacancies for such men at gymnasiums have increased to such an extent that, I am told, there is still a shortage of competent teachers for private instruction. As concerns the first rudiments of science, they are probably more numerous, while it is next to impossible to find a man capable of teaching the various sciences and arts at a level as high as that obtaining in the upper classes of a good public school in town. However, quite apart from the lessons as such, life in the city greatly widens the horizon of a young person by the closer contact he has with many others, and that at a time in life when the character has already taken on a more definite shape and self-control ought not to be lacking, so that there is also little reason to fear evil influences. Looking at my own life experience, I am most satisfied with the fact that I had my first schooling in the country, with the family, and later in town at the school. Possibly it would have been even better had I been sent to school a year or two earlier.

Thus I found this proposal quite acceptable. If it had been carried out I would have added a second proposal however, namely to establish, in the interest of the landed nobility and particularly of that section of it which does not follow a military career, a special institution under the name of *lycée* or a *polytechnic* for the serious study and practical application of the exact sciences. This should be done preferably in association with the neighboring provinces of Livonia and Courland so as to lighten the burden on small Estonia and obviate the need for excessive austerity in appointing such an institute. As concerns the status of the students, I envisage it as freer than in the schools and less free than at universities. I had the intention to submit a proposal of this kind to the Diet, but did not carry it out when I was informed that the decision was made to retain the lower classes of the Knights' and Cathedral School. Also, there was some talk about founding a polytechnical institute in Riga, which I thought might satisfy these needs in the course of time. Thus the proposal remained unsubmitted.

Still more to the point would be the observation that having finished school one still had the opportunity of acquiring the necessary knowledge in physics and chemistry in Dorpat. This is very likely and, in part even certain, since today there are students who work extensively in the chemistry laboratory of which there was not a trace in my time. But are lectures there on mechanics in any degree comprehensive? If treated from the mathematical aspect only, the material required for mechanical design and construction is not touched on at all. Be that as it may, I would advise the nobles to make inquiries both at the Polytechnic in Riga and at the university in Dorpat in order that they may see to the interests of the young farmers. A special laboratory for the use of future farmers does not seem to be out of place. It should not be difficult to find a suitable instructor in Dorpat.

It is obvious that I am searching for means to satisfy the increasingly urgent need for widespread knowledge and skills in the exact sciences, without, at the same time, changing the prevailing structure of our schools and without displacing the philological studies in particular, these having taken root and being relatively easy to find competent teachers for. It is possible that in the course of centuries these studies will have to yield altogether to the natural sciences. But let us not hasten their demise.

I may yet be permitted to make an opportune remark concerning the vast Russian provinces of the state, a remark that is almost forcibly pushing itself to the fore. The Russian provinces are now the scene of a heated debate as to whether or not the classical languages ought to constitute an essential part of all higher education. The struggle in itself is gratifying, since it gives these studies a standing which, due to their limited direct applicability, they have never enjoyed, and also because among the protagonists of these studies are also to be found native Russians, even such who are known, rightly or wrongly, to be Germanophobes*. Yet I think these protagonists go too far when they agree with the claim, which a professor in Kazan pronounced against me in 1863, to the effect that barbarism would destroy it once the classical languages no longer constitute the basis of school education.

It is my belief, however, that barbarism would be destructive or, to be more precise, that school education would fail to achieve its aims if the gathering of knowledge came to be regarded as its essential task rather than the exercising of the mind. Yet, whether this exercising of the mind is to be regarded as achievable solely, or at least pre-eminently, through the classical languages, has to be dealt with as a separate question.

Since the introduction of Christianity, school education in all of Europe had its beginnings in the church. All schools were originally church schools. Classical studies were introduced only gradually, as the Latin language, at least in western Europe, was not only the church language but the common language of the educated classes, and thus also became the language of the schools. Because Greek was the language of the New Testament it therefore could not be neglected entirely. When the old classics, which had been totally neglected because of religious fervor, were rediscovered, their contents and form began to exert an attraction. They awakened the desire to study the history of, and everything else associated with antiquity and to spread knowledge of it. One sought all education on this path of classical study. But mathematical studies also became valuable as they were recognized as the basis of astronomy, geography, and the nautical sciences. Natural sciences developed only much later. Yet in France, the natural sciences have already partly displaced classical studies. The Germanic peoples, on the other hand, especially the English and Germans, have held on to classical studies with greater tenacity. Even among them, however, the science-biased "real-gymnasiums" and polytechnical institutes have started to gain some ground

---

*The inhabitants of the Baltic provinces were most gratified on reading a recent article in a Moscow paper in which recognition is accorded to the fact that scientific education and, in particular, classical studies are more widespread in the Baltic provinces than in other provinces. Still more to be appreciated was the value placed on education in general, and not only for young men but also for women. Families of very limited means take it as their sacred duty to make every possible sacrifice for the education of their children. Not infrequently, a remote relative will step in, where the father is missing, to provide means for the education of a young member of the family.

It seems to me that, in the other provinces, in the many educational establishments where the state accepts the young people and takes care of all their needs, the natural obligation of parents and other members of the family have been greatly reduced. It will not be easy to restore the proper proportion unless the state will consistently follow the rule to accept as public servants only the most capable subjects, regardless of where they received their education, and not according to privileged graduation certificates.

on classical studies. In Russia, the educational system is obviously much closer to its ecclesiastical cradle than it is in western Europe. It is indeed questionable whether it would benefit the Russian people to retread the whole long path taken by the scientific education of the Germanic peoples in order, in a few centuries perhaps, to turn more to the exact sciences. What is more, compared with the Germanic peoples, the genius of the Russian people has a stronger bent for the practical and is less inclined to immerse itself in antiquity and lose sight of the present. The Germans have certainly profited from this propensity of theirs and from this development of their educational system, but equally certain is the detrimental effect these have had. To a people that is practically almost at the crossroads concerning the direction to be taken by its educational system, my advice is to go both ways at the same time: to set up schools for a thorough classical education as well as others for an equally thorough education in the exact sciences, and to have them exist side by side, especially in the big cities. Anyhow, there can be no reason why everybody should pursue only the same sphere of knowledge. In any case, such a one-sidedness has a self-perpetuating effect in that it will not produce the teachers required to break out of this circle. Also, for the development of the trades in all their ramifications, a wider dissemination of the exact sciences is an urgent need in Russia.

Returning from these vast distances and undecided big questions to our modest Cathedral School and bidding it farewell, I can only express my urgent and heartfelt wish that it will always retain the principle of placing pupils in their respective classes according to their progress in different subjects, not only according to a single subject. I only know that several years after my departure, this arrangement was abolished but was supposed to have been reintroduced when my two sons studied there. What the situation is now is entirely unknown to me. But I feel a real need to declare that I regard it as an irresponsible cruelty to arrest the educational advance of a young person just because he cannot, or even does not try to, make progress in a certain subject. A pupil was sent down from the specifically classical gymnasium in Königsberg because he sat for two years in the same class and could not be promoted even after that. The only criteria for promotion were the classical languages. This pupil went on to become an excellent man, not just in a practical field but as a prominent theoretician in a field far removed from philology. Obviously, what he lacked was not aptitude but interest in the languages, evincing, as he did, only too lively an interest in other subjects. The great Linnaeus, because he felt an overwhelming interest in free nature, revealed so little interest in the Hebrew language that his school intended to send him down to his father who, in turn, wanted his son to become a shoemaker, as he was obviously unfit for a clergyman.

But for a farsighted man who took him under his wings, and but for his own determination in later years to make up for what he had missed earlier,

Linnaeus would have become a cobbler. How many a human life is stunted in less spectacular circumstances, because the path prescribed for it was too narrow! How often does this break or bend a person's character, that rudder of life! Yet, what a man does in his life depends more on his character than on his wealth of knowledge.

* * *

Too far carried away by the discussion of the school and its problems, I seem to have lost sight of myself. There is not much more to tell except for the fact that after staying three years at the school, I left it with gratitude in my heart in the summer of 1810, so that I could begin my medical studies at Dorpat. This departure, however, was also to include a confirmation ceremony together with some fellow pupils leaving at the same time. We would have preferred to receive the blessings at the hands of Pastor Holtz, but he had died before the end of the semester, after he had taken over the office of rector in an active capacity and shortly before the expected nomination to this office. We were thus confirmed by Superintendent Meyer.

6. Dorpat University
(1810-1814)

With youthful hopes I went on to Dorpat University. When approaching from the north I first had a view of the town, including the old, imposing ruin on Cathedral Hill, now converted into the library, it seemed to me that I saw light irradiating the entire surroundings like the light emanating from the Christ child in Correggio's painting.—But I am unable to look back at the time spent in Dorpat with the same degree of satisfaction that I felt for the years spent in Reval. Not that I, too, like almost all of my fellow students as well as our successors, did not retain an abiding attachment to our alma mater, or that the joyful days of happy independence and the memory of many excellent friends has vanished from my heart. Nor will I deny the fact that if my Dorpat memories do not present as clear a mirror as did my Reval recollections, the blame is partly my own. First of all I had chosen a profession, practical medicine, which did not correspond to my inner organization, and for which I could not find the right approaches in Dorpat. But with all my striving for objectivity, I cannot deny the fact that, at that time, the university suffered from several shortcomings which have fortunately been rectified today and which may all the more be pointed out to give proof of the considerable progress that was to be enjoyed by future generations.

Yet some peculiarities that appear as shortcomings to me will be retained by Dorpat in the future also, notwithstanding all efforts by the administration. These are related to its situation. However, my judgment in this respect is possibly one-sided. I am referring primarily to the smallness of the town. Visits to and comparisons between many universities have convinced me that larger towns having universities are better for the education of young people than smaller towns. The intellectual horizon is wider, the educational facilities are richer, recreational possibilities for the students are more varied and there is less medieval crudeness. While students should feel like independent masters of themselves everywhere, those in small towns all too easily come to feel themselves masters of the town as well and sometimes, by extension, masters of the surroundings without defined borders, i.e., of the world. It could be objected that at small universities professors are much closer to students and therefore have much more influence on them, to the benefit of their education, than in larger universities, where the professor, having given his lecture, moves on to other activities, caring little about how the seed that has been sown comes up. This advantage of small universities is very real indeed, but to turn this into a reproach against universities in larger towns can be justified only with respect to universities in very big cities, especially in capital cities of large states. If there is a choice, such universities should be selected only for the last stage of education because they have the best and most varied scientific facilities, and a student who has already passed the *propylae* of the scientific edifice and has begun to penetrate into the inner sanctum, will gladly be helped even by the professor who, facing a tyro, might be inclined to think: "Well, you either swim or sink." However, it is not the very large towns which I hold most suitable for a scientific education, but the medium-sized ones. In my opinion, it would have been highly desirable if Riga had been selected for the University of the Baltic provinces. But with us, as was also the case for a long time in Germany, the main idea was to remove youth from the noisy world while studying so that nothing would disturb them. Better that they should not disturb themselves! On the occasion of the founding of the first university in our provinces, by Gustavus Adolphus in 1632, at its restoration in 1680 during the prolonged efforts for its rehabilitation, up to the actual founding of the new university in 1802, it seems that only such small towns as Dorpat, Pernau and, lastly, also Mitau were considered. Dorpat, it was said, lies in the center of the country—that is an argument that ought to be heard. But it was also said that Dorpat had no other sources of prosperity. That is an argument which, it appears to me, ought not to be heard. A university should not be considered a means to commerce.

In Germany, which in our day is crisscrossed by railroads in all directions whereby students are able to travel to larger places within a few hours and at small cost, the disadvantages of smaller localities will be less felt today than the advantages of having all auditoria and other facilities used by the student situated in close proximity. For some professions, these advantages may indeed outweight the disadvantages, but for the medical student the absence of large hospitals and their contribution—cadavers—is certainly a significant drawback.

In the meantime, however, Dorpat is about to progressively reduce these disadvantages. The town is growing rather rapidly, and there are now twice as many inhabitants as in my time. It also has a cheerful and comfortable countenance, with numerous gardens in its center. The Cathedral Hill, belonging in its entirety to the university, was even in my time well-planted with trees which have developed magnificently, and now constitute a major adornment of the town. The immediate surroundings could have been more pleasant and inviting as far as the students were concerned; this was all the more desirable since almost all the gardens within the town were, and still are, in private hands, with only one or two being made available to some large associations in town. None, in my time, were available predominantly for the recreation of the students and their exposure to fresh air. This was supposed to be the function of Cathedral Hill and on pleasant summer days it was indeed used for this purpose. But there were no facilities to enable students to settle down for a few hours and stretch their limbs, such as were maintained by every German university. The smaller universities provided these facilities primarily for their students; the larger ones also enabled their students to mix with other people. The absence of such a meeting place was felt still more strongly by us during our long winter. Both in Germany and the Baltic provinces, the main idea behind the selection of small towns for universities probably was a desired enhancement of the students' continuous and undisturbed attention to studies. Yet, when there are no meeting places, as was the case in Dorpat between 1810 and 1814, another kind of disturbance easily develops, one which is much less educational than the theater or similar places of recreation found in large towns. For young people to stick to their books from morning to evening would be against nature. At most, this can be expected from scholars of an advanced age and not infrequently is paid for by a loss of health. Scholars of this type also rarely miss the family circle. At a university, however, there are in addition to those who take their studies seriously and devote sufficient time to them, also not a few who, rightly or wrongly, spend much less time at them. Both those who need momentary relaxation and those who relax more or less permanently require a place of retreat so as not to disturb those who want to proceed with their work. In Dorpat, visits to one's room—sometimes by fellow students who just wanted to while away some hours—were a great disturbance, especially when many students lived together. I felt this difference particularly during my stays in Vienna, Würzburg, and Berlin, where I had no chance evening visitors of this type, and the only people coming to see me were those with whom I had some business. Relaxation and recreation were sought in public places. An attempt was later made in Dorpat as well to remedy the situation by setting up, with the professors' support, an academic club to serve as a meeting place for professors and students. As representative of the students during the last year of my stay, it was my duty to initiate the first negotiations concerning this subject with Prof. Parrot. However, the project was realized only much later.

I was more irritated by another matter, that concerned only the narrow circle of Estonians, than by these unwanted visitors who, in any case, only rarely dropped in on Assmuth and myself. When I came to Dorpat, I found that all students were organized into *Landsmannschaften*, groups of fellow-countrymen, that conformed to the geographical borders of the provinces. These associations, being covert, were valued all the more by the students. Thus, without having been asked, I found myself a member of the Estonian contingent which, if I remember well, was rather small, consisting of nineteen persons. I do not know how it happened that two students had been elected as Seniors (Chairmen), neither of whom were to my liking or should have attained positions as representatives. Probably none of the other older students, among them the later Dr. Rauch, had been prepared to accept these time-consuming positions. Thus it happened that one of the new seniors was a student who, so far as devotion to study and morals were concerned, could serve as the opposite of a model. Since according to traditional student rights, newcomers had to keep quiet and be properly drilled by the other students, we newcomers indeed tried to keep to ourselves, until our time of influence came. Anyhow, we friends from the Cathedral School were quite satisfied with each other's company. We were in fact rather drearily normal, much to the annoyance of the aforementioned senior, who regarded himself both obliged and authorized to rectify this situation by setting about to instruct us in the full-blooded tone and repartee of the real student. This must surely have been a sacrifice on his part as he was bound to find us very stuffy because we intentionally tried to appear slightly Philistine. As for me, I have always regarded Penelope, that universally accepted paragon of womanhood, as one of the dullest personages of antiquity. I would not have remained her suitor for long. How much more interesting is Helen!

The exact opposite of that morally corrupt but witty senior was the second representative, a good-natured young man of little talent, easily enthused, without really knowing what about. I would have liked to avoid the company of both. There were more interesting and estimable persons among the Estonians; how many more could thus be expected from all the provinces together. Therefore, even in the first semester, I found this segregation-by-origin system quite repugnant, and regarded it as a senseless restriction of the possibilities of my selecting for social intercourse those people that appealed to me most, in other words, a useless and indeed harmful restriction of academic freedom. When in the following semester, however, the previously described second senior visited me in order to reproach me for having no contacts with many Estonians while socially meeting even Courlanders (his own words!), I became thoroughly disgusted with this nonsense and promised myself that once the first year had passed and I had achieved some standing in the Students' Council, I would make an effort to have this restrictive practice abolished, and would further instead a grouping of students according to faculties. This aim was achieved earlier and easier than I had believed possible, and I cannot claim to have played a very important role in this matter. But this episode caused me to involve myself more deeply in student affairs than I would have otherwise. Even earlier, the strongest *Landsmannschaft*, the Livonian, had already more or less dissolved its association, and only the Courlanders and Estonians, whose ambition to assert themselves was spurred on by their smaller number, still maintained theirs. Only in my third semester were these associations dissolved, in a ceremony not lacking in solemnity. I now had what I wanted; for the remaining three years of my stay, the official division according to faculties was retained in all official negotiations. I could now see for myself, however, that while this arrangement, because it was official, had the advantage that only those students were elected as representatives who enjoyed the confidence of most and who also had some standing with the professors, it did not quite satisfy the wishes of the young people, possibly just because of its official stamp. There are always some ambitious persons who feel they can assert themselves to greater advantage under the cloak of secrecy. Thus, the *Landsmannschaften* were later reintroduced, and continued to exist for a long time, more or less with the knowledge of, but ignored by the professors. At present, students' organizations are recognized with the result, I hope, that no individual who does not have his fellow students' confidence can set himself up as a representative. Yet I wonder if other, less legitimate associations do not exist, or if such associations will not be formed? The clandestine is too seductive and mostly has an unwholesome effect. To begin with, it is bad for the future citizen to accustom himself to act against regulations of the state. In this respect I have become stricter, if anything. But even now I am not so morose as to grudge youth its full measure of youthful gaiety. Even a measure of youthful boisterousness well becomes the years of bright hopes, and some trifling acts of thoughtlessness are as forgivable as they are natural. I only hate to see them degenerate into rudeness. This also seemed to be the predominant view of professors in my time. All of them, or at least the majority, seemed to be of the opinion that the university could prosper only if it was not reduced to the state of a strictly supervised school. But I cannot approve of the fact that some of the professors in my time not only thought and lived like students, to put it mildly*, but also used to talk to the students as liberally as did the students among themselves. Greater events, through which I lived later, have taught me the rule that a prince should always think in liberal terms, but never speak in them. I believe the same rule should apply also to the less important relationship between the university's senate and the student body. If I use here the ambiguous word "liberal," it goes without saying that I refer only to differing degrees of academic discipline and deference. Of revolutionary ideology for which, I am told, Dorpat was later scrutinized, there was at that time not the faintest trace, nor could there be, because nobody knew anything about the organization and circumstances of the state and, to tell the truth, people cared less than would seem decent. Only in great events, such as the War of 1812, did we participate, following as we did the general trend of emotions, or else leading it with youthful hearts. As I look back on it, Napoleon's campaign showed precisely how little political education we had. We regarded it as nothing but a predatory invasion. I do not remember that any student viewed it as the expression of a political conception. Speaking generally, we were altogether too young. There were only a few students who, after finishing school, had some experience of life, and most of those were rather tired out. I knew only two who preserved some

*More about this can be found in Burdach's autobiography *Rückblick auf mein Leben*, pp. 214–265.

freshness, and I felt attracted to them because they widened my horizon. Later, during my visit to Jena, I had a similar experience, when I found several young men who had participated in the Great War of Liberation and now wanted to finish their interrupted studies. I wish that there were always some men of this sort in Dorpat, men who are already beyond their first youth but who live with the students. They bring with them a truer appreciation of time and a wider view of life. When at a later period I read with great interest the autobiography of Goethe, I came to realize, not without a feeling of envy, how many interesting personalities he had had early and fruitful contact with. This only strengthens my conviction that segregation into small *Landsmannschaften*, if it is intended to monopolize and restrict social intercourse, is absurd and even harmful. One of the few pieces of advice which I tendered to two of my sons before they left for the university was to select for their closer contacts only fellow students who enjoyed general respect and who they felt were an intellectual asset to them.

Of the professors I met, I was particularly attracted by our physics professor, G. Fr. Parrot. His daily, rather detailed physics lectures extended over the whole year, which still left two-hour sessions on electricity and magnetism for the third semester. His lectures were lively and well-constructed, proceeding from the particular phenomena to general conclusions, in a manner to which we were accustomed from our mathematics studies. Unfortunately, the lectures in chemistry did not conform to this pattern. Following the almost customary practice, or I should say malpractice, they started with general questions and let the particular limp along after. Moreover, they were somewhat confused because the lecturer was at the same time also rector, and overburdened with work to such a degree that he seemed to have no time to prepare what he had to say in an orderly manner. For me, this circumstance spoiled the subject which in any case has been completely transformed since then.

The professor of natural history, Germann, had died shortly before my arrival. Prof. Ledebour, known as a most able botanist, came during my second semester. He made his name with his *Flora Rossica*, and was supposed to teach all subjects of natural history according to the old classification: zoology, botany, mineralogy, and geology. That at least is what the announcement of his course stated. As far as I know he never lectured on the latter two sciences. Soon after his arrival the academic senate made an effort to obtain a separate chair for these two subjects, which was fully justified, as even at that time these sciences and the former, the biological sciences, had moved far apart. Negotiations were so protracted, however, that during the four years of my stay there were no lectures at all on mineralogy and geology. I did not attend any botany lectures, except for a short survey of the most important families, which one semester was presented once a week in a public lecture. For systematic botany, Prof. Ledebour was for me more of an enlightening friend who readily provided me with books. I waited most expectantly for zoology, although Ledebour had almost no lecturing experience in that subject and would have liked to refuse everybody who wanted to take his course. Finally, however, he put together a notebook from which he lectured. With the upper classes, he restricted himself to systematics, and as he was not much at home in systematics either and managed to convey the impression that he was poking fun at himself, and furthermore, in conversation made no secret of the fact that he was not familiar with the subject, his lectures were not much of an attraction. But my interest revived when we arrived at the Mollusks, partly because of the varied shapes of their shells—sometimes very elegant, sometimes rather quaint—of which there was a substantial supply, painstakingly prepared for each lecture by Ledebour, and partly because of some anatomical notes based on Swammerdam which Ledebour had worked into the lecture. However scanty the information provided on Echinoderms, Medusae, and Infusoria, it held my interest because of the unusual shapes.

Both Parrot and Ledebour soon opened their homes to me, for which I am very much obliged to them. Contact of this kind is always stimulating and enlightening for the student. This occurred again somewhat later with K. F. Burdach who was appointed Professor for Anatomy and Physiology in the summer of 1811. In Dorpat, Burdach's lectures were followed with the greatest interest, as they were brilliant even for the most common demonstrations, possibly too detailed sometimes, and tinged with nature philosophy*. But this was precisely what one longed for in Dorpat. Most other lectures suffered from a surfeit of rather useless scholarship with which the professors tried to show off, as well as from a lack of spirit. Occasionally we were warned darkly of nature philosophy as of a bogeyman, without there ever being anything more specific about the harm liable to befall us, because none was known. The natural result of this was to make us even more curious to meet this spectre of which the professors seemed in terror without their actually having made its acquaintance**. Burdach at first also lectured on general anatomy, to be sure, not at the microscope as is the rule today, but in Bichat's manner. Still, this provided us with some understanding of organic structure, which was very valuable. We were most impressed by his *Geschichte des Lebens* (History of

---

*[Ed. note: "Nature philosophy" is a technical term for a type of biological thinking popular in early nineteenth-century Germany.]

**Such vague warnings usually have the effect of stimulating curiosity. Prof. Balk frequently cautioned us against animal magnetism (Mesmerism), without bringing proof of the fancy and deception involved. As a result we of course read Kluge's book on the subject, and as it was written very temptingly, at least some of us became followers, clandestinely, that is. I myself was cured by the senseless gibberish of Wolfart's lectures in Berlin. By no means do I completely deny the existence of situations described. I believe I have seen them to some slight degree and even to have experienced them myself. But I would hate to have to hear such a lecture on the subject again.

Life), a kind of embryology. Unfortunately, I was unable to make use of all of Burdach's lectures as I had already attended Cichorius's for most of the necessary descriptive anatomy, and many of the other lectures I was supposed to attend in my first year were not given at all and had to be made up for later, e.g. zoology.

In fact, the various chairs were only partly filled, a circumstance that compelled me and my contemporaries to a rather confused cramming in later semesters. This induces me to take a closer look at several of the university's failings.

In the first place, the university was as yet too young, only eight years having passed since its foundation. It is true that during this short period a quite satisfactory amount of scientific equipment had been acquired for the different departments. For its part the government had spared no expense and had acquired entire collections; others, such as that forming the basis of the zoological collection had been donated. A botanical garden had been laid out that could be considered satisfactory for students; an observatory was founded that was soon to become famous; the various clinics, the anatomical institute, the library, and a very large main building had been built with great munificence. But it appears that great mistakes had been made in the selection of the original staff of professors. A not inconsiderable number of so-called scholars, who for years had been working as practicing physicians, private tutors, or in similar positions, natives or immigrants, had been appointed professors, and they brought with them the obsolete contents and obsolete methods of their fields of study for, since the days of their own studies, they had had no opportunities—some for as long as twenty years—to participate in the progress of their respective subjects. Apparently it was not yet permitted to appoint scholars from abroad. The otherwise rather detailed publication *Die Kaiserliche Universität Dorpat während der ersten fünfzig Jahre ihres Bestehens und Wirkens. Druckschrift zum Jubelfeste am 12. und 13. December 1852* (The Imperial University at Dorpat during the First Fifty Years of its Existence and Influence. Published on the Occasion of its Jubilee on the 12th and 13th of December 1852) is rather unclear on this point. All that can be found in it is a chance remark in a footnote on p. 33, to the effect that "The necessity to restrict oneself to scholars from within the borders of the Russian Empire has prevented the realization of a plan, devised in 1800 by the then President of the Board of Governors, Privy Councilor Carl Otto von Transehe, to go abroad at his own expense to try to induce such men as . . . (then follows a list containing many impressive names) to accept an appointment in Dorpat." Except for this chance remark, the blame for the selection of these superannuated persons would have to be attributed to the aristocratic board of that time, as on p. 23 of the text, the book clearly states that in 1800, after the provisional appointments of the first professors had been set in motion the same year, the first commission of the nobility had reserved its right to proceed with the selection and presentation of still more lecturers. However, the choice having been altogether limited to the home country where no university as yet existed, it was as good as impossible to find competent men for all subjects. The above quotation shows that the board was most anxious to recruit outstanding men from abroad, even if this involved financial sacrifices, as shown by the offer of the President of the Board, Transehe*.

In the first years after its foundation, the university paid salaries substantial enough to attract very competent men in their prime, even from Germany. Soon however, after the great wars of 1807 and 1812–1814, the rate of exchange became so low that the salaries, paid in bank script (paper money issued by the French revolutionary government) lost most of their attractiveness. Despite this, it was still possible between 1810 and 1811 to engage such outstanding men as Burdach and Ledebour. How much easier would that have been in the first years (1799–1800). It would have been possible to raise the new institution at once to the level of the German universities. As it was, this was achieved only later by strenuous effort and not without internal struggles.

It would have been hard for me to point out the weaknesses of Dorpat's first years, had I not been certain that Dorpat later ascended to a much higher level, and had I not accorded the pleasure of joyfully recognizing this splendid development of my native university with a full heart in my old age. The turn for the better was primarily due to the rector of many years, Gustav

---

*The pertinent information in the report cited is so indefinite and given with such mental reservation, that I am indeed not sure whether my interpretation is the correct one. Therefore, I should mention the fact that while I am writing these lines, the documented history of Dorpat University, which later Herr. W. v. Bock has begun to publish in the *Baltische Monatsschrift* (Baltic Monthly), Vol. 9, has not yet advanced to the founding of the new university and will not have arrived there when these pages will have to go to press. No doubt, this history will reveal the entire course of events. One must accord grateful recognition to those sections that have appeared so far and that give documented proof, though wryly, but not without justified indignation, of the fact that the long continued efforts of the nobility to restore the former state university have thus far been totally disregarded, if not intentionally ignored. In any historical description, the foremost aim must be the truth, if one does not want to lay oneself open to the accusation of partiality. Herr von Bock has been pushed toward such a position. It is our sincere wish, however, that coming to the new period of the university, he will forget all bias and as supreme judge may present whatever can be said about both sides, in particular including the extent to which the previous board may have been to blame in being removed according to the usual methods. Struggles seem to characterize the first years of all universities. I am familiar with the history of the founding of two universities where not the slightest pretext for a clash existed between scholarly and aristocratic pride. As a result, learned conceit caused the scholars to quarrel among themselves. With one university, for instance, the question was whether or not nature philosophy was to prevail. Its victory notwithstanding, nature philosophy is now unfit for battle.

Ewers, who took the reins firmly in his hands. Responsibility in a single individual is always more effective than responsibility of a multitude. On the other hand, the insight of a group is certainly greater and, above all, more varied. We often confuse the two and tend to believe that the signature of the many constitutes a greater safeguard for the state. I believe this opinion to be wrong and hold that if a capable and not egotistical man is placed in a position in which his honor and prestige are closely interwoven with the thriving of the institution, and if he is obliged to make use of the counsel and discernment of a larger group, his unrestricted activity will be more fruitful than that of the group. Coming from a man who claims to have behind him a scientific career, this statement possibly sounds peculiar. The foregoing does not deal with trends in science itself, however, but with the conferring of official positions. According to my experience, it is much better for this purpose, if the vested interests of a group are prevented from making themselves felt either overtly or covertly, especially in a country in which bonhomie appears to constitute a major obstacle to progress. Without intending or being able to judge all the steps taken by Ewers, or even their underlying principles, as I was not present, but I was told of them in Königsberg, I cannot but conclude from the entire picture, as well as from the results, that Ewers deserved extremely well of the home university in that he succeeded in gaining the full confidence of the then minister, and in that he had the courage, regardless of much dissension, to gather all the reins into his hand. I never had close relationship with Ewers (once even a rather unpleasant one, about which perhaps later). I would probably have disapproved of his religious views, as well as those of the minister, von Lieven, which were much talked about, but both were devoted to their work—a quality that cannot be overestimated. Although among those appointed in the beginning there were such excellent men as the physicist G. F. Parrot, the number of professors whose conduct was anything but a model for the students, or who failed to command our respect because of their low scientific qualifications, was still relatively large. Some were very infirm, so it almost seemed that they were appointed in order to ensure them a decent subsistence. For this reason it took years for the university to win recognition in the country. People made fun of the infirmary, and when the medical faculty appointed two professors named Styx and Balk respectively, I still remember as a pupil having heard people laughingly say that now that the faculty had succeeded in safely paving the path to the underworld, nobody need any longer Balk at the Styx [The German pun actually runs "... the faculty has now placed a Balken (beam) across the Styx in order to make the path to the underworld safe"].

Such defects tainted the whole. Thus methodology and academic guidance were placed in the hands of a man who was originally a poet, but due to an early infirmity had come to prefer the prose of lecturing on history at a fixed salary, to the uncertainties of poetry. He was already quite decrepit, and dragged himself to the rostrum only with great effort. From there, in a feeble voice, he lectured on book titles and diverse learned nonsense which even then seemed to me quite out of place, although I did not yet know how easy it was for a professor to impress a student with his erudition. Eventually it was medicine's turn, and the mental equipment required to master this science above all was a perfect knowledge of the Latin language. To this everybody agreed without, however, admitting the need for a complete course in Roman literature. It was common knowledge, after all, that prescriptions were written only in Latin, and that in anatomy and other disciplines only Latin terms were used. A subsequent lecture was dedicated to the indispensability of the Greek language, because Hippocrates and Galen had been very great physicians. One wondered somewhat: were not these old gentlemen squeezed quite dry by now? Yet if one absolutely insisted on drawing straight from these sources, one had better see to, and even augment, one's Greek. In the next lecture, the necessity was expounded of knowing the Arabic language, since Rhazes and Avicenna were also great physicians. That was too much for me! Was I supposed to learn Arabic as well, and to a degree enabling me to understand the medical authors in the original better than in a passable translation? Right after this lecture, the lecturer finally lay down on his sickbed, never to reappear. That was certainly the best part of his whole course of lectures.

Much later, long after I had given up medicine, I had occasion to look through Hippocrates for quite different purposes, to arrive at a fuller understanding of certain particulars. Therefore, I speak from firsthand experience when I state that, quite apart from language difficulties which, particularly with Hippocrates, are not inconsiderable, a long study is required to enter the world of physiological and physical concepts of these ancients and to transform them into more contemporary ones. Without such transformation the concepts remain totally incomprehensible. To this must be added the fact that works attributed to Hippocrates are of such disparate character that critics so far have been unable to determine which of these works are indeed to be ascribed to the famous medical practitioner and which not. Some are written by an unbiased observer, some are the expression of a preconceived hypothesis. I had a good laugh when I remembered that broken-down poet who, for a fee, lectured to me on Hippocrates and Rhazes. In the same way, using any old book, I could have lectured to him on Confucius and Zoroaster about whom I knew as little as he knew about Hippocrates and Rhazes.

It will be admitted that such lectures are likely to have the effect of cooling down youthful eagerness and ambition. But totally absurd lectures do have the advantage of arousing definite opposition. What I had expected and had not found, in fact, became clear to me and when I became associate professor in Königsberg nine years later and found the chair for Methodology and Cyclopedia of Medicine vacant because none of the older professors agreed to take it, despite the fact that the subject was demanded by the ministry, I grasped the opportunity to give a course of lectures in methodology which was rather unique. It extended only through the first two weeks, but was given daily. It was free of all scholastic trimmings as well as of book titles which, for other than anatomical subjects, I would have had to borrow anyway, and was aimed only at practical advice. In addition to attending Dorpat, I had spent some time at three other universities, had paid shorter visits to others and, from my own observation, I could relate some frightening examples of the total ruin of some unprincipled subjects, of the consequences of too irregular study and of the false shame which leads people to deceive themselves as well as others by trying to cover up defects. I was altogether practically-minded, to such a degree that I offered the following advice when I referred to independent study and books with a bias toward nature philosophy which exerted a strong attraction on young people—and often most strongly on those whom nature or schooling had not equipped with a capacity for clear thinking: "When you read a book, try to see whether you are able to present in a few words the essential contents of a carefully read chapter. Should you fail in this, be convinced that the book is not written for you, or not yet suitable for you. Put it away. There are many other good books that will suit you." As for morals, I refrained from taking the absolute position of the priest, but advised the students never to forget that ribald student songs were but the poetic expression of youthful dissociation from the Philistines, and in no way contained experience of life. The common parents' warning of "Don't let yourself be led astray," I suggested modifying into "Don't lead yourself astray," because if one were true to oneself, one held to the tiller and could always turn aside from a wrong path. Thus, I tried to speak not like a book, but like a man who had had some experience in life. Not that I can offer proof of the efficacy of this method, nor is it certain that all of my audience grew into normal human beings, at least, if such was the case it went unnoticed. But that one or the other did take my advice to heart, I can believe, because once, late on a dark, autumnal evening, almost at nighttime, a student came to see me to thank me for the day's lecture (where the above advice was offered). He said that he could not forgo the pleasure of conveying his thanks immediately. I have received many tokens of attachment from former students of mine, but remembering this Nicodemus in the night has always been particularly refreshing.

Now, that I have interrupted my tale to sing my own praise, justice requires that I also add some reproof. I did not give this self-invented lecture of mine more than three, possibly only two times, I do not remember exactly. In order that my moral advice might be accepted more readily, I tried to appear like an older friend rather than as a professor, and to this end, I adopted a rather boisterous tone. I found it rather difficult to give repeat performances in this style, however. I do not know whether the full-bottomed wig, which is said to creep slowly over a professor's pate, had already become stuck to mine to such a degree that I was quite unable to pull it off by then—be that as it may, I found it impossible to reappear and use that tone again. Yet to play the earnest and stern moral philosopher without the official black robe, I felt neither called upon nor able to do. The examples which I could point to were drastic—tragic enough, yet I had already repeated them several times. If every course had had its Nicodemus—well, that would perhaps have made it easier for me to continue. However, there was only that one, and no more, and I could no longer enjoy giving the ethical component of those lectures. As for the methodology of study, I believed that I could provide rather useful advice in the field of anatomy. The other subjects, however, I was not sufficiently familiar with, and a critical evaluation of my own experience could easily have been seen to be the criticism of my colleagues.

I would not have permitted myself this digression, if I did not have a suggestion to make. I know very well that in the end, the students teach one another. At small universities, however, where there are rarely any students who have already studied at other universities and have more experience of life in general, this mutual instruction is not worth much. Would it not be helpful if, at the beginning of a course, and limited to a few days, one of the lecturers were to provide practical methodological advice, always bearing in mind the entire course of medicine, as given at this university? It was my mistake not to have done so. If such a lecturer also wants to dispense advice about a way of life, independent study, etc., it must be his own decision. I regard a methodology embellished with unnecessary learning and a plethora of book titles, stretched out over a whole semester, as being as absurd and useless today as it was then.

To base my claim concerning the incompetence of many of the lecturers first appointed at Dorpat on the one example of an expiring man would be rather unfair. Therefore, I am compelled to resume my survey. At a somewhat later period, I had to take pharmacology (*materia medica*). But how it was presented! In alphabetical order, but not, as one could have guessed, according to a natural principle of order so that flowers, foliage and roots of a given plant would be listed together, but according to preparations. Thus, *Radix Rhei* and *Radix Salep*, that is, the purgative rhubarb root and the nutritive salep, were immediate neighbors not far from *Radix Valerianae*; *Herb Althea* next to *Herba Menthae pipertae*; *Emplastrum Cantharidum* adjacent to *Emplastrum Cicutae*, and following *Emplastrum adhaesium*. It is not necessary to be a medical man to realize that when pharmaceuticals are jumbled up to such a degree that the related are torn apart and the most heterogeneous linked according to the order of the first letter of accidental names, the beginner will find all this beyond his comprehension. The reason for this practice was probably the intention of avoiding anything hypothetical. But this is as if, in teaching geography, one would prefer to go by a geographical dictionary, just qecause certain towns and districts once belonged to, or in the future, might belong to different states. This would be the surest means of preventing any real understanding, the exact effect which the above lectures had. Any ancient subdivision into *Roborantia, Solventia, Sudorifica, Carminativa, Emmenagoga,* etc., would have been better. Chemical analyses as classifying principles or information on tests performed concerning the effects (of drugs) of course could not yet be expected at that time, although they became common practice later. In order to round off the nonsense, the more important preparations were associated with a series of diseases in which they are used, and it appeared that the Herr Professor took particular pride in compiling a list that was as complete as humanly possible, usually ending with *menses suppressi.* That the latter disorder accompanies the most heterogeneous diseases we already knew before we had visited the clinics. For the sake of this useless and offensive completeness, lectures on pharmacology were spread out over two semesters. In view of all this, how then did these students who wanted or were supposed to become practical physicians acquire some pharmacological knowledge? This was done partially in the clinics and partially by looking it up in books in which the pharmaceuticals were listed in groups. Here again it was seen that by their very absurdity the lectures had an effect quite opposite to that intended. For unless the alphabetical arrangement was provided for mere convenience, the intention must have been to keep us away from hypothetical assumptions, against which the teaching staff of Dorpat used to caution us strenuously. Since every student sensed what he lacked, however, books were sought which grouped the objects systematically. Even before Burdach had arrived in person, the first edition of his pharmacology book had appeared and was widely used in Dorpat, although this three-volume work was rather expensive for the usual student's pocket. Those who could afford it bought it and had to lend it out to others. Thus perverse lectures also have their use.

Nor do I know the purpose of an excessive completeness. Pharmaceutics, which preceded pharmacology, also extended over two semesters, the first dealing with the pharmaceuticals according to their preparation, the second with the raw materials according to their characteristics. The professor for this subject was indeed a master of his material; instead of selecting the more important preparations and explaining them clearly and lucidly, however, he aimed at the utmost completeness, and thus became hurried and often confused. As for raw materials, he not only went through all the so-called obsolete pharmacopeia but, also as far as possible, through anything which had been mentioned anywhere at any time. It is true that he had a fairly complete pharmaceutical collection and had some preparations ready for every lecture so that they could be looked over before and afterward. But there were too many of them—sometimes forty or more—and after the lecture, one had to leave at once, as other professors also had this penchant for completeness. It was altogether too much for me. It seemed as if my memory, which had stood me in such good stead at school, had left me. The only names that really stuck were those that had a proper rattle and clatter to them, such as *Tacamahaca rubra*, apart, that is, from the common ones which I had already encountered as a medical amanuensis. It was of those that I would have liked to have heard more rather than of all these materials which were characterized as obsolete and useless. Was that also not a case of confusing an academic lecture with a work of reference? Such confusion, however, is not a rare occurrence and at that time was even more prevalent among Dorpat's jurists. Certain lectures, e.g. those on the complete code of Roman laws, were not only given daily throughout the entire year but even twice a day during the last weeks, and every word had to be taken down religiously. This was probably preparation to train them to write their own comments. "That which you have in black and white is safely carried home," said Mephistopheles. But should it not be the task of a lecture to present the student with material that he can and should carry in his head if he is going to be effective in his profession?

Already in the first semester and in anatomy, one of the most indispensable subjects, I was forced to take a course of lectures which I disliked. Prof. Isenflamm had just left, and the university was looking for a successor of repute. There was another anatomist in Dorpat, working as a prosector, Prof. Cichorius, who, because of his peculiarities or for other reasons, the senate did not want to fill the vacancy. It was my misfortune, however, that he was the only lecturer in anatomy when I arrived, and a very odd fish he was in every respect. The blinds in his lodgings were drawn all day long, and it was said that he sat in the lighted room in a dressing-gown or a fur coat. In the anatomy class, however, his tall figure always appeared in a long uniform-coat with a very broad, white neck cloth which, covering his chin, reached up to his mouth and was suspected of hiding a goiter which, however, nobody had ever seen. Imbued with the importance of his profession, he seemed to have fortified himself with spirits before each lecture, due to which practice he frequently hiccoughed. From time to time he harangued us, and moving his body vigorously, declared that when he lectured, he lectured in the name of the Czar. Exhortations of this kind were delivered whenever he heard or noticed that we were snickering (we never laughed out loud). This was provoked by the quite incongruously florid language with which he tried to impart elegance to his lecture, as well as by his dialect which was not only unusual, but also hard to understand until one got used to it. So far as I remember, he quite consistently pronounced the hard letters as if soft, and the soft letters as if hard. Thus, after the first week of lectures a student asked me in all seriousness whether I could help him to locate the *Ossa jabidis*, as he could not find it in his book. Cichorius had always pronounced *capitis* as *gabidis* and the above student, coming from the border of the Mark (Brandenburg) and Pomerania, in turn converted the *ga* into *ja*, rendering the word completely incomprehensible. While I quickly accustomed myself to this dialect, I very much disliked his long-winded presentation, delivered in a monotonous singsong. Perhaps for better spacing of the terms in which anatomy is so rich, Cichorius used to intersperse his presentation with questions and answers, to which one had to pay attention if one did not want to lose the thread. This made memorizing in the course of the lecture doubly difficult. When, for instance, he had mentioned a gland and wanted to describe its position, it went, "Now where is that gland located? Well, that gland is located between...." All these ornaments were delivered right into the air of the room without looking or pointing at the preparation, the lecturer's body swaying to and fro. How different were the clear, I would even say pellucid lectures of Döllinger on descriptive anatomy. I did not study with him but sat in on his lectures several al times. He spoke slowly, and stopped for an instant with every new name so that the attentive student had the time to repeat the name to himself. Not one superfluous word was said. This was the example on which I later tried to model my own demonstrations, remembering as I did the excessive byplay that, with Cichorius, used to make it so hard for the principal facts to sink in. Nobody could reproach Cichorius for a lack of zeal, but his zeal was turned in the wrong direction. He needed six hours per week for his lectures on osteology, not because of a surfeit of facts, but because of proliferating nonessentials. Burdach's lectures on general anatomy dealt more with general aspects, and were easily comprehended and committed to memory.

But now I must finally move on to practical medicine to which I had looked forward with great expectations, as the disciplines preceding this course were less to my taste than I had hoped. Practical medicine was mainly the domain of Professor Balk, who was not only professor of pathology and therapeutics and head of the medical clinic, but in my time had also taken over the surgical clinic, whose designated head, Dr. Jochmann, was too busy being sick most of the time. Professor Balk was a man of talent and great devotion, and he was also regarded as a most competent practitioner. Unfortunately, there were some unsavory rumors abroad concerning his private life, and although I had no proof of this, it had the effect of preventing me from taking a liking to him. His lectures on pathology and therapeutics, which went into great detail, were taken down by most students word for word, like a holy codex. One of them had even acquired the art of stenography, so as not to lose a single word. I, too, took down as much as I could without, however, having the stenographic manuscript dictated to me, as did many others. I was not, however, overly impressed by all this comprehensiveness. The descriptions of *Radesyge* and *Lycanthropism* seemed to me rather superfluous. On the other hand I would have liked to have seen more stress on the main symptoms of common diseases rather than their being blurred by the mass of other symptoms mentioned. After all, it is these main symptoms which primarily guide the physician. I had hoped the clinic would supply the missing knowledge.

The first patient examined in my presence suffered from a pronounced nervous fever. After he had been examined at great length, and Professor Balk had also stressed several symptoms such as the stupor, the greatly reddened eyes and their peculiar luster which he called glassy, the decision was: "Give valerian." Why specifically valerian? I was compelled to ask. Balk occasionally liked to walk about on the rostrum and to hold forth on the sublimity of science, the value of rational treatment, and the wretchedness of routine. Yet of what use were all these Jacob's ladders to me when I needed a bridge from a glassy eye to valerian and, if possible, a very simple and solid one? At this point it became obvious that what I needed was a grouping of the pharmaceuticals according to their effect, as well as a grouping of the diseases according to the important changes in the organism, as expressed by the symptoms—in short, exactly what is being done to produce a solid basis for practice today. I hoped that continued visits to the clinic would give me more certainty, and I believe I can attest to the regularity of my visits there. However, with the exception of a few cases, my judgment still remained uncertain. When, in a case of distinct pneumonia one sees a clear relief immediately after blood-letting, one has a definite idea of the previous state, as well as of the newly created one. But in most cases it seemed as if Balk was acting by a certain instinct, or according to rules familiar to him but which he was unable to communicate to others. I am almost inclined to think that a consistent schooling, especially in mathematics, spoils a man for medicine. One has become used to proceeding in one's thinking step by logical step, and that is hardly possible even today, when pharmacology and pathology have advanced so much further. I was forced to realize more and more that I either lacked the instinct of providing the missing links, or, to return to the previous image of building bridges, that I perceived the gaps too clearly. It was with genuine envy that I observed the ferocious zeal with which various pharmacist's clerks and barber's assistants (which latter, though entirely lacking in Dorpat, are still to be found in the south of Germany) copied prescriptions, memorizing every word of experience, well-founded or not, and boldly went off to practice. I myself was far more undaunted as Glanström's helper prior to my university studies, than when I had left the university and my head was buzzing with remarks concerning rational methods which collided with sundry fragments of information which I was unable to put in order.

What I have just said about Professor Balk's teaching is to be understood more as an expression of the inadequacy of the times and my own inability to bridge the gaps than as criticism directed against Balk. At times he was quite practical, offering us purely empirical knowledge. His only failing was his proclivity for riding the high horse. Yet the most brilliant cure I ever performed I owe only to him. He had told us once that a mixture of sulfur and *Elaeosacharum Millefolii* was particularly effective in the treatment of irregular hemorrhoidal movement of the blood, and in the discussion of the case that was presented, the mixture had worked remarkably well. I memorized such simple precepts easily; it was the lofty theories that confounded my poor head. Some time after I had finished my course of studies, my father's nose almost suddenly turned a glowing red and, in addition, became covered with a spotty rash looking like a white powder. At just that time he was supposed to receive a Grand Duchess at the borders of the province in an official capacity. "You must rid me of this," he said in a paternal imperative, "I can't receive the Grand Duchess like this." None of the lectures had ever mentioned such noses, nor was it thinkable that this could be the effect of wine as my father drank wine possibly only twice a year. I knew, however, that several days earlier he had taken a cold bath, when his hemorrhoids were exuding. When I learned that the hemorrhoidal flow had stopped at once I took this as an indication of his problem, and prescribed the aforementioned mixture. After a few days, the rash disappeared, the redness of his nose was reduced to a hue quite natural for many persons, and his journey to the reception could be undertaken.

Professor Deutsch's lectures on obstetrics dealt mainly with the practical aspects. I did not take the first so-called theoretical part of these lectures and tried to replace them by studying on my own. The result was that the theory of the various forceps, etc. impressed itself on my mind much more deeply, although I am now of the opinion that the comprehensiveness with which this branch is being taught is now something of a luxury. From the practical part of these lectures, which I did take, I came to realize how these disciplines should be treated: the essentials should be enlarged upon, and they should be presented as graphically as possible, in an unstilted manner, and without academic trimmings, drawing from one's own experience. These lectures, too, were to stand me in good stead long after I believed I had forgotten them. Professor Deutsch had frequently talked about the efficacy of blood-letting in cases of delayed labor. He was so emphatic in stressing the advisability of this remedy—despite the prevailing prejudice against blood-letting—provided, of course, that the patient was in good health and particularly of a plethoric constitution, that his words made a lasting impression upon me. Later, in Königsberg, when my wife was about to give birth for the first time, her labor came on slowly although strongly on the first day, abated toward evening, and stopped altogether during the night and on the following day, while she grew progressively weaker. The old practitioner who advised us on the first day was to celebrate his silver wedding anniversary on the second day, and I did not want to impose on him if I could help it. Also, I was not sure but that he was prejudiced against blood-letting. Therefore, I took counsel with my friend and neighbor, the botanist Professor Eysenhardt, and, without asking the old man, we decided on blood-letting. Almost immediately after that, vigorous labor began again, and delivery proceeded successfully.

The clinics as practical training ground for medical students were all open and fully functioning. I only wished that the assistants who were in charge during any absence of the professors had been more mature persons. But they were mere students. Before they entered the clinics, students had no opportunity at all for practical work. There were no chemical laboratories for them and no physiological institute, a facility that is altogether of a more recent origin. What irked me most, however, and what I felt even more at a later date, was the lack of opportunity to study the anatomy of the human body by actual dissection. Although suitable rooms had already been prepared in Isenflamm's time, in my time no dissections were performed by students, partly because of the presence of two prosectors, one official, the other unofficial. The Catalogue of Lectures listed Cichorius as prosector, but because of the value he placed on his long-winded lectures he had no thought for the practical training of his students. Later, when Burdach arrived, such training became impossible. The number of cadavers which came to anatomy was too small, a consequence of the limited size of the town. Burdach and Cichorius gave their respective lectures quite separately, thereby doubling the demand for fresh specimens. What is more, Burdach had brought along an assistant and unofficial prosector in the person of a Herr Pietsch, and what wasn't needed for lectures he retained for his private investigations, defending it manfully against the claims of the students. I myself put in such claims several times, but succeeded only once in carrying off one arm which, without any instruction, I then proceeded to dissect at home with several friends. The student who has had the opportunity of taking part in practical anatomical work during a winter semester cannot imagine the grinding work involved in sitting at home, trying to acquire a complete anatomical knowledge from books, and that especially at a time when copper anatomical engravings were rare and costly. Only one of my acquaintances had Loder's anatomical tables, which were in great demand. This home cramming was usually reserved for the last period, as preparation for the examinations, when one locked oneself in and tried to learn the whole of anatomy by heart.

How different things are now at Dorpat! Students work in the chemistry laboratory and in the physiological institute and with such thoroughness that substantial contributions have already been made to science in these laboratories. The population of the town has grown to twice its previous size, despite which arrangements have also been made to procure cadavers in winter from other towns, sometimes from considerable distances. This last-mentioned arrangement was an achievement of the board under Duke Lieven of whom it could have been assumed that his religious beliefs would have made him object most strongly to such provisions. This goes to show that this man knew how to distinguish between genuine religiosity and prejudice.

I cannot leave Dorpat without mentioning with sadness the gaps in the lecturing program that prevailed during my stay, some for part of the time, some for the entire period. When I arrived there was no lecturer for natural history, a subject I would have liked to have studied, especially in my first semester. No lectures at all were given in mineralogy and geology during the entire period of four years, leaving a noticeable gap in the study of natural history. An omission of similar importance to the study of medicine was the absence for the entire four years of my stay of lectures in surgery, as well as of a course in practical surgery. The former Professor Kauzmann had left in 1810. Later, a successor was appointed, but he appeared to be ill most of the time. At least, he never got around to starting his lectures and heading the surgical clinic.

It seems to me that in this respect, Dorpat has still some way to go. Gaps of this sort occur in every university from time to time. Yet in Dorpat they are not filled rapidly enough, the less rapidly when the selection is careful, which in recent years the university must generally be given credit for. Foreigners who have been appointed cannot always sever their previous connections at once, even if they wish to do so. Professors are liable to fall ill for extended periods, or to undertake scientific journeys which keep them away for years. Thus I had a son in Dorpat who was eagerly applying himself to geology, when his professor disappeared for an extended period, forcing him to interrupt his studies in this field. If such a thing should happen in a small university in Germany, one simply moves to another university without being forced to leave a gap of any importance. With our provinces this is not as easy, even if it were permitted. Even in my time at Dorpat it was constantly repeated that whoever wanted to obtain a position with the state had to finish his studies at a native university. I found this very unjust, and if such a regulation indeed existed, it should have been the concern of the academic senate to propose exceptions to be made in cases of serious gaps. As far as concerns the appointment of medical men, however, I found that little, if any, attention was paid to the source from which they drew their knowledge and skill.

Since Dorpat University has risen to such a level of excellence in recent years that we are proud to see her as the model university of the empire, efforts should be made to produce a generation of future professors from among the non-tenured lecturers. The best of these could become eligible for professorships at Dorpat or other universities of the empire. This would also afford the authorities an opportunity to appraise the lecturing abilities of the aspirants. Dorpat would become the nursery of the Russian Empire, and the lecturers out of self-interest would strive for perfection of their knowledge of the Russian language. Vacancies would be filled much more successfully by these young men than by the so-called tenured lecturers who, growing old and turning gray, sometimes serve as mere stopgaps for the frequently quite heterogeneous disciplines of an entire faculty. At the same time, substituting would provide these young lecturers with opportunities for continued training. Because I have no knowledge of the particular conditions prevailing at the university, I shall refrain from elaborating on this proposal any further. *Dixi et salvavi animam meam* (I have spoken and I have saved my soul).

I must now return to myself in order to finally arrive at my graduation.

Of the lectures I attended which were not directly associated with my subject, I remember Morgenstern's characteristics of the Greek and Roman classics according to Quintilian, Huth's lectures on popular astronomy which I found very interesting because of the lecturer's clear exposition of the latest investigations of the elder Herschel concerning the stellar system, and some private lectures on horticulture by the botanist Weinmann.

Circumstances permitting, the botanical excursions were also continued. To this end, as was customary with students, several short journeys were undertaken on foot and in a group. I was everywhere the importunate instructor in botany. Once our merry group even went by foot from Dorpat to Reval. I had heard a great deal about journeys on foot in Germany and wanted to prepare myself. As a grammar-school pupil, I had already walked from Piep to Reval with such overwrought zeal that it took me less than two days to cover the entire distance of about 110 versts (1 verst = 0.6629 miles). On arriving at Reval, however, I suffered such a severe nose bleed that it took great efforts and almost ten hours to staunch it.

The botanical excursions in Dorpat kept me less from a diligent scholastic regimen than my participation in student affairs. While it is true that there is also an educational aspect to young people's striving to influence their equals, I have no doubt now that at least as far as I was concerned, the profits accruing from these activities did not balance the losses in time and interest in the lectures. Although the high spirits and independence of the students did appeal to me, I really had no stomach for their noisiness, and if I made an effort to overcome this dislike, it was only in order to appear as one of them.

A special episode in my life was a temporary move to Riga.

When Napoleon invaded Russia in 1812 and an army corps under Macdonald, comprising more Germans than French, was encamped near Riga, after the flooding of Courland, the opposing Russian army corps and, in particular, the town of Riga, were in the throes of a typhus epidemic. A great many doctors died at Riga while the hospitals were overflowing with wounded, and even more so with typhus cases. Still more had to be accommodated in barns and whatever other large buildings could be found. At this point the authorities approached Dorpat University with a request for young doctors, or at least older medical students. Out of youthful enthusiasm and patriotic feeling, twenty-five young men volunteered. Many probably also hoped to see and learn a lot. I myself thought that I could not very well stay behind, although my clinical course had only just started and I had every reason to doubt my talent for careful observation. But it was said that one had to do something for the Fatherland, and as for typhus, none of us was unduly worried. Yet the disease cut us down like fresh fodder. Of the twenty-five, only one was spared, who contracted a large furuncle which might have diverted the fever. The remaining twenty-four fell ill within a few weeks; but only one of us died. The rest of us recovered, due partly to our youthful constitution, partly—may my sceptical attitude be forgiven—perhaps because of lack of treatment. For individual persons, particularly outsiders and students to boot, to be treated by experienced doctors was out of the question. The indifference and apathy that came over people living near the scene of battle in a town in which the thunder of guns is heard in the streets every day, and where death reaps his harvest without hindrance, is really incredible. As for me, I was billeted with a comrade in a burnt-down suburb, in a small house that was spared by the fire. Glaser, my comrade, was the first to be struck by typhus. Indifferently I saw him lie down, knowing well that my turn must come soon. A few days later, while working in the hospital, I felt a great dullness in my head, and had no doubt that I had contracted the disease. I returned to my quarters and sat down with great effort to write a letter to my parents, to succeed in which enterprise I believed I had first to drink a glass of wine. I felt at once that this only increased the numbness. That decided my view on the proper treatment for typhus. Some time before that, Professors Parrot and Burdach had carried on a heated debate as to the use of vinegar against typhus and we, too, had discussed the subject. I now decided for vinegar and had a bottle of it as well as one of water put near the bed, into which I then crawled with the same apathy which I had observed when I saw my comrade lie down. During the first days I was still conscious enough to take some vinegar from time to time. I also noticed that the landlord's daughter, who lived on the other side of the hallway, slightly opened our door each morning, no doubt to find out whether or not we were yet ready to be buried. On our side of the hallway lived only an old soldier who was given us as a servant and who now celebrated his leisure by being dead-drunk all day long. I soon lost consciousness completely, and I do not know how long I lay in bed like that. I was first wakened from my stupor by my comrade who, having recovered before me, stood by my bedside and said laughingly, "You are all covered with red blotches!" This piece of news left me quite unmoved, and I lost consciousness again. Within a few days, however, I too had recovered. Although my strength returned only slowly, a delightful feeling of well-being returned soon enough. It took time, however, until I was in a condition to visit the hospital again. The other students had fared similarly. All of them, whether they liked it or not, had had a taste of the "wait-and-see" method of treatment.

I cannot claim to have gained much medical knowledge from this experience, but I did see the horrors of war and those beyond the battlefield, and how human life is treated with the same indifference with which we crush an ant that happens to cross our path. After my arrival, I was at once posted to a field hospital that had just been set up in a barn. When I entered, the barn was only half filled with patients, but new cases were continually carried in so that when I left the barn after several hours it was already almost completely filled. Next morning there was no more room in the barn, which now held 300 persons. Only now did they start to set up stoves which were indeed ready after as little as two days, and were kindled on the third day. Yet for three days the sick had been in an unheated room and in the meantime a sharp frost had set in. Every day a number of dead were carried away. Who had time to determine whether they had simply frozen to death or had died of a disease? And of what use would such an inquest have been? At first, a head physician was available to whom I was supposed to turn for guidance. He limited himself to a very few prescriptive formulae, because the hospital pharmacy stored only a few medicaments. Before I managed to get used to this situation, quite new to me, the head physician was transferred after two days to a newly set up field hospital elsewhere. I now had to take care of half the hospital, that is, 150 patients. The other half was the responsibility of Dr. Levy, whom I had already met in Dorpat when he was an older student to whom I could turn for advice now and then, but only in haste, since we both had difficulties in coping with all the patients. Even if we were to spend no more than an average of five minutes with each patient, 150 patients would require 750 minutes, that is, twelve and a half hours. These problems were still further increased by the fact that many of the patients were prisoners of war. They were mainly Prussians and Bavarians who were glad to learn that the doctor spoke German and who used the opportunity to bring up all sorts of small requests, not to listen to which would have been more than cruel. To be able to voice their requests and have them granted to whatever extent possible was more of a comfort to them than any amount of medicine. As it was, with doctors' visits continuing from early morning until total darkness, the November days permitted no more than an average of three minutes per patient. Given these conditions, I am astonished that I was able to stand my ground even for as long as fourteen days before I fell ill.

During the time that we were unconscious, word came through that Napoleon's army was not only in full retreat, but that it was in fact disintegrating completely. Macdonald's corps, too, had to withdraw, and when we crawled out of our various holes we found the scene completely changed. No guns were thundering any more and everybody heaved sighs of relief. The hospitals began to empty, and there were again more doctors available. We were glad that there was no more need for us and, in the first half of January, we returned to Dorpat. Whether we were of great use to the state is a matter of doubt.

Resuming my studies at the beginning of 1814, I entered upon a second period of suffering, the so-called preparation for final examinations. Of that period there is nothing to be told. The examination itself, however, which took place on a very hot day in June, I cannot pass by altogether, because however unedifying that day was at that time, later recollection of it became very amusing. Also, it is only the anatomical-physiological part of it to which I shall refer. That part was all in the hands of Professor Cichorius because Professor Burdach had already left Dorpat in January, 1814, following a call to Königsberg. The first question I drew referred to the muscles of the lower extremities. The answer was as could be expected from one who was once present at a demonstration and had subsequently tried, with the aid of books only and without benefit of anatomical work, to memorize a complex muscular apparatus. I was able to demonstrate some muscles quite well, some remained rather rudimentary in their exposition, and others were complete failures. There are altogether too many of them. I do not mean to imply that nature created some of them in excess of actual needs, but for a poor medical student who must be able to demonstrate all bones, ligaments, muscles, nerves, vessels and viscera on a single day, as well as to show his mettle in physics, chemistry, zoology, botany, pharmacology, pathology, etc., there are definitely too many. Cichorius' face darkened perceptibly. Next, I drew a question in physiology: How many kinds of organization are there? I would like to know whether Cuvier or Meckel, who were still alive at that time, could have answered that question, in fact, whether any of the presently living luminaries of physiology and zootomy would try a hand at it without myself equipping them with Ariadne's thread for this maze. However, I provided an answer which was excellent, so excellent in fact that Cichorius' face broke out in brightest sunshine. Let it be known then—for the sake of all peoples and all times, I cannot but reveal it—that there are but two kinds of organizations: fully fluid and semifluid, there being no fully solid ones. Whence do I know that? Why, from Cichorius' lectures, naturally. Where else could this bit of wisdom have come up? Burdach had never given the whole of physiology, only "The History of Life" that I had studied with him. As my registration card had to show proof of my having taken the major courses, I had had no choice but to study physiology with Cichorius. That physiology lectures in 1812 or 1813 were bound to be a rather meager affair, no one would doubt today, but the scantiness of Cichorius' physiology could only be described as exquisite. Although I now seem to remember only very little, this particular piece of nonsense about the fully fluid organizations which yet did not flow apart, seemed even then too colossal not to be retained by the memory, all the more so as it was by no means an occasional remark, but was treated as a major tenet, a mainstay of science. The explanations made some mention of *Medusae* as proof of the fully fluid organization. Thus it was not blood that was referred to, but animals swimming about in the sea that were fully fluid in consistency but were yet cohesive.

After the doctoral examinations, one breathes more freely and approaches one's dissertation with enhanced self-confidence. I had long toyed with the idea of preparing a monograph on the *Carices* of Livonia and Estonia, because I took pride in the fact that I know more about the local types of this genus than others. When I mentioned this idea to Ledebour he did not try to dissuade me and even seemed to agree to some extent, but with such a doubtful expression that I grasped his meaning. Burdach disapproved of such a dry subject. Both were right, Ledebour more in what he did not tell me directly, but let me find out by myself. He provided me with several monographs of this kind, on perusing which I realized what subtle punctiliousness and what a large amount of material must go into such an enterprise if it is to amount to anything at all. Not intending to spend that much time on the *Carices*, I gave up the idea altogether. What is more, upon leaving the university I accused my herbarium of being a waster of time and decided not to take it along on my forthcoming journey, but to stash it away somewhere and leave it to its fate.

I then selected a more general subject, the diseases of the Estonians, to which choice I felt entitled, having frequently seen them in their illnesses, but primarily because I had wandered about much in my botanical fervor, and the many swamps I saw did not at all conform to descriptions of Livonia as I found them here and there in books. These descriptions often fitted only the southern parts of Livonia with its extensive sandy ground and the sea coast. Even the name of Livonia has its origin in sand, probably because the German immigrants took the word *liv*, which the Estonians and possibly also the Livonians use for sand, for the name of the country.

As for my dissertation, *"De morbis inter Esthonos erdemicis"* ("On diseases endemic among the Estonians"), its value is bound to be similar to that of most dissertations written about such general subjects by inexperienced young people—namely, very slight. Despite that, it was now and then mentioned in our journals—by non-medical men, it appears—because it seemed to convey a feeling of concern for improvement of the conditions of the Estonians.

But some trifle of mine had been published even earlier than that: a review, written in the Estonian language, of a textbook for midwives. Now, while the idea of a student-reviewer soon after that became offensive to me, the responsibility for this precocious piece of criticism must be laid at the door of Burdach. The latter, in cooperation with Al. Crichton and Joh. Rehmann, had begun to publish a journal with the title *Russische Sammlung für Naturwissenschaft und Heilkunst* ("Russian Collection for Natural Sciences and Medicine"). In addition to original papers, it also was to report on everything that had appeared in print in Russia pertinent to the aforementioned fields. Among other material they had received was also that work in the Estonian language, and as Burdach knew that I was fluent in that language, he had asked me to read that particular work and let him have my opinion in writing. This I did willingly, without, so far as I remember, knowing the eventual purpose. The young reviewer pointed out some errors committed in language or translation which seemed due to the translator's lack of familiarity with the subject*.

The month of July and the better half of August went into the actual writing and printing of my dissertation. According to regulations, however, I still had to perform a more extensive operation on a cadaver before I would be permitted to defend my thesis, which then would be followed by the bestowal of the doctor's diploma. During this entire period, the anatomical laboratory did not have a single cadaver. The vacation extended throughout July, and although the new semester had started with the first days of August and the clinics had filled up again, not a single one of the results of their art had yet been delivered to the anatomical laboratory by the time the dissertation had been completely printed, except for the title page. In vain did I protest that I had no opportunity to take a course in operations and that, moreover, I did not intend to become an operating surgeon. The Dean would hear none of it; regulations had to be observed. Thus I roamed the town like a starved vulture to find somebody on the point of death. In a military hospital I found a patient who, according to the assurances of the good-natured medical officer, was bound to die within two days. What student would doubt the word of an old practitioner ! To be on the safe side, I allowed three or four days and had the twenty-fourth of August set on the title page of the dissertation as the day it would be defended. But on the twenty-fourth, the patient was not yet dead. As the title of the dissertation could not be printed without the Dean's consent, I should have at least been allowed to defend it on this day and to have the drawing up of the diploma postponed. Only the Dean, Prof. Styx, was unwilling to do even this, although it would not have infringed upon any regulation. The man whose death I waited for so anxiously, because several fellow students had already assembled in Dorpat to travel abroad with me, preferred to die only on the twenty-sixth or twenty-seventh. One day later, I cut off his leg and had someone attest to this fact. However, I was still required to perform a special operation under the supervision of Professor Balk. The criticism and solemn graduation finally took place on the twenty-ninth. From this account it can be seen why the date printed on my dissertation is not also that of my graduation. Strangely enough, the intelligent Dean did not insist on having the title page of the dissertation reprinted, the costs for which I would gladly have borne myself. Instead, he gave me a piece of advice to the effect that I should not put too much trust in a prognosis. Yet he himself had trusted the prognosis, and only a hearsay prognosis which he learned from me at that.

I had prepared everything for a journey abroad, and after a day or two, I departed with a few fellow students who had been waiting for me.

After I had passed the examination, I told my father that I could not pos-

*See Works VI, 1.

sibly start to practice without becoming more sure of myself and, in particular, without filling in some substantial gaps in my training. He did not utter any objections although his large family and the low rate of exchange must have made it difficult for him to sacrifice a goodly sum for my journey abroad. Thus, under the guise of a fee for my brilliant cure (related earlier, see p. 97), he gave me a sum which may indeed be called a princely fee, and which, according to my preliminary information concerning the cost of living in Germany, I calculated would last me for one and a half years. I had an inkling, however, and certainly a secret wish as well, to extend this trip for an even longer period. Therefore, I asked my elder brother, who had settled down in the meantime, whether he could raise a similar sum for me should the need arise, by taking a loan. Well, the need arose and he did take the loan. For the second part of my stay in Germany, I lived on borrowed money.

I don't believe it superfluous to mention this circumstance, in order to explain my sensitivity to the fact that Dorpat had not offered me suitable facilities for practical study in several essential fields, especially in anatomy.

7. Journey to Germany. Vienna
(1814-1815)

I was now a doctor of medicine duly graduated, but a doctor who had little confidence in himself, and not much more in medicine as a whole. If a patient, appealing to my conscience, had asked me whom to choose as a doctor, I would have had to answer: "Take anyone but me." But this was truly going to be rectified. In Vienna, so I was told, there were large hospitals where one could see much, where practical medicine could be studied. Moreover, Hildenbrand's work on typhus had recently appeared and had created a great stir, especially among us here, where the disease had raged so horribly in the hospitals and had always been treated with irritants only. Hildenbrand, it was said, had now shown for the first time that, at least in its initial stages, typhus was of an inflammatory nature and had to be treated antiphlogistically. That irritants were of no help when I had been ill with typhus, I can vouch for myself. So it was Vienna for me.

Immediately after my graduation, I left Dorpat with the students who had waited for me, and we were joined by two more students in Riga. Students are rather like burdock heads; they are found mostly in clusters. There were now six of us, going on to Königsberg, and not always in the most sensible way. Connection with Germany had been cut off in the past so frequently and persistently, that young people at least had very little knowledge concerning the best ways to travel there. Thus, in Memel we waited long for the wind so that we could go by boat to Schaken and thence by land to Königsberg. The long way from Königsberg to Berlin we traveled in a freight coach. As there were six, and later seven of us, we would have done better and saved both time and money if we had taken a special mail coach. Young people learn the hard way, however. Nowadays, of course, one buys a railway ticket and no more questions arise. In Königsberg, we stopped for two days to see Burdach again, and he gave us a very friendly welcome. I am astonished that he did not enlighten us as to more reasonable modes of travel. Or maybe he did, but we had exaggerated ideas about the expense of foreign special mail coaches.

In Berlin I met Pander, the future embryologist and paleontologist. He had been there for one or two semesters already and he tried hard to talk me into staying in Berlin. He spoke enthusiastically of the zoological museum, of the botanical garden, and of all kinds of lectures that he attended. This was all most enticing, but after all, I wanted to become a real practitioner, and I was afraid that such alluring beauties would only distract me. So I stood my ground and decided not to pay attention to all those sirens. Had I not left my herbarium behind? Instead, I visited Sanssouci and similar novelties of which one had heard.

Then, together with Dr. Sahmen, I set out for Vienna. On the way we studied the works of art in Dresden, the beauties of a miniature alpine region in Saxony's "Switzerland," the historical monuments of the town of Prague, but I shunned every botanical garden and every zoological collection as a consuming fire.

We arrived in Vienna and at once took lodgings in the suburb of Alser where the large medical institutes, the hospital, the maternity ward, and Josephine Academy and its various branches are also located. For this reason, this particular district always accommodated, in addition to the local medical men, a large number of foreign doctors who came to round off their medical studies. Most of the foreigners took their noon dinner at the restaurant *"Zum goldenen Hirsch"* (At the Sign of the Golden Stag). Among them were a number of interesting personalities, and since here young people from different regions of Germany, Switzerland and sometimes even England, came together, all of them already quite mature, I now found what I had always missed in Dorpat. The dinner table was presided over by a man who was later to become a famous surgeon, Dr. Chelius.

I threw myself head over heels into practical medicine, that is, simultaneously in all branches, regularly visiting the ophthalmic clinic of the famous ophthalmologist Dr. Beer, participating equally regularly in his course on eye surgery; being present at the visits and operations of the brilliant Professor Rust in the hospital for surgical cases; following Professor Boer during his visits in the maternity hospital; taking part in a private course on the theory of dressings, as well as in another on surgical operations; and starting to read several practical treatises. All of this was quite interesting and enlightening. I was particularly attracted to the ophthalmic clinic of which I had seen nothing in Dorpat, and also to Rust's treatment of surgical cases. But he dealt mostly with the more important operations, such as trepanations, lithotomies, and the use of heated irons in cases of so-called spontaneous dislocations. On the other hand, I was more interested in becoming more confident in the treatment of ordinary cases, which Rust left to the junior staff. He had already written a book on ulcers and was now less interested in them, and regarded his demonstrations, to which I think he was not even obligated, more as the rounding-off of his earlier lecturing and as a justification of his wide reputation as an operating surgeon. What I needed, rather, was an ordinary surgical clinic. As for Hildenbrand, the clinician for internal diseases, it was for him that I had come in the first place. On this point, however, I was badly let down. That winter, it seemed, Hildenbrand had decided to experiment with the "wait-and-see" method. His assistants marshalled a continuous flow of minor cases, mostly catarrhs, which were subsequently cured with very simple means, or even without anything more than rest and good diet. That light illnesses could also be cured without medical intervention, however, was wisdom not easily come by. Hildenbrand used to appear with a large cluster of students who surrounded him like the coma of a comet, he himself constituting its nucleus, and a rather solid nucleus at that as he was a large, heavy man. During the first of these visits, this nebulous coma was so large that I could not make out any of the foreign doctors I knew and was unable to reach all of the beds because when Hildenbrand, being the comet's nucleus, entered one space after the other between the beds, he was at once surrounded by part of the coma which filled the space, a substantial part of it protruding like the comet's tail. Therefore, I adopted the strategy of skipping the space that was just filling up and taking up position in the adjacent, still empty, space. In this way I managed to penetrate every other space between beds. As is the common practice in clinics, each patient had his observing clinician who, having arrived at his patient's bed, started to read out, in tiresome detail and in Latin, his observations since the last public visit. Everything was mentioned, the slightest change in pulse rate, passing coughs, the type of sleep, down to the smallest symptoms. Hildenbrand listened, or at least appeared to listen, adding very infrequently a word or two, to correct a Latin expression. I was astonished to see only patients with very minor illnesses and to hear only one remedy mentioned: Oxymel simplex (honey boiled with vinegar). I did not trust my ears and as, in any case, I did not clearly understand what was said at the beds which I had skipped, I went to the clinic the next day, but not during visiting time. I could then read unhurriedly the patients' records fixed above their beds. These records listed the name of the disease as well as the medication administered. Indeed, I found Oxymel simplex ordered everywhere, with possibly here and there a minor admixture, which I do not remember now, but which could have had only a slight effect. The diseases were given different names, but were never more than minor afflictions, mostly of the chest. There was never a real pneumonia or any other definite disease. I have no doubt that Prof. Hildenbrand wanted to demonstrate the fact that the so-called healing power of nature was capable of taking care of minor indispositions, so long as one did not interfere. At the same time, students were being shown the natural course of minor illnesses; otherwise, the detailed histories would have made no sense. I never had doubted the fact that catarrh could be cured even without medical treatment. To hear this repeated at twelve or sixteen beds (I do not remember the exact number) at the cost of one and a half hour seemed to me too big a sacrifice, and I decided not to return until the "wait-and-see" (observational) method of treatment was done with.

At the "Golden Stag," the meeting place of the foreign doctors, little mention was made of Professor Hildenbrand's medical clinic. They spoke more about Professor Kern's surgical clinic as a curiosity. Professor Kern let the healing power of nature manifest itself in a different way. He treated all wounds, whether from operations or any other cause, and ulcers as well, with the aid of pieces of cloth, soaked twice daily in warm water. No further dressing was used, and he loudly proclaimed the advantages accruing to the state due to the saving in adhesive bandages and binders, and naturally the advantages to the patient of the simple treatment. The charlatan aspect of his method made him an object of derision, whereas Hildenbrand was respected; people regretted only that he had now adopted only the "wait-and-see" method, to observe which nobody had the time. Professor Kern, being also frequently attacked by his colleagues, made a great effort to obtain recognition for his method. It was even said that he tried to win over the physicians of the sovereigns who had assembled in Vienna on the occasion of the Congress. A young doctor from Dorpat was once invited by Kern to join him in his carriage, where he asked him what the opinion was in Russia of his method, to which the young doctor had to give the mortifying answer that he had never heard of the method before.

I visited his clinic under the guidance of his assistant. They were not simple pieces of wet cloth that were laid onto the wounds (they would have dried too fast), but so-called compresses, larger pieces of linen, folded several times, that were laid on without further dressings if they could remain in position without such. In cases where they were liable to slide off, they were held by a larger piece of linen. In other words, the simple ointment commonly used wherever a piece of skin is missing, had been replaced by a wet piece of cloth, which is frequently done even today and all adhesive bandages were avoided as much as possible. However, when I saw the stump of a man's leg which had been amputated at the thigh and in which the femur protruded from the fleshy parts by almost half an inch, I was inclined to believe that this man would have preferred later that adhesive bandages had not been spared but used to pull the fleshy parts over the bone. Among the alleged ulcers treated, none were cancerous or otherwise serious, except for syphilitic ulcers, which were also treated with embrocations of mercury as well as warm water. Kern was said to have been a good operating surgeon. I was present at a few operations only, because it was difficult to see anything at all, unless one had been specially recommended to the surgeon. I found more valuable the private course in surgical operations which I took with a few fellow doctors under Kern's assistant.

I was in a peculiar situation. I had forced myself to repudiate the natural sciences in order to devote myself exclusively to practical medicine, to which end I had turned to Vienna. And now, in Vienna, all the most prominent representatives of medical practice such as the therapeutist Hildenbrand, the surgeon Kern, and the obstetrician Boer—all taught that nature should be left to her own devices, very rare cases excepted. Boer himself had spent his entire life fighting against artifice and artifacts, even against the use of forceps during deliveries. Do not interfere with nature, she knows how to help herself! Likewise, during my stay in Vienna, only a single operation took place in the great maternity hospital there. The other two gentlemen had turned to the "wait-and-see" method later, only because medicine as a whole was moving away from violent and one-sided methods. Whenever I remembered how well my fellow students and I were served by the lack of professional treatment in Riga I found it hard to disapprove of this method, but I thought it improper to devote so much time to it. There are certain to be many cases in which merely waiting can only be harmful. It seemed to me that such cases should have been considered to a greater extent, rather than demonstrating the benefit of waiting and carefully selecting cases which would bear out this theory. I, at least, would have benefited more from the opposite procedure, as I was already a rather doubting Thomas when I arrived, and longed to be rid of my doubts.

Nor did I find the proper course to follow in the other clinics. With Rust I saw many interesting cases, but they were really too interesting for me, that is, too rare. I would rather have reduced dislocations and set fractured legs, but Rust left such work to his junior staff, who performed it outside of visiting hours. What was left for us to see was the dressings. What could I profit from these rare cases which I would never encounter in my practical work if I were unable to treat the common ones with competence? The treatment of spontaneous dislocation with hot irons was wonderfully effective, since patients started to walk straight, without limping, immediately after treatment, although the limp tends to return after a longer period. This was something to tell about, something still new. But it could not be expected to have occasion to treat such rare cases. Beer's ophthalmic clinic seemed best suited to my needs, because similar cases kept returning and I could feel my diagnostic confidence increasing.

While I thus kept on reasoning, and without really being conscious of it, I fell victim to temptation—a twin temptation, that is. Two natural-history collectors appeared at the "Golden Stag," Herr Wittmann and Herr Jan. They offered the assembled medical men dried plants, wood books, i.e. wood samples in the shape of books containing inside foliage, blossoms, and fruit belonging to each tree, as well as insects and the like. Courageously, I refused everything as being a sheer waste of time. Then, Herr Wittmann offered to lecture on edible fungi. I had seen and classified a great many plants, but knew nothing about fungi. As there were to be only a few lectures—eight, I believe—I took this bait. The lectures were arranged, but they turned out to be pretty much built around Trattinnik's book on edible fungi, which book Herr Wittmann honestly enough offered up for sale after the lectures. He did not care at all about scientific renown, he was only a collector by trade, a *coureur des bois*, who was after a few gulden, so that he could continue his excursions. A harmless and amiable breed, these collectors! I for one was quite pleased to find myself again in the company of creatures who neither moaned nor wanted to be cured, and all that without the close hospital air ! This was the first temptation and took place in winter.

The second temptation was just in the making. In addition to some other Livonians in Vienna, I found a friend I had come to like and to respect earlier at Dorpat, Dr. J. Friedrich Parrot, son of the professor of physics mentioned earlier, and the same man who, with Herr von Engelhardt, had earlier measured the elevations down to the Caspian Sea, had repeated them later, and had climbed the Ararat. Upright in the fullest sense of the word, yet not passively so, as is often the case, but forceful and competent in everything he undertook, he was of a strong character at an age earlier than is usual in young people. He attracted me immensely, and I do not remember when I ever felt so compliant, I would even say so submissive, toward an equal as I felt toward Fr. Parrot, although we were of the same age*. Parrot had arrived in Vienna in a most beautiful Indian summer several months before I did. Immediately on entering the town, he had discerned a prominent mountain peak on the horizon and, being an experienced mountaineer, he was so greatly drawn to it that the moment he had found lodging and had put away his baggage, he

*I did not want to suppress saying a few words in the text in memory of my friend who died so young. I remember with pain the wrong done to him when efforts were made to deny his claim to having climbed the Ararat, and even the official investigation that he had initiated did not appear to pronounce in his favor. Because he had these findings published, having promised to do so, the doubts persisted for some time. Abroad these doubts have evaporated by now, as far as I know, but in Armenia the inaccessibility of the peak is still tenaciously upheld. The Patriarch himself adheres to this opinion, and Armenia is really a kind of priest state full of monasteries ruled by the chief monastery, Edshmiadsin, and these in turn rule the people. During my travels in the surroundings of the Caspian Sea, I also managed to visit Armenia, my immediate aim having been the Alpine Lake Gokcha which was particularly rich in fish. At that time I took the opportunity to visit Edshmiadsin and the Armenian Patriarch Narses. I was witness to the determination and indefatigability with which this Armenian Pope denied the possibility of climbing the Ararat, and yet at the same time, how shrewdly he did so, in that he never cast aspersions on the veracity of living persons, relying exclusively on the legends of the Saints. It so happened that a few years before my visit, General Chodsko and a party of soldiers had climbed to the top of Ararat and had spent one and a half weeks there, using goniometry to determine the position of the mountain tops. Not only must this visit have become known in the entire country, but it must also have caused quite a stir. One of my younger companions asked the Patriarch what one was supposed to think of that visit, whether it took place on the true top. "My son," replied the old man with apparent guilelessness, "St. Jacob himself did not manage to reach the top; how could mere mortals succeed in doing so today?" Whatever peaks human beings were going to attain, he always had a still higher one, possibly floating in the air, which St. Jacob wanted to reach and from which he was pushed back again and again. Obviously, the wily man could not even be accused of defamation since he was referring to the summit which St. Jacob failed to reach, any other summit holding no interest for him.

Any person who knew Dr. Fr. Parrot will agree with me that for him to commit an offense against the truth was quite impossible.

marched off toward that mountain without having asked the way, or even for the mountain's name. Only on the way did he learn that the mountain was called the "Schneeberg" (snow mountain). He climbed it without a guide and without undue effort. He spoke to me most enthusiastically of this mountain and the adjacent mountain ranges, thereby arousing in me the strongest desire to visit the Schneeberg too. I had never yet seen a real mountain range: I took the "Switzerland" of Saxony, including Lilienstein and Königstein for what it was, a phenomenon of erosion. Parrot was ready to join the party at once, but since the mountain is snow-covered for a rather long time, we had to postpone the undertaking to the transition of spring into summer. Even before the expedition to the Schneeberg, however, the coming of spring drew me frequently to the enchanting environs of Vienna. Perhaps no other town has surroundings of such variety, so richly bordered with comfortable settlements bustling with cheerful people, and a gradual transition from picturesque hill country to majestic, even somewhat somber mountain ranges. Considering also the multitude of flowering plants quite new to me, it was most natural and therefore forgivable that I soon found hospitals and clinics to be horrible places and that all my good intentions were somehow lost without my being really aware of it. The only clinic I still visited regularly was Beer's, the private courses having come to an end in any event.

The trip to the Schneeberg took place, I think, around Pentecost and was to lead us through charming Baden into the stark mountains and right up to the summit of the Schneeberg. As I came out of the forested region, passed through the scrub timber, and finally into the full Alpine vegetation, that is, seeing conditions in nature which I had known from books only, my rapture knew no bounds. We still found snow on some slopes and in some hollows; the mist covered many peaks, melting on one side, re-forming on the other; the light, pure mountain air, the incomparably beautiful and variegated view*, the feeling of standing higher than other human beings, but not alone, being with a faithful and experienced friend—all this only enhanced my joy. Our confidence, however, involved us in a peril that could have had a very serious ending. Parrot, who had been there before, knew where to find a mountain hut located at the foot, or already on the slopes, of the Schneeberg, where we spent the night. He had hoped to hire a guide here, but an important festival

---

*I cannot understand why in Reichard's *Passagier* (seventeenth edition), the comment on the Schneeberg reads, "The view is rather extensive, but it hardly justifies the effort of the climb." The writer of these lines must have chanced upon a very misty day. To me it appears rather that: "This view is comparable to that offered by the Rigi." What the Rigi has in majestic mountain peaks, the Schneeberg compensates for by the many clusters of human habitation seen from its top. However, as the top of the Schneeberg is rather broad, one has to move about from point to point to enjoy a panorama in sections, so to speak. It is true that the Schneeberg was the first high mountain which I had climbed. My impression of it was therefore all the more intense.

was due on the next day and the local people firmly refused to come along, thinking that it was much too early for a successful climb because there was sure to be much snow higher up. When Parrot declared that in that case we would go by ourselves, they laughed and assured us that we would never make it. Nevertheless we started out and reached the top without undue difficulties. There was no more snow on the top, but it was still thoroughly wet, with much wet snow on the slopes and in the hollows. The Schneeberg, an easy two days' trip from Vienna, at a height of 6,567 feet, is the most prominent mountain in the vicinity and almost constitutes the eastern boundary of the mountain system. It rises very gradually, and from Buchberg is more easily climbed than any other Alpine mountain that I have known. Despite its moderate height, its broad top is of an entirely Alpine character. It was there that I first saw the Alpine flora, which was entirely new to me. The view is most beautiful, although not as imposing as that from the Rigi, because there are no glaciers to be seen. Instead, one has a view on one side of the densely settled lowlands of Lower Austria right into the Hungarian plain, including the large Neusiedler Lake, and on the other side an immense chaos of mountains. Having enjoyed our long stay on the summit we then turned back in a somewhat reckless mood, brought about by our effortless ascent. We soon reached a slope steeper than any we had seen before, and enjoyed the crumbling rocks which rolled down from beneath our steps. Having descended this difficult slope, we saw a depression on the side, which we followed, thereby imperceptibly being led into a tight ravine or gorge at the bottom of which a narrow brook ran. We followed the ravine so that we might get down faster, and had only enough room to be able to walk beside the water. At times, however, whenever the brook came too close to one of the rock walls, we had to wade through it to be able to continue on the other side. Suddenly it began to rain. We had been unaware that the sky had darkened. The more experienced Parrot called out that it was essential to get out of the ravine, as the water would collect there. But the rock walls were extremely steep and much too high to climb; thus we had to advance along the ravine as fast as possible, despite the fact that it turned farther and farther away from the general direction of Vienna. Since there was no possibility to come out of it, we had to go forward as fast as we could. After several hours had passed, the ravine became somewhat wider, but we now encountered fallen tree trunks and rock fragments in it. At the same time it had become so dark that climbing over them required using our hands to recognize them. Finally, the walls became lower, the ravine wider, but it was now totally dark. It was late when we saw a light and, completely drenched, we reached a charcoal burner's hut where we could stay for the night. We discovered now that we, set over against the Vienna side, had arrived in a narrow valley. The next day, this narrow valley, which bore the name "Höllenthal" (Hell's valley), appeared a paradise to us compared to the gorge in which we had been squeezed, since it was more than twenty times as wide as the ravine and had a flat bottom of detritus. We had to walk in this valley for over half a day, and only in the evening did we reach the road to Vienna.

With these excursions, I again became addicted to botany. I had brought back several Alpine plants that had to be classified. Twice a day I ran to the library to compare my plants with the large copper-engraved works by Jacquin and Host, and with gratitude and humility I express my appreciation of the willingness with which the librarians removed these valuable works from the shelves twice a day and carried them back again, all in the service of a person completely unknown to them. Never again have I encountered such friendly readiness. The library regulations, however, were observed equally scrupulously. In vain I asked that these tomes be left, at least between twelve and two o'clock, in the locked reading room. At that time, I also started to seriously pursue this field in Vienna by looking up Host and Trattinnik, because it began to dawn upon me that medicine would not become my profession after all. I had had occasional opportunities to get acquainted with an aspect of practical medicine which was as new to me as it was repugnant: the antagonistic and slanderous way in which medical colleagues spoke of each other. Professor Zang, whom I visited occasionally, spoke very disparagingly of Professor Kern who in turn talked similarly of all other surgeons. But the height of disregard was achieved by the otherwise good-natured Boer. On a certain occasion he put some questions to the midwives who were being trained in the maternity hospital, and when he received answers which were not to his liking, he said loudly, in the presence of all the foreign doctors who accompanied him, "Well, that's Steidele for you, that ass." Professor Steidele was especially in charge of training midwives. This lack of urbanity might at that time have been characteristic of Viennese doctors, but to me seemed quite unthinkable among scientists.

Whenever I felt happy with my botanizing on the neighboring mountains, and as soon as I sat down to rest or take in the view, I felt as if my wicked *alter ego* were asking, "What will be the end of all this running around?" I was well aware of the fact that being acquainted with several hundred types of plants did not amount to anything much. Thus I had either to devote myself completely to botany, or remain faithful to medicine. I had not yet given up the ophthalmic clinic and wanted to give myself another chance with Hildenbrandt. But again I found very trivial cases and an equally dumb clinic; on every chart I again read *Oxymel simplex*. There was no doubt that Hildenbrandt was collecting material for a work on the natural course of illnesses or on the "wait-and-see" method. His last work, *Meditationes clinicae*, I have not read. If it does not contain some of the same kind of material, it is quite possible that he simply did not manage to prepare it, since he died in 1818. This time I cannot even attest to the universal and exclusive use of *Oxymel simplex*, because I found the clinic unbearable and ran away, straight to the lovely hills of Vöslau to contemplate my future under God's clear sky.

The seriousness of life gripped me hard by the throat. I could honestly say that I had achieved some confidence in ophthalmology and, practicing it, I would do even better. But how and where would I be able to practice ophthalmology when right now I had no confidence at all in the rest of medicine and, given my basic doubts, could entertain little hope of ever achieving it? I would not have minded practicing the "wait-and-see" method but one did not have to be a physician for that, and in order to become director of a hospital, one had first to make one's name in private practice.

The natural sciences, on the other hand, offered much brighter prospects. While systematic botany seemed somewhat empty to me, its practice, as far as it entailed roaming, made me happy—especially in the mountains. The important point was perhaps to extend the botanical studies over the entire globe. But even then, what about the future? I knew that there was room for one botanist only in our Baltic provinces, and that vacancy had been filled recently. It would be still better, I thought, if I had the opportunity to study systematic zoology. But mostly I played about with a vague presentiment concerning comparative anatomy, about which I knew little or nothing but of which I thought highly. Maybe somewhere I could also find an opportunity for a thorough study of geology which in any case would have led me more into the mountains. I thereupon decided to leave Vienna and to look for a haven for the study of comparative anatomy or geology in Germany. Should this attempt fail, I would return to seek out the hospitals again in winter, possibly in Berlin. But to stay in the sickrooms in summer I considered a sin against the Holy Spirit. Yet, I first wanted to visit the Schneeberg again and penetrate deeper into the mountain ranges. Parrot had already left; therefore, I went all by myself, in the middle of the summer, found more new Alpine plants, and walked as far as Mariahilf and felt again inexpressibly happy in the mountains, even though I was alone.

Solitude is welcome if one has to put one's thoughts in order, and was twice welcome to me in the mountains because I did not feel at all forlorn but completely at home. From the mountains, I had once again to return to Vienna where, as a reward for the good decisions I had arrived at, I now completely abandoned myself to the naturalist's vices, and visited for the first time the natural-history museum and the botanical garden; gathered information on interesting regions; bought books on the Austrian flora as well as various touring guides by Schultes; and then, I set my sail for the west, without as yet knowing the place where I would drop anchor. My first stop was Linz, whence I turned off to the Traunsee, Ischl, and Hallstadt glued to the rock like a swallow's nest. Having returned from this so-called Salzkammergut to Linz, I moved on to Salzburg. With Salzburg as my center, I made many trips to wonderful Berchtesgaden up to the end of the Königsee, climbed the 9,000-foot "Wazmann" with its sharply pointed peak, and visited Reichenhall,

Hallein, and Golding in preparation for future geological studies. But my itinerary also did not neglect the Untersberg, since I knew that Dr. Hoppe had been collecting Alpine plants here for years, which he sold.

On this excursion, and without my being aware of it, developments were initiated which were to decide my future.

Thanks to my habit of roaming, I had become a proficient hiker who thought himself a match for anybody. Even in the mountains I felt practically indestructible, much less in the plains. Therefore, I planned to set out in the morning from Salzburg, reach the Untersberg, climb the mountain as high as possible, and return to Salzburg by night. At the foot of the Untersberg was some kind of an inn, where Hoppe used to stay. Arriving there, I was told that he was not there at the moment, having left with another gentleman for the Glockner, I believe. I hired a guide for the Untersberg, roamed over the mountain in all directions, and by evening was back at the inn to have some food and continue to Salzburg. My guide threw himself flat on the floor and declared his inability to go on. It is true that he had had to carry the portable herbarium which I now had to shoulder myslef. Just when I was about to leave, the innkeeper came along with a guest book in which he asked me to write a few lines. The idea did not appeal to me very much as I was in too much of a hurry to write something either witty or poetical as I found written by others in the book. Therefore, I only noted my regret not to have met the famous Dr. Hoppe, as I had wanted him to resolve some botanical doubts for me. So, I left and on the way was rewarded by the most magnificent Alpine glow I have ever seen. The Alps to which I was so much devoted seemed to bid me farewell with gratitude, as from now on it was to be the plains for me. I stood still for a long time, to enjoy the spectacle fully. When it was over I continued walking for some distance, but before I reached the town I lay down on the ground and fell asleep. The night was rather chilly and I caught a bad cold that kept me in Salzburg for several days, after which I was on my way again. I was only a few days under way, when in a small town—it must have been Wasserburg—two men stopped me and asked whether I was Dr. Baer. Replying in the affirmative, I had a good look at the two who seemed very curious. One of them was an elderly man in what appeared to me to be peculiarly sagging apparel. The other was in his prime, with dark hair which I immediately envied as my own fair hair had always annoyed me. The name of the older man was Dr. Hoppe, that of the younger, Dr. Martius, the future expert on palms. They had arrived at the Untersberg inn soon after I had left, had read my deep sigh for botanical enlightenment, and Dr. Hoppe in his kindness was ready to provide it here and now. However, I had sent my herbarium to Munich in advance and could not show them anything. On the other hand, since I had left the mountains behind me, I had begun to be tormented by the thought that I was marching on without at all having a clear destination. On the spur of the moment, therefore, I asked the two gentlemen whether they knew where one could study comparative anatomy. "Go to Döllinger in Würzburg," said the younger of the two. "If you care to look me up in Munich, I will give you a small package of mosses for the old man. He likes to busy himself with them in his leisure hours." I expressed my gratitude, for now I had a definite aim. I think that this entire roadside congress took less than five minutes. For me, however, it assumed great importance, as will be seen in the next chapter.

But for the delay caused by my cold, this meeting would not have taken place.

8. Würzburg
(1815-1816)

In Munich I went to see Dr. Martius who was already preparing for his journey to Brazil, and indeed obtained from him the package of mosses for Döllinger. This was important to me as a means of introduction and I felt all the more obliged as my entire claim to the recommendation to Döllinger was based on a chance encounter at the roadside and my wish, expressed very urgently and even passionately, to find some place for a thorough study of comparative anatomy. I now had a definite aim, and this circumstance in itself did much to raise my self-esteem. Along the entire route from Vienna to Munich, the larger inns presented me with registration forms on which, for the benefit of the police authorities, I was supposed to indicate where I was going. I would have liked nothing better than to tell the police that I did not yet know, but I was rightly afraid that such candidness would land me in their tender care.

Without haste, I set out to see the sights of Munich, the picture gallery and other art collections, then moved on via Landshut where I met the craft of botany in the person of Schultes and, if my memory serves me right, also attended a students' meeting, and via Regensburg to Nürnberg where the works of art from the German Middle Ages and its transition to more modern times caught my interest. From Nürnberg I took a detour via Erlangen to see the place where my father had studied, and in Muggendorf I visited the famous caves with their archeological finds, finally arriving in Würzburg in the early fall of 1815.

As soon as I had found lodgings, I went to see Professor Döllinger, handed him the package of mosses from Dr. Martius, and declared that I wanted to study comparative anatomy with him and therefore I had come to Würzburg. "This semester I am not teaching comparative anatomy," replied Döllinger with the imperturbability and leisureliness characteristic of him, opened the package, and began to examine the mosses. I was thunderstruck, because the possibility had never crossed my mind that these lectures were given in the summer semester only. Still less did it occur to me that instruction was also possible without lectures, since all I had experienced was lectures without guidance. Undecided as to what to do now, I stopped. Should I stay in Würzburg and again make the sickrooms my main task, or should I look for another place to study one of the other natural sciences? Döllinger looked up from his mosses and, seeing me still standing before him, he looked at me for some time and then said in the same slow manner of his, "Why indeed lectures? Get yourself some animal, dissect it here with me—and bring then some others." This was an invitation that was much to my liking, as I wanted first of all to find out whether this subject would be more to my taste than medicine. I accepted his invitation with alacrity, and since he left even the hour to my choice, I appeared the next morning with a leech from a pharmacy because, being a complete stranger to the town and its environs, I could not find anything else at such short notice. Following Döllinger's instructions, I had also procured some fine instruments. The leech was temporarily put in oil to suffocate it, and I was shown a small wax-lined dish which I was to buy for dissecting under water. In the course of all these preparations, it must have become obvious to Döllinger that I was totally unfamiliar with finer anatomical work. Now and then, when the opportunity presented itself, I had indeed cut open some mammal out of curiosity, but I did not have the faintest idea how to approach an invertebrate. All the more reason for my being obliged to Döllinger who was ready to go to the trouble of instructing me, once he saw how great a store I set by it. When this, to me, unforgettable leech was about to be dissected, and Döllinger drew my attention to the fact that the digestive cavity was closely adjacent to a muscular layer which, in turn, was contiguous with the outer skin, I was so anxious not to proceed clumsily that I progressed with extreme slowness. Döllinger, who finally reappeared at my table at the end of an hour, praised my caution and produced the monograph by Spix, which he lay before me. I now had some idea of the parts to look for as well as of their position. Having obtained permission to take the monograph home for thorough study, I found that dissection proceeded rapidly the next day, and before the day ended, all essential parts had been laid bare. I had gained an understanding of the structure of this animal, not only by having seen with my own eyes, but also by having dissected with my own hands. This method of instruction suited me eminently. There then followed, one after the other, dissections of the most varied animals, sometimes invertebrates, sometimes vertebrates, in a sequence either dictated by chance or determined as a result of discussions. Döllinger found monographs for all such objects, and I quickly realized that it was most helpful if I studied these monographs first. Whenever a special manipulation was required or at least useful, such as the removal of shells from shellfish or snails, Döllinger would give a demonstration first, then leave the dissector to his own devices, busying himself mostly with his mosses, which he softened and then spread in an orderly fashion on stiff paper, probably also studying their spore capsules under the microscope. Later he also performed other work or read a book. From time to time, at intervals of one or two hours, he looked in to see how far I had progressed, pointing out some details which he thought merited attention.

Even before I had spent two weeks in this manner, I felt that I was on the right track, at least on a track suitable for me. The academic semester had not yet started, and I could use all my time for the dissection of various animals. I bought not only Cuvier's Comparative Anatomy, but also whatever monographs could be found in Würzburg. The more I saw for myself, the more intelligible and attractive became the works of others on other forms of animals. I was extremely gratified by the fact that each evening I could tell myself that I had increased my knowledge to some extent and that, looking back over longer intervals of time, I could indeed discern the increments of this growth and perceive that they were substantial. My self-confidence, almost completely shattered in Vienna, was being restored again, and this had such a salutary effect on me that I was able to fend off—not out of carelessness, but in full awareness—the agonizing thoughts as to where all this was leading, and whether I believed that zootomy was going to secure a position for me in this world. As a first stage, I intended to acquire sufficient knowledge and first-hand experience in comparative anatomy to become fully oriented in this science, so as to be able to form general abstractions from my own detailed collection of the particular. It soon became obvious to me that, in its creations, nature was pursuing certain general themes which it proceeded to vary in the different species. In Cuvier's Comparative Anatomy, this insight is somewhat masked by the arrangement of the work, which deals with the different anatomical systems in succession. His Zoology had not yet appeared. It was a masterful exposition of that toward which an inner urge drove me. I was enraptured, therefore, when later, shortly before my departure from Berlin, I became acquainted with the book. Yet I think it was just as well that I did not come upon a similar work at Würzburg, and that instead a need for it was awakened in me and animated my interest in zootomy. My present tentative plan was to continue the following winter with medicine, after having achieved that desired comprehensive view of comparative anatomy, as it was only by practical medicine that I could expect to make a living.

Having made these plans and taken these decisions, I took upon myself only a little heterogeneous work, once the lectures had started, as I had come to know the joy of studying by myself. I attended the obstetrical clinic of Siebold, so as not to miss that opportunity and a course by Professor Wagner, the exact title of which I do not remember. My fellow students with whom I dined called it nature philosophy, because all general speculations were regarded as nature philosophy, and all the more so, the less they were based on solid foundations. I was very eager to take a consistent course of lectures on the philosophy of Schelling. Nature philosophy was spoken of everywhere, and mentioned in many books, yet short of going through Schelling's writings one after the other, it was hard to grasp its meaning. Thus, I signed on with Wagner, although Döllinger had told me I would not find much. I found, indeed, a highly peculiar schematizing of both objects and relations, something which I found stimulating at first because of its novelty, but which soon appeared as empty as it was labored. I found it impossible to attend the lectures to the end. Because every being tended to differentiate itself into its opposite, and the equalizing of the differences created something new, all relationships had to be expressed by a fourfold, or rather quadrangular, formula. This was the simple basis of the theory. At times, the quadrangular formula appeared to fall into place quite naturally, at times it seemed very comical. In the family, for instance, father and mother constitute the natural difference, the child or the children being the natural consequence of the opposing action of the differences. This, however, leaves us without the fourth corner. The latter, we learn, is filled by the servants, who are thus an essential part of the family! If Schelling were to be held responsible for all such frivolities, his burden would be very heavy indeed. My longing for philosophy was stilled for some time. Döllinger himself was an admirer of nature philosophy, but of a more serious and solid variety. For my part, I preferred more positive matters for the time being. Together with some others, I took a course in practical pharmacy given by a chemist's assistant, and, in the afternoon, also participated in dissection exercises under old Hesselbach. This still left me sufficient time to busy myself primarily with comparative anatomy, with Döllinger I studied nothing but physiology in this first semester; however, given the state of that science at the time, it could not but be rather meager measured against practical needs. Döllinger was too honest to embellish the lectures with bombast or general philosophical speculations, which he himself had gone through and had left behind. But I fully enjoyed being permitted to dissect with him.

I now experienced for the first time the advantage of occupying myself continuously, or at least predominantly, with one single discipline, an experience which was to repeat itself to an even greater extent later when I became a lecturer. I am, therefore, a decided admirer of the institution of the unpaid lecturer. I often had occasion, then and later, to ask myself whether our entire university arrangement was not all wrong, in that it compels us to pursue many subjects at one and the same time, in fractional doses of forty-five to fifty minutes, after each of which we hurry on to a completely different one. Would it not be better, I had to ask myself, if one could pursue the subjects in succession, so that one could spend several weeks on one or, at most, two subjects and only then go on to others? The important and essential would no doubt be retained much better. As far as clinics are concerned, it is admittedly difficult to reduce the time, but how much more useful would the clinics be if the medical student in the last period of his studies were to do nothing else but observe and use good books to read up on the cases observed? For all the subjects mentioned, I regard separation in time definitely superior to simultaneous lectures in quite disparate sciences, especially when the student is overburdened with lectures, which will always be the case whenever the cardinal stress is put on an extreme comprehensiveness. All too often the hour-long occupation with heterogeneous subjects results in the student's saying to himself on the eve of such a hectic day, "All this confuses me as badly as if a millstone were turning in my head"*. In order to quiet his brain fibers, vibrating from the multifarious stimuli, he is likely to cease thinking of his day's work altogether. As a rule, a lecture provides little more than a stimulus, while ripe fruits are attainable only by studying on one's own. If a lecture is meant to enrich the memory, be it with images or with names, these will fail to impress themselves deeply during the lecture, and they will certainly be forgotten much more easily than when a conscious effort has been made to memorize them in one's own good time, staying with the subject until familiarity has been achieved. When the main stress is on developing concepts and conclusions based on these, as in philosophy, the lecture is admittedly of greater importance than in subjects dealing mainly with masses of facts. But here, too, studying on one's own, making use of a book, has the advantage of enabling one to follow through a whole train of thought time and again, to find out whether it concurs with one's own thinking and needs or not. A series of philosophical lectures would have to be taken down word by word if it were to be used in this manner, but while assiduously doing so, it would be hardly possible to make a critical assessment of the philosophical structure. It would be better, therefore, if the notes were available beforehand, either in hectographed or printed form. Judicious guidance, however, will always strive to further and intensify independent study, of both philosophical and empirical subjects; guidance, that is, by an experienced and circumspect man who is completely at home in the respective subject. It is quite clear what I am driving at. It is not that I now consider the professors superfluous, having been one myself for many a long year. I do believe, however, that they should make it their concern to guide the students in their independent study more than has until now been common in several subjects. Such guidance would have to be different for different subjects. Indeed, in disciplines that aim less at enrichment of the memory than at the training of judgment, the circumspect professor will recommend different works for independent study, depending on the individual student and his needs. After all, we do not act differently in common life, when we recommend those books that appear to fit the aptitude and educational level of those seeking our counsel.

The fact that at good universities today, students in chemical, zoological, and physiological laboratories, in anatomical institutes and in clinics, are taught to observe, and investigate by themselves, is itself proof of the increasing recognition of the need to induce the student to study on his own. The objection may be raised, and quite rightly so, that even in other subjects those professors who take any interest at all in their subject as well as in their students, gladly give them advice on their independent studies. While I do not doubt this, I would also like the state to adopt this point of view, instead

*[Ed. note: from Part I of Goethe's *Faust*.]

of regarding the lectures predominately as the be–all and end–all of education, as if lectures were a physical quantity that could somehow be poured into heads. Once the conviction has become general that independent study, or at least the craving to know, is the means to attain knowledge, this fact is certain to be given attention in the organization of universities. If, however, independent study is recognized as the essential ingredient of education, the imperfection of an intellectual training divided by the hour becomes obvious. How is a philosophical presentation to be properly assessed, compared with others, and digested, when it is immediately followed by something quite different; when the student, thirsting for knowledge, has just been introduced to the World as Will and the World as Idea, and still hardly knows whether he has solid ground under his feet or whether he floats in the ether as mere Will or mere Idea of himself; when immediately afterward another sage cruelly pulls down his soaring spirit by enumerating the different varieties of mice as distinguished by the length of their tails or the color of their pelts or by trying to impress upon him the important difference between a *folium ovatum* and a *folium cordatum*; or when yet another, a chemist, confidently demonstrates to him that whatever cannot be weighed has no real existence at all, and that he himself was no more than the amount of organic matter indicated by the balance? The tormented soul, squatting on the flat earth, now feels himself a mere quantity of matter. But at this moment a physiologist ascends the rostrum and declares that the vital processes, the internal developments which were already shaping matter in the plant had developed into a sense of self in the lower animals; into self-consciousness in the higher animals, into cunning selfishness in the apes; and into clear self-knowledge in man. The dejected student raises his head again, feeling something like an upgraded ape, but does not really know where the vital process may have originated, or how many grains it weighed. Above all else, he should think this through for himself, but he has no time for this. Next morning he is given further explanations, as he is shown conclusively that the Will was the Cause of all Effects. Now he also knows the origin of his vital process, which is, of course, his own Will. He then wants to put some order in whatever he has heard so far. I wonder whether he will succeed.

I take the aforesaid more seriously than one might believe. The fact that the student is exposed simultaneously, in separate classes, to men who set out from entirely different premises while treating each other with sublime disregard, I find most objectionable. Every philosophy, so far as I understand the matter, carries only a relative truth, for which reason there is benefit in philosophy only to the degree that one is able to roam in it with confidence. An absolutely true philosophy with which the world could be constructed has yet to be found, and the past holds out little hope in this respect, inasmuch as it proves that philosophers have again and again set out from a few well-worked basic views which must thus be considered as innate in the mental make-up of man. If this is true, it follows that the various philosophies offer no more than a yardstick with which to measure the world rather than means with which to construct it. Is it now helpful, one may ask, if the future virtuoso of the yardstick is handed quite different yardsticks all at the same time, each of them based on a different supposition? In other words, is it helpful if the future thinker is exposed to idealistic, materialistic, and dualistic points of view simultaneously? Is it not likely that this simultaneous onslaught might confuse him rather than help orient him?

But how to remedy the situation? One will surely not want to force the naturalists among the professors to adopt a uniform system? By no means! It should be possible, however, to introduce a more extensive separation in time. When a student—to remain with philosophy—has become used to, and trained in a particular philosophical trend of thought, he will be able, depending on his individual bent, either to translate the philosophical reflections of others into those he has accustomed himself to, or to replace the familiar with the new, if the new be more appealing. A general objection to this will be that "a wider separation in time would prolong studies beyond measure." Yet it is worth a trial! Such an experiment would reveal that quite a number of disciplines can be acquired in a much shorter time by studying them primarily on one's own, whereas at present they are stretched over one or two semesters simply because courses happen to be arranged by semesters.

But leaving aside philosophy which, by the way, I should like to place at the end of one's studies, rather than at their beginning: this would enable the young man to order the positive knowledge which he has gained onto the philosophical scaffolding later acquired, and to then assess the basic premises underlying his knowledge. The habit of beginning with philosophy appears to be founded on the exaggerated value accorded to logic in the past. The opinion, however, that a man is unable to think consistently unless he has taken a course in logic is as absurd as the assumption that a child could not walk until it knows what a step is and how it is done. Man thinks because he has the faculty for it, just as he walks because he has the faculty for it, yet he will be unable to do either until the faculties have been developed together with the organs.

Let us remain with medical studies! Anatomy, everyone will readily agree, is both an essential and a very sizeable part of these studies. It is usually spread over at least three, if not four, semesters. The first semester osteology is given as preliminary groundwork, followed by the rest of descriptive anatomy, which takes two semesters. If microscopic anatomy is not given concurrently with this course, it is likely to occupy a fourth semester. At some universities, practical anatomical work is begun only when the course on descriptive anatomy has been concluded and, to a great extent, already forgotten. Thus, the study of anatomy spills over into the fifth semester.

Now I should like to ask all anatomists whether they would not be prepared to take a young man of some eagerness and average intelligence and, within half a year, introduce him to and familiarize him with the entire anatomy of man to such a degree that he would have everything essential for the understanding of physiology and pathology, at his command, and also as much as is required for surgical operations. In addition, would not the young man at least have seen everything else which is not frequently met with in medical practice, such as the muscles of the back, to the extent that in case of need he would be able to orient himself rapidly with the aid of his textbook and his anatomical atlas—provided that during this semester our eager student would not engage in any time-consuming activity other than studying human anatomy? Then he would certainly have time enough to dissect for several hours a day, and he would not only have learned to use, but would indeed himself use the microscope. What he has seen and heard will reinforce each other, and once a coherent and clear understanding is formed, the substance of future lectures will be increasingly retained by the memory, which will loosen its hold only on those matters to which no connection arises in subsequent lectures. Without doubt, if a single person could gain a sufficient amount of knowledge within one semester, why not a whole group? In any case, it is an advantage during practical work to be able to compare several specimens and thus to observe the same features several times over. Anatomy teaching would naturally take place during the winter semester. In the subsequent summer semester could be studied botany, zoology, comparative anatomy, and descriptive pharmacology, as related sciences; or physics, chemistry, and physiology, but each of these sciences limited as far as possible to a period of one semester and, if necessary, be studied twice daily. If there could be kept in mind the basic principle of aiming at succession and of avoiding conjunction of totally heterogeneous subjects, it would be discovered that at present several subjects are unnecessarily spread out to adapt them to the duration of a semester. Why stretch, like rubber, general therapy to cover a whole semester if it is impossible to fill it with real content? Would it not be better to treat it as the concluding chapter of pharmacology (*Materia medica*) or the opening chapter of special therapy? Why the stretched-out theory of the various levers and forceps in obstetrics of which, in the end, only one particular type is recommended? Of the obsolete methods of surgical operations, starting from the ancient Egyptians? Nowadays, the theory of surgical operations will, of course, have to start not with the Egyptians, but with Stone Age man who, having no metal tools, probably used flint splinters for his operations. When holding forth on furuncles and felons, professors of surgery aiming at completeness will not fail to mention this fact, even if they have nothing to add of their own, and even though students, if they have heard of flint tools, are usually able to infer that much by themselves.

"Faced by such exorbitant demands the professors will surely go to ruin," some might think. I do not believe so, knowing very well that a professor needs much time to keep pace with the progress of his science and that for himself, it is also most desirable that he contribute to this progress. All that would change, I believe, is the division of his time. If, for instance, the professor of anatomy were to be very busy during the winter, he could be completely free in summer, and so with the others more or less.

It would be wasted effort on my part, however, to further elaborate these opinions and to draw up a detailed timetable, as I am well aware that it is very slow and difficult to change the established order of things. Not for a moment, however, do I doubt that such a change is bound to come in the course of time, and I have already pointed out that the practical activities which are gradually being introduced in various fields of study do indeed serve as proof of the irresistible force with which the importance and necessity of independent study have been asserting themselves. As concerns the other aspect, namely the avoidance of completely heterogeneous activities following each other at intervals of three-quarters of an hour, so will one perhaps concede to me that I do not value a mere notion, if everyone wished to ask himself about the circumstances under which he fell in love with a particular science. Did it happen when it was administered to him like poison in small doses, intermittently, and at prescribed hours, or when he had opportunity to immerse himself in it? Or let us, in our minds, consult an ancient Greek who, according to his national character, is supposed to have had a feeling for propriety and proportion. What would he think of taking a young man who is supposed to acquire much knowledge, not only a plethora of facts but also a well-ordered way of thinking, and instructing him first for an hour in philosophy, then in anatomy or botany, then in chemistry or physics, always being cut off by the stroke of the clock (assuming that our ancient Greek was familiar with striking clocks and with the above sciences)? Would he not answer rather that these continual interruptions were bound to have a confusing, or at least dulling effect and that it would seem better to him if the activities were to be less varied but more sustained? With children, the situation is different of course; their attention flags more easily and makes frequent interruptions a necessity. Also, young pupils are less frequently required to merely listen, and are given more active tasks in most subjects. At a later age, however, the mind is less inclined to passive reception and more to independent action. It is just then that the student is asked to digest and absorb what is said by others in rapid succession. The student is treated like a sack into which one attempts to cram as much knowledge as possible, as if one were baling cotton. When he is examined, however, he finds that he has retained and assimilated only those subjects, of the many he has been taught, in which he was actively interested or had been repetitively diligent; in other words, he knew only those things he had dwelled on at length.

Yet, unless I forcibly put a stop to it, this subject is sure to lead me too far afield. I shall therefore attempt to compress into a few sentences that which I wish to make clear but cannot accomplish in detail without producing a special treatise.

The purpose of universities is the scientific education of mature youth. This purpose is served better and to a more lasting effect by encouraging and guiding independent study rather than by a surfeit of pronouncements. Love for the subject is the soil in which the seed sprouts and bears fruit. This love is more aroused by sustained, rather than by regularly interrupted and mixed activity. Professors should be more concerned about their students' progress than about the completeness or even elegance of their lectures whenever elegance is not an integral part of the lecture. I prefer lectures to constitute postscripts to, and corrections of the students' own work.

Some might be inclined to think that such principles, while possibly suitable for the education of experts, such as future professors, are less suited to the education of the large number of officials, preachers, and general practitioners, etc., which the state requires. It appears to me that the principle of stressing the importance of independent study is a useful one for more limited needs also. Only those in this field who are appointed to watch over the interests of the state or society, i.e., the members of the various faculties, will have to decide on what they regard as essential for the scientific education of competent citizens, what is useful, and what is merely ornamental. They will have to see to it that the essential is not missing from any education, that the useful only seldom, and that the ornamental is only regarded as an encore when the essential has been fulfilled. For the surgeon it is essential to know the structure of the regions he is going to operate on, useful, if he is able to compare and choose between the major methods for each operation; but to babble about the methods of operating at the time of the Pharaohs is no more than tinsel, which is hardly worth the minutes wasted on it and is positively harmful when the most trivial operations, such as bloodletting and the like, are not properly practiced.

I must beg the reader's forgiveness for this digression, which was brought on by my vivid memories of Würzburg where my activities were most concentrated, as opposed to Berlin, where I unfortunately heaped upon myself work of the most heterogeneous nature, as I shall have to relate later on. The ideas sketched roughly here are at least the proper ones for my organization, as my life's experience has convinced me. I am aware, of course, that in order to make these ideas effective and fruitful, they would have to be elaborated and applied in several directions. In recognizing the value of the sustained pursuit of a particular subject, I have quite unintentionally and unawares slipped into a crusade against superfluous scholarly trimmings and against the cyclopedic treatment of trivia, as well as against high-flown and thus quite vacuous introductions to lectures. Against such scholastic frills and sundry embellishments I have an aversion which is either congenital or else was acquired gradually in the course of my medical studies. Already at Dorpat I felt an inner revulsion whenever I thought I could discern that particular whiff of learned air which the professors were so fond of giving themselves for their own greater glory. If instead of mentioning a large number of book titles which presumably were to be found in the textbooks, Professor Balk had tried harder to instruct us in the confident assessment of pathological symptoms and in the treatment of diseases, he would have attracted me far more.

Döllinger placed me directly in the midst of things, by letting me begin with the dissection of some animal, to be followed by others. Thus, I soon gained material for my own comparisons, and the different forms which I required to this end were quite familiar to me, as I had actively explained and investigated them myself. This way of passing on from the particular to the abstraction is not only the natural way—because a valid abstraction can be arrived at only through proper knowledge of the particular—it is also the most fruitful way of teaching, although the Germans frequently display a predilection for putting the abstract first. I have always found that when one lectures on the vertebral theory to students who, with considerable effort, have learned osteology in the usual manner by demonstration of details, that not only do they perceive the vertebral form in the skull, but they also recognize a fundamental type in the different vertebrae and that they are deeply moved by this. On the other hand, I have seen how other students to whom osteology had been presented by first demonstrating the general vertebral type and then turning to modifications, were left completely cold, possibly because they felt more confused than enlightened. They were not familiar with the details, the particular; still less with the abstracted generality of which they could have no total conception, as the latter can develop only from a multitude of particular images, not yet assimilated by them. Thus, it appears to me a difficult and unrewarding task to point out to a man not used to close observation of plant forms that the entire plant consists of a series of leaf areas and internodes, while another, however, who has seen leaves and their various positions, with calyces and integuments, with corollas, stamens, pollen tubes and fruit shapes often enough to have a working knowledge of them, will feel as if the scales fell from his eyes, as if he were looking into a sea of light, at a demonstration of plant metamorphosis according to Goethe. It is more or less as I remarked earlier (p. 23), referring to the study of arithmetic. Abstractions can be made only by proceeding from concepts which have been thoroughly assimilated, at least those are the only valuable abstractions. We will possibly return to this later.

I have offered the preceding remarks only by way of homage to my worthy, dearly beloved, and deeply revered teacher, Döllinger. Distance and obligations of an official position did not permit me to lay flowers at his grave when his mortal remains were interred; yet I will not neglect to say some words of gratitude for the love and selfless dedication Döllinger had for his students, and to speak in recognition of his method. If these words should spur on even a few of the academic teachers to something approaching his sacrifices, Döllinger's work would have an effect extending even farther into the future, bearing rich fruits for science. To equal him completely is a goal hardly attainable. I shall attempt to elaborate on this point.

Döllinger was a teacher through and through. To achieve a place of honor for himself in the history of science did not appear to be his ambition, at least not during the time I made his acquaintance. Nevertheless, he felt the strong urge to achieve complete understanding in the subjects he dealt with; and when he published a treatise he did so to share the results of an investigation or even of a philosophical reflection with others as well. It was thus enlightenment which he saw as his aim, not self-assertion. For this reason, when investigations of his students, even if initiated and guided by him, were published under their names, this did not seem to him to be a sacrifice on his part. Even the description of very rare objects—such as the human ovum described by Samuel—which did not entail protracted investigations, he left to them. Their task in such cases was to work through the literature which had been indicated by Döllinger in general terms. His lectures had the same character. There was no trace of self-advertisement and thus of ostentatious scholarship and rhetorical frills. His only, unalterable aim was the enlightenment of his audience, which he strove hard to achieve. It was this attitude that captivated his students. In reply to the question about the secret of his teaching method, he is said to have answered, "I clearly explain the main problem, leaving aside the marginal and incidental"*. This, his own explanation, completely characterized his teaching methods. Thus, his lectures on descriptive anatomy were unsurpassable in their precision and lucidity, always presenting the essential and never containing a superfluous word, as I have already mentioned on page 95. I myself was particularly gratified by his avoidance of every unnecessary word, since the excess and distracting verbiage in Professor Cichorius' lectures had been a serious impediment to my understanding. I very much regretted not having attended any but the last of Döllinger's lectures on anatomy. His lectures on physiology had the same character, and if they were somewhat meager, it was because the science itself was relatively undeveloped. On some selected subjects, however, in which his knowledge and understanding had become more comprehensive and positive, he was more exhaustive, for instance on blood circulation. Bichat's theory, that the pulse was caused not by a progressing blood wave but by the propagated thrust against a continuous column of blood, had been elaborated by Döllinger, who spoke about it with such a wealth of evidence that he at once convinced even those who had come holding the opposite opinion. On the other hand, questions for which there

---

*Ph. Fr. v. Walther: Rede zum Andenken an Ignaz Döllinger ("Address in Memory of Ignaz Döllinger"), p. 27.

were simply not enough facts available at that time to give a complete answer, he treated in a very cursory manner. At most, he heaped sarcastic comments on commonly held beliefs which he regarded as erroneous or faulty, adopting to this end a rather vernacular mode of speech, to bring the faults out all the better. His philosophically trained mind clearly saw the gaps in the available knowledge, without being able to fill the gaps, a slow process requiring painstaking chemical and physical investigations which were still a thing of the future. He never attempted to bridge these gaps with philosophical deductions, which was all the more remarkable as he undoubtedly had a philosophical mind. Earlier, he had studied the philosophy of Kant with zeal and then he was carried away by Schelling with whom he had personal contact. Given his critical mind and well-controlled imagination, however, he probably soon realized that Schelling had taken the most difficult tasks of philosophy and had turned them into the points of departure—the pedestal, so to speak— for his philosophical edifice. Later he did not like to talk of this period and saw the future of physiology in empirical observations which were then to be comprehended in the spirit of philosophy.

He much preferred to lecture on comparative anatomy (in the summer), because here he proceeded with definite facts. Yet, in this subject, too, he avoided all scholarly glitter and sham, touching only on the differences between gross anatomical organizations. His lectures could not be called comprehensive, even for his time, yet they were uncommonly stimulating, as was his entire personality, because everywhere he had his eye only on the essential.

In all these respects Döllinger has probably had predecessors and will have successors, though not many. Purkinje, too, has let his students publish the most important histological discoveries made under his guidance and, indeed, with his participation, being mindful only of scientific progress. Other teachers, too, will have striven after this same lucid and impressive lecturing. There will also have been some professors here and there, who, driven by their love for knowledge and truth, were more likely to reveal the gaps in their sciences than to hide them. But in one respect Döllinger has possibly had no predecessor, and is likely to have no successor his equal: his dedication, indeed his self-sacrifice to the interested student. I have no clear conception of those ancient times when adepts of science were only few and far between, and when these adepts were sought out by equally few students coming from afar to glean from them the secrets of their knowledge or skills, and being ready, in return, to perform the services of a famulus. As I have said, I am not sufficiently familiar with those times to use them for comparison, but it may be seriously doubted whether—since those days when numerous students at the universities crowded around a teacher—there has been a single teacher whose dedication to the individual student searching for knowledge equalled Döllinger's. It was not a public laboratory especially appointed for this purpose, but rather Döllinger's own lodgings and in fact, usually the very room in which he himself was wont to pass the time and work in, that served many a budding scientist before me as a workroom, and was intended to serve many others afterward. Like everything, this situation, too, must have had its natural antecedent and adequate cause. It probably began with Döllinger's asking young people in whom he had discerned desire as well as talent, to perform under his own eyes some work in which he himself was particularly interested, so that he was able to supervise and guide them, and have immediate access to the results. The dissertations of Wohnlich, Samuel and Schönlein*, for instance, were worked out in this manner, before I had arrived (although Schönlein's dissertation was still at the printers).

Thus it was originally Döllinger's desire to see certain physiological and anatomical questions solved, or brought nearer to solution—such as, for instance, the difficult problem of the sexual functions of the snail—without having to attend to collecting the material and performing the special investigatory work himself. As Döllinger cared more about accretion to his knowledge than to his name, he found it quite natural for the young dissectors to publish these works under their own names. He also saved himself the bother of looking up and compiling the details from the existing literature. Given Döllinger's simple, open, and genial nature, such cooperation usually resulted in a very affectionate relationship between him and his special students. I could not name a single one of the latter who was not totally devoted to Döllinger, and he, too, grew very fond of these students of whom he expected no more than that they would preserve their attachment to him. Never during the years of my contact with him did I hear him utter the slightest word of reproof to any of his students, yet he was never slow in expressing a hearty affection for one or his recognition of a student's talents if he found him to be bright. My predecessor as special student and in-house dissector was Schönlein, who later made such a name for himself as a clinician. Döllinger justifiably had great expectations of him. A few days after his dissertation had been published and successfully defended, Schönlein, his baggage on his back, appeared at Döllinger's rooms where I happened to be at work, to bid his farewells. Döllinger was visibly moved and asked him to wait for a moment, as he wanted to accompany him to the gate. With such affectionate relationships as this, Döllinger looked upon his students as a personal enrichment. In the course of time, he also began to extend his guidance to those who, unlike his senior students, did not take it upon themselves to pursue a task set by him, but wanted him to introduce them to comparative anatomy, as I reported earlier (p. 119) with regard to myself. As he could hardly expect

*Wohnlich: *Dissert. de Helice Pomatia et aliis huic affinibus animalibus e classe Mollusc. gasterop c. tabula aenea*, 4. 1813.

Samuel: *De ovorum Mammalium velamentis dissert. c. tab. aenea*, 8°. 1816.

Schönlein: *Von der Hirnmetamorphose*, mit Kupfert. 8°. 1816.

After my departure, many other dissertations appeared in addition to Pander's.

an early contribution to science from me, it must have been my fervent desire—which he must have read in my face—that induced him to accept me. I cannot tell with certainty whether he had already had students of this kind before my arrival; however, I am inclined to think so, since Martius was so positive in recommending Döllinger when I expressed the wish to be introduced to the elements of comparative anatomy. For some time I was the only student of this kind, and then some others were added, also beginners. Still later we were joined by a man more advanced in his studies, Christian Pander, who was to engage in an investigation through which Döllinger's school was to become so important to the development of natural science.

Before relating how I became the happy instrument of Pander's move to Würzburg in the spring of 1816, and before reporting on the beginning of his investigations, I beg to add a few words on Döllinger, as well as to bring the report about myself up to the spring of 1816.

Ignaz Döllinger, born in 1770 in Bamberg, first studied medicine in his home town, then in Würzburg, Vienna, and Pavia. Later, in Bamberg, he lectured on various medical subjects, specifically pathology, symptomatology, and therapy, but also on physiology. When the university in Bamberg closed down in 1801, he was transferred to Würzburg where he lectured on physiology and anatomy with its branches, namely comparative and pathologic anatomy. His distinctly philosophical bent led him, as mentioned earlier, toward the philosophies of Kant and later Schelling, but it was this selfsame disposition that again drew him away from Schelling when he felt the need to understand the essential core of things more than to possess a system, a scheme into which the entire world could be fitted. He thus aimed more at broader knowledge, and studied mineralogy and geology, about which he has even written, as well as botany, for which he prepared himself a herbarium. His special predilection was mosses, which he collected to his dying day. Zoology and its ramifications were too closely related to zootomy to be neglected by him. But he is also said to have lectured on experimental chemistry. In all these different sciences, with the sole exception of the knowledge of mosses, it was only the essential, the important, that attracted him. It was as if his occupation with mosses, which he himself regarded as no more than a pastime, had completely satisfied his need for the special, the particular. This fact permitted him to be at home in so many subjects, and also made him such a stimulating person to come into contact with, as he had thought about the most different subjects and had formed his own opinions. Even concerning everyday matters he liked to express himself in a way which was the result of his own reflections and which sometimes, like an oracle, challenged the interpretative power of his listeners.

He was very much a natural wit. His public appearances, therefore, were awaited with great suspense, as he always liked to intersperse his lectures with sarcasms which were very much feared in certain quarters. He once said in public that obstetrics was no more than a branch of surgery, i.e., of the medical craft, as levers and forceps were merely artificial extensions of the fingers—an utterance greatly shocking those who liked to declaim the sublimity of surgery in general, and obstetrics in particular. He was always concise, never voluble. With the students working under him, he never felt the need to assert or demonstrate his knowledge and skill, unless specifically asked by the student himself. Indeed, it was regrettable that he was not more wordy and did not volunteer more of his knowledge. The students' need to always draw him out possibly contributed to creating a certain distance between him and them. On the other hand, he liked them to keep him informed of news from the scientific world which they might come across in journals. To search the daily papers himself for news or minor items of interest for his studies was apparently not at all for him, although he never balked at thoroughly studying even the most difficult works when he had reason to believe that they contained some deeper insights. Since he never accepted any kind of fee for his instruction, despite having a large family, he never lacked appreciation on the part of his students, with whom he liked to maintain completely informal relations as long as they felt themselves his students, and he liked to take short walks with them in the summer in the vicinity of the town, or more extended ones to the village of Sickershausen, where Nees von Esenbeck then lived with his family; I had first met him at Döllinger's and later frequently visited at Sickershausen in the company of Döllinger, D'Alton, and Pander.

So, during the winter of 1815–1816 I worked assiduously at comparative anatomy with Döllinger, using the evenings to peruse the pertinent literature. Soon, however, I felt the need to also participate in practical exercises in human anatomy. Such a course was given under Hesselbach, who for many years had conducted it according to a strictly traditional form, and now, in his old age, had become so taciturn, that he guided his students more with signs and gestures than with words. At a later point when discussing the dissection exercises in Königsberg, I shall take the opportunity to return to Hesselbach. That I did little else apart from anatomy, I have already remarked upon (p. 122). I should not, however, like to omit completely mentioning a short visit to the therapeutic clinic. When I came to Würzburg, Prof. Friedrich, the professor of therapeutics was seriously ill, and no one knew when his clinic would open again. He was regarded as a very good practitioner and as an excellent clinical teacher. When after some months he had recovered and resumed his lectures, I was eager to see him in his clinic. His simple delivery, which expressed an abundance of experience communicated in the simplest manner, was uncommonly attractive, and I felt that if it was at all possible to turn me into a practitioner, I would have to have such a teacher. But as soon as he wanted to give me a patient, I took to my heels. I had plunged too deeply into comparative anatomy by then to use an hour in the late morning for anything else. The degree to which the lecture, occasioned by a case of herpes, had caught my interest, however, may be judged by the fact that I still remember its essentials completely. The circumstance that the information conveyed by that lecture was to be used by me later with spectacular success (similar to the cases mentioned earlier on page 97) may have been a factor contributing to its being so memorable.

In retrospect it now seems curious that I took such a dislike to the profuse embellishment of so many of the lectures in Dorpat, and that in Vienna, where, true enough, I only visited the practical institutions, the exclusive reliance on Nature's healing power in all the clinics, appeared so boring to the eager student, regardless of the importance of observation as such, while in Würzburg all the teachers seemed to deal with the material in an unpretentious, simple, and straightforward manner. Even the pure inanities of Professor Wagner seemed to be no more than a satirical comment on the philosophical schematizing of his time, although this was not quite his intention.

Singing the praises of the unhampered natural course of the disease was a necessary and salutary reaction to the preceding Röschlaub period of "Sturm und Drang" in medicine. That the clinics, those institutions for the training of young doctors, were exclusively used to exalt the "wait-and-see" method, however, could only happen in Vienna, where all instruction by salaried staff had to be given free of charge. Had the professors been permitted to accept a fee, they undoubtedly would have taken good care to make the clinics interesting as well as instructive. Without this incentive they transferred to the clinics all the observations they wanted to make of the "wait-and-see" method.

My studies in zootomy and anthropotomy, pursued assiduously and without much interference during the winter of 1815–1816, made me feel so happy and content that I refused to be overly worried by my prospects for the future. In fact, however, they were anything but rosy. Since my arrival in Würzburg, I had been living on money which my brother had borrowed for me, and which I had to repay. The loss incurred in the transaction was very substantial, as the rate of exchange had dropped considerably after the great wars. From a letter which my brother wrote on the occasion of a money transfer in the fall of 1815, and which remains in the family, I can see that the ratio of banknotes to silver was about 412 to 100, their real value thus being less than one-fourth of their nominal value. With youthful optimism, I hoped that the means for repayment would materialize eventually. But as in Estonia there was not the slightest chance to earn a living in anatomy, I realized the imperative need not to give up my hope for a career as a practitioner. For the time being, I intended to continue to devote myself to the activities which were to my liking, while promising myself to resume my medical studies with renewed energy in Berlin. In the meantime, I corresponded intensively with my former fellow students from Dorpat, who were spread out all over Germany. Some of them showed up for short visits in Würzburg, only one of them staying on, namely Dr. Sahmen, with whom I shared my lodgings. Others were staying in Berlin, Vienna, Göttingen, Jena, and Heidelberg; still others had moved to Paris and Italy. I very much longed to see some of them again, and since Jena was located roughly centrally to their German abodes, I conceived the idea of all of us converging on Jena during the Easter holidays of 1816, as it was to be expected that many of them would change their places of residence in any case at this time. Since this suggestion was instrumental in Pander's move to Würzburg and in his research, as well as in my own on embryology, I should like to report on this meeting in greater detail.

As early as January 1816, I conveyed this suggestion to my friends in Jena, where Ulmann, the present bishop; Assmuth, frequently mentioned earlier; Dullo, also a theologian; and Holländer lived, asking them whether they would be in Jena around Easter, and whether they would undertake to forward the invitations to the other towns as well. I also had the not very bright idea of writing my letter on a quarto-sized sheet in such a way that the lines on the back were written so that they perpendicularly crossed the lines on the front side. After that, I cut the sheet into four equal pieces, sending each of my fellow-students one of those quarters in a separate envelope, so that, by himself, none of them should have been able to make head or tail of it. Since they were living together, a fact which I did not know, they soon put two and two (or should I say one, two, three, and four?) together. Yet this jest, however cheaply brought off, seemed to excite them, and they decided to present me with a challenge. After Assmuth had tentatively agreed to my proposal, I received on the twenty-ninth of February a ceremonious invitation to a "Livono-Courono-Estono-Ruthenio Congress" as they called it, to take place on the twenty-ninth of March. Appended, also, was the decision to publish a congress newspaper under the title of "Der nordische Baer" ("The Northern Bear" [a pun on the author's name]) of which I was sent a proof sheet. It was cut out from a large sheet of paper and had the shape of a bear. It was divided by lines into six columns in the manner of newspapers, which were filled with news from traveling fellow students, written in different languages. The whole thing was then cut into twenty different, interlocking pieces, so that its proper assembling took some time. This humorous vein in the preparations probably contributed to the high spirits of the large number of persons who came to Jena from Berlin, Vienna, Würzburg, Heidelberg, and Göttingen to meet in merry company, and to tell one another of their past experiences. Having thus collected information, some, then and there, were to decide on their future studies.

Christian Pander, whom I had come to know and like while still in Dorpat, was also among the guests. Pander had early decided to devote himself entirely to the study of the natural sciences, although fatherly foresight urged him in the direction of practical medicine. Since, in contrast to the rest of us, he had neither to regard these studies as an accessory to medicine, nor keep an eye open for a future position in Russia, he had left Dorpat two or three semesters before I did, and had turned to Germany, staying first in Berlin, then in Göttingen, whence he came to this meeting in Jena. With overflowing praise I told him of my Döllinger, and so persistently tried to persuade him to move to Würzburg, where I would stay for another half year, that he finally decided to do so. I am not certain now whether I had told him at that time that Döllinger was looking for a young man ready to spend time and not inconsiderable financial means on a thorough investigation of the development of the chick in the egg, but I believe I had. Pander himself is far away at the moment and therefore not available for questioning. Be that as it may, Pander came to Würzburg without first having accepted Döllinger's proposal. He did not come with me as I asked him to, however, but said that he had to return to Göttingen first, to wind up his affairs.

I have asked myself at a later point, whether our innocent meeting (which was given the high-sounding name of Congress only because that word happened to be in the air at that time) did not contribute to that quite different meeting on the eighteenth of October 1817 at the Wartburg, to which students in Jena had invited delegates from various universities, and which had a definitely political flavor. That meeting, through the enthusiasm of some persons, may or may not have precipitated the wretched deed of Sand, but it certainly caused the hunting of persons suspected of so-called "subversive activities."

At that time there were in Jena many young people who had participated in the Wars of Liberation, and who were now continuing their interrupted studies. I found a closer acquaintance with some of them rather rewarding, as they had a more serious attitude to life than one was used to in Dorpat, where, with few exceptions, only regular students gathered. Who knows whether these young people, having become used to regarding themselves as fully active citizens of the state by virtue of their army service, did not read a political tendency into our meeting? We were so far removed from political considerations, that the very correspondence which initiated our meeting can serve as ample proof of how little our imaginations were fired by changes in the government. I still keep my part of this correspondence, and while it would lead too far and is not interesting enough for me to publish here any greater amount of it, some paragraphs of the "Congress Regulations" bear quoting, just to indicate the tone and direction:

"d. The afternoon, as a rule, is to be devoted to investigations into the state of the Country, by ambulatory inspection throughout the neighboring countryside, of the ruins of castles, the mountains, valleys, etc."

"e. Important investigations concerning the empire's brews will be performed in the evening. Herr...... is hereby appointed acting president of this section."

More prosaically expressed, this means that trips to the countryside surrounding Jena were to be undertaken in the afternoons, whereas the evenings were to be spent in a beer joint. This facetious note, once struck, was amplified during the meetings proper. One of the participants from outside Jena, a good-natured, but rather phlegmatic theologian, was elected Archbishop, and soon after enthroned as Pope, whom we were duty-bound to venerate. It was decided that each number of the Congress Newspaper had to carry a bulletin reporting on his state of health. When we learned that nature had bestowed the gift of sleep on "His Holiness" with much greater generosity than on other mortals, it was proposed to weigh "His Holiness" each evening and each morning, to find out how much weight "His Holiness" was pleased to lose in his sleep by transpiration. Of the Congress Newspaper, however, there appeared little more than the specimen number.

Occupied as we were with that and similar follies, we heard no political opinions, even from the former warriors. When in the years 1819 and 1820 the authorities were busy with tracking down "subversives," taking childish utterances of quite immature persons as serious portents of the times, I became afraid (being by that time a teacher in Königsberg) that it was precisely the significance attached to what were mostly no more than expressions of foolishness, for certainly little of it was more serious, which was liable to confuse the unaffected minds of the students, giving them an inappropriate sense of importance. I must confess that my opinion has not changed essentially. Our own time is without doubt more disquieting, but possibly it would not have come to such a pass had yesteryear's follies been treated as such from the very beginning.

Because of my penchant for walking, I had come to Jena on foot, despite the approaching spring. On the way I had visited, and crawled about in, the coal pits of Ilmenau, a visit that was made possible through the good offices of the mining superintendent, Voigt. The return trip was also made on foot. While trying to go over a ridge still covered with snow in the Thüringer Forest, however, I had the misfortune to sprain my foot, and could not go on. A good-natured student from Würzburg who had accompanied me found a sled in a neighboring village; thus I was pulled across the mountain. On the third day, my foot was again usable.

Spring had already passed into summer when Pander arrived in Würzburg with the intention, at first, of pursuing the practical aspects of comparative anatomy. To this end, he soon introduced himself to Döllinger, to whom I had spoken about Pander's impending arrival, his financial independence, and how this had permitted him to devote himself exclusively to the natural sciences, in which he was most interested*. Döllinger, in greater detail than

---

*In this, as I later learned, I had erred, inasmuch as Pander's father did in fact wish him to finish his medical studies.

before, then repeated his wish to find a young man who would, under his supervision, investigate the development of the chick in the egg, and at the same time, however, also be able to defray the costs of such an undertaking. He, Döllinger, had himself begun this investigation earlier, but had had to give it up, partly because of the costs involved, partly because of the continuous supervision which the incubator required. As he was aware that I was very much interested in this project, in which I hoped to take part, possibly he thought it superfluous or even unseemly to put this proposition to Pander right after he had arrived. Having made Pander's acquaintance, however, Döllinger seemed to be much taken by his personality, and appeared to feel that he was the right man for the project. On the occasion of a walk to Sickershausen, where Pander and I accompanied him, Döllinger again spoke first with me, of the ramifications to be expected from a thorough study of the development of the chick. I at once told Pander of this latest conversation, and Pander declared his readiness to take on the project. In Sickershausen we discussed the details, and it turned out that Döllinger had been turning the whole project over in his mind for some time now, as he now declared that, to achieve full understanding, it was necessary for the different developmental stages discovered to be drawn not only accurately but also artistically, so that they could serve for copper engravings to be prepared later. Thus, it would be most desirable if a draftsman and engraver could be found united in one person. Such a person, he proposed, was d'Alton, an incomparable artist living nearby, who had in the past published an anatomy of the horse with excellent illustrations, but was now without work. Pander agreed to all of these suggestions.

In a letter to Pander, which prefaces the first volume of my book *Ueber Entwickelungsgeschichte der Thiere* ("On the Embryology of Animals") (p. VI), I have already spoken about the conception of these investigations. I shall have to repeat it here, partly because my own investigations are connected with it, partly in order to refute some erroneous information found in writings which would appear to be based on the sources. Thus, Dr. Ph. Fr. v. Walther's "Address in Memory of Ignaz Döllinger," p. 84, reports that Döllinger had first approached d'Alton "... for the purpose of investigation and graphic illustration of the animal foetus from all classes of vertebrates." Pander is said to have joined them in 1816. This is completely erroneous. Not only did I never see d'Alton in Würzburg prior to his engagement by Pander, but I was also present at the conversation during which Döllinger, to ensure the success of the investigations to be undertaken, suggested that d'Alton be engaged and induced to move to Würzburg, by offering him a regular, monthly remuneration. Subsequently, it was decided that Döllinger would write to d'Alton, to inquire as to his financial demands. D'Alton came to Würzburg only after Pander had agreed to these demands, that is, in the middle of July 1816, about six weeks after Pander's arrival. D'Alton's past was somewhat shrouded in darkness, and I do not know how well-founded the rumor was according to which he had changed his original name of Dalton into d'Alton. It was mainly his engagement which was the cause of the very considerable costs of Pander's investigations since these, including also the publication of the Dissertation and the Contributions, took much longer than originally foreseen. D'Alton was a highly talented artist, as was borne out later in the publication of the work on the skeletons of mammals. Until his arrival in Würzburg he was a complete stranger to investigations on embryology but being a very intelligent man with a good grounding in natural history, he was bound to have picked up the requisite knowledge quickly. He had already published his "Natural History of the Horse" in two large folio volumes, of which the first dealt with the different breeds, and the second with the anatomy of the horse. After the Würzburg research, he accompanied Pander on a journey through the Netherlands, England, France, and Spain. It was at that time that he prepared drawings of the skeleton of the Megatherium which later, when d'Alton had obtained a position in Bonn, appeared in a deluxe edition, "The Giant Sloth, *Bradypus giganteus*, described and compared with related species by Pander and d'Alton," to be followed in eleven additional installments and in similar form and design, studies of the skeletons of Pachyderms, the Carnivores, Ruminants, Rodents, Quadrumana, Edentata, Seals and Manatee, Cetacea, Marsupials, Chiroptera, and Insectivores and, lastly, the skeletons of ostrich-like birds. This work, embellished with most beautiful illustrations, is primarily d'Alton's achievement although many of the skeletons were sketched during their joint travels.

According to the foregoing, the memorial address was thus in error when it reported that Pander, having arrived in Würzburg in 1816, joined Döllinger and his friend d'Alton, to participate in investigations already under way. Elsewhere a still more definite opinion is expressed to the effect that this line of research should in fact be regarded as performed by Döllinger. This statement should be regarded as quite baseless, as the three men wanted the investigation to be regarded as a joint effort. The very fact that the publications, composed by Pander, appeared under his name only, indicates that the others acknowledged his greater contribution*. Therefore, I regard it as not inappropriate to report on the preceding discussions. I can still add a few details concerning the first initiatives in which I took part, before d'Alton arrived in Würzburg. Later, I maintained frequent contact with all three of them, although no longer participating in the project.

There can be no question that Döllinger had earlier carried out a series of

---

*Pander not only signed the *Dissertatio inaug. sistens historiam metamorphoseos, quam ovum incubatum prioribus 5 diebus subit.* 1817–8., and the *Contributions on the Embryology of the Chick in the Egg* (*Beyträgen zur Entwickelungsgeschichte des Hühnchens im Ei*). 1817. Fol., but also the reply (*Isis* 1818, vol. II, pp 512–514) to the doubts expressed by Oken (*Isis* 1817, No. 192).

investigations on the development of the chick and was familiar with the operation of the incubator. Apart from his own claims, this was also obvious from the expert manner in which he treated the egg to get the growing embryo under the microscope. Today, this simple method is, of course, well known, and in general use: First, the section of shell above the air space is knocked in, causing the entire yolk to sink. The germinal disc, including the embryo which, after several days of incubation, has moved close to the shell, is thereby moved away from the shell. After that, a larger section of the shell above the embryo is opened and the entire yolk poured into a dish containing water. A disc-shaped section is then cut from the yolk sac and, provided development has not progressed too far, the germinal disc is carefully detached from the yolk sac and, floating on water, brought under the microscope either with or without the developing embryo. Today I believe this practical but simple method has, by tradition, come to be generally acknowledged and employed.

However simple this method appears, it must not be assumed that it was hit upon on the first attempt. If that were so, there is no doubt that the development of the embryo in the first days would have been completely understood at a much earlier time. Haller in particular would inevitably have discerned several earlier stages in which no heart is visible. Since it has long been known that, regardless of how the egg is being held as long as its longitudinal axis is horizontal, the embryo is always at the highest point, it seems only natural to try to open the egg carefully just above the embryo. This practice, however, easily leads to injury to the embryo or the germinal disc, unless one first causes the yolk to sink. The same also applies to the subsequent steps. It will be difficult to discern anything during the first days of incubation, unless one succeeds in observing the well-cleaned embryo under higher magnification. I doubt whether Haller or any of his predecessors, with the possible exception of Malpighi, ever discovered how to do this. And long after Wolff and even Pander, Home presented us with embryology of the chick, which manages to tell us little more than that the chick grows progressively larger. Kaspar Friedrich Wolff may indeed have used the same method, but since he did not describe it, it had to be rediscovered.

Döllinger had thus worked out this most practical method by himself, for which he had a very distinctive talent. It is also undeniably to Döllinger's credit that the splendid execution of this investigation was not initiated by mere happenstance, but that he purposefully worked toward it and arranged and supervised it in such a manner that it was bound to lead to success. The surmise, however, that Döllinger had already had a coherent picture, and that all that was left to Pander was merely to go over certain stages and have them drawn, must be strongly denied. What interested me most was the way in which a disc-shaped body such as the so-called "cock's tread" (germinal disc), was able to turn into an embryo with an abdominal cavity and a protruding gut. At first I participated in the investigation to find an answer to this question, but nobody seemed able to enlighten me on this point. Also, the first experiments were far too groping to provide an answer. Yet it was precisely this process that had been rather exhaustively investigated by Kaspar Friedrich Wolff. His description, however, was too long-winded and involved to be easily understood.

Thus, Pander indeed enjoyed the advantage of being able to utilize Döllinger's previous experience as well as his proficient methods. But if one wanted to get down to a truly developmental level, one had to begin the entire investigation anew and pursue it persistently. This, to the best of my knowledge, was indeed what had been done primarily by Pander, just as it was he who also first understood Wolff's publication, bore the costs of the project all by himself, and took care of the incubator. Döllinger, as he also did in other research, merely reserved his natural right to be kept fully *au courant*, and to check the results to convince himself. It was for this reason that he accepted Pander into his house.

In the beginning, the investigations yielded very few positive results, as each earlier stage could be understood only from a later stage, and that stage from a still later one. Faster results would have been obtained if, right at the beginning, the decision had been taken to investigate in the reverse direction, from the later toward the earlier stages, as should be the sensible way in every developmental process of which the final result is known. Still, because one prefers to understand a process from its very beginnings onward, it is almost always this course of investigation that is selected. Since at the beginning the results were not only slow in coming but also limited to conjectures, I soon ceased to take an active part. I thought to make better use of my time by engaging independently in other research and, above all, by devoting more time than I had in the preceding winter to human anatomy with old Hesselbach. I hoped that Pander would occasionally inform me of the results of his work. Yet it seems that complete understanding of processes which one does not find described everywhere is only attainable by continuous preoccupation with them. That, at least, is what I felt when in late August on the occasion of a visit to Nees in Sickershausen, I had the opportunity to talk to Pander. I asked him, now that the research had been going on for several months, to give me an explanation as how the germinal disc turned into a closed body. It was obvious to me that Pander already had a clear, and probably correct picture of the process. I also remember distinctly that he took a handkerchief, spread it on his palm and, by bending his fingers, brought them close to each other, thus trying to demonstrate the formation of the umbilicus. His use of visual aids notwithstanding, the process did not become quite clear to me, possibly, I now believe, because I could not visualize the detaching of the gut. Thus, when I engaged in these investigations in Königsberg, I had to start more or less at the beginning.

The summer semester of 1816 was, by the way, also a very cheerful and stimulating one. Somewhat earlier I had made the acquaintance of Nees von Esenbeck and his intelligent and affectionate wife. Nees, who had just finished his work on fungi, helped me to a first understanding of these cryptogams and of the algae on which he spent much time, as he also did on insects. Thus, there were frequent visits to his small estate near Sickershausen, a two-hour walk from Würzburg. Sometimes I went alone, more often with Döllinger and Pander, and later with d'Alton as well. Döllinger was very fond of occasional intellectual stimulation in cheerful and witty company, and he didn't let a holiday or vacation pass by without availing himself of the opportunity for it. D'Alton was even more eager for lively company where he could show off his wit, and we enjoyed being their faithful companions. Nor did we limit our range of action to Sickershausen. From there we sometimes moved on to the small town of Mainbernheim or to Mergentheim, the places where families included in Döllinger's and Nees's circle of acquaintances lived. Now and then we visited parish fairs in neighboring villages. We also went on trips to the nearby mountains, converging from several sides to spend the day together. I have forgotten the name of these mountains, but I believe it was the same Schwabenberg on which, after my departure, the trio which was still brooding, describing, and drawing, spent another four weeks with all their paraphernalia, continuing their work in the open air. Thus there was always a refreshing mixture of work and merry company, and it was this conversation on the occasion of those meetings that created new tasks and had a most stimulating effect on the work. It appeared to me as if Nees von Esenbeck, who had shut himself in almost hermetically for years so that he might finish his work on the fungi, was now strongly feeling the need for human company, and it was usually he who initiated these excursions. This mood of his also might have been caused by his certainty of soon being elevated to an official position, to which he had long aspired. We all knew that the university at Bonn was about to be founded, and that Herr von Altenstein not only had promised Dr. Nees a professorship, but was also consulting with him and Professor Goldfuss about the establishment of the university and the selection of professors to be appointed. Nees, known in the past in only a narrow circle as a devoted, well-informed, and philosophically inclined natural scientist, had not only made himself a name with his work on the fungi but, through his close connections with Herr von Altenstein, he had also become an influential person whose favor was courted by many. As is now known, he was soon appointed president of the Leopoldine-Carolingian Academy, having accepted a call to Erlangen in 1818. At the end of that year, the deed of foundation of Bonn University was signed and Nees, appointed there, left Erlangen for Bonn in 1819. In Bonn, assisted by a substantial yearly contribution from the King of Prussia, he obtained for the publications of the aforementioned old and venerable academy wide recognition and, indeed, respect.

For us young people, these repeated meetings with brilliant men and women were most stimulating. These gatherings were also attended by such medical men as Dr. Siemers and three Greeks, of whom one in particular, Vogorides, was a man of wide education; they were studying in Würzburg and were devoted not especially to anatomy and physiology, but to medicine in general. Other participants included several transient doctors who were in Würzburg for only a short while. Yet, at the same time, we discerned the first signs of conditions which were later to dim the memory of the president of the Leopoldine-Carolingian Academy.

* * *

During my stay in Würzburg the first steps were taken which were to determine my future. Professor Burdach had sent me friendly letters now and then, both to Vienna and to Würzburg. On replying, I never failed to give him some idea of my life and doings. Thus, in January 1816 I received a letter of the ninth of the month in which Burdach informed me that he was at last in a position to set up the long-projected anatomical institute. A building had been bought, but what was still missing was a prosector. He asked me whether I knew a young man, either in Würzburg or elsewhere, who, by his diligence and skill, would be suitable for this position. He offered a salary of 300 Thalers in addition to free, decent, and well-heated lodgings. If I knew such a person, he should write at once, and also produce documents attesting to his skills. I believed I could recommend young Hesselbach, the Würzburg prosector's son, who had studied anatomy and anatomical techniques with his father, in whom he also had a model of loyalty and devotion. Young Hessel bach readily agreed, and Burdach gladly accepted his application. As he (Burdach) wrote me in March, he even gave him preferential treatmen compared to his treatment of other candidates, and had undertaken the necessary steps with the ministry to ensure his employment. Yet while Burdach expected his imminent arrival, Hesselbach, although already in possession of the travel expenses, hesitated to depart, allegedly because he was still waiting for a letter of appointment. Such a document, too, wa procured, after I had reported Hesselbach's demand when, in the last day of July, old Hesselbach fell sick and died shortly thereafter. His son now declared that he was withdrawing his candidacy for the Königsberg position and desired to stay in Würzburg, probably because he had received assur ances that he would obtain his father's position. After I had informed Burdac of the situation on the ninth of August, I received a most cordial letter from him on the twenty-fourth, in which he asked me whether, now that the posi tion was again vacant, I felt inclined to accept it? If I wanted to devote my self to practical medicine, he would withdraw this offer. If, however, I had scientific career in mind, he thought that several years in Königsberg woul be as good a preparation as any. Even if I wanted to stay in Berlin until th

Easter holidays, he was prepared to wait that long. Although the prospects of a future in practical medicine were anything but alluring, I had lived with the idea too long, and had thought too little about the possibility of a scientific career at home and even less about such a career abroad, being so attached to my homeland, that to give it up seemed a decision I was not capable of making at the time. Yet the chance to move for several years in the scientific sphere and in the company of Burdach at that, appeared so attractive that I did not refuse the offer, provided I could stay in Berlin until Easter. As I perceive from later letters, my answer must have been a rather equivocal one. The decision came later.

9. Berlin
(Winter 1816-1817)

At the end of September, 1816, I left Würzburg to go to Berlin, where I intended to spend the next winter. Again I preferred travel by foot to any other mode of locomotion. Dr. Lindt of Bern, whom I had befriended when still in Vienna, and who had recently come to Würzburg, decided to join me.

I would like here to inject a word about travel by foot because given today's time-saving travel by rail this sort of change of scenery has by now probably become extinct for long distances, except perhaps in mountain areas or in terrain on which specific observations are to be made. It was not the expectation of lower expenses which made me prefer this mode of travel, experience having already taught me that the longer duration of journeys on foot and the greater number of overnight accommodations involved made expenses approach those of vehicular travel. It was rather the feeling of greater independence, the possibility of stopping whenever one liked, as well as the contact with different classes of people that attracted me. In my travels, therefore, I liked most to put up in small towns or larger villages. In these places the innkeeper, the servants, and the few guests are all real persons, some friendly, some coarse-grained, but always of interest to the stranger who wants to know the people, their mode of living, and their opinions. Food to fill one's belly could be had everywhere, even at the remotest spot in the mountains, if one only found a house that was inhabited. In the large South-Russian steppe, on the other hand, such an optimistic view would be rather out of place.

In later years I have also made frequent use of the railways, but have been bored to distraction by the type of hotel owner who receives the traveler on the stairs, bows deeply and then at once disappears never to show himself again as he is always busy making out the bills; by the waiter who rushes toward the traveler, snatching from his hands whatever the latter wants to take upstairs; and by the servant who, with equal aplomb and silent efficiency moves one's knapsack upstairs and later down again. I have always wished that all these speechless persons were replaced by machines one could trust and that instead of the multistoried hotels with their endless menus one could always have those modest inns with their jovial keepers who like to talk about themselves and their immediate surroundings.

How to convey the poetry of earlier modes of travel to future generations at a time when the innkeeper regarded his guest as a member, if temporary of the family, taking part as he did in its objectives and needs, trying to further the former and satisfying the latter? Today the traveler is regarded as no more than a source of income. But it would be futile to try to describe conditions which have to be experienced to be understood. I can only regret that for this truly undreamt-of saving in time, the present generation has to pay such a price.

Our journey by foot from Würzburg to Berlin, while not particularly enlightening, was yet richer in poetic interludes than we had bargained for. Helped along by the most beautiful weather, we made our way across the Fichtelgebirge to Eger and Carlsbad where we arrived too late in the season to meet visitors taking the cure but, nonetheless, saw the localities. When we moved on, however, in the direction of the Erzgebirge to reach Annaberg, the weather changed drastically. When we left Carlsbad, the sky was already overcast; it became more and more cloudy, and when we were crossing the mountains a persistent rain was falling, accompanied by wind. The path across the mountains was quite soft by now, and we had to struggle on, wading through the mud. Before we reached Annaberg there would be no opportunity to continue our journey in what now seemed a much more sensible way. My jovial companion, Dr. Lindt, repeatedly cried out, "I have seen some bad roads but the road to Annaberg beats them all!" The umbrellas which we had produced were of little avail, since the wind drove the rain sideways against us. From the chest down our clothes were soaking wet, and the mud not only clung to our boots but since from time to time we tried to find easier ground by moving through shrubbery, it also spread over our linen trousers. In this deplorable state, we at last reached Annaberg in the afternoon in full hope of now being able to dry ourselves and change our clothing. At the town gate, however, we encountered a rather sly guard who first looked us over carefully and then declared that the burgomaster wished to see us. We expressed our thanks for this act of outstanding courtesy of the burgomaster, who was a complete stranger to us, but we thought that we would first find an inn, to change and have some food. The crafty guard, however, would have none of it and insisted that in this town it was the burgomaster who allocated accommodations. When we answered rather impatiently that we could not very well appear before the burgomaster in this dripping-wet state, the guard became still more insistent and assured us that it was precisely in this state that the burgomaster wanted to make our acquaintance. As he seemed prepared to use force by calling together some townspeople, we finally followed him of our own free will, to find out what indeed this was all about. When we arrived at the town hall, the guard ordered us to wait in the antechamber while he himself, with a rather self-satisfied air, went into the burgomaster's room where we heard him whisper secretively. We were now requested to hand over our passports, which we did. Soon after that, the burgomaster emerged, appearing somewhat embarrassed, and asked us several questions. When he had satisfied himself that our answers agreed with what he found in our passports, he apologized most earnestly. It appeared that two days ago a countess had been robbed outside the city gates of Annaberg. Of the two robbers, one had been fair-haired and slim, the other dark-haired and stout. A reward had been offered for their capture, and the not very bright guard had hoped to collect it. It so happened that Dr. Lindt was dark-haired and, for his age, quite stout, while I was blond and slim. The guard's mistake was thus quite pardonable. To make up for the blunder, the burgomaster invited us to stay in Annaberg till the next morning, when we would be able to be present at the melting of a large quantity of silver. We accepted his invitation and, on the next day, witnessed the so-called brightening of a mass of several thousand pounds of silver.

I entered into another adventure due to my interest in the great German war of liberation, and since I have not yet had an opportunity to demonstrate that interest, I might as well give an account of this adventure.

We were already beyond Chemnitz and quite close to Berlin, when we met a student friend of mine from Dorpat who, like myself, traveled on foot, carrying his all with him. I let Dr. Lindt continue on his own and went with this fellow to a nearby inn where, over a glass of beer, we exchanged experiences. While we talked, I suddenly realized that it was the fifteenth of October and that, if I immediately changed direction for Leipzig, I would arrive there early enough to be able to visit the field of battle on the 18th of October. I counted my cash and found that it amounted to no more than two and a half Thalers. As I had money waiting for me in Berlin, I had not been pinching pennies. To try to walk from here to Leipzig and from Leipzig to Berlin with such a small sum seemed a rather daring undertaking. But this in itself was a challenge to me. Thus, I started at once for Leipzig, where I duly arrived early on the seventeenth. To derive full benefit from my visit, I bought several descriptions of the battle, which I read on the battlefield on the eighteenth. Instead of a monument, to my dismay, I found only a wooden cross which was about to topple over, and this four years after that great, decisive victory! But no more of that! My financial means for marching on Berlin were already reduced to a minimum, when the magistrate at Leipzig did me the undeserved honor of exacting from me four good Groschen for endorsing my passport. For this deed I have never forgiven him because when I had settled all my bills, I was left with a sum that, even with extreme abstinence, would barely last me to Berlin. Indeed, on the last day I had to walk nine miles from Treuenbriezen to Berlin, and had only six pfennigs to eat on. Having arrived in Berlin, I set out to look up a fellow student, and when I did not find him at home, I simply lay down on the floor in front of his door, my knapsack under my head, and slept soundly until he arrived.

* * *

Surveying my stay in Berlin during the winter of 1816–1817, I cannot but regret deeply that I did not make as good use of it as I might have, had I altogether abandoned my efforts at practical medicine. Although I knew I had a position waiting for me, and although I had experienced the advantage of devoting oneself to a single subject only in Würzburg, I still held to the belief that an independent existence could be based only on practical medicine. Contrary to all my experience, therefore, I decided that I could not give up medicine and, following my former resolution (page 121), proceeded to overload myself with lectures, clinics, and similar periodically recurring activities to such a degree that if two persons had shared them, each would have been fully occupied. Three times a week these activities followed each other so closely that I had barely time for my noonday meal. When Baerends' clinic took only slightly longer than usual, I could only eat standing up, hat on head, in a students' tavern which I had to pass on my way.

When I arrived in Berlin and had acquired the Catalogue of Lectures, I was delighted by the abundance of lectures in the natural history disciplines. Yet I persuaded myself to make daily visits to the hospital, where I was particcularly attracted by the visits of Professor Horn and also accompanied Professor Rust, who had moved to Berlin while I was at Würzburg. In addition to this, the fellow student with whom I had lodged and who spoke with such enthusiasm of the clinic of Prof. Baerends, whose amanuensis he was, induced me to enter my name for it as well. I, too, was most impressed by this clinic, but did not appear to be able to muster the required energy, and not infrequently became impatient when the clinic occasionally went beyond its allotted time and prevented me from attending the lectures on crystallography. In addition, I attended Professor Wolfart's lectures on animal magnetism and was present at the magnetic treatments. I wanted to be able to form my own opinion on this controversial subject. The book by Kluge, as I have mentioned earlier, had at that time temporarily won me over to animal magnetism. In Würzburg, however, I had had an experience that rather shook my belief in the trustworthiness of the observations of these allegedly secret or not yet understood forces of nature. One day, the news was spread that a metal diviner and her divining rod had been brought to town, and that Professor Sp. would show her to the medical men and natural scientists the next morning in a certain garden. I went to that garden, and Professor Sp. introduced a robust peasant girl as the metal diviner and declared that a copper plate had been buried in the garden and we were now about to see how the divining rod would show her the place. The experiment was performed in such a manner, however, that it was practically impossible not to find the plate. The night before the demonstration there was a frost. In the morning, several young doctors buried the copper plate in a straight section of a garden path, and one could clearly see up to which point the hoarfrost had been destroyed by the steps of these doctors. But also, followed by the entire party, the girl was led to the path she was to walk. However, when she approached the spot where the copper plate was buried, the young, miracle-seeking doctor who had buried the plate moved to her side and, finally, to right in front of her and behind the burial place, so that to pass him the girl would have had to knock him over or push him aside. Naturally, the divining rod, the tip of which had first pointed upward, started wobbling when the doctor stepped to her side, and moved downward when the metal-diviner's way was blocked. The miracle seekers exulted at the miracle, while others, among whom I counted myself, grumbled at the crude way this experiment had been interfered with. The miracle was concluded with another yield of metal, when those present were invited to donate some money, and since they readily followed this invitation, the miracle girl brought home a not inconsiderable sum. Some time later I was visited by my friend and former roommate, Dr. Weisse, and he told me of a woman, a supposed metal- and water-diviner, whom he had visited and found to be a fraud. Later he published his experiences with her. Quite possibly this was the selfsame girl, who had married in the meantime, since she knew how to make money without doing any work.

Thus, I had arrived in Berlin harboring considerable doubts. While the cases just cited do not quite belong to the domain of animal magnetism, they do demonstrate the extreme readiness of the believer to be deceived. On the other hand, I was still quite eager to learn the truth and, if possible, to form a definite idea of the magnetic state. Wolfart's lectures lingered for an unconscionable time on general reflections and uncritical historical reports on the miraculous exploits of Gassner, Mesmer, and others. Still, in his clinic, one saw a not inconsiderable number of persons who came daily for treatment, sat down at the large tub and stroked its metal rods with their hand. About half of them fell asleep. Others were magnetized only with the aid of metal rods, or by movements of the hand. This clinic was held at two o'clock in the afternoon and some of the visiting doctors were heard to grumble under their breath that the patients at the tub had probably had their midday meal and were now simply taking their afternoon nap, possibly helped along by the manipulations at the tub. Indeed, their sleep often looked quite ordinary.

During the first weeks, I observed these proceedings with some doubts, yet without being able to reach any conclusions, and at the same time I read several publications on animal magnetism. I was so fired by a fervent desire to arrive at a clear picture that these efforts had an effect on my nervous system which transported me to a state which I thought resembled that of a magnetized person. I had visions at night which were much more vivid than ordinary dreams. In part, these visions brought back to me the sweetest memories from the past, but with a tenderness which can only be felt, not expressed in words, and with additions which, at least for my personality, were rather remarkable. Thus, I once dreamed of a flutist who, amid lonely surroundings, played a melody that penetrated to the very core of my heart.

I was able to repeat it in the morning, and still found it sweet, but my susceptibility was greatly reduced. I call the melody that I believed I had heard very remarkable, because I had never before dreamed of music and although I am not insensitive to a striking piece of music in the waking state, none had ever made such a deep impression upon me. Also, the melody was quite new to me, and if I had ever heard it before, I must have lost every recollection of it. Another night I dreamed that I was being magnetized, the magnetizer pointing a finger of one hand against my chest and one of the other against the lower part of my back. Suddenly, a very broad, blue beam of light shot through my body, from one magnetized point to the other. Several days earlier, one of the patients in the magnetic clinic mentioned such a beam of blue light which he claimed to have experienced. I felt as if this light beam had altered the tone of my nervous system. It had become more sensitive; what was present in earlier visions reappeared on later nights, e.g., the melody, and it had the same emotional impact, but left only a faint recollection upon waking. Each night, however, I had the feeling that the visions of the previous nights had become alive again, and I felt as if I were now capable of understanding, or rather sensing, the innermost profundities of nature and its workings. Of this deep understanding I was at first unable to carry over into the waking state more than the consciousness or the belief that it had indeed been there. This I regretted and decided that, prior to my falling asleep, I would try to concentrate all my thoughts on certain questions of comparative anatomy. I indeed succeeded in making these questions the objects of this clairvoyance; in other words, I seemed to have a much deeper understanding. Since in the waking state, however, I had the fervent wish not to lose this deeper understanding again and, as a start, to have it repeated the following night, I gradually succeeded in observing this phenomenon more closely, in making myself wake up at the right moment, and in retaining this deeper insight in my memory. There could be no doubt now that this apparent deeper understanding was but what my waking mind also told me, only with less insistence. Quantitatively, my understanding had not increased, at least not measurably, but it had reached deeper levels, being now mirrored in the perceptive sphere. I wonder whether "clairvoyance," i.e., "clear seeing" is after all no more than "deep feeling"? In addition to these hallucinations induced by my scientific activities, I later experienced others also, for which I could adduce no cause, and which recurred many nights in succession, making no sense at all. Thus, one night, there appeared a gnome or dwarf, carrying a pyramid and slowly walking past, followed by a second, a third and, eventually, a fourth. The following night they were there again, behaving exactly the same way. This phase continued for about two weeks, during which a kind of conscious observation of these hallucinations became increasingly pronounced. I became angry with those silly visions, and it was as if this caused them to become more timid. Eventually I worked up such a rage that the fourth gnome preferred not to appear at all. This, in fact, signaled the end of all the nocturnal revelations, the desired as well as the uninvited. My health, which was undoubtedly debilitated in the beginning, had been restored again.

I experienced the observation and assessment of my own hallucinations again much later in Astrakhan, during the crisis of a malaria attack which lasted for several hours. The list of visions is too long to be listed here. The aforementioned, entirely unrelated visions I also take more for a symptom of a return to health, while the beginnings I am inclined to diagnose as a pathological state resembling that of being magnetized, which might have been the result of excessive preoccupation with animal magnetism. Thus, I am not a complete sceptic; I believe in somnambulism, although I have seen only very few genuine cases, and would like to believe that some, if not many of those falling asleep at the tub were doing more than just taking their afternoon naps. Wolfart's observations, however, I found to be completely uncritical. Suffice it to relate the following. Professor Rust once visited Wolfart's clinic, and when Wolfart presented a boy who had been suffering from acutely inflamed eyelids which, according to Wolfart, were much better now, having been treated with a magnetic rod, Rust carefully looked at the boy's face and said quietly, "I would not be surprised if that were so, as for the last six weeks I have been treating this boy with precipitate (mercuric) ointment." Wolfart seemed to be amiably embarrassed, but did not utter a word. He never inquired whether his patients were also using other medicaments, and since his clinic did not charge anything, many patients made use of it in addition to other arts of healing. Even less could Wolfart's lectures satisfy me. When, after a long-winded, completely meaningless introduction, he finally arrived at the magnetic treatment, singing the praises of the excellence of its effect but not teaching which cases should be treated this way and which that way; when he went on to explain the design of the tub, which should contain crushed glass, water, maize, metal, and diverse other items, without showing the why and wherefore, I saw clearly that as far as I was concerned, this senseless hodge-podge went against my nature. I felt that I could not continue this way, and thus my efforts came to a temporary end, temporary, that is, until such a time as more sober and scientifically conducted observations might again invite me to study animal magnetism.

Now and then I also visited Professor Osann's clinic, thereby coming in contact with Hufeland.

My contacts with Rudolphi and Rosenthal were of a more serious nature occasioned by my frequent, if not quite regular, visits to the dissecting room. Here, future doctors were trained in a manner quite different from that practiced in Würzburg, which fact made me observe closely as well as draw some comparisons, as will be discussed in greater detail when I review my own activities in this sphere (Chapter Eleven).

Of the natural history lectures, I attended Erman Senior's lectures on electricity and galvanism, and Professor Weiss's on crystallography and geology, which were delivered with great zest and which I found uncommonly interesting. Due to my heavy work load, however, I was unable to follow them up with the necessary homework. Link announced a series of weekly public lectures on Cryptogamia, which I could not leave untouched, especially as Link, whom I had visited on Nees's recommendation, had been kind enough to identify for me the cryptogams I had recently collected. His lectures, however, did not proceed beyond algae. Shortly before the end of the semester, I found myself at a public lecture by Horkel; the course would have attracted me very much had I heard of it earlier, or found it in the lecture catalogue. A student acquaintance of mine, who otherwise had no particular interest in physiology, told me of these lectures as of a curiosity, mentioning the fact that throughout the entire semester Horkel spoke of nothing but of the chick in the egg, and of the honeycomb. What my acquaintance regarded as rather comical was what attracted me, as I sensed that the basis of his philosophical reflections was the development of the chick as typical of the formative, and the work of the bees as typical of the active life in its social form, which we call instinct. This was indeed the case, and I was sorry not to have been able to attend more than two lectures, in which Horkel mainly developed the views of Giordano Bruno. Yet Horkel's thoroughly philosophical lectures so little attracted the masses that even after I had joined them there were only six persons in the large auditorium, "a few swimming in the vast deep" (Vergil). In contrast, how full was the auditorium of the quadripartite Wagner a year ago!

Of all these heterogeneous doings of mine, the closest to my heart was my predilection for comparative anatomy. Not only did I like to turn to my Cuvier, in the evenings, but to test myself at public lecturing I succeeded in enticing some of my fellow students to attend a miniature course in comparative anatomy given by myself.

Neither did there lack other distractions and interruptions in this semester. My parents having agreed to my moving to Königsberg (if not very enthusiastically), I had declared my definite acceptance of the prosector's position there in December, 1816, and was now asked by Burdach to have a look at the collection of anatomical specimens from the estate of the late Professor Senff of Halle and, provided I found it worth the money, to conclude the transaction for the new collection in Königsberg. Professor Senff's widow had already accepted the offer of 1,200 Thalers. My task was to ascertain that the collection was indeed in as good a state as she claimed it to be. Senff had been professor in obstetrics and, as such, had had opportunity to collect many instructive specimens relating to human embryology. These specimens were treated with great circumspection, I would even say, elegance. The number of other specimens was not large, but as these, too, were well done, I could only compliment the owner and close the deal.

This journey, undertaken during the Christmas holidays, also helped me to make the acquaintance of J. F. Meckel, the most famous anatomist of his time, whose collection I studied at length; of the botanist Kurt Sprengel, also a luminary in his science; as well as of Ersch and Krukenberg. Furthermore, I had the opportunity of renewing my acquaintance with Dr. Friedländer, whom I had met in Vienna and who had become a lecturer here.

At the end of the semester, I was charged with the task of packing the Senff collection and having it shipped to Königsberg via the inland canals. I also had to go to Leipzig to carry out various errands. This expedition took the better part of April. In Halle I now made the acquaintance of Weinhold, and in Leipzig of Rosenmüller. My acquaintance with Meckel grew more intimate, although he was at first rather annoyed that Senff's collection would not stay in Halle. When I told him that I would start my lectures in Königsberg with the structure of the invertebrates, and when he discovered through talking to me that I was quite knowledgeable in the subject, he appeared to be rather interested.

Both journeys to Halle and back were made by ordinary mail coach and over bad roads, a mode of travel in which the speed of progress stood in inverse ratio to the amount of sleep it afforded. I still vividly remember the vehicle, called the "Royal Prussian Mail Coach." It differed from the barrel of Regulus only inasmuch as it was not the points but the heads of the nails and bolts keeping the framework together which protruded on the inside. On the return trip from Halle, I sat near such a projecting head which, at every pothole in the road, hit me in the head, and against which my head fell whenever sleep claimed its right. Embellished by a goodly number of large bumps, I arrived in Berlin.

10. Farewell to the Homeland
(Summer 1817)

Having packed Senff's collection and loaded it onto barges that were to pass along the Prussian inland canals, all I had left to do now was to pack myself off to Königsberg, to which end I again made use of the ordinary mail coach. This time, however, it was less of an ordeal, either because I had obtained a better place, or because of the advanced season, which found the roads in better repair. Nonetheless, I was much impressed by the extraordinary progress made when, eleven years later, I traveled the same road from Königsberg to Berlin in the stagecoach in less than three days. In 1817, using the ordinary mail coach, this journey required more than a whole week.

My first stay in Königsberg was only a very short one, to acquaint myself with my future circumstances. When I accepted the offer of the Königsberg position, I was still attached to my homeland with all the fibers of my heart. Both my parents were still living. I not only revered them greatly, but there had never been any conflict between us, not even of a temporary nature. Also, all my brothers and sisters, that is, those who had survived childhood, were now grown up, and there had always been complete harmony among us. Furthermore, in Berlin I had received the news that my brother was to be married in the summer of 1817, to a lady whose acquaintance I had made earlier. Many of my friends from the Dorpat period had remained in our homeland, others had returned there from their travels, still others were about to return. I myself had roamed about the world for three years and longed to strike roots back home—but where and how I did not yet know. It was thus quite natural, I believe, that I remained undecided for a long time when I was offered the prosector's post at Königsberg and, thereby, a scientific career. Had the same opportunities presented themselves in the Baltic provinces or in St. Petersburg I would not have hesitated for a moment. When I finally accepted the offer, I did so under the condition that, after my three years away from the homeland I would be able to return to bid it farewell.

When I arrived in Königsberg, Burdach thought it most expedient if, after a short stay, I were to set out for home, since the anatomical institute was in any case not very active in the summer, and as the Senff collection would not arrive for some months. Therefore, in May, 1817, I set out for Estonia, using the ordinary mail coach, and traveling via Memel, Mitau, Riga and Dorpat. Of the journey itself my memory has retained only the fact that I undertook it again in 1819 but with a different companion, a Finn, the first having been a Rhinelander. Starting from the border of Courland, the Rhinelander was amazed by the many coniferous forests, while the Finn expressed similar wonderment about the many deciduous trees. For me, these differing utterances have always remained a striking proof of how differently one and the same object may be assessed from different standpoints. Finland is almost completely covered with conifers, except for truly marshy land, and deciduous woods are no more than isolated, pleasant interruptions of the coniferous mass. The Rhinelander, on the other hand, is unaccustomed to coniferous forests.

At home I found more changes than I would have expected after a short absence of three years. The abolition of serfdom, decreed by the Diet, seemed to have created a serious, expectant mood, as if people were preparing for a new age. I even found the use of some provincialisms in the language discontinued, without anyone's being able to explain how this had come about. Possibly, it was the reestablished contact with the outside world that had wrought these changes. To report on my reunion with, and subsequent farewell to my family appears inappropriate to me. Suffice it to say that the wish, and indeed conviction, was expressed everywhere that this move abroad would be a temporary one, a transition to a position in the homeland. I myself, also clung long to this view.

Having accompanied my brother and his young wife to their new home in Metzaken, and having stayed with them for a short while, I returned to my father's home, to set out on my return trip in the last days of our July, or the first days of August according to the Gregorian calendar. Some additional stops and delays notwithstanding, I found myself in the new position before the end of that same month.

11. My First Official Position as Prosector and Lecturer in Königsberg (1817-1819)

When I returned to Königsberg, the second half of the summer semester was still in progress. As a prelude to my future activities, I at once started on my previously announced lectures on the structure of the invertebrates. Using the best sources, I tried to inform myself on animal forms with which I was not familiar through my own investigations. In addition to students of medicine who were still at the beginning of their studies, I was also honored by the presence at my lectures of Professor Burdach. Essentially, my course consisted of demonstrations based partly on specimens, inasmuch as they could be prepared on the spot, and partly on illustrations. It was thus not a lecture designed to be copied word by word, but to provide the audience with a conception. As Burdach had rarely in the past dealt with lower animals, he, too, took some notes. It was precisely this circumstance which could have ruined my entire relationship with him right at the beginning. At that time, a fellow student from Dorpat, von D., whom I had befriended because of our common interest in botany, passed through Königsberg on his way back to Germany. He stayed with me for several days and was also present at some of my lectures. Soon after his departure, he gave notice in a letter that "he would become the herald of my fame," a statement which I accepted with indifference, taking it as a piece of flattery. Only in 1818 was it brought to my notice that he had spoken rather boastfully of my lectures in a Baltic journal, using a tone calculated to offend those of my friends who had remained at home. He did not fail to stress the fact that Burdach, too, was one of the note-taking participants. I myself have never seen this report and do not know whether Burdach has ever heard of it. But the selfsame D., who thought that fame could be conferred that easily, managed to completely block his own career by similar assault tactics. As for me, he wanted me to move to Dorpat as soon as possible, so that the two of us would be able to work together on the flora of Livonia. When, at a later point, I passed up transfer to Dorpat, he wrote me a very angry letter, asking me among other things "whether I had gone completely crazy to want to stay in that . . . hole."

Before the beginning of the winter period, Burdach wanted the new "Anatomical Institute" to be inaugurated with all due ceremony. The building housing the institute, though not new, had been substantially altered to

157

arrange for the most essential facilities needed in a mortuary: a device for lowering and hoisting the cadavers, as well as a well-lit dissecting and demonstration room. Other rooms were set aside to house the collections of anatomical specimens. Up to now, Königsberg had not had an institute for the teaching of anatomy, that is, an institute set up by, and belonging to the state. For a considerable period of time, there were only two professors of medicine at the local university, one for the theoretical, the other for the practical aspect of medical instruction. Only gradually was instruction in anatomy turned into a special, salaried, position. In 1745, Professor Büttner, at his own expense, put up an anatomical demonstration building which the state had purchased for 500 Thalers after his death. Since, however, his anatomical specimens were acquired not for Königsberg, but for Berlin, and since Büttner's successors used to prepare specimens only for their own immediate needs, there was no anatomical collection belonging to the state. Arriving in Königsberg (in March, 1814), Burdach found the building left by Büttner in a state of imminent collapse, containing only two defective skeletons and one dummy used for training in the application of bandages. It was a fortunate circumstance that, by the time Burdach had come to Königsberg, the Prussian state had already risen to greater glories and the allied armies were converging from all sides on Napoleon's capital. But even earlier after the previous disastrous war of 1807, the Prussian state had adopted the principle of compensating for the physical might that had been lost by developing the spiritual resources of the people. As a consequence of this decision, the greatest efforts were made to raise the level of all institutes of learning, from the elementary to the highest. In this spirit, an observatory was built in Königsberg in 1811, seeing which, Napoleon, passing through Königsberg on his way to Russia, is said to have called out in amazement, "Is the King of Prussia still able to build observatories?" After the victorious conclusion of the last great war, the attitude of the Prussian government toward scientific institutions was, of course, even more favorable. Burdach thus succeeded in obtaining not only a special building for what is usually called an anatomical theater—including the sums required for the alterations, as well as a substantial yearly budget for miscellaneous expenses, for the personnel, the prosector, and the attendants, for the acquisition of objects for scientific investigations, and for a library—but also a further sum for a decent initial stock of instruments and specimens. It was decided to acquire the collection left as private property by Burdach's predecessor, Professor Kelch, and subsequently the aforementioned collection of Senff. The latter collection had arrived and had been unpacked during my farewell visit at home. Only one jar was found to have been broken, and when I returned, I found both collections already well-ordered in white cupboards, where they afforded a rather eye-catching spectacle. In fact, the entire building was well furnished.

It was this new "Anatomical Institute" that Burdach wanted to inaugurate solemnly and, at this opportunity, to present to the board and the public at large. The thirteenth of November was selected for the ceremony. Burdach read a paper on the history of the foundation of the institute and on past conditions of anatomical instruction in Königsberg. He had asked me to give an address, too, and I spoke on Swammerdam's service to science and on his life, which had been painful because he was so far ahead of the opinions and, particularly, of the scientific requirements of his time. His life, as described by Boerhave in his preface to the *Biblia naturae*, had attracted me since I had started with my zootomical studies. Earlier, Burdach had published a paper "On the Task of Morphology," which was to serve as an outline of the institute's program. The two inaugural addresses remained unprinted. At a later point I rewrote my own address, as I could not find its original draft, and included it as the first, in chronological order, of a collection of addresses recently published*.

In this newly inaugurated institute I now began my official activities as prosector and lecturer. The institute was situated near the city walls, on a slope called the Butterberg. Like Rome, Königsberg prides itself on being built on seven hills. I was given official quarters in the building of the surgical clinic, very close to the anatomical institute. Since the botanical garden and the observatory were in close proximity to the anatomical institute, a small academic circle soon formed itself and compensated for the fact that I lived at a considerable distance from the center of the rather widely spread town. All the more persistently did I haunt the institute in the mornings and afternoons. As one cannot very well live in an anatomical theater, the proximity of my residence was no small advantage. An even bigger boon, however, was the fact that the institute had a nice library which was growing rapidly. Burdach had bought all the usable pertinent books in the fields of anatomy and physiology from the estate of the late Professor Kelch, and he was also using a sizable sum from the yearly budget to increase the number of such books. Since later on most works on zootomy were acquired upon being published, and efforts were made to add gradually the most important works of the less recent literature also, there was no lack of opportunity to study the history of anatomy and physiology and, in the case of current investigations, to look up the opinions of other authors on a particular subject. I believe that, quite wrongly, such specialized libraries are usually neglected in similar institutes. Even if it is impossible to have a complete library, certain standard works should be available, especially such as are required for frequent reference. This is of particular importance for the younger lecturers; I myself have experienced the advantage of having access to reference works right in the work room. Much time is saved, and when

---

Addresses given in scientific meetings, and short papers of scientific content. Vol. 1, *Reden* (Addresses). St. Petersburg. Schmitzendorff, 1864. 8.

one is familiarizing oneself with a science, time is worth much more than mere money. The older professor is likely to have gradually acquired some illustrated works on human and comparative anatomy, or larger compendia and reference works such as Haller's *Bibliotheca anatomica* and his bulky *Physiology*, which, however obsolete it may appear, systematically presents the knowledge which preceded him. It takes time until the younger lecturers will own such works and if, in order to find out when a certain anatomist has lived and what he has written, he is sent to a public library, his progress will be very slow indeed, especially in Königsberg, where the university library was located in the farthermost section of the town and was open to the public only twice a week, and that for no more than two hours. Also, it was rather poor in the anatomical-physiological field.

In the first winter there was much to do in the institute. Burdach had charged me with part of the lectures. I therefore had to read and to supply fresh specimens for Burdach's, as well as for my own lectures; the collection had to be extended and, above all, I had to oversee the dissecting exercises of the students.

As I could well believe that, but for the lack of opportunity for anatomical training in Dorpat, I would have turned to anatomy much earlier and would perhaps have desisted from making attempts, against my natural bent, in the direction of practical medicine; and as at any rate my extended stay abroad, necessitating the borrowing of a substantial sum, the repayment of which seemed now much more problematical than ever, was a direct consequence of this gap in my earlier education, I saw it as my sacred duty, in my own official position, to now give the students as much opportunity to train in practical anatomy as I possibly could. It is thus clear that I took those practical exercises most seriously.

In Würzburg I had seen these exercises pursued in a very different manner and with different results, which I consider quite useful to compare in order to point out the respective advantages of both methods and to outline a way of combining these advantages.

In Würzburg, the dissecting exercises followed the anatomical subdivisions closely. According to an arrangement of long standing, one dissected either muscles, or vessels, or nerves, or, finally, the so-called viscera. For each course, a special fee had to be paid, which entitled the student to work on the system concerned (i.e., on the muscles, nerves, etc.) through all the main parts of the human body. As these fees were rather high, most students worked through only a few systems but, when the cadavers were distributed, they demanded all the material they required. On the other hand, it was hardly possible to go through more than two systems per semester, working, as one did, very neatly and thus slowly. This compulsive drive for careful work seemed to emanate from, and spread through the very walls. Dr. Hesselbach, who was always to be found in the dissecting room, usually at a special table, was probably the originator of this stress on neatness when dissecting. An old man then, the monotony of his job had made him so taciturn that he pre-ferred to instruct by means of signs rather than words. A student who had an arm lying in front of him, inner side up, and the *Arteria axillaris* laid bare as far as he could, but unable to reach its extreme branchings, called Hesselbach. The old man got up, went to the student's table, turned over the arm, and without saying a word, indicated with his finger the point from which the student was to work toward his original incision. Pointing out the *Musc. in-fraspinatus*, Hesselbach made a hopping motion with his finger to indicate that this muscle had to be detached from its insertion, if one wanted to follow the course of the *Art. circumflexa scapulae*. One could have thought that he was mute. Once the specimen was ready, which usually took several weeks, he demonstrated it completely, however. He was also ready to dry expertly any specimen, which he often did with those of vessels, to serve as a souvenir. In addition, some specimens were paid for not by those who had prepared them, but by other students who wanted to show their parents a specimen of diligence and erudition. As can be seen, Hesselbach did not pass up the opportunity to make the dissection exercises lucrative. Indeed, this might have been the cause of the discord which was said to have existed between him and Döllinger in the past. In my time, Döllinger hardly ever appeared in the dissection room. During my stay, I remember having seen him only once, and he stayed for no longer than a quarter of an hour.

The method I encountered in Berlin was completely different. The number of students was larger, but so was the number of cadavers. These were distributed in main sections according to the list of claims. Whatever a student subsequently did with the arm or leg he obtained was nobody's concern. Rudolphi, professor of anatomy, and Dr. Rosen-thal, prosector, were usually present in the mornings, the latter also in the afternoons. They were, however, busy in an adjacent room with their own work. From time to time they appeared in the dissecting room and then the students asked for help and advice, which they did not refuse, but it was obvious that they tried to disappear again as soon as possible. In general, the students were thus left to their own devices. Indeed, many were not auda-cious enough to call on the professors. Most of the students worked very fast, using their textbooks to bring out the main features and not caring at all for precision in dissecting. Obviously, there must have been some who did pay attention to proper technique and precise execution—was not Schlemm a graduate of the dissecting rooms of Berlin University? Yet, generally speak-ing, the drive for rapid conclusion of the work was so predominant that, upon my first visit, I was rather scandalized. I soon realized, however, that, while their scalpel work might have been sloppy, these students were all the more serious in their study of anatomy proper. Usually, two students were work-ing on one specimen. They would have brought along a textbook, with the aid of which they tried to find their way about. On finishing their work, they would go over it again, guided by the textbook, inasmuch as a demonstration by the lecturers was not to be expected. I even saw some older students who had dissected during the previous winter, who were walking about, their textbooks under their arms, partly to have a look at the specimens and brush up their knowledge, partly to give advice to the beginners. In other words, the stress in Berlin was on the study of human anatomy, while Würzburg emphasized technical skill. In Würzburg, a student carrying a textbook in the dissecting room was a rare sight, and still rarer was the student who actually used it. Learning proper was postponed until the prosector's demonstration. Since, however, such a demonstration is not remembered well enough, and since during dissection no one paid much attention to naming the parts at hand, the insertion of muscles, etc., very little real anatomical knowledge as such was acquired in the dissection room. What was acquired, and at a great expense of time, was merely neatness and precision in the execution of dissections. Most specimens of vessel and nerve branching were well worth preserving, and it is not improbable that this emphasis on precision originated with Hesselbach, who wanted to enlarge the university's collection rapidly, using the students' dissecting work to this end. In the course of time this attitude had become self-perpetuating. There can be no doubt that more stress should have been put on independent study. In Berlin, on the other hand, the active study of anatomy was the predominant idea, and this could be achieved only by having the students study on their own. Even the very rapidity was a calculated means to this end. As the parts to be dissected were distributed twice a week, everybody tried to have done with his portion within three days, both the dissection proper and the subsequent examination with the aid of the textbook, so as to be ready to start on a new part when one's turn came on the next distribution day.

Having decided in Berlin on the prosectorship I had been offered, I had ample reason to compare the advantages and drawbacks of the two methods, and I tried to combine the former in Königsberg. I was present in the dissecting room both in the mornings and in the afternoons. Instead of there being a demonstration by the prosector, which I had come to regard as definitely harmful, the student had to demonstrate his specimen to me when he had completed his work, and he was able to do so only if he had first gone over it carefully. Even when the student was dissecting, I consented to give advice only when he could show that he had first tried to find his way himself. All students were supposed to bring their textbooks along. As this was not possible in each case, since many students lived a long distance away, I made sure that Hempel's *Anatomy*, belonging to the institute, was always available, right in the dissecting room. In addition to the latest edition of Hempel, which already incorporated the most recent discoveries by Bock, the more concise textbook by Rosenmüller was also frequently used. At that time the polytypography technique was not yet known. As a student who works with extreme neatness cannot very well go over the whole of anatomy in the course of a single semester, and as, on the other hand, the great number of lectures he has to attend will hardly permit him to devote two winters to dissection work, I strongly advised my students to treat some objects with the greatest possible care but, once their skill with the scalpel had attained a satisfactory level, to proceed rapidly, having only the speedy exposure of the detail in question in mind.

As to the timing of the dissection exercises, my advice was to place them in that winter semester in which the student was also attending anatomy lessons and not, as was the student's initial tendency, to postpone them to a later semester. Even then, I was convinced of the usefulness of simultaneously engaging in related activities, a conviction that I have explained in greater detail earlier (pp. 122 f).

Because of problems of conservation, no anthropotomic work was undertaken during the summer semester which instead was an occasion for zootomic exercises that took place on certain days. The subjects for these exercises had to be brought along by the students themselves, unless they happened to be found at the institute.

For dissecting work on human cadavers, a fee was charged, which was set at the modest amount of five Thalers, as most students in Königsberg had only limited means at their disposal. That a special fee should be paid for this course, I still regard as most useful and even necessary. Not only is overseeing this type of work more time-consuming than lecturing, and much less satisfying for the lecturer, but the very fact of monetary sacrifice involved increases the value of the course in the eyes of the students. In both Würzburg and, perhaps, even more so in Berlin, students were very vocal in their demands for dissection material because, having paid for them (in Berlin, two Louis d'or), they wanted their money's worth, if not more. In Russian universities, with the exception of Dorpat, no fees were charged for either the lectures or the dissecting exercises. I have seen a university in which no dissecting work was done at all, surely a serious omission in a medical curriculum. Therefore, when I was asked for an official opinion on this problem, at a later point, I declared that, according to my experience, not charging a fee for the course in practical anatomy had a deleterious effect. This course is very time-consuming for both teachers and students, and is all too easily neglected unless both parties have a clear interest in it. Moreover, I seriously doubt that a reasonable understanding of the human body is attainable without putting a hand to it, so to speak. I am altogether for the charging of a special fee for all lectures and would prefer to save the student expenses by avoiding the unconscionable stretching of the medical courses, by fixing the fee at a moderate level, and by officially exempting the really impecunious from all payments. At the time I was in Königsberg, the Prussian Ministry of Education put great stress on payment of fees, because this was held to enhance the value of the lectures in the eyes of everybody concerned. Once, the university was even reproached or admonished by the ministry, which claimed it had information to the effect that several professors at the university were not accepting any fees at all. The ministry, so the missive said, did not contemplate abolishing the custom of fee-paying and would prefer the professors to attract the students by virtue of the quality of their lectures rather than by exempting them from paying fees.

My students might well have been obliged to me for the zeal which I brought to the dissecting exercises. I, in turn, owed that zeal to my own earlier privation in this field and my later attempts to make up for it, accomplished at the price of an indebtedness which now began to worry me more and more.

As I mentioned earlier, Burdach had asked me right at the beginning to take care of the anatomy lectures. While he used to arrange his lectures according to the different regions or sections of the body, dealing with the head and the trunk during the winter semester and with the extremities during the summer, I chose the conventional way, following the anatomic systems and giving osteology during the summer semester and the remaining systems in the winter. The first method, which proceeds according to the sections of the human body, had indeed the advantage that the skeletal part of the section dealt with is still fresh in the mind when one moves on to the muscles, nerves, etc. Since, however, all anatomy textbooks of that time were arranged according to the systems, a corresponding organization of the lectures greatly helped the students to realize old Wehrmann's principle of *Repetitio est mater studiorum* ("Repetition is the mother of studying"), to which I subscribed as well, and which proved particularly valuable for anatomy. After the first year, therefore, I arranged "refresher meetings," held every Saturday, to deal with the subject of that week's lectures, during which those present were requested at random to demonstrate their recently acquired knowledge. Naturally, some of the students did not show up on these Saturdays, but then I knew who my absent friends were, and I believe that for those who did appear, and who always constituted the larger half, the inducement not to postpone this recapitulation was to be of value. For the lecturer, on the other hand, these repetitions are somewhat tedious. In addition to lecturing on the anatomy of human beings, I also lectured on the anatomy of mammals, with special stress on domestic animals, and gave a first course in anthropology, of which more will be said at a later point.

The number of medical students in Königsberg was not large. Since all students also had to pass a state examination in Berlin, the examiners for which were mostly also professors of that university, the better-off students from East and West Prussia preferred to move to Berlin as early as possible, some even right at the beginning of their studies. Given the small number of those who remained, the formation of a closer relationship between the lecturers and their students was all the easier. By and large, devotion to study was quite satisfactory. I always remember with pleasure that Dieffenbach, later so famous as a surgeon, was one of my students during the first year of my lectureship. He was a very assiduous anatomist. Also among my audience during the first or second year was Professor Baum, later professor of surgery in Göttingen; Professor Reichert attended my lectures for about half a year at a later period; Professors Grube and Burow, however, were particularly close to me for several years.

During the first two years I could do but little for the enrichment of science. In the first winter I had my hands full to make myself completely at home in human anatomy. Whoever wants to guide the practical work of students does not enjoy the advantage of the lecturer, who can prepare himself beforehand, as he must be able to furnish an answer at a moment's notice. Nonetheless, I found time for some dissection work on animals, as shown by a series of preparations and entozoa which I was able to incorporate into the anatomical museum even during my first year. Also, I had found in the basement of the anatomical institute a number of undetermined animal specimens, among them a holothurian which went under the title of "Indian Birth," with its intestine preserved in its entirety; a starfish; and other welcome booty. All this, however, could serve only for my own enlightenment and practice. During summer and in the following winter I busied myself with dissecting such animals as were occasionally available in Königsberg and whose anatomy still offered some scope for new observations. These included the elk of the Lithuanian forests, the seal, the porpoise (*Delphinus Phocaena*), and the Baltic sturgeon. Most of my dissecting work was devoted to the latter, while my investigations of the porpoise belonged mostly to a later period. When Burdach invited me to contribute a paper to the second yearly "Report on the Royal Anatomical Institute at Königsberg," I offered him, under the title "Remarks from my Zootomic Diary," some results from research dealing with these animals; in particular, however, with the sturgeon whose anatomy had not been very well known, which offered me many opportunities for new observations or for verification of older ones. Only the brain was omitted in this paper, as I thought that without illustrations its structure could not be made understandable. I had already investigated and correctly interpreted it in its individual parts, and still possess the illustrations I prepared at that time. I intended, however, to devote a special paper to the brain, which I found of particular interest because of the fact that here the origins of the trigeminal and the vagus nerves are so uncommonly distinct. First, however, I wanted to compare these origins with those of fish of quite different classes. Yet before I could realize these intentions, Stannius had published his investigations of the sturgeon brain.

At the request of old Professor Hagen, who had written a detailed treatise on the Lithuanian aurochs (*Bos Urus L.*, or *Bison Europaeus*), I produced "Vergleichung des Schädels vom Auer mit dem Schädel des gemeinen Ochsen" (A Comparison of the skull of the aurochs with that of the common ox). Since this article was to be presented at a popular level, without going into any details, it could hardly say more than had already been said on the same subject by Cuvier. Even without this limiting condition, however, I doubt whether I could have made any comments of greater significance, since Cuvier appeared to have grasped everything essential. Of greater importance was the fact that, through my brother-in-law, who at that time was superintendent of forestry in the Grodno district, I was able to obtain up-to-date information on the aurochs population in the forests of Grodno.

I cannot refrain from mentioning a special branch of literary activity which I ventured into in the spring of 1819. A certain Mrs. Dennebecq had brought a rather interesting and well-kept collection of living animals to Königsberg from abroad. I had visited this menagerie several times, and had tried to classify these animals. Then I had published in the *Allgemeine* (*Hartung'schen*) *Königsberger Zeitung* (Hartung's "Universal Königsberg Newspaper") an article comprising a list of the systematic names, as well as information on the countries of origin and modes of life of these animals, all in a style which I thought was appropriate for the larger public. The article was very well received by the public and for the benefit of the owner I had a number of special reprints prepared which were sold in the menagerie as guides to visitors who wanted to take a closer look. The owner of the menagerie must have made a nice profit from these guides, since I was told on a later visit to St. Petersburg that she had ordered a second edition. As far as I was concerned, this first attempt of mine resulted in my soon becoming the patron of all those who exhibited curiosities of nature: animals, freaks, or developmental anomalies such as albinos, dwarfs, etc. This patronage carried with it the privilege of repeated access to such exhibits, and, most important, first claim to whatever animal, happened to die, which they did from time to time. These publications, naturally, gave me an occasion to read up in the available literature on the objects to be reviewed. During the rest of my stay in Königsberg I continued with this kind of journalistic work, even more so when, in the course of time, I was appointed Professor of Zoology.

Until the death of Kant, the University of Königsberg was very much neglected by the state. Königsbergers, while claiming that East Prussia was treated by Berlin as a sort of Siberia, remained nonetheless the most loyal supporters of the Royal House and the most zealous champions of Prussian honor. Because they rightfully considered themselves the cradle of Prussia, they took the warmest interest in the greatness of their offspring who had emigrated, and were thus patriots such as any state could have wished for. Due to the difficulties and infrequency of communication of those times, however, a type of local patriotism had developed in the form of what might be termed

Old Prussianism. I quite agree with Burdach's judgment that these new "Old Prussians" were characterized by honesty, capability, and extreme conservatism. Mostly due to the latter, but also because Germans were rather slow in moving to this remote province which did not belong to the German empire and, for a long time, was harassed by the Poles, the university, founded as early as 1544, was long staffed predominantly by natives. As a consequence, local conditions, the history, and the geography of the country were the subjects of many works of enduring value, while, right into the first half of the eighteenth century East Prussia's share in the general development of the German people and of the sciences remained slight. (For this purpose, Copernicus, born in Thorn in West Prussia, has to be considered a citizen of the Polish state.) In the course of the eighteenth century, however, East Prussia was to become powerful in the development of the German people, and along with this spread a high luster over Königsberg. Although Gottsched emigrated to escape the recruiting officers of Friedrich Wilhelm I, he held on to his Old Prussian patriotism. German minds must have found it curious that it was a son of the little-regarded East Prussian province who wished to become the reformer of German literature. Soon, however, Hamann, Hippel, and Herder proceeded to show that, by its earlier displacement and Germanization of the ancient Prussians, and by cultivating German education, East Prussia now had the right to regard itself as a German country. The apex of glory, however, was attained by Königsberg at the end of the century through the immortal Kant. He turned it into a focal point of precisely that science for which, next to the Greeks, the Germans may rightly claim to be most gifted. If they now wanted to draw nourishment directly from the source of their very own spiritual needs, they had to leave their own country and emigrate to East Prussia! Besides Kant, a lasting impression was also left by Chr. J. Kraus, a man of great erudition and a sharp mind. In his later years, he devoted himself mainly to the science of economics, he was an early proponent of the principle of free trade, and he drew enthusiastic students. All these men had arrived at their important positions by dint of their own efforts only, the state having contributed but little. The number of chairs at the university was small, the university library very poor. The university statutes in force had not been changed for over a century, and were of a distinctly medieval character. Thus, the faculty deans were required to make sure that no innovative matter crept into dissertations (*ne quid novi insit*). During their graduation exercises, doctors of medicine had to swear a solemn oath to use neither magical nor insufficiently tested methods, etc. Institutes and collections for natural sciences of more recent origin were altogether lacking, as was an observatory. That there was not even an anatomical theater I have already noted (p. 157 f). For a long time, the only representative of the natural sciences at this university was Karl Gottfried Hagen who lectured on chemistry and pharmacy until his death (1829), but earlier also on physics, mineralogy, botany, and zoology. On these subjects, he had produced independent works. He was able to be active in all these disciplines only due to the fact that, being the owner of a pharmacy, he had become a wealthy man. Only after the deaths of Kant (1804) and soon afterward Kraus (1807), and after the Court itself had stayed at Königsberg for a prolonged period, in the wake of the disastrous battles of Jena and Auerstadt and the loss of Berlin, did the government seem to realize how very greatly it had neglected Königsberg University. Even before the nation had found its feet again, following the Wars of Liberation, Schweigger was called to Königsberg to set up a botanical garden and teach botany; Bessel to build the observatory which was to become so famous in later days; Burdach to teach anatomy; Herbart received the professorship of philosophy. Also for other subjects new men were called to Königsberg from afar: the famous Lobeck for philology; Gaspari for geography and statistics; Mühlenbruch for jurisprudence; for theology, Wald, Vater (the Polyglot), Kähler, and Dinter. It appeared that the government intended to efface the provincial character which was felt more strongly at this university than elsewhere, and which the government possibly felt was to be blamed for the university's relative backwardness in the newer disciplines. It redounds to the credit of the Old Prussians that they most heartily welcomed and accepted these men. After many foreigners from other universities had joined Königsberg University in this manner, a start was also made to review the completely obsolete statutes. This undertaking, however, was interrupted in 1819, when the hunt began for "subversive machinations." The statutes were finally reformed only in 1843.

As can be seen from the foregoing names, I found myself in most respectable company, many members of which were exceedingly kind to me. These included, in addition to Burdach, my neighbor Schweigger, the amiable and equally witty Bessel, and old Hagen and his son, the political economist and government counsellor. But all these men were by far my seniors in years and had established reputations, whereas I had yet to make my name. Even the historians Voigt and Drummann, who had arrived at about the time I had, were my seniors in age and maturity. Here I was, then, far away from those with whom I had spent the years when one simply presents oneself as one is, and also accepts others just as they are. It is, therefore, quite understandable that, despite everything, I felt rather deserted, and I am certainly not ashamed of the fact that I longed to be transferred back home, all the more so as I did not relish the prospect of a prolonged prosectorship, seeing as how Burdach was still in the prime of his life. My former fellow students urged me to move to Dorpat and, without my active participation, took the initial steps to effect such a transfer, with von D., whom I have mentioned above, probably being the most active of them. When I learned of it, negotiations were already under way. I was supposed to become prosector under Cichorius. I consented but, given the peculiar character of this man, I made the condition that a special document be drawn up defining my future position. As I knew that the authorities in Dorpat were not too happy with this man's mode of life, I had hopes that the powers-that-be would arrange my position to be fairly independent. But it turned out quite differently. There was no doubt that Cichorius himself was charged with the formulation of the document, which, according to official procedure, was perhaps not to be avoided. Accordingly, Cichorius, on his part, did not fail to formulate things in such a way that he was entitled to order me to the anatomy laboratory at all hours—those ordinary ones, which it was his duty to determine, as well as extraordinary ones, which it was his privilege to establish. That I was to dissect for him and, if I wanted to lecture, also for myself, I could have expected. I was primarily to lecture on osteology and syndesmology, so that students should never lack the opportunity to start on their course of studies. To this must be added that the above document, signed by the president of the board, Prince Lieven, and including also the official invitation, arrived much later than I expected (as I had no experience of the snail's pace of such negotiations in Russia), namely in January 1819, when I no longer counted on it. Meanwhile, in December 1818, Döllinger had informed me by letter to the effect that Berlin had offered him the professorship of anatomy in Bonn, with the right to choose his own prosector, and that he had proposed me as prosector. These negotiations between the Prussian ministry and Döllinger must have been broken off soon, as I heard nothing further about it. But even without this intermezzo I could harbor no illusions about my prospects in Dorpat. To be dependent solely on Cichorius for everything seemed too risky. Therefore, I declined the offer of the prosectorship, explaining that the definition as formulated related me not to a position, but to a person. Rather hurt by this document, and remembering the sacrifies required of me to compensate for Dorpat's failure to afford me an opportunity to train in practical anatomy, I could not refrain from dropping a few remarks in this vein, which was of course quite uncalled for. Whether it was the explanation of my refusal that caused greater offense, or the appended *sotto voce* remarks, I do not know. But my friends were quite appalled and let me know that I would never have a chance again in Dorpat.

In the meantime, fate was preparing different circumstances for me. Schweigger was not only a botanist, but also liked to busy himself with the lower marine animals, especially with the coral family. He had made substantial discoveries in this sphere, among them the finding that some structures, which until then were taken as corals, were in fact true plants which, in their youth, were green but which proceeded to calcify gradually in the course of time. He gave a lecture series on corals and corallines, which I attended too. He felt no calling, however, to deal with the higher animals. It was, moreover, his ardent wish (in which he was supported by the Minister, von Altenstein) to spend some more years on scientific travels before finally settling down. Having perceived that I liked to dissect animals of all kinds, and being convinced that zoology today should be pursued only in conjunction with zootomy, he approached me with the proposition that I take upon myself the lectureship in zoology at Königsberg, and establish a zoological museum. This proposition was very attractive to me, but I did not know what to do about it, since nobody in Königsberg had ever contemplated a special professorship in zoology, not to speak of a zoological collection. I must have his efforts to thank for the fact that, when as early as 1819 I was appointed assistant professor (entitling me to a raise of 300 Thalers over my previous salary of the same sum), I was also asked, unofficially that is, to initiate the setting up of a zoological museum for Königsberg University. Officially, the matter was made public by the ministry only at the beginning of 1820.

Also, early in 1819, I developed a deep affection for a Königsberg lady, Auguste v. Medem, and, as assistant professor, I did not hesitate to ask her to become my wife, subject to her parents' consent. As the latter was forthcoming, too, I seemed all set for Königsberg. I now felt the strong urge once more to bid farewell to my homeland, and this time for good—my previous farewell having been regarded by my family as no more than a furlough for a short period. Undertaken in the late summer of 1820, this journey was not limited to Estonia, but also included a short side-trip to St. Petersburg, in order at least to have seen the capital of my fatherland. At the beginning of the winter semester, I was back in Königsberg.

12. My Second Stay in Königsberg. The Museum and Professorship in Zoology (1819-1829)

Every circumstance seemed to coincide to make me feel at home in Königsberg and to turn me into a warm supporter of the Prussian State. A few months after my return I married and thus set up my own household which was soon blessed with children. There were four sons, one after the other, then a daughter and, in 1829, a fifth and last son. My ties with my homeland, on the other hand, became progressively more tenuous. In the first year of my marriage, in 1820, I had already received the sad news that my good mother had died. In 1824 my father, who had long enjoyed the best of health and an almost youthful vigor, fell ill with dropsy. He came to Königsberg to seek help, and there, in the following year, I had the painful task of laying him to rest.

In the meantime, a number of young lecturers gathered in Königsberg of my own age, some even younger; all were of the generation which I had missed so much in my first two years. Now that I had a family of my own, I had less emotional need of them than would have been true earlier; however, there were men of such charm and, indeed, excellence among them that my life was greatly brightened by them. The first to arrive was the botanist, Dr. Eysenhardt, who was appointed by the Ministry to substitute for Schweigger, who had left about the middle of 1819 on a long journey. Dr. Eysenhardt, a young man of the purest character, was thoroughly educated in the natural sciences. As he lived in the botanical garden not far from me, he became a very close friend of the family. Unfortunately, he died after a few years due to a pulmonary hemorrhage caused by tuberculosis.

Those who followed Eysenhardt were now younger than myself. While I had little occasion to seek the company of the lecturers in the law faculty, with the possible exception of Abegg, I was most attracted by the physicist Dove, the physico-mineralogist Neumann, and Ernst Meyer, the sharp-witted botanist who had replaced Eysenhardt. I also had friendly relations with the theologians Hahn—who later moved to Breslau—and Olshausen (later of Erlangen), who lodged with my mother-in-law. F.W. Schubert, the historian and statistician, busied himself mainly with the history of his own fatherland, as befits a Königsberger, and was important to me because he made efforts to have me naturalized. At Bessel's I frequently met the younger Jacobi, not-

171

withstanding the fact that our respective scientific fields were miles apart. The elder Jacobi belongs to a somewhat later period. I felt drawn toward von Bohlen also, not only because of the novelty of his field but because of his amiable character, which helped him to strike roots in and become acclimated to what must have been very difficult surroundings for him. We, who had no more than heard of Sanskrit studies, were very glad to be able to learn something more about this subject, but it should not be forgotten that Königsberg was the seed-bed of classical philology, and has always had something exclusive. The two principals of the local gymnasiums, Gotthold and K. Struve, were both philologists, the one exclusively, the other predominantly so. First and foremost, however, was Professor Lobeck, who had been active in Königsberg for a longer period of time, and who by his thoroughness and stupendous diligence—which exceeded the bounds of the credible—had built himself a great reputation. Although he did not hold too high an opinion of natural history studies, he was still inclined to regard them as a harmless scholarly pastime, which compliment we returned by calling his long-cultivated classical philology antiquated hairsplitting. But he was most contemptuous, and indeed derisive, of the polyglottism of his colleague, Vater. He seemed rather happy when the latter left us in 1820, but when the Sanskrit teacher appeared a few years later to defile the pure waters of classical philology, there was new material for derision. Soon, however, Lobeck's scorn turned into disquiet, as he saw how a language even more ancient than Greek, and richer in forms, could be treated with the same thoroughness. The only pity was that Bohlen had been brought to Königsberg, where there were absolutely no sources for his studies. Other newcomers found more auspicious conditions. It is much to the credit of old Hagen that he accepted all of them with open arms, although Eysenhardt, Dove, Neumann and I—as zoologist—dealt with sciences that belonged to his domain. But he was also quite conscious of the fact that these sciences had by now grown beyond his reach. Chemistry and pharmacy, on the other hand, were not touched by anyone, so long as he lived. Being a man of honor, he was respected by everyone and, thereby, brought honor, and also some converts to the Old Prussianism for which he stood. On the list of young lecturers were a number of brilliant names, many of whom, however, intended to leave Königsberg. Others, such as E. Meyer and Bohlen, died young. When I returned to Königsberg after a long period of time, I found only the worthy Neumann left, along with Schubert.

I received the friendliest reception and found much intellectual stimulation in circles outside the university as well. It would be too much for me to mention them all here. I must, however, note with gratitude the friendly attitude with which I was met by the brilliant governor, von Schon, and the venerable justice, von Wegnern. I felt particularly drawn to the former. Burdach introduced me into the homes of the erudite and jovial principal of the gymnasium, K. Struve, whose wife was a Livonian, and of Hirsch, the public health officer. I first knew the latter's son as a student, and developed the closest bonds of friendship with him when he became a medical practitioner (he is now clinical professor). Another man who interested me was the lively and witty Dr. Motherby. Some of the faculty, among them Ellendt and Lucas, together with some clergymen and Dr. Hirsch, had formed a circle which met regularly, and which I also joined. Such popular scientific societies such as the Medical, the Economic, and the German societies, which elected me a member, contributed even more to my getting acquainted with people from the most diverse layers of society. All three strove more toward intellectual diversion rather than scientific inquiry. The German Society, for instance, was rather at a loss for an answer when asked as to its purpose, which nobody really knew for certain. The usual explanation was that it had been founded by Gottsched and, since then, simply kept going on. The people met, a member would have prepared an address, and the others would listen, particularly on occasion of patriotic festivities, the King's birthday, etc. It later took on a more historical direction under Schubert. The Economic Society had a better defined aim which, however, had also become somewhat obscured in the course of time. I shall return to this society at a later point. Here I should like to note that this society included craftsmen also, not mechanical engineers or higher artists, but just craftsmen, the most educated ones from this class whom I have ever met. They had had no more than a general school education, not a scientific-technical one, thus their longing for a school with a technical trend, which I mentioned on pages 62–63.

Of the social gatherings at peoples' home I did not much like those that took place at noontime if, according to national custom, they were associated with an endless struggle with a long series of dishes. Much more to my taste were the evening parties, to which one used to invite a large number of guests, so that issuing one or two invitations per year brought one's whole circle of acquaintances to one's home. These parties were not so packed as to impede moving about freely, but crowded enough to obviate the need to stay too long with one's neighbor, and one could make the best of this freedom of movement. At these gatherings, members of the university were always present, but never exclusively or predominantly so. This prevented the coteries, of which there is never any lack in scientific circles, from assuming those impassioned and indeed repugnant forms to which they sometimes are prone in universities of small towns, and for which Halle was, for several years, a forbidding example. Taking into account the number of students, and remembering the aforementioned long-standing neglect, Königsberg must be considered a small university. However, due simply to the size of the town, with its almost 70,000 inhabitants, substantial merchant class, and the large number of public agencies, the university was spared the damage incurred by similar institutions in small towns. Although not enjoying the advantages, neither did it suffer the drawbacks of cities of royal residence.

The moderate size of the town was very much to my liking. As it straddled the road from Berlin to Petersburg, it enjoyed visits from virtuosi and actors passing along this road. There was also a permanent theatrical group, although of mediocre quality. The town itself, though slightly antiquated—especially in its castle, which was a patchwork of many different periods, still had some very appealing parts, particularly the castle pond and the gardens surrounding it. The immediate environs of the town were also most charming and varied. I particularly liked the fact that social life organized itself along lines corresponding to the educational level, and also that, due to the town's moderate size, it was possible to make the acquaintance of most, if not all the people of consequence without being dependent on a certain class. Nor was it necessary to look up all these people, since the larger evening parties offered ample opportunities for such meetings. In fact, social life was such that a man in a scientific position frequently felt the need for solitude rather than the desire to seek the acquaintance of people.

I soon felt completely at home and, without really being aware of it, began to harbor feelings of Prussian patriotism. One of the legacies of the great war of liberation was a noble and dignified self-confidence, a splendid but quiet striving for progress, and a great respect for education. At that time, this striving was not an effort against the government, but for, or rather with, the government. Thus, when the persecution of seditious intrigue started, nobody in Königsberg was ready to believe that there was a real occasion for it, and, here at least, it was this very campaign that spread the first ideas of such seditious endeavors. It is true that the school's graecophiles cried out about impending barbarism, when a regulation was to be issued making it no longer obligatory to teach the Greek language to secondary-school students, but they were allowed to rage. It is also true that many complained of the interference with their studies or trades caused by their stint of military service. In general, however, people were proud of the new defense system, which drew men from all classes of society for the defense of the fatherland. Least of all could I detect any trace of tension between the standing army and the citizenry. This was probably also due to the fact that many volunteers from all classes of society had fought in the Wars of Liberation; furthermore, young people had to undergo a period of military training. The officers whom I met appeared to be very well educated, and did not at all exhibit that frivolity for which Prussian officers had been reproached in the past. To me, the note of aversion toward the army which is now heard in the halls of government as well as in the press is, therefore, as unexpected as it is incomprehensible. Great changes must have taken place.

At that time, people were proud of the position achieved by the Prussian state, an achievement to which all classes felt they had contributed and, consequently, were happy with every evidence of further progress. Remembering now the joyousness with which I greeted the establishment of the *Zollverein* (a customs union), I must indeed have been a Prussian patriot. Also, I always believed that the Prussian state was the best governed one—and I still do.

If only because of this patriotism, I tried to acquaint myself with the history and characteristic features of East Prussia, and this, of course, also included the flora and fauna of this province. In furtherance of this endeavor— and since, in any case, one cannot very well be a Prussian patriot without having visited the amber mines—I undertook several journeys on foot through Samland before it became known for its seaside resorts, and later made trips to other areas as well. The results of these hikes were some small contributions to Hagen's *Chloris Borussica*, and the report on "botanical walking tours along the Samland coast" in the journal *Flora*. These tours were all the more important to me, because they afforded me the opportunity of observing the *Medusa aurita*, of continuing my anatomical work on the sturgeon, and of visiting the breeding grounds of several fish. Best of all, they permitted me to investigate the stagnant waters for their variety of inhabitants.

My most pressing task now was establishing the zoological museum. This was no easy job, as none of the elements required to this end was at hand. The ministry refused to grant a specific sum until it was convinced that a serious start had been made, but to make such a start was very difficult without money. Not being able to grasp the fact that no such collection had ever existed at Königsberg, the ministry inquired of the university board about the fate of previous objects of this kind. Prompted by this inquiry, a search was instituted, resulting in the discovery of three objects which were given to the King as presents, namely, a cassowary egg, the nest of a titmouse, and a stuffed bird, the plumage of which had been moth-eaten to such a degree that only the heavier shafts were left, but nothing of the vanes. From the shape of the beak and the two longer tail-feather shafts, one could surmise that these derived from the *Prionites Momota*. These three objects, one of which had to be declared completely useless, were given to me as the basis of the zoological museum. Undoubtedly by order of the ministry, Professor Lichtenstein, director of the zoological museum at Berlin, sent us eighty small stuffed birds from North and South America, all probably duplicates, but not a single hummingbird or other similarly rare bird among them, which would have made this consignment interesting for the larger public also; for that he was too keen on his own museum.

There was, in fact, a collection of natural history objects in Königsberg, belonging to a Frau Hennig, a widow. However, the collection had been brought together in part, without scientific knowledge and quite uncritically, and was said to contain objects which had never existed or which made no sense at all, such as the scrotum of a whale, fossilized fossils, etc. Moreover, the owner put an exorbitant price on it, so that I had to give up the hope of ever possessing it. Therefore, I had to take a different path. Counting on the patriotism of the Prussians, I published an appeal in the newspapers, announcing the founding of a zoological museum, and calling on the "friends of natural history in Prussia," I asked for suitable objects, especially of the local fauna.

Thus, many parts were gradually coming together to make a whole. In the meantime, however, we also lacked a taxidermist, and I arranged for a dexterous barber's apprentice by the name of Ebel to be sent to Berlin to be trained in taxidermy. Upon his return he was to observe, hunt, and stuff birds, so as to get together, in the course of time, a collection of the local fauna.

It would be pointless to mention the minor difficulties and complications caused by the collision between youthful zeal on the one side, and an uncertain board which had not the slightest idea of requirements of a zoological museum, on the other. But I cannot omit the unforgettable beginning. Having received the birds from Berlin, I reported that I had ordered three small cabinets to accommodate the gift birds, and asked for payment. In answer, I was asked who had authorized me to order these cabinets. According to standard procedure, an estimate had to be submitted and would be scrutinized. I had the carpenter prepare an estimate which was duly submitted. This estimate was first checked in Königsberg, and then sent on to Berlin. After several months, I received the reply that Berlin felt that three cabinets were too many for the few objects mentioned by me. I had to explain that, by now, we already had more objects than the three small cabinets could house. Before the new authorization could go through, new needs had arisen. Had I waited that long, the fate of the Berlin birds would have been that of the *Prionites Momota*. The cabinets that I had ordered so precipitately, yet at the right time after all, were at first put in a small room in the anatomy museum. In the meantime I had been casting about for special premises, since that minute room could not possibly accommodate the zoological museum. Soon a newly built house was rented nearby, in which I also received an apartment. In 1822, this house was already filled to such a degree that I was able to compose a guide bearing the title, "Companion Through the Zoological Museum of Königsberg" and the Zoological Museum was opened to the public twice a week.

The appeal to Prussian patriotism had fallen on very fertile soil. In particular, the head foresters of the entire province sent us everything that did not seem very common. Although some of the animals arrived in a rather useless state during the summer months, it was still possible to learn something about the country's fauna. Whatever was in a useful condition was stuffed. Such contributions would have been impossible had the museum not obtained a permit exempting its volunteer suppliers from postal fees. To obtain predatory birds in their various hues, I came to an agreement with the government, according to which they would accept the receipt of the museum for predatory birds sent to it, in lieu of the claws every head forester was required to deliver as proof of his activity in reducing the number of predators. As is only right and proper, the contributor's name was mentioned on the label of the object. Following the example of the Berlin museum, the labels were given different colors according to the different continents, and the labels of Prussian animals were prominently marked with a special frame. Patriotic zeal was so great that, had a number of collections existed in the country, most would surely have been combined to form one large collection. But, as indicated before, except for Hennig's, there were no collections worth mentioning. This statement notwithstanding, we did obtain several items: an insect collection from the estate of Kugelan, an entomologist from Osterode. Fortunately, this was kept in separate small boxes, so that about half was in a satisfactory state of preservation, while the other half had been rather seriously damaged by mold. Through the generosity of Dr. Andersch we received a rather pretty collection of Prussian butterflies; a gift from Professor Hagen, senior, of a collection comprising 125 glass jars with Surinamese animals preserved in spirit; and we also received a gift of money—200 Thalers from the magistrate to enable the museum to buy the shell section of the Hennig collection. Other animals from foreign parts were acquired from commercial sources. Later, on the intercession of governor von Schon, the assembled Diet raised a certain sum through contributions from its individual members. Least progress was made in acquiring the large foreign mammals, as I preferred to have something of all species for teaching, as well as for my own studies, to using money to acquire the costly skins of the large mammals. The initial tightfistedness shown by the Königsberg board and the ministry in Berlin notwithstanding, a budget of more than 1000 Thalers, quite considerable for a provincial museum, was granted after a few years. The authorities could not fail to be impressed by the great interest shown by the public as well as, I may add, my own zeal.

The large number of local animals sent to the museum brought in its wake a very extensive correspondence, which I tried to keep within manageable bounds by periodically reporting in the newspapers on the objects received. These reports appeared under the soon familiar headline: "To the Friends of Natural History in Prussia." Indeed, I made it a habit to correspond with my friends, both known and unknown, through the newspaper. Since at the same time I continued in my role of the devoted patron of menagerie owners, classifying and publicly reviewing their collections, my appearance in the newspapers was quite frequent.

My relations with the patriotic well-wishers of the museum gave rise to a desire, expressed from all sides, for a textbook dealing with the animals of Prussia. Most head foresters were not familiar with the more recent literature. A few had acquired one or another of the older, good books, in particular Frisch's *Vorstellung der Vögel Teutschlands* ("Introduction to the Birds of Germany"), a work containing many large and very good illustrations, but which unfortunately, treated predatory birds in their early plumage mostly as altogether different types, and which also lacked the commonly used systematic names. People could not understand why I always called the animals by names which differed from those mentioned in this work. In my announcements in the newspapers, I occasionally recommended the most suitable and instructive works, but it appeared that their prices were far beyond the means of the head foresters. Even the *Taschenbuch der deutschen Vogelkunde* ("Handbook of German Ornithology") by Meyer and Wolf (ten Thalers plus one-and-a-half for the supplements) was too expensive, and Naumann's work could be mentioned in these newspaper columns only as an unobtainable treasure. I was, therefore, repeatedly requested to prepare a low-priced handbook on the local fauna, particularly the vertebrates. I did not feel the slightest inclination to do so, firstly because the list of local animals was growing only very gradually and secondly, I was committed to some anatomical work for the near future. Therefore, I arranged for Ebel, the curator, to compile an *Ornithologisches Taschenbuch für Preussen* ("Ornithological Handbook for Prussia"), based on the animals we had obtained, using material from the better works on birds. The book indeed appeared in 1823, comprising a preface which I wrote, as well as an appendix discussing the desiderata of the museum. Later, using the material from the museum, work was begun on a *Fauna Prussica* by Herr Lorek, a teacher at the Fridericianum Gymnasium as well as a skilled draftsman and copper engraver. I do not know whether this work, which had progressed as far as the mammals and most of the predatory birds when I left Königsberg, has ever been finished*. I myself made use of the objects which entered the museum only for occasional short notices. On the occasion of the opening of the zoological museum, I prepared a short article, "Zwei Worte über den jetzigen Zustand der Naturgeschichte" ("Two Words on the Present State of Natural History"), published by Bornträger (1821, 4°), the aim of which was to show Prussian friends of natural history the extent to which the systematic catalogues had grown in recent years. At the same time I also kept my eye on the university's newly appointed government representative who, after a consignment of insects had been received, demanded that a classification be produced at once and who, when I told him that this would take a considerable time, became rather suspicious and had made some inquiries about the professor who, on the spot, was unable to call any and all insects by their names.

I made use of the fossil fragments of mammals which we had obtained, as well as of some previously published reports, to prepare a two-part dissertation: *De fossilibus mammalium reliquiis in Prussia repertis*, 1823, 4°, of which a very limited number of copies also reached the bookshops. The reason for this two-part effort was that at Königsberg, as at many old German univer-

---

*In Engelmann's *Bibliotheca historico-naturalis* I found only 3 brochures mentioned. That many had already been prepared at the time of my later stay in Königsberg.

sities, it was the custom to present one's dissertation twice, once *pro loco*, and again, if one wanted to join the faculty. One was permitted to postpone these dissertations but until they had been completed, one was listed in the catalogue as Designated Professor. I disposed of this formality on two successive days.

The fossil mammalian remnants were mostly those prevalent in the topmost strata of a large part of Europe. I was struck by the large number of fragments of antlers of various sizes, as well as bones, for which I had no explanation. Today I would probably see most of them as tools from the so-called Stone Age. Among the objects received, there was an elephant tusk, resembling that of the African elephant. It was allegedly found on Mount Rombinus near Memel. However, since there were still dried remnants of soft tissues on the tusk, I could not declare it a fossil.

Some unexpected consignments of Prussian birds—*Larus minutus, Fringilla erythrina, Ibis Falcinellus, Ciconia nigra* etc.—induced me to write an article, "Ornithologische Fragmente" ("Ornithological Fragments"), which appeared in the tenth volume of *Frorieps Notizen,* and was followed by several more short notes. Other short articles, such as "Beitrag zur Kenntniss des dreizehigen Faulthiers" ("Contribution to Knowledge of the Three-toed Sloth") and "Ueber Medusa aurita" ("On the Medusa aurita"), were more of a zootomic nature and appeared in *Meckels Archiv für die Physiologie* (Archive for Physiology). A larger work entitled "Beiträge zur Kenntniss der niedern Thiere" ("Contributions to Knowledge of the Lower Animals") I handed over to the K. Leopold. Carol. Akademie. It consisted of seven different treatises which together were intended to utilize zootomic investigations of particular animal forms in the lower orders to draw conclusions pertaining to systematics; it concluded with a treatise "Ueber die Verwandtschaftsverhältnisse unter den niedern Thieren" ("On the Relationships among the Lower Animals"). The material for these investigations came mostly from the bodies of stagnant water around Königsberg.

That surroundings of Königsberg would offer little material, as far as the systematics of higher animals was concerned, was quite obvious. Even the commercial establishments dealing with natural history specimens did not carry the lesser known foreign animals. Because of these circumstances, my literary activities turned mainly in an anatomical-physiological direction, which I shall turn to at a later point. Yet, altogether, I liked to occupy myself with zoology, regarding it as complementary to zootomy.

This was also reflected in the character of my zoology lectures: I always considered the inner structure together with the outer, discussing the manifestations of life and, in the higher animals as well as in insect groups, also habits and customs. More detailed treatment was accorded only to such animals as were of particular importance to human existence, either through their usefulness or their harmfulness. By and large, I followed Cuvier's system, though not slavishly. I was never able to regard the mollusks as more highly organized than the insects. I further went along with Cuvier in that I accepted genera including subgenera or indeed subgroups as such. This was the only way to survey all known forms of organization. With the insects, however, I had to stop at the larger subgenera. The museum was organized on the same principles, which also determined the labeling of the animals. The old, familiar generic names for the larger groups were retained as far as possible, the names of the subgenera being inserted in parentheses between genus and species. Even today, if I had to manage a zoological museum—a small, provincial one, that is—I would adhere to the same principles, because I believe that zoology has been harmed, rather than helped, by the proliferation of generic names. To begin with, this has scared away large numbers of amateur naturalists. Within the scientific family itself, it has created a situation where zoologists now have difficulties communicating with each other. If I speak of *Rhodeus amarus*, many a zoologist who does not specialize in fishes will hardly know what I am talking about. If, however, I were to add *Cyprinus amarus*, he would at least have a general idea, as it may be assumed that every zoologist is somehow familiar with all main classes according to their old names. I have not the slightest doubt that there will have to be a return to the use of the more comprehensive generic names to characterize the species. I have discussed this problem with zoologists, and most often have encountered the objection that one could not very well set a limit to the precision of an investigation. Certainly not! But this was never the intention. My argument was that we should not forego the advantage accruing from Linnaeus's happy inspiration of using the first, generic name to indicate the family character, and the second name to indicate the species and their special qualities, just as in ordinary life an individual is also distinguished by two names, his family name and his given name. The surfeit of finely distinguished genera of the moths have brought students of lepidopterans to the point where most of them use only the species name, as the one being generally known. In this way, the many generic names have been reduced to a scholarly ballast, quite useless because they are not generally accepted. To this must be added the fact that the boundaries of these newly established genera were liable to shift according to the different opinions of different naturalists. Certainly nobody should be compelled to accept the border line between *Abramis* and *Leuciscus* at the point set by someone else. But it seems obvious to me that had the old generic name of *Cyprinus* been retained, those shifts would not have caused this onslaught of synonyms, the proliferation of which, far from benefiting zoological knowledge, had in fact become a burden. One of the results of this phenomenon is the fact that zoologists have now taken to specializing more or less according to the animal classes. That I did not unconditionally stick to Linnaean nomenclature whenever substantial differences in structure or modes of life demanded a separation, goes without saying. But this question deserves separate treatment. At this point I just want to state my position in this respect.

Returning to my lectures, it should be noted that, given my way of combining the elucidation of the inner structure with systematics, and my striving to provide a complete survey of all organizations (as far as was known at that time), it was quite impossible to cover the material within one semester, even with daily lectures. My lectures always extended well into the second semester, and it was only during the last two months that I offered some general reflections on animal organization under the name "comparative anatomy." As the details had all been dealt with by then, I could afford to move on to general considerations. I would approve of such a division of the subject matter even today. An insight into the structure of an animal form is possible only when one can survey all the essential components of the organization in their mutual relationships. Other concepts, on the other hand, such as the vertebral theory of the skull, of the general skeletal type, of the main forms of the nervous system, and similar building blocks of a future theory of organic structure, are best understood not in their particular manifestations, but by comparing entire series of such manifestations.

At times I was worried lest my zoology lectures were too detailed, especially for the medical students who were expected to demonstrate in their examination some general zoological knowledge. I saw it as my duty, therefore, to also provide a very concise survey with particular stress on officinal animals. Thus, one summer (about 1823 or '24), I announced a very general course in natural history, believing that students, especially medical students, would very much welcome it. However, only a single medical student enrolled, and these lectures, the preparations for which took me far more time than the more specialized and detailed ones, altogether attracted no more than seven or eight students. The medical students declared their preference for the more detailed zoology course which also included zootomy. I subsequently discontinued this general course in natural history but, from time to time, gave lectures on special subjects: the history of zoology and zootomy; fishes; insects; prehistoric animals. Cuvier's epoch-making paleontological investigations were novel and still in progress at the time. I was enchanted by his lucid presentation, and a lot of midnight oil was burned over his work, for the study of which my environment offered little enough incentive, but to which I felt irresistibly attracted.

After the tragic death of Professor Schweigger in Sicily in 1821, the ministry nominated me for a full professorship in natural history specializing in zoology. The Royal Letter of Appointment, dated January 18, 1822, also stipulated my retention of the prosectorship, as well as a salary increase of 300 Thalers.

Altogether I now had a salary of 900 Thalers, as well as some pecuniary benefits which came to me by virtue of my joining the faculty. The most sizable of these benefits was attached to the office of the prorectorship to which the full professors were elected for turns of half a year each. The permanent *Rector magnificentissimus* was the Crown Prince, the future King Friedrich Wilhelm IV. As I was told, however, his relations with the university were limited to the yearly occasion of his birthday when he accepted the felicitations of the university, conveyed during a festive ceremony. In his stead reigned whoever was elected at the moment to be *Prorector magnificus*, or rather, in fact as a time-honored custom [*sic*]. The prorectorship, which I held twice, consumed little time, while carrying an extra income of about 300 Thalers. There had existed in Königsberg numerous endowments since old days, from which the rector (prorector) of the day was entitled to draw, as well as other funds which were exclusively assigned to him. Some of these funds provided a curious proof of the former penury of rectors, and of the willingness of rich men to alleviate this penury in their wills. Thus, I remember one of these charitable endowments which granted the rector ten Thalers to conduct himself in splendor, whenever Königsberg expected distinguished guests. Although the times were past when ten Thalers would provide even a modicum of splendor Königsberg was rather inexpensive to live in and, above all, the professors, following the custom prevailing at German universities, lived rather frugally. Being an Estonian by birth, this thriftiness appeared to me exaggerated in some respects. My economic position now appeared to me to be such, since the loans I had assumed for my Würzburg years having been paid off with the aid of an inheritance from my mother, that I felt I could afford to indulge my craving for good books. During my early years, I had bought with true hardship and real privation such indispensable books for daily use as the four volumes of Meckel's *Anatomy*, and similar works. I was, however, unable and unwilling to buy myself, in addition to the anatomical works, the most indispensable works for the classification of animals we received. In this field, the university library was particularly poor. When I proposed the acquisition of several works, I was told in the most friendly terms that an unpaid lecturer had absolutely no right to propose books to be bought by the library. What a curious rule! Nobody is more eager for intellectual nourishment, nobody, as a rule, is better informed on the demand and supply of the times than the unpaid lecturer who has not yet immersed himself in extended investigations dealing with a narrow subject, and nobody has less means to acquire for himself the books he needs—and this very person is to have no right to indicate his requirements! When I became assistant professor I was allowed to propose purchases from auction catalogues. But these proposals were subject to approval by the library. Once I found the twelfth edition of Linnaeus's *Systema naturae*, the last edition which he had attended to himself, in an auction catalogue. I ordered it, together with several other works. Linnaeus was struck off the list, however, because the library had an earlier edition, the tenth, or was it the eighth? Since the minister at that time, Stein von Altenstein, was himself a naturalist, I turned to him and reported to him on the state of the library, and that without more massive assistance, his plans to establish a zoological museum in Königsberg were quite unrealizable. Following this meeting, the minister granted the library a lump sum of 1,000 Thalers, the use of which, however, was left to my discretion. In the past, I had indeed been reduced to asking old Professor Hagen for the use of his private library which, however, was also slightly obsolete. Without that extraordinary grant, almost no zoological classification would have been possible, yet after the acquisition of some major publications, such as the *Linnaean Transactions*, it had about melted away. In an earlier official expose, Professor Vater, then head librarian, pointed out to me that the acquisition of natural-history works had to be kept within certain bounds, since the library staff had made an estimate as to approximately how the early budget should be distributed among the various major subjects. Accordingly, medicine was to be granted 200 Thalers, and since natural history was considered a preparatory subject for medicine, it could not receive more than fifty Thalers. I was so touched by these fifty Thalers for zoology, botany, and mineralogy, that I developed the strongest urge to stay away as much as possible from the public library as well as from the calculations of philologists. I therefore included in the draft budget for the zoological museum also a small sum for the acquisition of books, and the budget was duly approved. As soon as my own means permitted, however, I was hard at work enlarging my own library, more on the zoological side than on the anatomical, since the library of the anatomic institute was quite considerable in this field and was growing daily. Thus I decided to devote the entire income from my turn of duty as prorector to my own library, which swelled considerably, since 300 Thalers, judiciously invested at various auctions, went a long way. But the saying, "l'appetit vient en mangeant" holds particularly true for victims of bibliophilia. This appetite is never sated and such experiences as related on page 52 have a short-term effect only. As I was spared the last stage of this disease, in which one searches for rarities without regard to their usefulness, I had scraped together a rather nice library when I finally left Königsberg in 1834. Thus, although entomology was by no means the subject for which I collected in particular, I possessed Réaumur's *Mémoires pour servir à l'histoire des insectes*; Rösel's *Insectenbelustigungen* ("Fun with Insects"), including the supplementary volume by Kleemann; de Geer's memoirs as translated by Göze; Panzer's *Fauna insect. Germ.*; Lyonnet's *Traité sur la chenille, etc.*; Huber's *Fourmilles*; Kirby and Spence's *Entomology*; Jablonsky's *Natursystem der Insecten* ("Natural System of Insects"); all works by Fabricius, Meyen and Schäffer; Swammerdam's *Historia insect.*, except for the *Bibl. natur.*; and many minor works. On fishes I had not only the complete works of Artedi, but also the large edition of Bloch's work on native and foreign fishes, Klein, Gronov, Gouan, Lacepède, Meidinger, Nilsson, Faber, and, of the older authors,

Rondelet, Salviani and Gessner. My collection of literature on intestinal worms was so complete that, in 1834, there were hardly any of the very old (and now quite useless) works missing.

My successors will possibly have had grounds for complaining that I did not acquire more books for the university library, but I really did not know what to do with that third of fifty Thalers per year, and when I demanded a larger work for the library, for instance the large ichthyology by Cuvier and Valenciennes which had just appeared, I was treated to such a wringing of hands and gnashing of teeth that I preferred to inflict upon myself whatever privations were associated with the acquisition of books*. It is true that the university library had a very limited yearly budget. But I have never heard of a serious attempt to have it increased. Prior to the nineteenth century, the library must have been exceedingly poor. Later—I do not know exactly when—a royal library was attached to it. Yet for all the subjects that had not been taught in Königsberg for a long time, it remained very poor, as is borne out by the fact that Linnaeus's *Systema naturae* was available only in a very old edition. But since the ministry was earnestly trying to raise the level of the university, it would undoubtedly have increased the means available to the library if the appropriate picture had been drawn, as can be seen from the fact that my own private efforts resulted in a grant of 1,000 Thalers. In Königsberg, the old custom still prevailed, according to which only philologists could be librarians. If the philologists were fluent in several modern languages, there can be no objection to this custom, but especially with the so-called classical philologists this is by no means the rule, and it is my experience that of all the separate branches of scientific study, it is classical philology which maintains, in the most single-minded manner, what I earlier tried to describe with the expression exclusiveness. Its study makes a rather limited use of a scientific apparatus which comes from the past and, although continuously reworked, almost necessarily regards all newer branches of scientific inquiry as irksome weeds. By no means does the study of philology automatically lead to a manifold bibliographic knowledge, and therefore does not in itself constitute any certificate of proficiency for the position of librarian. The situation was different in the sixteenth century. Because the most valuable part of literature consisted in the newly printed old classics, it was obviously the philologists who were the natural librarians, just as in the Middle Ages this business fell equally naturally to the monks. In the nineteenth century, literature has greatly extended its compass, in spite of which the classical philologists have not abandoned their priority claim to the positions of librarians, quite as in

---

*I would have easily allowed myself to be persuaded to leave the bulk of my library in Königsberg, for very moderate compensation, as it was no small matter to transport such multivolume journals as the *Annales de physique, Annales des sc. naturelles* (prem. série), Ferussac's *Bulletin*, etc., had anyone made such an offer. As it was, I did not want to originate such a proposal.

German universities of the old school, where the professor of philology is necessarily also professor of speech and, as such, is charged with the publication of the lecture catalogues, although all traces of oratory and poetry have long since disappeared from them*.

*At Königsberg University, the statutes of which, as already mentioned, stem from the sixteenth century, the original statutes having been changed only slightly toward the end of that century, Professor Lobeck naturally would also be professor of speech and, as such, editor of the lecture catalogue. This business, however, seemed to him so much below his dignity that he did not attend to it himself but, so people said, left it to some student or other. Our lecture catalogue thereby gained the character of classic negligence. A catalogue appeared for a summer semester that was to begin on October 25. A lecture which Professor Neumann had described for the German lecture catalogue as: *Ueber die Fortpflanzung der Wärme in Mineralien* (On the propagation of heat in minerals), read in the Latin translation: *De vermium in corporibus solidis propagatione* (On the propagation of worms in solid bodies) (Summer 1831). The anonymous translator had thus read Würmer (worms) for Wärme (heat). I was present when Professor Neumann reproached his colleague Lobeck for this blunder. The only answer he got was, "Well, why do the gentlemen not announce their lectures in both languages at the same time?" Yet if one wrote in Latin, one laid one's work open inevitably to word-for-word scrutiny and was never sure how one's Latin effort would wind up. Lobeck would scarcely have approved of the expression *in mineralibus*, yet it was all the same to him whether it was worms or warmth that propagated in minerals, since the classics had never bothered with such problems. Having been present at the above interlocution, I was prepared for another. In the German lecture catalogue where my name appeared, I found it spelled with an umlauted a (Bär). I went to see the secretary of the university and explained to him that inasmuch as I had seen my ancestors' handwriting, I knew that they had for at least two centuries spelled their name æ, which, if he pleased, I should like to perpetuate. He shrugged his shoulders and declared that he had nothing to do with the lecture catalogue and did not know who its editor was. I turned to the government's representative. He, too, assured me that he had no connection whatsoever with the lecture catalogue, which was Lobeck's responsibility. I thus applied to Lobeck who informed me in the most charming cadences that he really could not work up any interest in the spelling of a name which was known neither in Attica nor in Latium. I ventured the opinion that the lecture catalogue was certainly a sort of a document, but Lobeck did not want to rate it that high. Still, he did me the favor, at a later opportunity, of dissolving the umlaut into its components. A short time after that, however, the umlaut reconstituted itself, presumably because a new student had taken over. Lobeck never revealed the identities of these students, however. Our lecture catalogues were the first to raise my doubts as to the validity of the then current theory of spontaneous generation, since the catalogue's creators were not to be discovered; on the other hand, however, the catalogues had certainly not created themselves. It was at that point that I decided to speak in public on the spelling of my name, since even graduates of Königsberg University did not always observe the proper orthography, relying rather on some yearly volumes of our lecture catalogue. In Königsberg my claims were heeded only after I took the opportunity to step on some sensitive toes. This opportunity presented itself on the occasion of a dinner party attended by Governor von Schön, as well as by the government representative. The talk turned to poetic license, and I claimed that the greatest poetic license was to be found in our lecture catalogue. I proceeded to give them

(Contd.)

But what, indeed, is the subject that qualifies a person for the position of librarian? According to my opinion, general history of literature. Whoever is seriously pursuing this study, for him what is now becoming established as an independent library science is hardly a weak sideline to his studies. If no student of the history of literature is available, the most suitable man from among the aspirants is probably the one who works hard to enlarge his own library. He, at least, has some experience of the ways and byways of the book trade, and will not lack some knowledge in the history of literature, so that he will only have to follow new directions along tracks already familiar to him.

In view of the difficulties in communication at that time, people at Königsberg University should have taken particular care to enlarge their library. To a much larger extent, the same holds true for the Russian Empire, where I regard the enrichment of the libraries in the major and university cities as the most urgent need for the advancement of serious studies. There, unlike in Germany, it is impossible to visit the rich libraries of such towns as Berlin, Göttingen, Vienna, or Munich at the cost of only a few hours' travel. Many a scientific enterprise had to be interrupted in Russia, because a work which seemed important for comparison and reference was not at hand.

Governor von Schön appointed me censor for the natural history subjects. Such an appointment was accepted as a tribute, since the power of decision as to whether or not something could be printed was supposed to be entrusted to the most judicious. Burdach was censor for medical writings, Voigt for historical. While this position was, in principle, unpaid, each approved printed sheet carried a payment of two Groschen, so that for a medium-sized volume the censor was paid two Thalers. As not much printing was done in Königsberg (most books written in Königsberg went to press in Germany), one did not make a living from censoring. I myself did not make more than ten Thalers a year from the office of censor but, on the other hand, it was an easy

chapter and verse, concluding with the case of the dancing master who had died of cholera two years ago, yet, for the third time now since his demise, was using the kind offices of the catalogue to offer his dancing lessons. Herr von Schön burst out laughing. The dancing master was left to rest in peace, and the spelling of my name was given its due, if only for a few semesters; in winter 1833–34 the æ turned umlaut again, possibly due to the contractive effect of the winter cold.

As I am now dealing with the spelling of my name, I should also like to remark that I never used the additional "von Huthorn" as it appears in our birth register, because I regard this senseless "Huthorn" either as a simple spelling mistake, or a wrong reading. The family estate of a family by the name of Baehr, in the archbishopric of Bremen, from which my great-grandfather claimed to have descended, was called Hethorn. (See Mushard: *Monumenta nobilitatis antiquae Bremensis et Verdensis*). In German gothic handwriting, the letter $\varkappa$ (e) easily assumes the shape of a u or n, when the connecting bar becomes too long. This, I believe, is the way in which, in 1749, the name "Huthorn" was created in the Vienna chancellery. I have been unable to find another derivation for it.

task. One did not have to worry about single words or expressions. All one had to do was leaf through the manuscript to see that the author did not profess any destructive tendencies. This was never the case in Königsberg at that time, because wherever such a tendency might have existed, it dared not to come into the open, the general temper of the town being against it. Assessment of historical or political works might have been more problematical. While censorship of books and shorter writings was in the hands of professors and other qualified persons, the newspapers were censored by the police, who were given special instructions from time to time. We others were given no directions; it seems that the authorities relied on our good sense and judgment, as well as on the fact that every author knew he was to be scrutinized by an expert whom he wanted neither to incense nor to embarrass by some disguised attack on the rulers of the world or of the country. As to myself, I regard a sensible censorship as definitely necessary, and I quite approved of the way this institution was organized because, first of all, the governor, if dissatisfied with the efficacy of a censor, could appoint another without fuss and hesitation until the right man was found, since nobody's livelihood was jeopardized. In the second place, no author could complain that narrowness and ignorance had prevented him from enlightening the world, as other authors would have recognized the good sense of a censor, if he were deserving of such recognition. After all, he was more than a mere censor. I have not formed an opinion as to the proper handling of newspaper censorship, and have had no experience in this field. I also do not have the slightest doubt that in times of political fermentation, suitable supervision of daily newspapers is difficult and laborious because the newspaper editors have an interest in the increase of ferment, to stimulate the readers' appetite for more. Censorship of serious literature, on the other hand, I would organize in such a way as to base it on the integrity of a man of sound judgment. Special instructions seem rather out of place in this matter, because they can never be made to cover all exigencies and eventualities. If a mistake is made in the application of such an instruction, this will only serve to debase the institution of censorship *per se*. At a later period, I wrote a long treatise on man, not for a journal, but for a book, in which I characterized the main groups of man according to their social structure and organization. On the lowest level I put the New Guineans, especially the Southern New Guineans. After I told the reader that the individual member of the tribe had no property other than his weapons and whatever he carried on his person, but that the country was divided into hunting regions in which every member of the tribe could hunt, although none had exclusive possession, it occurred to me that it was precisely this state of deepest barbarism—and, as no stores were laid in, of greatest human misery—which corresponded perfectly to the communist ideal. Therefore, I added that this was in fact the state to which the latest benefactors of mankind aspired (at that time, communism was still a novelty). I admit having felt some satisfaction at having been able to adduce such striking proof of the absurdity of communism, using an often described example from real life. This treatise was to be translated into the Russian language. When I saw the printed sheet, I was astonished to discover that my lethal blow against communism had been deleted by the censor. Why? Because it was forbidden to write about communism. Yet I had not written about communism at all. All I did was to take the opportunity to demonstrate its absurdity, using a striking example and, in fact, taking some pride in having made use of this opportunity. Chance remarks of this sort are often more effective than special articles, the intentions behind which are liable to be suspect. Several years later it was reported that the theory of communism had been discussed by a group of young people who had no idea of the different social conditions of man. It was precisely these young people for whom this book had been written.

At another time the censor deleted the word "terrestrial" from the sentence "Man is the highest product of terrestrial creation." I was particularly interested in this word, however, as I take it for a serious error when naturalists consider man as the highest possible organism, seeing as how we have not the slightest idea of possible organisms on other planets. Still earlier, the word "weise" (wisely) was excised from Schiller's verse, "*Was er weise verschweigt, zeigt mir den Meister des Styls*" ("What he wisely withholds, shows me the master of style"), presumably because of a quite, to me incomprehensible aversion of the censor to wisdom. A verse with an amputated foot is no longer a verse, and only intentional withholding, not withholding as such may be regarded as facility of expression.

Having mentioned one of my avocations, I might as well recall another which I fell into although I tried to keep away from it. There was a keen interest in Königsberg in the common weal or, as you would call it today, in public welfare. As often as newspapers repeated their "appeals for charity" in the wake of fires, floods, etc., they were always successful. Here must also be mentioned the fact that, before the Great War, the continental blockade notwithstanding, the town had engaged in a lively commerce, the greater part of which was with England, which the French government knew, but which it apparently tolerated at this remote point, so that it should not break out elsewhere. After the Wars of Liberation, commerce in Königsberg receded from its unnaturally high level, as the nearest and most natural channels were reopened everywhere. The working classes who had become improvident during the prosperous pre-war years, found it increasingly difficult to make a living and had to look elsewhere for direct help. The wealthier classes who had considerably improved their financial position during the years of brisk trade were prepared to extend this help willingly. This state of affairs, however, gave rise to a usurious literature in petitions and a troublesome pressure from supplicants. While I found it hard and unjust to refuse them all, I could not find the time for a closer check of their circumstances. To me, this appeared to be a task more for the female sex and for leisured gentlemen. I therefore began to think about a charitable organization which would collect a voluntary Poor Tax from all well-to-do citizens, and which would appoint several relief officers for each district into which it would divide the town. These officers would first investigate the circumstances of the supplicants, then, together with others, decide on the relief allowance and watch over its proper use. That unsupervised relief could only increase begging became clear to me, even good-natured as I was, when I was truly touched by the urgent petition of a man who asked for no more than the money needed to buy himself a shovel and other utensils required to become a road builder, as his present trade would not feed him. Somewhat later, I learned that this man had sent the same letter to many others and had almost always obtained the assistance he asked for. Instead of starting to build roads, however, he occupied himself with making copies of his first, effective letter! He was a strong man! Why was he not actually given a shovel and wheelbarrow, and why did nobody check up on him, I thought. It would have been better for him, both physically and spiritually, than training himself to be a copyist of his own letters. So as not to become personally involved in the realization of my plan, I kept it to myself for a long period of time. But when a preacher most earnestly exhorted the wealthy to take care of the poor in his Christmas sermon, I felt I had to make use of the occasion to publish, in the last issue of the *Königsberger Zeitung* of the year 1822, an anonymous public appeal under the headline "In Celebration of New Year's Day," without committing myself to more than a contribution. Only to the preacher did I reveal that it was his sermon which decided me to publish the appeal which he would read in the newspapers, and that I hoped he would agree to head the society as, anyway, a man of the cloth was best suited to this kind of activity. The preacher, however, strongly protested his unsuitability. Professor Hahn, on the other hand, declared his readiness. Soon I had to give up my anonymity, however, as the town's Welfare Board seemed to have been offended by my appeal, and published a rather explosive declaration condemning it, carrying sixteen signatures in issue No. 6 of the newspaper. In its passion, the Board went as far as declaring, "One believes oneself placed among the heathen and infidels, reading in the appeal: 'the poor seek the sustenance which is denied to them by their work at the doors of the wealthy!' That is an untruth, etc., etc." A counterdeclaration on my part, in which I asked to be shown those points in my first article which the welfare board had construed as a slur, was returned by the newspaper which claimed that it could not be published because of the censorship laws. A second article was given the identical treatment. Therefore, I had no alternative but to pay a visit to the head of the censorship authorities, President von Auerswald, to find out about the censorship laws which my rather even-tempered explanations had apparently run foul of. It turned out that the censor's scissors in this case had

been wielded by the very private hands of Mayor Horn, who had felt affront-
ed by my appeal, although it was directed at those who engaged in private
charity, often without first making closer enquiries. My last reply was printed.
It was, of course, quite impossible now to continue hiding behind my anonymity, in consequence of which I could no longer avoid taking a more active
part. First and foremost it was Professors Burdach, Kaehler, Hahn and
myself who appeared as champions of the enterprise, in which we also had the
effective support of the Governor, who expressed strong disapproval of Mayor
Horn's behavior. To deny publicly the existence of begging was indeed
audacious and made the Mayor many more opponents. The Mayor, however,
secretly continued his opposition and was said to have cast aspersions on
those professors who sat on the society's governing board, namely Burdach,
Kaehler, Hahn, and myself, as being revolutionaries trying to curry favor with
the masses. For this he was most strongly reprimanded by the then minister,
Schuckmann, since the Chief of Police also sat on the board, and the Com-
manding General as well as the Governor were active members. In his ire,
Horn, in many respects a talented man, caused himself so much harm that he
was not reelected as Mayor.

Burdach, who had also published a brochure, "Some Words about the
Private Charitable Society of Königsberg in Prussia," became its first chair-
man. I tried to keep away from this job, not because of any modesty on my
part, but because I had begun some extensive anatomical research, and I was
also certain I had very little talent for such a post. All the same, in one of the
following years I was obliged to accept it and am unable to report that my
opinion concerning my talents has changed in any way.

For a number of years, this society did very beneficial work in Königsberg, as contributions kept flowing generously: over 2,300 Thalers were
pledged in the first year, and Burdach obtained another 1,000 Thalers from
Berlin. A considerable number of members declared their readiness to look
up the poor at their houses. Basing its actions on their reports, the board
then decided on the kind and amount of support to be extended. The board
saw as its main task helping such persons as were of reasonably good behavior, and who showed a will to work, but lacked the means to acquire the
necessary tools or the skills and opportunity to assure their employment. The
preferred procedure therefore was the provision of small advances to acquire
work tools, which were procured by the relieving officers. Soon, a special
work center was established, where material for work was distributed, particularly to women. Payments were made for the delivered, finished articles
which then were sold by the society. At a later date, a school was set up, in
which the children of the poor were taught and instructed in handicrafts. The
morally corrupt, as well as invalids and those too old to work, were not supported by this private charitable organization, but were referred to the
municipal welfare authorities.

The experience I gathered while working with this society may be summarized as follows: 1) among the persons seeking aid, but by far among those who strove to obtain their most urgent needs by their own work, that they felt encouraged and to some degree even honored, when it was explained to them that it is unworthy and brings no lasting relief if a man who is able to work approaches strange people and begs for money, thus becoming a burden on society instead of a useful member. We knew several poor women who were over eighty years old, and hardly able to see, and yet who appeared every Saturday at the society's institute to draw fresh cotton and deliver their spun yarn, however meagerly paid for, although the town would have had to care for them if they had declared themselves unable to work; 2) there is more selfless human kindness in evidence than I would have expected, most frequently among the female sex, but also with quite a number of men. I still remember with the greatest respect a Frau Kleeberg, a doctor's wife who for several years spent her Saturdays at our institute, receiving finished work and handing out new—in addition to her usual visits to the poor on other days of the week. Still more recognition is due to a man who headed the society's school and gave lessons to the children of the poor. Although he was unable to volunteer his services, having lost his small means as a merchant, he contented himself with a salary of 200 Thalers and a very small apartment, and was highly satisfied if, at the end of the year, the board granted him a small bonus of about thirty Thalers. He found full satisfaction in his work with the children.

Combining these two findings, one becomes firmly convinced that it is primarily the wealthy section of the public which must bear the blame for the spread of crass begging, as the latter proliferates in a climate of indiscriminate charity. On the other hand, a civilized city will always find compassionate human resources for the organization of well-planned and well-supervised charitable activities.

Yet the great difficulties involved in the successful continuation of such an enterprise did not fail to make themselves felt, due primarily to the fact that the benevolent, who dedicate themselves to the service of the poor with selfless devotion, rarely act with the required firmness and circumspection, and are easily put out of countenance when their recommendations are not accepted to the degree expected by them. Sometimes, too, some individuals show an impatient zeal and are not satisfied with one branch of charity, but want to expand in all directions, before this one branch is fully consolidated and its requirements completely determined. In Königsberg it was particularly the charity school and the soup kitchen (which, strictly speaking, were the responsibility of the municipal welfare board), as well as other facilities, that were set up too soon, before work distribution had been expanded as far as it could and should have been. This was the fault of one enthusiast in particular; he was always ready to sacrifice his time, but not his ideas and plans. In his autobiography (p. 343), Burdach has more to say of this person. Another difficulty was to find a permanent head for the society. Most of them stayed for no more than one year. The fact that it was mostly professors who were elected to this position in Königsberg was a serious drawback, as it is precisely these persons who are most niggardly with their time. To my mind it is the military, of whom some had volunteered as relief officers and had even agreed to serve on the board, who are most suitable for this post as in times of peace they usually do not lack leisure, and their very profession seems to endow them with a certain firmness. Since the Officer in Command, General von Borstel, had volunteered as a relief officer, however, no other officer could be persuaded to accept a post that would give him the final decision on any remonstration brought before the board.

Since due to the above-mentioned overextension, after several years of fruitful activity, the society was no longer able to find employment for all those seeking work, the House was again, and with increasing frequency, treated to speeches which for many years had been answered by referral to to the private charitable society. As a result, contributions fell off, and when I left Königsberg in 1834, the effectiveness of the society did not go much beyond the distribution of work to persons of the female sex, and to running the school.

Let us now return to my scientific pursuits.

As upon my appointment as full professor I was supposed to retain my position as prosector, my official work at the anatomical institute continued as before. In winter I supervised the daily dissecting exercises of the students, and in summer I had them perform zootomical work once a week. The lectures in human anatomy continued more or less unchanged, except that now and then I let myself be persuaded to arrange my lectures according to the regions of the human body. Some animal experiments were performed at Burdach's request, particularly such as were intended to demonstrate the difference between sensory and motor nerves according to the descriptions of Bell and Magendie. The first of these experiments was carried out as early as 1818–19. The situation changed in 1826, when Burdach approached me with the proposition to take over the directorship of the anatomical institute in addition to that of the zoological museum. He wanted his son to become prosector, and thought that in such an event it was somewhat inappropriate to remain director of the anatomical institute. This was the gist of his quite unexpected proposal, and I find it unfortunate that in his autobiography he prefaces the report on this change with the remark, "It was rather unfitting that Baer, since 1821 full professor and member of the medical faculty, was at the same time still prosector." I had definitely made no efforts to retain the prosectorship. Without consulting me, this had been decided upon by the ministry and duly ordered by the King. I was led to believe and still do that the ministry acted in recognition of my interest in the disssecting work of the students, possibly encouraged to do so by Rudolphi who, as early as my first trip to Königsberg, had expressed his dissatisfaction with the fact that until 1817 anatomical work in Königsberg had been sadly neglected. Be that as it may, this new proposal, however unexpected, was quite welcome, since the time-consuming prosectorate was becoming rather burdensome, as I had started extended research, and the endless repetitiveness of the dissecting room was beginning to weary me.

I was now professor of anatomy and zoology, which was brought about by my having moved from anatomy to zoology, having been attracted to the latter particularly by the great variety of structures and forms. In any case, there was little scope for more extensive systematic work in Königsberg. With my successor, Rathke, who had more or less the same academic antecedents, this combination was still adhered to. At a later date, the two subjects were again separated.

It seems appropriate to intersperse at this point some reflections concerning the most successful way in which to improve the universities. In Königsberg, the ministry succeeded in reshaping the university and extending the studies within a very short time and, as far as I could make out, with a very moderate financial outlay. Having formerly aimed at no more than the scanty instruction of students of medicine and jurisprudence—apart from theology, philology, and history (primarily local history)—the university's relative backwardness was not evident as long as the stars of Kant and Krause graced its academic skies and, one may add, as long as Hagen in his youthful vigor attempted to embrace almost all the natural sciences. After those two luminaries had stepped down, and after the natural sciences had greatly developed and had in part changed their structure so that zoology came to depend on zootomy, and geology could no longer do without paleontology, nor physics without a thorough mathematical grounding, the ministry began to invite to Königsberg a number of men of well-established reputation, to teach and to establish institutes. Subsequently, the ministry sent a large number of very young lecturers to the university who had just finished their studies, and who received extremely low salaries. Most of the men had to start with 300 Thalers; others, if I remember rightly, at 200 Thalers, while some local men who applied for a position in Königsberg were not given any salary by the state. It should be kept in mind that the institution of the *Privatdozent* (the unsalaried lecturer) at German universities was originally characterized by the fact that such a person started his career at his own risk, depending only on whatever fees he could extract from his hoped-for audience. Many of these young lecturers, who had been posted to Königsberg by decree, tried to move away again, because they felt that Königsberg was too far removed from the center of German science; indeed, not a few succeeded in being sent elsewhere. Those who revealed some inclination to stay on, however, and whose lectures found favor with their students and with the board, while they themselves were found acceptable by the educated classes in the city, were soon granted raises of the stipend which were just enough for bare subsistence, but not more. These stipend raises were, however, rather unequal, and depended solely on the ministry. Thus, one of the young lecturers at that time obtained no raise at all and could not but feel that the authorities simply did not want to advance him any further, for which reason he soon gave up his academic career altogether. The first raise was followed by others, always in accordance with the reputation one had made for oneself as well as allowing for one's needs, as stipends stayed unequal all along and the government did not disregard the fact that one had to feed a large family or none at all, and also took into account any additional income or private means. Thus toward the end of my stay, my pay was 1,200 Thalers, with an additional yearly income of about 250 Thalers. This method made it possible to reshape the university within a few years without changing its statutes and to introduce entirely new subjects without having to retire any of the older professors, or even possibly reducing their income—which never happened. On the other hand, when a professor was regarded as superannuated, a younger lecturer was made available for the same subject. It is obvious that the minister and his councillors did not proceed without consulting with the university's board which, in turn, could obtain information from the faculties. Little became known through intermediate inquiries, however, and it was always the minister who appeared as the person in charge. This procedure is broadly the same as that followed by the other German universities. With the latter, however, the process of rejuvenation is more gradual and, being less in demand, fewer *Privatdozents* are paid a stipend at the beginning of their careers. Also, with most universities, the shorter distance to the center of German life was bound to cause fewer difficulties than was the case in Königsberg until the railroad was introduced. It is only thanks to the latter that Königsberg now feels itself a German university for all practical purposes: whether it takes seventeen or six hours to reach the capital, and whether one pays a few Thalers more for the journey appears to me of no consequence.

As much as these conditions in Germany are common knowledge, I consider it worthwhile to mention them again, because I found that Russia followed somewhat different principles, and I would like to express my opinion on their respective advantages and disadvantages. When in Russia one intends to raise the level of a scientific institute, one changes first of all the entire organization, imposing on it a new form, in which all subjects of study are laid down exactly, not only as to their number, but also as to their scope and extent. The common procedure is thus to establish an exactly defined framework which is then filled with content. But is it not exactly this line of action which impedes development over a longer period of time? No matter how circumspectly this framework has been designed, it will be appropriate only for the time of its creation, not for the future. To illustrate this, I need only remind you of the fact that it is but recently that scientists have learned to investigate the different animal tissues under the microscope, bringing about the development of a special branch of anatomy. Pathology, too, has learned to examine alterations of tissues, as well as expectorated matter, thereby gaining a better understanding of many diseases. This could not have been foreseen. Many a clinical teacher may be a competent practitioner without being familiar with the use of the microscope, if he finished his studies more than twenty years ago. Still more frequently, the opposite will be found, that a young man is very skilled with the microscope but far from having enough experience to diagnose the character of a disease from its general symptoms. Given the earlier structure of the institutes, this state of affairs could not possibly have been anticipated. How, then, to solve this problem? The simplest solution would be to staff every clinic with both a clinician and a microscopist. In Germany, this is exactly what happened quite of its own accord, through the *Privatdozent*—because it is mostly the latter who goes in for new directions and branches of the various disciplines. The advantages of the less rigidly determined framework are still more strikingly illustrated by the history of the physiological institutes. They are of quite recent origin. Purkinje, who was then in Breslau, was the first to propose setting up a special institute for anatomical-physiological research quite separate from the dissecting rooms. As he was a scientist of renown, his proposal was accepted. Before a quarter of a century had passed, such institutes had spread over all of Germany, and have contributed not a little to the development of science. How would that have been possible if the use of university funds everywhere had been decided upon beforehand?

For a long time our own (Russian) universities, beside professors, had only their assistants, for the institution of the *Privatdozent*, that nursery of future professors, was completely absent until now. Dorpat was the first to introduce it some years ago, but each faculty had only one salaried *Privatdozent* who, it stands to reason, also served as a substitute whenever the professors went on a trip. This is altogether an arrangement quite different from the institution of the *Privatdozent* as known and practiced at German universities. It was only very recently that the category of the *Privatdozent* was also established at our other universities, and that without any limitation as to their number, thereby creating that seedbed so indispensible for the rapid spreading of new branches and new forms of old-established sciences. Only thus is it possible to keep, and soon make use of, budding talent, rather than discouraging and losing it. If reorganization of the university in Königsberg was next to impossible without granting salaries to the *Privatdozents* posted there, it is still less possible in Russia, since opportunities to secure a living by participation in a journal or similar work in the scientific field are much scarcer. But to fix the salaries only at a later date, as demanded by the regulations, seems to me rather less helpful than the gradual and nonuniform increases which are the rule in Königsberg. And why have the higher authorities, as it seems to me, given up so many of their prerogatives?

The fact that the state is making substantial sacrifices to further the development of the universities with the new regulations must be recognized with the utmost gratitude, as it is no doubt desirable that a state of such political weight should participate in equal measure in the intellectual development of humanity. To further this end, the number of academic disciplines which should have their own professor has been greatly increased. Increasing the number of disciplines, it is true, also increases the number of teachers, but at the same time restricts the range of their activities. Thus, physical geography, for instance, has its own professor. The disciplines associated with this subject are probably also taught at every German university, but I doubt whether they have their own professorship. Usually, a physicist would lecture on meteorology, a geologist on the general attributes of stagnant and flowing waters or hydrology.

With the non-prescribed and therefore more lively development of the universities, everything which has drawn scientific interest and merited scientific treatment in recent times has been passing into the body of teaching matter through the institution of the *Privatdozent*, provided the number of teachers is not too small. As much as I welcomed the increasing number of lecturers who were hopefully expected to exert an educational influence by their social contact with their environment, and not only from the rostrum, I deplored the proliferating departmentalization. If, for instance, a university has two physicists, one of them undoubtedly will lecture not only on the application of physics to the earth, but also on any other physical discipline with which he is particularly familiar. Yet with the rigid division introduced in the organization of the universities, it will be regarded as nothing short of criminal trespassing, if not an outright declaration of war, if a younger lecturer, employed alongside an obsolescent physicist and charged specifically with lecturing on the physics of the earth, dared to try his hand at the theory of light by demonstrating and explaining, say, Bunsen's spectra. Light, not being of earthly origin, he could be told, did not belong to his domain. If, however, he were appointed as a physicist, the two physicists would either agree on a division according to their respective skills and experience, or else they would compete with each other in their lectures. In both cases, the students would gain. With a less rigidly prescribed subdivision of the disciplines, the government would also be in a position to make the best use of the qualifications of the individual. It is this remark that is prompting me to the present digression. In Königsberg, Burdach, who saw his literary activities as his particular calling, desired to limit himself to lecturing in physiology and completing his major work on this subject. As both I and my successor Rathke, approached zoology predominantly from the zootomic standpoint, it was possible for both of us to be charged with the anatomy lessons (which

Burdach wanted to be relieved of). If the zoologist had been mostly an entomologist or altogether a taxonomist, this transfer could not have been carried out. In other circumstances, it is possible for a zoologist to be better qualified to lecture on paleontology than the geologist, or for a chemist to be most knowledgeable in mineralogy. In other words: rigid predetermination of the outer form cannot be a substitute for, but often constitutes an obstacle to, an inner ambition. A pinch of rivalry, on the other hand, nourishes ambition.

Finally, I must give expression to a conviction of mine, which I know will not meet with approval either now or in the near future, because it deviates greatly from commonly held views and commonly prevailing conditions. As far as I could ascertain, it was the widely held opinion that justice demanded that all professors—full and associate, as well as the lecturers with fixed salaries (the former Dozents)—be paid identical salaries within each group. To me, this equality appears to be unnecessary, restricting as it does the influence of the government or the board. Today—as long as the rate of exchange is more or less stable, that is—the professor is very well paid, a most desirable state of affairs for a man who not only tries to keep up with the developments of his science, but also strives to contribute to this development. Much time is needed to merely follow a science in its growth; much more, however, is required to produce a substantial work based on one's own research. It would be desirable that one could find more time than is possible. It is therefore quite sensible not to compel such a man to search for additional means of existence, a principle apparently adopted by the government, because one or, at most, two lectures per day would not otherwise merit such generous remuneration. If, however, a man of scientific endeavor and ambition is compared with another who, having once prepared his lecture notes, goes on using them for his daily lectures until the day of his retirement, what kind of justice is it that demands an equal salary for both? "This should not happen any longer," one is inclined to think. Indeed, it should not, but such an aim would be better served if an authority, either the board or the ministry, were to express its appreciation by grading and progressively increasing salaries. This, of course, presupposes an ability on the part of the board and the ministry to indeed recognize scientific zeal and thoroughness. Such an ability must be assumed, however, since without it no positive action could be expected at all. Or again, what kind of justice opposes a salary increase to a lecturer, a former assistant, who for many years has substituted, and possibly more than substituted, for an ailing professor, just because—if I understand the rules correctly—the sick man refuses to die, while another lecturer is rapidly advanced because a suitable opening has materialized early? More freedom of action to the authorities whom, to be sure, I must assume to be benevolent as well as judicious!

But enough of these remarks which, for all I know, will be heeded only in the far future, since today popular opinion holds otherwise. I only intended to express my conviction that this popular opinion was based on a fallacy, possibly on a misleading comparison with work in an office. In an office, however, the clerks are supposed to devote a number of hours to others, while the professor must work not only for his lectures, but also for his own improvement and for the advancement of his science. If anyone not acting this way is given equal treatment with others, this seems to me to be less a measure of justice than of convenience. As far as the authorities are concerned, the graded salary determined only by equity, as practised at German universities, is far less convenient, to be sure. That it was precisely this practice which raised the level of German universities so highly is an undeniable fact, although it must be admitted that blunders are liable to be committed here and there, even with discriminating administrations. Did not the Prussian Ministry of Education let the illustrious Helmholtz move to another state where he found a more appropriate sphere of activity!

Such inequality, one keeps hearing, must breed envy. In answer to that, may I say that, far from doing any harm, some envy among teachers has in fact an invigorating effect. In Germany, more pernicious cases of envy have a way of taking care of themselves by emigration. Since in Russia all universities are subject to the same government, an evaluation of lecturers, should it ever be introduced, must not be the responsibility of both the minister and the members of the board, so that the possibility may be kept open of obtaining the recognition one feels is one's due at another place.

If I were asked to comment on what appeared to me to be a frequent failing of the German universities, to the extent that I have become acquainted with them, I would say that at times scientific achievements are valued above devotion to and ability for teaching. Considering the ultimate purpose of universities, teaching ability should really count for more. Teaching ability and devotion, however, are not always concomitant with scientific proficiency. But this, too, is a situation in which a freer disposition by the authorities can help by engaging a *Privatdozent*.

To return to my own story, the anatomical work I undertook consisted in part of occasional zootomic investigations, in part of drafting an anthropological work designed for the larger public, and, finally, of sustained observations in embryology.

The zootomic investigations were partly a continuation of dissections begun earlier on the more remarkable animals of Prussia, such as the sturgeon, the porpoise, the seal and the elk, and partly dissections that arose as opportunity offered. The anatomy of the sturgeon was brought to completion, although I published only a short paper on the lateral line of this fish (in *Meckels Archiv*, 1826, Illustration 1827). The sturgeon whose scutes, particularly those of the head, clearly indicate the type of vertebral division, afforded me an opportunity for writing a treatise "On the Outer and the Inner Skeleton," which took the form of an open letter to Professor Heusinger

Meckels Archiv, 1826). In it, I opposed the typical identification, then being attempted, of the exoskeleton of the arthropods with the bony skeleton of the vertebrates, and strongly upheld the ring shape as the original type of the exoskeleton. This letter seems to have left its mark, and has won recognition also at a much later date, for instance by Professor Bergmann, although I went too far in claiming that exoskeletons differed from endoskeletons in their texture as well. That was before Purkinje's pioneering work on the internal texture of bones.

I particularly persisted in the dissection of the porpoise (*Delphinus Phocaena*), obtaining at least one each spring and sometimes even two specimens. My intention was to prepare an anatomical study comprising all the organic systems of this animal, as typical of the cetaceans. A preliminary report was published in *Isis* of 1826 under the title "On the Porpoise (*Delphinus Phocaena*), Preliminary to a Comprehensive Anatomical Monograph on This Animal." Later I published a more detailed study, "The Nose of the Cetacean, Illustrated by an Investigation of the Nose of the Porpoise" (*Isis*, 1827). In this publication I attacked, on anatomical grounds, the current view of the water spout; I continued this attack in *Isis* of 1828, and resumed it later from St. Petersburg. Today, the erroneous view that the vapor spouts ejected by the exhaling whales consist of water taken in by way of the mouth has been more or less abandoned, although some professors still seem unable to do without it. At a later date, during my last stay in Königsberg, I presented a paper to the Leopoldine-Carolingian Academy on the greatly developed venous plexus in the abdomen of the porpoise. It was published in Vol. XVII of *Nova Acta*. But the complete monograph, which included a list of all the muscles as well as the description of the intestine and the vascular and nervous system, remained unprinted because I could not find a publisher. I had nine plates drawn to imperial folio size, and intended to have the work printed in that size. This, it turned out, was too much for German publishers. I turned to Cuvier, who was kind enough to offer me the hospitality of the *Mémoires des Savants étrangers* of the Paris Academy. In this case, however, the work would have had to appear in the French language, with the added difficulty of having to reduce the plates to quarto size. Being conscious of the great sensitivity of the French with respect to the correct use of their language, I did not dare to translate the work myself, neither could I find a competent translator nearby. To have the German manuscript translated in France seemed too risky, as I could not expect Cuvier to make a special check of such a translation. A short time later, Cuvier died. What is more, I began to have some doubts, as I found some discrepancies in the description of the muscles, prepared in different years. Finally, I also discovered some variations in the skeleton, particularly in the sternum, which, in the specimen last obtained, showed a lacuna in the center. The thought began to haunt me that the specimens that were so similar outwardly might in fact be two different types. Today I am inclined to regard this suspicion as unfounded, and to ascribe these small variations to the low degree of typicality of the cetaceans. These variations were also pointed out by my colleague Brandt, an experienced zoologist.

Later, when I had moved to St. Petersburg, I hoped to find an opportunity there for new investigations and for a critical revision of this monograph. The journeys to the far north were in fact partly undertaken in this hope. But it seemed as if my plans for an investigation of the cetaceans were definitely out of favor with the fates. When I came to Archangel for the first time (1837), a large school of white porpoises (*Delph. Leucas*) had just been caught at Sjusma, in the vicinity of Archangel. Yet when I arrived, all I found were skeletons littering the beach. Near Novaya Zemlya, where such catches were also frequent, none were made during my visit. In 1840, I made an effort to arrive in Archangel at an earlier date, but that year no school showed up that could have afforded me an occasion for interesting comparisons. The porpoise is a rare visitor to these waters, and the fact that it was often sighted off the Shetland and Orkney Islands came to my knowledge only very much later and at an advanced age. When information reached me to the effect that Professor Eschricht had made an extended study of the cetaceans and had collected a wealth of material, I had no doubt that he would soon publish a comprehensive anatomy of one of the porpoise types, and regard my own work as totally antiquated. Unfortunately I was wrong in my first assumption, and Eschricht published an excellent and comprehensive work which dealt only with the whales proper. In 1858, I personally offered him my monograph in case he should ever try to tackle the porpoises as well and could in any way make use of my own work. Before the transaction could be carried out, however, Eschricht, a man apparently in excellent health, suddenly died.

On the seals I have occasionally published some papers; others I held on to, until a suitable occasion would arise. Thus, the venous plexus in the abdominal cavity of the common seal, described and illustrated by Professor Burow in *Müllers Archiv* of 1838 (Plate VII), had been investigated by me and, already drawn by the then student Burow who was kind enough to help me with his drawing skill.

As no opportunity presented itself for a comparative investigation of a stag, the elk afforded me only little material for publication. I should like, however, to mention the interesting fact of the varying number of ribs of the elks, some of which were dissected in Königsberg for the local museum and some for other museums. The normal number, to be sure, was thirteen pairs as in most ruminants. But twice I saw an additional false rib on one side, and once I saw fourteen pairs of ribs. The last rib was sometimes free in the flesh. This seemed to reveal a tendency, in the larger ruminants, to an increase in the number of ribs; therefore, the fifteen pairs of ribs which Cuvier found in the American bison as opposed to the number found in the European bison or aurochs, did not, to my mind, signify any specific difference, since the ani mals are otherwise very similar in both their outer and inner structure. On one of the elks I noticed that the larger of the numerous cysticerci which had encapsulated in its omentum were encased in a very thick-walled, leathery shell which I sent to Rudolphi, together with its contents. My attention was also drawn to the remarkable difference in the mucous membranes of the anterior and the posterior walls of the soft palate. I have not observed such a sharp difference in any other animal in the lining of the tracheal and the esophageal tubes up to their crossing. I was also interested in the numerous hippobosci infesting all elks during the autumn, but would have liked to have seen them also during other seasons, for which no opportunity presented itself, as the elk could only be hunted in the autumn, and that only with special permission.

Other, more common animals were investigated as occasion or need arose, and yielded material for various smaller or larger papers. The "Contributions to the Knowledge of the Lower Animals" (*Nova Acta Acad. Caes. L.C.*, Vol. XIII) have already been mentioned, as has an investigation of the only medusa found near Königsberg (*Medusa aurita*). Because Rosenthal's revised version did not give to this last-mentioned description that recognition which I believed it deserved, I referred to my original version in a paper published in *Isis* of 1827, col. 847. In the 1828 volume of the same journal, col. 627, I disputed the views of Raspail, who had declared the *Aspidogaster* and other mussel parasites which I had described in the aforesaid "Contributions" to be mere "shreds of skin," and who saw in the different Alcyonaria only different developmental stages of the same type. I strongly defended the different nature of these types, which is now hardly in doubt. I also published some papers on the structure of our mussels (*Unio* and *Anodonta*), first on a system of water vessels found in these animals (*Frorieps Notizen*, Vol. XI), later "On the Path Taken by the Eggs of Our Fresh-Water Mussels to Reach the Gills, Including General Remarks on the Structure of the Mussels," and "Remarks on the Generation of Pearls," which appeared in *Meckels Archiv*, 1830. I also found occasion for some work on intestinal worms. Some living specimens of the *Bothriocephalus solidus*, which I found in freshwater, as well as many small sticklebacks (*Gasterosteus pungitius*) each of which accommodated in its abdominal cavity a large worm of the above type, appeared of such interest that I prepared a report for the Naturalists' Society in Berlin, which published it in its *Proceedings* (Vol. I, p. 388). At that time, general opinion held that intestinal worms could exist only in the insides of animals, and Linnaeus's report of having seen living tapeworms in open water was therefore met with doubt. Although some of the worms I had found were already weak, others were quite strong, and as some of the sticklebacks I had found had their abdominal cavity torn open by the worm which, compared to this limited space, must be considered very large, the bursting out of the worm must be seen as something quite natural or, at least, frequent. Today the fact is accepted that a considerable number of these parasites spend only part of their life within their host animals, and another part outside of them, when they are able, or indeed compelled, to live in the water. At that time, however, the opinion that all internal parasites, with the exception of insect larvae, were originally created in the host animal and did not invade it from the outside was so generally held that whoever believed in another possibility of transfer than that from the devoured to the devouring animal, was pilloried as a scientific fossil. Thus, when I found that mussels living in some water basins near Königsberg were almost teeming with parasites, while in other waters these parasites were entirely absent, I did not dare to opt for an introduction from the outside, which appeared to me the simplest explanation (*Nova Acta* XIII, pp. 553–555). I merely postulated a hereditary predisposition to generate these parasites.

A camel which had been brought to Königsberg sick and died soon after had occasionally produced from its mouth what looked like a bubble. A student by the name of Richter was entrusted to carry out an anatomic investigation on the cadaver which disclosed a fairly large fold of mucous membrane in front of the soft palate which, when forced out of the camel's mouth, could well have appeared to be a bubble, resembling as it did the bubbles often seen in camels in heat.

Altogether one may say that, considering the relatively small number of students graduating during my stay in Königsberg, many dissertations dealing with anatomical subjects were prepared, as well as some with zoological content. Without being able to vouch for the completeness of this list, I do remember the following: L. Jacobson: *De quinto pari nervorum animalium*, quarto with two engraved plates, 1818; Leo: *De structura Lumbrici terrestris*, quarto with two engraved plates, 1820; Reuter: *De lingua mammalium et avium quaedam*, octavo, 1820; Arendt: *De capitis ossei Esocis Lucii structura singulari*, quarto with engraved plate, 1822; Richter: *Analecta ad anatomen Cameli Dromedarii*, octavo, 1824; Lietzau: *Historia trium monstrorum*, octavo, 1825; Blumenthal: *De monstroso vituli sceleto*, octavo with lithograph plate, 1826; Koch: *De Talpae europaeae oculo*, octavo with engraved color plate, 1828; Neumann: *De Anodontarum et Unionum oviductu*, octavo, 1827; Kleeberg: *Molluscorum Borussicorum synopsis*, octavo, 1828; Rosenbaum: *De singulari cujusdam foetus humani monstrositate*, octavo, 1828; J. Jacobson: *Phalaena Noctua Gamma*, octavo with color plate, 1829; Berlack: *Symbola ad anatomiam vesicae natatoriae piscium*, octavo with lithograph plate, 1834; Burow: *De vasis sanguiferis ranarum*, quarto with engraved plate, 1834. These dissertations should be regarded as the work of the candidates named on the title, as they were charged not only with the formulation of the dissertations, but also with the investigation involved, although they required counselling with respect to the literature with which they could not be expected to be familiar. Whenever a candidate could not be convinced of the fallaciousness of his opinions, I thought it my duty as dean or examiner of his dissertation to let him state these opinions freely. Thus, J. Jacobson, having investigated the damage caused by the extraordinary proliferation of the caterpillar of the owlet moth, expressed his belief in spontaneous generation. As he stubbornly clung to this view, I did not try to prevent him from putting it in print, but I published a paper myself in which I treated such views as archaic.

A few words on my lectures on anthropology, before going on to the investigations connected with embryology. As early as the second winter of my stay in Königsberg, I had begun a series of lectures on the anatomy and physiology of man, designed for a mixed, nonmedical audience. Quite apart from the additional income from the fees which, at that time, I could not afford to regard with indifference, I saw in these lectures a challenge to devise anatomic demonstrations that were simple and easily comprehended, and to go on from basic anatomic knowledge to an understanding of the spiritual or mental life of man, and relate this life to those phenomena of nature that are not compounded of mere material changes. The lectures also included the physical and mental variations found in mankind according to the different races. This last subject caused me little worry or work; at that time people were generally easy to please. Blumenbach's representation of the five main races, increased to six by Peron's work with the South Pacific Negroes, and slightly modified by comments from Rudolphi, Cuvier, and Heusinger, seemed to suffice and could even be maintained in face of the further subdivisions by Bory de St. Vincent, Desmoulins, and others, which followed in rapid succession. Now that the question as to the variations and affiliations of the human race calls forth far wider interest and is being investigated by far more scientists, one would certainly be hard put to paint a clear-cut picture in answer to this question. Times have changed in this respect, too. Compared to the past, many more details are known today; yet, even better recognized is the fact that, as the differentiation and distribution of the human race is concerned, the unknown by far exceeds the known.

What attracted me was not this aspect of the subject, but the desire to obtain insight into our spiritual or mental nature and its relation to the corporeal and, indeed, to the world as a whole. It appears quite appropriate for me to say a few words concerning this matter, since this striving for insight is an integral part of my personal development.

The philosophy of Schelling, I said to myself, cannot be as empty as claimed by some of his detractors since many men of science are still sustained by the warmth of its rays. I, therefore, tried to make its acquaintance, although by shortcuts only, as my other professional duties on the one hand did not permit me to go through the complete works of Schelling and other authors of nature philosophy and, on the other hand, I was instantly put off, whenever I sensed some pretentious nebulosity, however attracted I otherwise felt by that daring flight toward the dawn in search of the source of light. As far as I remember, Oken's *Nature Philosophy* was the only larger work of this type which I had studied with any degree of thoroughness. The striking incisiveness of expression and the consistency of reasoning characteristic of this work appealed to me, but my most emphatic resistance was roused more often than not when, for instance, the author treated the negation of all limitation on the one hand, and the absence of all qualities, on the other—in other words, the absolute and nothingness (zero)—as identical, thereby arriving at the postulate: "God is self-conscious nothingness," a contradiction in terms if there ever was one. In the end, these recurring contradictions had a greater effect on me than the daring flights through mist and dawn, undertaken on the wings of the aesthete's yearning imagination, to find the source of light. Although such flights held a certain appeal for me, probably because I myself had originally harbored such yearnings, it soon occurred to me that, once the source of light becomes fully visible, mist and dawn quickly dissolve and, conversely, as long as the latter reign, the sun has not yet fully emerged.

Meanwhile I had erected for myself an intellectual scaffolding—although home-made and only slowly pieced together, partly with ideas of others which I had found congenial and partly with the fruits of my own supplementary cogitation—which seemed to span the whole range from the directly perceptible to the most general insight. This structure satisfied me completely for a whole winter, and I became my own most faithful disciple. But, alas, the doubts did not fail to materialize and soon loosened the foundations of the edifice. What bothered me most, because it increasingly began to tease my critical faculties, was a sentence that, at that time, seemed to me to contain the ultimate understanding of the world: "The (original) unity develops into a plurality; unity and plurality combined constitute totality." Did such a statement in fact contain an objective truth, I had to ask myself and if so, had it any validity except for the man who had derived it as the ultimate abstraction of many "sub-abstractions" of distinct experiences and observations and, what is more, who is also able to reproduce this derivational chain at any moment? For him alone, the statement is no more than a kind of mathematical formula, and a very vague formula at that, which, one might say, makes it in fact unmathematical again. Generally speaking, by the use of a highly refined abstraction, the genealogy of which is not directly before one's eyes, the intellect is able to prove whatever the heart desires. Once I had become critical, I could not disregard the fact that, contrary to my former belief, my scaffolding was by no means built from the foundation upward, but rather, as I gleaned, from the top downward, and was therefore a fantasy. It became gradually clear to me that however much my spiritual needs strove for complete and all-embracing comprehension, my talents permitted me only to advance from the specific to the general by abstraction, which still left me very much removed from the top.

I need not point out that, seen from this aspect, the philosophical part of my anthropological system progressively lost both weight and luster. I had hopes, however, of being able to rehabilitate it according to new principles in the course of time.

As I had promised my lectures in their entirety to a publisher, and as the illustrations were engraved long ago, I delivered the first half of the manuscript in 1823, and the second in 1824, both halves comprising the first volume which dealt with the corporeal aspects of life. Mental life, as well as comparative anthropology according to the races, etc., I reserved for a second volume. *Embryology*, for which I had begun very special research that seemed to be promising but had not as yet led me to the discovery of the mammalian and human ovum, was also intended for this second volume. The latter never appeared, however, primarily because I was too carried away by my research for my studies on embryology, and also because the treatment of the psychological section, as I had attempted it in my lectures, was no longer to my taste, which now favored a more empirical attitude along the lines indicated, for instance, by Kant. I simply did not have the required leisure. Already during the editing of the first volume, I could not escape the fact that I could produce in the special physiological part still not much certainty. Chemical investigations first began with Berzelius. The rather recent distinction between sensory and motor nerves held out some grounds for hope for a clearer understanding of the physical basis of consciousness, and provided some persuasive reasons to postpone publication. But the anatomical institute claimed my time in winter, and the first half of summer was necessarily dedicated to the *Embryology*. I would have been free during the second half, had I not agreed, first to substitute for Professor Eysenhardt; when he had to go on a journey for reasons of health, leaving me in charge of the botanical gardens, the botanical demonstrations, and the field trips, and later after his death. The first time I felt obliged by friendship, as I lived nearby; the second time to accommodate the board. From the financial point of view, there was nothing in it for me, since I was not entitled to a special remuneration. But the botany field trips involved still held some attraction for me as I regarded botany only as a neglected, not a rejected, mistress. Was it not Eysenhardt who had given me and some others a private course on fungi and confervae?

My numerous appearances in the newspapers, my anthropology lectures given to a mixed public, and the recent publication of these lectures, had gotten me perilously close to a slippery slope, particularly hazardous for a man of science: the routine of speaking to a large, nondiscriminating public. In such a situation one easily acquires the habit of relying unquestioningly on the authority of others, and it was only due to the *Embryology* that I managed to divest myself from these paths. Perhaps in the future one will be able, in this sphere as well, to be enlightened solely by the works of others. At that time, this was impossible; that is, if one strove for real understanding.

As it is my own work on embryology, to which I owe whatever claim I may have to a place in the history of the natural sciences, it seems in order to report further on these investigations here, in addition to what I have already related in a communication to Pander with which I prefaced the first volume of my work, *Ueber die Entwickelungsgeschichte der Thiere, Beobachtung und Reflexion* (On the Embryology of Animals; Observation and Reflection).

My interest in these investigations had its roots in Würzburg, in particular in the investigations initiated there by Pander in cooperation with Döllinger and d'Alton. As I soon had to give up participating in these time-consuming studies, I did not succeed in understanding their work. Early in 1818, Pander gave me his Inaugural Dissertation presenting an account of the changes which an incubated egg undergoes during the first five days, which, however, was incomprehensible to me. Soon after that he also gave me his *Beiträge zur Entwickelungsgeschichte des Hühnchens im Eie* (Contributions to the Embryology of the Chick in the Egg), including beautiful illustrations which excellently depicted the different stages, and which, together with the dissertation and some of my own investigations, gave me a complete understanding of the matter.

The lack of comprehension which the dissertation encountered, far from being limited to myself, must have been rather general. I would like to treat this subject in greater detail, because it was precisely this lack of understanding which was a great spur to me, as well as to others, to engage in special research. The frankest expression of this incomprehension came from Oken, who merits credit for being so candid—in his errors no less than in his insights. He himself had done some not inconsiderable work on the development of mammals, and had indeed perceived the continuation of the gut into the yolk sac, but had thought that he had thereby grasped the entire process of metamorphosis. He complained bitterly about the incomprehensibility of the description by C. F. Wolff who, much earlier, had carried out some very special investigations on the formation of the gut in the incubated chick. Oken therefore awaited with great curiosity the outcome of the Würzburg investigations and when he had obtained the dissertation, he at once reviewed it, in almost the last issue of the 1817 *Isis*. He reprinted essential sections word for word, and his comment alternated between words of praise and the strongest expressions of his lack of comprehension. For instance, having printed the beginning of the report on the state (of the chick) at the forty-second hour, he added, "As in Wolff, we do not understand. And would not, if we saw it. We would like to know if anybody does." After reproducing some more lines of the text, Oken again blurts out, "We do not grasp a single letter. It does follow Wolff, but precisely because of that, we do not understand. If indeed the alimentary canal is, so-to-speak, cut off below and if it protrudes like a trumpet with an open, free, clear, aperture, we are ready to eat our hat, etc." One would have had to eat much more than one's hat, if proof had been brought for the above statement, but it is precisely the description of how the end of the section of the alimentary canal already formed bends and continues in an entirely different shape that Oken failed to understand. In conclusion, Oken says, "After everything has been said and done, we must finally confess our failure to understand. We certainly do understand the development of the gut, but we do not understand Wolff's description of it, nor that of the present writer."

Some months later, the *Med. chirurg. Zeitung* (1818, No. 44) printed a review by Gruithuisen, who first cites from the two works of Pander, thereby appearing to indicate understanding and approval. But then, the reviewer suddenly stops and declares: "Drawing preliminary conclusions from the reviewer's first dozen observations, one may say that the transparent matter in the germinal disc is indeed the true, primary ovum, corresponding to that of the mammals." This statement reveals a misunderstanding of such colossal magnitude that a second or third dozen observations would hardly have been able to rectify it, if indeed there was any sense in seeing in the common poultry egg, known to any child, a primary ovum in the nascent stage!

Whence this misunderstanding? In part, it is probably due to the fact that everybody believes he knows something about the embryology of the chick; in part, however, it is because people have tried, but never managed, to understand the only accurate description to have appeared so far of the metamorphosis of the germinal disc (the so-called cock's tread) into the chick with the membranes sticking to it. To this description, therefore, we must return. About half a century before Pander, this transformation had been very carefully investigated by C. F. Wolff. Already in his inaugural dissertation, *Theoria generationis*, this investigator had stressed the need to replace the hypotheses which then prevailed by accurate observation. Transferred to the Academy in St. Petersburg, he began work on a detailed description of the changes which the germinal disc undergoes during the first days of incubation, although this paper, divided into three parts, only bore the modest title: "On the Formation of the Alimentary Canal in the Incubated Chick." Particularly thoroughly investigated and described is how the body of the chick first lies with its abdomen completely open to the yolk, and how it subsequently curves, growing in front, from behind and at both sides, with the edges, however, coming closer together, until after some time only the umbilical region remains open, which also eventually closes. Equally completely is described how the amnion forms, as the upper layer of the germinal membrane, from the head end, from the tail end, and from the sides, is directed toward the back and begins to form a circular or rather elliptical fold which draws together more and more, until it has completely grown together so that the embryo now lies in a closed sac. Thus these processes, which to be sure change the aspect of the nascent embryo, were completely understood by Wolff, but he described them in most excessive detail, superfluously naming all transient indentations, cap-like coverings, and other minute details which appear at different stages, then soon disappear. The breadth of his representation was still further augmented by the fact that Wolff, having described a transformation in great detail, likes to recapitulate, repeating his explanations in different words, with the result that the reader who has not been very attentive, or who has not quite understood the first explanation, is easily led to believe that something new is being said. This unnecessary verbosity and the proliferating nomenclature were not at all characteristic of Wolff, but appear to have been adopted by him in order to be better understood, a tactic which achieved the opposite. In his dissertation, *Theoria generationis*, Wolff wrote very concisely. Yet since this paper won less recognition from the older physiologists of his time than he rightfully expected, he apparently believed that the very conciseness made it unintelligible. I assume this to have been his reasoning, because a few years later he revised his first work and published it in the German language, in much greater detail, and also took issue with other authors. It was not obscurity, however, which had prevented full recognition of his first paper by the physiologists, but rather the extravagant hypotheses concerning generation and development which held sway at that time, and from which the older physiologists in particular were unable to free themselves. I presume it was this same striving for lucidity which misled Wolff in his third work, prepared during the years 1766–68 and printed in 1768–69, into a truly monstrous prolixity that, as mentioned above, produced the opposite effect. For a long period of time, this work remained misunderstood and ignored, and it was only much later, in 1812 in fact, that a German translation was prepared and published by J. F. Meckel, who thereby gave proof of his understanding, or at least made such understanding appear very probable. All other anatomists and physiologists seem to have absorbed only isolated details. Pander, who went through the entire sequence of changes in his own observations, must have had complete understanding. However, since he was influenced by Wolff's overabundant terminology and overdetailed description, and since his dissertation contained no illustrations whatsoever, the obscurity was not relieved. Anyone analyzing Oken's exclamations of noncomprehension, and being familiar with the metamorphoses, will immediately realize that it is the formation of the umbilicus and of the amnion which he did not understand, that is, the very processes which Wolff described so excellently, if with disturbing prolixity. Oken quite rightly demanded schematic cross-sections so that these changes might be made more graphic. At a later date, Pander sent him an explanatory letter including some drawings of cross-sections which greatly facilitated his understanding (*Isi* 1818, p. 512 ff.).

As for myself, I did not understand Pander's dissertation any better than others. In 1819, I turned to my own research and to Wolff's description which, on first reading, remained incomprehensible, since the more one read on, the harder it became to keep in mind all the details described earlier, and whatever illustrations existed, referred only to a few later stages. I read and re-read Wolff's text several times in succession, however, and suddenly I realized that this awful long-windedness could have been avoided by stating quite simply: The beginnings of the chick consist in a thickening of the germinal membrane, the lower surface of which rests spread out on the yolk. Presently, the dorsal surface starts growing faster than the ventral surface, while simultaneously the rudiment of the embryo expands from the front, the hind end, and the sides toward the ventral surface, providing it with a wall, with the exception of the umbilical region which remains open for a long time, but eventually closes up, too. Thus the embryo ties itself off from the yolk in its whole circumference, while at the same time the lowermost layer of its structure transforms itself into the alimentary canal. The formation of the amnion can be represented in similar terms; by the constriction of the center of the uppermost layer of the germinal membrane above the embryo, causing the embryo to become enclosed in a sac. The separation of the germinal membrane, i.e., of the enlarged germinal disc, into several layers escaped Wolff, but was followed by Pander.

This simple conception notwithstanding, it was still necessary to understand the transformations within the initial rudiment of the embryo, and the comprehension of these processes was no doubt affected by my former work in comparative anatomy. From early on I had tried to perceive the basic types in the different organizations and, burning much midnight oil and giving private lectures (see above, pages 151 and 153) in 1816–17 in Berlin, I had attempted to work out such a system. In 1819 I had already written a treatise on the classification of animals and, as I could find no publisher, had begun to have it printed at my own expense, but stopped the printer after the fourth sheet*, partly because, as it turned out, printing threatened to become too costly for my financial circumstances at that time, and partly because the freshly initiated investigations connected with embryology absorbed me completely.

Proceeding from the view that the vertebrate type was a doubly symmetrical one, a view that was increasingly confirmed the farther I progressed, I did not take long to realize that the two parallel ridges which appear first and which Pander had called "primitive folds," were in fact the two lateral halves of the back, which, for instance, in congenital Spina bifida remain altogether separate, and that the vertebrae do not originate next to these "folds," but right in them, or, if you wish, below them, because in fact the part of the vertebrae formed first is not that which clearly projects into the "primitive fold," but is located deeper down. It is therefore definitely incorrect to say that the vertebrae originate at points adjacent to the "primitive folds." In fact, the expression "folds" is really appropriate only for the outermost layer

*See Writings, section "Articles Intended for Publication but Not Printed."

which, in a schematic drawing, indeed assumes the shape of a fold. I therefore proposed the term "dorsal plates" and, for the analogous developments toward the abdominal side, the term "ventral plates." These two developments appear to have their origin, one could say their axis, in a line passing through the center of the spinal column, and right through the center of the forming vertebrae, and is seen as a relatively dark line which I have called "dorsal cord" or, still better, "vertebral cord"*. This was earlier observed in cartilaginous fish in many of which it more or less persists, being particularly pronounced in some of them, especially in the sturgeon. I could not fail to notice that the ventral plates are the origin not only of the lateral walls of the entire abdominal area but, by detachment of the lowermost layer—as already observed by Pander—of the gut itself. The latter in turn produces its own extensions which have their origin in sack-like hollow bulges, initially simple, then gradually branching out, and which I called "evaginations." The different tissues of bones, muscles, nerves, etc. are gradually formed in the interior of the remaining ventral plates. All the heterogeneous parts of the back develop quite similarly from the dorsal plates: the interior of the originally homogeneous tissues, consisting of globules in a semitransparent matrix (in the frog these globules are particularly large), turns into quite heterogeneous tissues, as required by the different body regions. The spinal cord, however, is formed by a process of detachment. It was the development of the spinal cord that took me longest to understand. The opinion prevailing at that time—apparently also shared by Pander—was that the spinal cord was generated by a process of coagulation taking place in the initially open, later closed, canals left between the dorsal plates. Others mistook the vertebral cord for the spinal cord, although the former is located much deeper in the trunk of the spinal column. I finally arrived at the conclusion that the spinal cord is created by a detachment, a process of exfoliation one might say, of the inner surface of the dorsal plates on both sides, and that its characteristic texture is formed only very slowly. This process is difficult, if not impossible, to verify in the chick, because even if a leaf-like layer can be detached from the inner surface of the dorsal plates, it cannot really be shown that this layer has not been formed by precipitation from the liquid. Proof of the real nature of this developmental process, however, can be seen in the frog embryo, the entire surface of which is of a black color. Thus, the dorsal plates in the frog, which assume the shape of rounded, initially distant ridges, are black on both sides. These ridges soon draw together and coalesce at their upper edge. The canal thus formed is at first all lined in black. Soon, however, the blackness is reduced, the pigment becoming more diffuse through continuous transformation of the globules of which the dorsal plates consist. It is soon possible to detach an inner layer of a pronouncedly gray hue from the outer layer. This

*[Ed. note: Discovered by the author, this is today known as the notochord or chorda dorsalis.]

inner layer is in fact none other than the spinal cord which gradually becomes white only after progressive internal transformations. Just as the gut forms hollow evaginations, so does the spinal cord, or rather its front end—the brain, because it is not only the separate cerebral vesicles, but also the innermost parts of the sensory organs, at least the higher ones—the eye and the ear, and to some extent also the nose—which are formed by such evaginations. These latter then proceed to fold in upon themselves, becoming invaginations, i.e., hollow extensions of the outer surface. Now, since the dorsal and ventral plates themselves are not formed by coagulation or precipitation from a liquid, but by proliferation of the germinal membrane, which in turn is formed by a spreading out of the germinal disc, no part of the body whatsoever is to be regarded as a precipitation or coagulation from a liquid, right back to the germinal disc which, being in fact the nascent embryo, should be called germ or some other name more appropriate than cock's tread. Whatever liquids there are serve only for nourishment of the embryo and do not add any new parts by precipitation. In essence, the development of the embryo is mainly nothing but the beginning of growth; only at its initial stage does it assume forms differing from those of later ones.

This I consider to be the main result of my research, in addition to the certainty that development is determined by the type of organization. To be sure, the manner in which the germinal disc or germ itself is formed did not become quite clear to me at that time, nor, I must confess, is it today. Since, however, in the not yet fertilized eggs of many animals there can be discerned a spot, located at the point of the future germ and very similar to the latter, though less rounded and more deeply immersed in the yolk, I had no doubt that the germ, too, was itself a product of transformation. The animal egg, consisting as it does in the main of a yolk mass, should not be regarded as a collection of liquids, but as an organized body the substance of which is very soft, consisting of nothing but globules with a little matrix. Since, furthermore, budding in all its variations, very common in plants and also observed in lower animals, is able to produce independent organisms, I did not hesitate to regard all reproduction as a transformation of parts which had already been organized earlier. The scion of a plant organizes while still on the maternal branch, at first as part of the latter, gaining by this development the ability of becoming an entity independently of the maternal plant, from which it becomes detached either spontaneously, as do the bulbous buds of certain lilies, the buds of polyps, etc., or else artificially, as in grafting or in the eying or cutting of potato tubers. Even when the scion remains on the branch, it follows its own development according to the norm communicated to it by the maternal plant, since a graft, even when transplanted to a tree of a different kind, will bear such fruits as are characteristic of its maternal plant. Procreation by eggs appears to be different only inasmuch as the eggs are specially formed parts of the maternal organism, able to develop only up to a certain point beyond which they are incapable of full development, unless exposed to the effect of the fertilizing agent. From this moment on, given propitious conditions, they will follow the same developmental route as did their parents.

I must have arrived at these general results as early as 1821, because that year I gave a short course at the Medical Society on embryology comprising three lectures, the draft of which I still possess. In them, the transformations in the interior of the embryo are distinguished by only a few words, sufficient to indicate the sequence of events. I am therefore unable to determine to what extent I succeeded at that time in understanding the processes taking place in the interior. Near the more detailed end of the draft, however, I find that I put great stress on some observations of Pallas, according to whom butterfly eggs developed without being fertilized, and I used these findings to point out a certain very general correspondence between plant scions and eggs, however different they were in other respects. Today, many such butterflies are known. In some types, this kind of reproduction is even the rule and, according to the interesting observations of von Siebold, it appears that the eggs of the queen bee develop into drones without the need for fertilization. Now there can be no doubt of an even greater correspondence between plant scions and eggs. If there is no absolute difference between scion and egg, however, no reproductive process may be regarded as an absolutely new formation, but only as a continuation of an ongoing life process, a continuation that becomes independent with both the plant scion and the fertilized egg— occurring later with the former, earlier with the latter.

As to details, however, there was still much to investigate. It is almost unbelievable how hard it is to capture a certain short, transient moment, even with hens' eggs, of which a large quantity is available. Thus I had long been convinced that all hollow ducts maintaining contact with the alimentary canal were in fact evaginations of the latter, but I was unable to observe the lungs in their nascent state. Either I didn't find the trachea at all, or it had already branched out. Finally, after a number of years, I discovered on either side of the esophagus a broad, gentle, but quite distinct widening, such as is illustrated in the second volume of the *Embryology*, Plate IV, Fig. 16. It seems that all the evaginations have their beginning in such a broad base, but then rapidly constrict and branch out. Wolff already made similar observations.

In spring, hens' eggs were hatched in the incubator; in summer I searched for points of comparison in other animal forms. The incubator—which ruins one's health because one never has a good night's rest if one has to watch over its temperature oneself—was later replaced by brood hens. I would advise against the machine, unless one can afford an attendant.

I had not yet thought at all of publishing my findings, which I wanted to be more conclusive, setting myself rather broad aims; too broad, in fact, as I had to admit later. I had hoped to be able to follow the development of all larger groups of the animal kingdom, when, at the end of 1821, together with my colleague Eysenhardt, I received a written invitation from Professor Burdach to take an active part in a large work on physiology which he was planning. As no details were yet available, the work being still in the projected stage only, we were afraid that such participation would burden us with many new tasks, keeping us from concluding research already under way. Our answer, therefore, was rather more declining than consenting. Soon after, Eysenhardt fell seriously ill, and died in 1824. Nevertheless, I let myself be persuaded at that time to promise some contributions, despite serious doubts as to the wisdom of preparing material for a work the structure of which was to be determined by somebody else, and which, because of its all-embracing ambition, would lead one either to express one's views, even if they were preliminary and untested, or to hold back one's views, making it appear as if one subscribed to the views expressed elsewhere in the manuscript. One is liable to experience such dilemmas even with one's own works if they are not well defined. But there one is always able to express doubtful opinions in a doubting manner, or else to circumvent them. I promised, however, first of all a rather detailed presentation of the development of the chick and of the frog. This was intended for the second volume of the *Physiology*, the first volume having been largely prepared by that time, so that all I could do was to promise that, if ever I should find occasion for supplementary or emendatory remarks, I would not hold back.

Thus, on the title page of the first volume, I was already mentioned as an author of contributions. Part of the manuscript was sent to me; I added to it here and there whenever additions seemed necessary, and voiced objections to some claims that I felt were untenable.

In 1825, the manuscript went to Leipzig. When I received the printed volume in 1826, I could not help feeling some annoyance. What I had least expected was to have been listed as a witness to research on the generation of Infusoria in marble, granite, etc. (Burdach, *Physiology* I, p. 18). Not that I had doubted at that time spontaneous generation or primitive generation, as I preferred to call it in contradistinction to reproduction. But I simply was not present when the jars were filled and, therefore, could not know whether the jars were well closed and the ingredients pure. While I was indeed present for a short while during the inspection, I did not have the slightest inkling that this inspection was to serve as ultimate proof for spontaneous generation. I still remember that in one of the jars a considerable amount of what seemed to be a fluffy substance could be discerned even with the naked eye. This was evidently the same substance one often finds in substantial quantities in poorly-corked jars in which pharmacists keep distilled water over long periods of time. There can be no doubt that it was "distilled" water of this kind which had been poured into the rather small jar and, with the water, also a fair amount of such confervae. I do not believe I had seen this part of the manuscript prior to its going to press. For other manuscript parts which had been sent to me I had prepared remarks and additions. These were not suppressed, about which I would have cared little, as I had not felt any need to have them printed to begin with. However, here and there I did indeed find one of my remarks or expressions of doubts printed, but with altered text. Other remarks, intended as real contributions, appeared to have changed their location or had been split up and put into different sections, which was liable to cause misinterpretations. While there is no sense in going into details, it seems quite obvious that it would have been appropriate to show me the manuscript again, to let me see how my remarks, some of them comments or expressions of doubt, would appear after the last revision of the text. Now, while it is true that I had not made my agreement conditional upon such a postrevision checking, I somehow took it for granted, since we lived in the same town.

I would not have mentioned this feeling of annoyance had not Burdach uttered an accusation against me in his autobiography, which I think merits some comment, as I have agreed to prepare an autobiographical report and I feel an obligation to explain the fact of the double appearance of the work on embryology. It will most certainly be conceded that it is not any touchiness on account of this postdated expression of thanks or any need to justify myself which motivated me, considering that I have known the facts for over fifteen years without ever having uttered a word. Even today, the subject is very painful to me, as I am quite conscious of the fact that I owe Burdach much, and that it was indeed Burdach who had steered me toward an academic career. I believe I have never denied or disregarded this fact. Besides, Burdach was in many respects a charming and witty person, but if I say that he never had the habit of, nor felt the need for doing much dissecting himself, I do not think I am revealing a secret, as the situation must certainly be well known. While this state of affairs suited me fine in some respects, I hope to be believed when I say that it also caused me some difficulties which I think I need not elaborate on. Was it not natural that I preferred to work independently? Yet I may state that I never refused a requested contribution and that, provided I had arrived at a result, I never held back my views. Thus, even if Burdach's request for contributions was less than welcome, his having made it twice, I thought I could not refuse. Generally speaking, our relations at that time were less intimate than they had been earlier, and it seems that both of us tried not to accentuate our differences. I therefore cannot understand the need, after I had stepped aside, for the accusation concerning which I owe the gentle reader an explanation—which, however, I beg to postpone for a few pages, so as to keep to the proper sequence of time—because before my larger contributions to the *Physiology* were handed to the printers, other work was in full swing.

Prior to the publication of the results of my research on the formation of the different parts of the chick embryo, I deemed it important to learn more about the differences in development of the principal types of animals, as well as to compare the development of different classes of vertebrates. While there was no opportunity of observing members of the Echinodermata in Königsberg, I saw enough of other types to perceive the difference. That the Arthropoda start forming from the ventral toward the dorsal side in two parallel excrescences, I learned from the eggs of small crustaceans of the order Isopoda. I found it very difficult to follow the development of the molluscs, using, as I did, mostly the eggs of freshwater snails and the small field slug. Although I did not succeed in going beyond what was observed and described by Carus, the absence of any marked center line showed that here, too, the type develops very early, possibly from the beginning, and the spiral convolutions of the embryos in their amniotic fluid indicate the direction in which requirements of tissue building act as a force of attraction.

Much time was spent on a detailed and protracted investigation of frogs and, occasionally, salamanders. I promised to have a report on the development of frogs ready for the second volume of Burdach's *Physiology*, while elsewhere I published some reports on early malformations, for instance, a case of acephalia found in a pig embryo in the early period of gestation (*Nova Acta* Vol. XIV), and a double chick embryo on the beginning of the third day of incubation (*Meckels Archiv*, 1827). In the spring, some street boys brought me lizards, but their stages of development were all rather the same; they were probably caught while searching for suitable spots to bury their eggs.

Primarily, however, I was attracted by the embryology of mammals, both as concerns the development of the embryo itself and the changes in the ovum during that development. Although I could obtain only very few embryos from the earliest developmental period, those few showed such a striking similarity with the corresponding stages of the chick that no doubt was left as to the correspondence of the respective modes of development. That the embryonic membranes and the general form of mammalian ova vary greatly in different families has been long known. But attempts were later made to reduce these different forms to a basic form which more closely resembles the fetal membranes of the more mature chick embryo. It was Dutrochet and Cuvier in particular who produced very clever comparative studies dealing with this aspect. According to their views, much greater similarities would be found if one were to trace all stages back to the very beginnings in these animals as was done with the chick, rather than limiting oneself to single, randomly chosen developmental stages. First trying this path with dogs, I came even closer to the original form and saw the great similarity between the developing puppy and the developing chick, in the configuration of head and body, with a gut that was closed merely at both ends, but over most of its length was connected to the yolk sac through a slit-like opening. At a still earlier stage I saw the entire developing embryo spread out on the yolk. The ovum itself had only incipient, hardly visible villi and, under the microscope, looked not much different from a very small bird's egg without the hard shell. Going back to a still earlier stage, I found very small, semitransparent and, therefore, hardly discernible vesicles in the oviduct which, observed under the microscope, showed a circular spot resembling the germinal disc. I found even still smaller, opaque, round, and grainy-looking bodies; thus I was almost forcibly led to the discovery of the ovum as it lies in the ovary prior to fertilization, although I would never have had the courage to start my search from what was in fact its ultimate aim.

To point out the importance of this discovery, and to explain my aforementioned lack of courage, some words seem appropriate on much earlier research which had had the same aim. Albrecht von Haller (1708–1777), a man of the widest erudition and of a prodigous diligence, was without doubt the foremost anatomist and physiologist of the eighteenth century. He worked independently in almost all branches of these two sciences, publishing most important and, at the same time, extensive works in these fields. Naturally he was also especially interested in embryology. He closely followed the formation of the heart and the circulatory system of the chick, as well as that of its skeleton. He was, however, not satisfied with his own, occasional research on the development of the mammalian ovum. Therefore, in 1752, that is shortly before leaving Göttingen (1753)—where he held a professorship—for his native Bern, he found an assistant, a student by the name of Kuhlemann, for a series of investigations to be performed at certain intervals on pregnant animals, starting from the moment of mating, which was carefully noted. Sheep were selected for this purpose. Kuhlemann took upon himself the very considerable costs, the tending of the sheep, and recording of the instant of mating. He also brought the slaughtered animals to the dissecting room, where Haller himself performed the investigation. About forty sheep were sacrificed. While apparently well contrived, the enterprise had rather unfavorable results. Although Haller realized that the vesicles, which had been found in the mammalian ovary long ago and which had been named Graafian follicles or eggs, for their discoverer, must have an essential effect on the further development of the ovum, seeing that in animals which are not yet in heat these follicles remain closed, and that as soon as an animal has been impregnated, a burst follicle is found or, in animals that produce multiple litters, several burst follicles are found, which are soon filled with a yellow mass, known as the yellow body (corpus luteum). Although Haller more definitely confirmed those discoveries made before him, he first recognized the developing ovum in the uterus only on the seventeenth day and only quite definitely on the nineteenth day, by which time it is already quite large. Investigations on different animals which Haller carried out at a later date did not produce better results. He therefore concluded that initially, a fluid was secreted and led into the uterus, where it becomes mucoid and, much later, produces the ovum by a process of coagulation. According to him, the first membrane to be formed was the allantois which, in reality, is the last one. One misconception naturally produced another; this, however, is not the place to follow his chain of errors. It is certainly important to know, however, that, sustained by Haller's authority, the idea came to hold sway that not only the fetal membranes but indeed the embryo itself coagulated in mammals by a kind of crystallization from a noncohesive fluid. This was precisely the explanation given to me at Dorpat University as to the genesis of the mammalian and, therefore, also the human embryo*. Today, it is quite incomprehensible that nobody after Haller had thought of carrying out a similar series of investigations. People simply got used to regarding him as the highest authority in anatomy and physiology. He wrote thousands of reviews, reporting on almost all new developments in these fields, and whether or not a young author won recognition depended primarily on Haller's judgment. In addition to this, he himself produced a body of work of such dimensions that to "study physiology" in the second half of the eighteenth, and as late as the beginning of the nineteenth century meant in fact to study Haller's works. That a man with such a prodigious output might possibly not be careful enough in his research, nobody seemed to have dared to imagine.

Yet by no means did all physiologists subscribe to those views which appeared to be the direct outcome of Haller's research. Some continued to hold the earlier prevalent opinion, that the Graafian follicles were the actual, original ova, and that as such, that is, in the closed state, they would be received and transported by the oviducts. Others left the question undecided. Then, in 1797, an Englishman, Cruikshank, appeared with the claim that he found rabbit ova in the oviduct on the third day after mating, and that they were much smaller than the Graafian follicles of the same animal. He must not have been widely believed; otherwise the true conditions would have been established long ago. Other observers had taken various pathological structures for the original mammalian ova, thus compounding the prevailing confusion. Eventually, the small and early ova of rabbits and dogs were rediscovered by two French authors, Prévost and Dumas, who published their report in 1824, thus preceding my own report by a few years only. They had seen the first beginnings of the embryo and had made some altogether very pretty observations. It was unexpected, however, that they would pronounce against what they thought to be the excessively small size of the ova as given by Cruikshank. According to them, the smallest ova of dogs which they found were still about one millimeter in diameter; others had measured two to three millimeters. They doubted that ova as small as those Cruikshank claimed to have found could in fact be transparent and detected. They thus never en-

*This view is still retained in the first edition (1826) of Burdach's *Physiology*, Vol. I, p. 75, without the use of the term crystallization, however.

tertained the idea that the original ova might be opaque and, therefore, visible even at a much smaller size. Indeed, it appears that they had encountered the original ova in the ovaries, but did not recognize them as such, because of their opacity.

This was the situation when I began to immerse myself in the subject. As early as 1826, I had several times found small, transparent ova of one to three millimeters in diameter, as had also been seen by Prévost and Dumas, located in the uterine horns and even in the tubes proper. In 1827, however, I found significantly smaller, much less transparent and therefore visible ova in the oviduct. I had no doubt that these were indeed ova, as it was quite probable that, originally, the yolk mass would be opaque in mammals also. In April or the beginning of May of the last-mentioned year, I told Burdach that I could no longer doubt that mammalian ova came fully formed from the ovaries, and that I very much wanted to obtain a bitch which had gone into heat only a few days earlier. At that period, according to the observations of Prévost and Dumas, one should expect to find the Graafian follicles still closed in dogs but ready to burst. It was the generally accepted view at that time that the rupture of the Graafian follicle depended directly on mating taking place, which, however, is not the case. It so happened that Burdach had just such a bitch in his own home, and she was sacrificed. When I cut her open, I found several Graafian follicles that had already burst, but none of the others were anywhere close to bursting. When, rather dejected because hope was again unfulfilled, I looked at the ovary, I noticed a yellow spot in one of the follicles, then in some more, indeed in most of them, and always only a spot. Curious! I thought; what might that be? I opened one of the follicles and, using the scalpel, carefully lifted the little spot into a water-filled watch glass which I then put under the microscope. Taking a single look through the instrument, I recoiled as if struck by lightning, because I saw a small, well-defined yellow yolk mass. I had to try to relax a while before I could work up enough courage to look again, as I was afraid I had been deluded by a phantom. Is it not strange that a sight which is expected, and indeed hoped for, should be frightening when it eventually materializes? To be sure there was something unexpected in what I saw. I had never believed that the contents of the mammalian ovum would resemble the yolk of bird eggs to such a degree. As I had used a simple microscope with a low-power objective, magnification was only moderate, and the yellow color, which turns black on higher magnification and illuminated from below, was still discernible. What had so frightened me was the fact that I had seen a sharply delineated regular globule, enclosed in a strong membrane and differing from the bird's egg yolk only in the coarse, somewhat loosely fitting membrane. The small, opaque ova I had found in the oviduct had had a yellow-white coloring, no doubt because the yolk was already dissolving; the larger ones were transparent. Some more of the yolk masses not yet dissolved were removed, all of them also being seen by Burdach, who had soon joined me.

The original ovum of the dog had thus been found! It does not float in an indeterminate position in the interior of the rather viscous fluid of the Graafian follicle; rather it is pushed against the wall of the latter and held there by a wide ring of larger cells, which disappears in the very delicate inner lining of the follicles. In all bitches I have dissected since then, I have recognized this ovum in at least some Graafian follicles prior to their rupture. If the walls of the follicles are somewhat thinner than usual, and if the ovary does not contain much connective tissue and fat, the ovum is easily recognized. If, however, the follicle wall is coarser than usual, and particularly if the ovary is rich in connective tissue and fat, recognition is very uncertain unless the follicle is cut open. Naturally I began to search for the ovum also in other mammals, and in the human female. Here I found the ovum to be more whitish, rarely with a yellow tint, and rarely recognizable from the outside without cutting open the follicle and resorting to using the microscope. Follicles of this type were most frequently found in pigs. Their ova are less colored, but if the contents of the follicles are carefully observed under the microscope, they are always found, even in still very immature follicles.

I soon understood why Haller did not succeed in finding the sheep ova and then only saw them later when they had grown to a considerable size. In the sheep ovaries, the ovum is of a faintly white hue and thus scarcely perceptible. If, moreover, one does not know that it is pressed against the inner wall of the Graafian follicle, it is liable to remain in the follicle when the latter is opened by a small puncture, and its contents are carefully poured out. The ovum will be found, however, if the handle of a very narrow scalpel is used to scrape out the follicle and to let its contents flow into a water-filled watch glass. Now, in the uterus, and even earlier in the oviduct, the ovum rapidly absorbs the liquid collecting in these organs. Due to this process, the outer membrane becomes elongated and very thin, and adheres closely to the uterine wall. As certain projections of the uterine wall, peculiar to sheep, start swelling with the arrival of the ovum and at the same time pressing against the latter, the outer membrane is torn almost of necessity when the uterus is opened and the sooner this is done after the death of the animal, the more certainly so. If one waits a little while, detachment has a greater chance of success. I have frequently encountered this problem with pig ova, which also grow rapidly in length. The outer membrane of these ova penetrates deep into the countless folds characteristic of the inner surface of the uterus of these animals, thereby itself folding similarly. As long as the ovum is very young, it is impossible to detach its outer, very delicate membrane from all these folds; that is, if one tries to do so soon after the uterus has been excised. If, however, one waits some hours or half a day, detachment is much easier. As soon as the ovum has become larger and, particularly, as soon as a bladder-like structure, the allantois, growing from the embryo and rapidly increasing in size, has reached and nestled against the outer membrane, the ovum becomes more solid on the outside and, in this stage, has been long known. In ruminants and pigs, the yolk sac, that membranous extension of the embryo which grows around and encloses the now liquefying yolk, is drawn out, forming two very long, thin cusps. The embryo is formed in the middle, between the two cusps, remaining small for a considerable period of time, but easily recognized once its length is about two and a quarter millimeters, if one looks for it carefully. At this stage, however, the cusps are still very thin, almost thread-like and extremely delicate, so that they are liable to be overlooked and torn, if one is not prepared for them.

This being the situation, the failure of Haller's enterprise is easily understood. To begin with, he was unlucky in the choice of his animals. He decided on sheep, no doubt because their tending seemed to pose the fewest problems. Then he probably thought he had to open the uterus as soon as possible, maybe even while the latter is still undergoing peristalsis, which it does quite vigorously as long as the organ is still warm to some degree. By prematurely opening the uterus, he could not but tear the outer membrane of the ovum. Searching now in the opened uterus, he could find no ovum, looking as he did right into one, not knowing that its outer membrane was torn and that the viscous fluid he saw was in fact the contents of the ovum. During the early days, he could easily overlook or misinterpret the embryo with the two delicate cusps of the yolk sac, because during that period the embryo has the shape of a small, elongated cushion, and he would not have known how to interpret the delicate cusps, even had he found them. But that he perceived the embryo only after it had grown to a length of 13.6 millimeters and had acquired a heavy umbilical cord with blood vessels, is curious indeed, and can only be explained by assuming that, at that time, delicate and painstaking research was not the rule. Besides, Haller had also dissected bitches and other female animals both earlier and later, only to arrive at the conclusion that the ovum and the embryo were formed only long after mating, prior to which all there was in the uterus was a viscous fluid.

It was thus Haller's misfortune by his very renown to have produced and spread some utterly false concepts. These, having come to prevail, must also be blamed for the fact that Cruikshank's discovery in the tubes of rabbits of very small ova, which could not possibly be Graafian follicles, was not followed up to find their point of origin. A contributory factor to this omission might also have been the long-cultivated *emboîtement* theory, according to which it was assumed that all future generations were already preformed in the ovaries of their ancestors but, being infinitesimally small, could not be recognized. Although Wolff courageously fought this soon-to-be-forgotten hypothesis of Bonnet—who presumably intended it as homage to the might and ingenuity of the Creator—the idea of the extraordinary smallness seemed to have survived, as shown by the fact that ready opportunities were passed up to look for ova in very small mammals, while there was probably a desire for investigating elephants and whales. But recognizability happens to follow the opposite rule: it was precisely the Graafian follicles of hedgehogs and mice in which I recognized the ovum without having to open the follicle, using only moderate magnification.

Be that as it may, the fact had not yet been recognized that even prior to fertilization, indeed long before the onset of puberty, the mammalian ovum is already preformed within a Graafian follicle in the ovaries. Only Prévost and Dumas seemed to have encountered the ovum, but they failed to recognize it for what it was. This is evident from their report, according to which, upon opening a follicle, they had twice found a small, spherical body with a diameter of one millimeter, but different from the ova found in the tubes in their much greater opacity. They therefore seemed to have failed to grasp the fact that the original contents of the ovum must have been a yolk mass which in mammalian ova, could well be as opaque as in birds' eggs. Instead, at this point, they demanded a reexamination of the connection between the true ovum and the Graafian follicle. Also, the size of one millimeter diameter given by them is much too large.

Essentially, the mammalian ovum is thus a yolk mass similar to the bird's egg, only very much smaller. In dogs, the yolk mass, without the somewhat loosely fitting membrane, has a diameter of less than 0.11 mm, and including the membrane, about 0.23 mm. In most animals the yolk mass has a whitish yellow or yellowish-white tint; in dogs and probably other carnivores, the color is yellow. The surprising smallness probably has to do with the fact that these ova rapidly absorb the fluid flowing into the oviducts and the uterine horns, once ova have entered. At first they swim in this fluid, but soon they grow small villi which, in a manner of speaking, take root in the uterus and are met by similar outgrowths from the uterus. Now secretion from the maternal body becomes even stronger, but so does absorption by the ovum, so that all that is secreted is absorbed. At the same time, the blood vessels of both sides branch among each other, without actually fusing. Thus, the ovum and, as soon as it becomes recognizable, also the embryo, are nourished by the mother via the egg membranes.

In birds, all this is quite different. Once the bird's egg is laid, it can obtain no more nourishment from the mother, only warmth. Therefore, all the substances the chick requires for its formation must be brought along, as its dowry, so to speak. Nature has solved this problem by making the yolk mass which forms in the ovaries very large, and by adding around this yolk mass a large quantity of albumen which is also used to nourish the embryo at a later stage. Lastly, a hard, calcareous shell is formed, enclosing the entire contents. The egg is now ready, but it contains only a germ, not a formed embryo. The mammalian ovum, on the other hand, is completed only when the embryo is ready to be born. In accordance with the order of animals to which they belong, the more advanced ova of mammals differ widely in their outer form and the constitution of their membranes which cannot be discussed further here. It is enough to state here that these relationships are determined by the shape of the uterus.

According to what I have said, I am entitled to ascribe to myself the discovery of the true process involved in the genesis of mammals, man included, readily admitting that this was due less to strenuous research or brilliance of mind than to the acuity of my eyesight during these years, and to the conviction arrived at during my work with the chick. My eyes, which because of their near-sightedness have caused me many an awkward moment in every-day situations, have given me excellent service during anatomical research in that they made small pictures quite clear. Once I made an experiment with an audience of twenty, in which I found only one person whose eyes I was prepared to regard as superior to mine, since he could see near objects as well as I could, yet he was not myopic. My eyes were especially adept at recognizing the slopes of surfaces in half-transparent objects by their shading, which helped me greatly, especially with fish eggs. I must also regard them as extremely handy, remembering that, later in my life, I had once continuously observed the cleavage of the black batrachian eggs for nearly two weeks, yet when I wanted to have them drawn, the draughtsman—who was also a copper engraver—was blinded to such a degree after two days that he had to give up the work. It was particularly my left eye that served me so faithfully. But for the last twenty years it has been weakening and now even large objects produce only a blurred image. It has done its duty.

The conviction which I had came to during my work with the chick, and which indeed had acted like a preconceived notion, held that all apparently new formations were in fact during their development transformations (pp. 211–212). This idea helped me in discovering the preformed ovum, in which indeed it found its most rewarding confirmation. Since that time, I could not but regard all procreation as metamorphosis of already organized elements, an opinion which I have later elaborated in public lectures, part of which were also printed (e.g. in *Reden*). Although the eggs of the lower animals are often quite transparent, their contents are in no case, so far as I know, completely liquid, so that even here one is entitled to speak of them as organized.

The egg is, accordingly, an organized part of the maternal body, which almost always requires the intervention of the male procreative substance in order to develop under propitious conditions, into the corresponding animal according to its type. However, in which way and by what agency the male substance, having reached the egg that earlier was only a part and as such destined to die unless fertilized, now renders this egg capable of developing, that is, capable of becoming independent, is as yet not understood. Equally puzzling is the way in which characteristics of the father, too, pass into the new individual. Since then, many details have of course been added to my original description, in particular, proof that the release of the mammalian ovum by no means depends directly on mating, but in part on the estrous cycle and the associated stimulation of the ovaries. I find it hard to believe, on the other hand, that the act of mating has no influence at all, as has been claimed, because female birds kept in isolation, while laying eggs now and then, do so only very infrequently, provided they are birds whose natural life conditions have not been disturbed by domestication. Birds and mammals cannot be very different in this respect. With mammals, too, yellow bodies (corpora lutea) are found not infrequently after estrus, that is, indicating that the Graafian follicles have released their contents, even without mating having taken place. But after an act of mating, this occurs with greatly increased frequency. Therefore, there can be no doubt that release of ova which, it is true, the ovaries can effect by themselves, is greatly enhanced by mating. Concerning fertilization or the capacity for independent development, the general result of countless investigations to which mine have contributed nothing of substance, shows that it is effected only by direct contact between the ova and the male agent. The fact, mentioned earlier (p. 212) that with some butterflies and with the queen bee fertilization is not indispensable, therefore constitutes a still unsolved puzzle.

The general result of my own investigations must be distinguished from that of Wolff's, as is clear from what has been said. Essentially, however, the difference is not as great as it appears on first sight. Wolff had in mind primarily the so-called preformation or *emboîtement* theory prevailing at that time, according to which the embryo was always present in the ovum, completely formed, but too small to be seen. It was the preformationists, who had fought courageously and victoriously, that he had in mind, but he called their theory evolution, countering it with his own principle of epigenesis, the truly new formation of all parts and of the entire embryo. Here he patently went too far. It is true that neither head, nor limbs, nor any other parts are already present, but they become. Yet small they do not come into existence by truly new formation, but by a transformation of something already existing. The term "evolution" thus appears to me more suitable for these phenomena than epigenesis or new formation. Nothing corporeal is preformed, but the course which development takes, which is completely that taken by the parents and which, with very limited variations, as in parents, so it is the invisible, the course of development, that is preformed, and one can therefore state that the process of life is a continuous one through the entire progeny, a process that is only temporarily dormant (in the formation of the ovum, that is), and that creates new individuals by restarting its course after an act of fertilization or, with the formation of scions in plants, simply continues its course, since the scions, detaching themselves from the maternal plant to lead an independent life, began their life as part of the maternal body. The lower the organization of a living individual, the more reproduction becomes a mere extension in time of the individual life, so that with the very lowest stages of life, growth simply becomes division into several individuals.

It was never in doubt at that time, that alongside reproduction based on transformation, low organisms may also be created anew, giving rise to new series of reproductive cycles. Today this concept of spontaneous generation without parents has become highly problematic, the great majority of present-day scientists regarding it as completely refuted, although some difficulties remain unsolved. This applies particularly to the question of the origin of existing stocks and their series of offshoots. Be that as it may, the proof that mammalian embryos do not coagulate out of a fluid, but develop by a series of transformations from a previously organized corpuscle, was a weighty argument in the above matter. If the previously held view of the genesis of mammalian and human embryos from a fluid had prevailed to this day, the other view, concerning spontaneous generation of simple organisms in all sorts of infusions, would hardly have given way that easily.

I have dwelled on the present subject at great length, because there is no sense denying the fact that, to this day, I am very much pleased to have made that discovery, although I will be the first to admit that this was more a question of luck than of merit. I decided to publish quickly and sent a hurriedly drafted report in the form of a letter of thanks to the Academy in St. Petersburg which had appointed me a Corresponding Member. The report was entitled, "De ovi mammalium et hominis genesi epistola, etc." and I sent it off in the middle of July 1827 to Herr L. Voss of Leipzig. As there was only a simple copper engraving to prepare, I had no doubt that the paper would appear in the course of the aforementioned year; the text itself did not exceed a few printed sheets. Because of its subject matter, I believed I could also submit it to the great concourse which takes place in Paris at the end of each year; therefore, I prepared my letter to the Academy in good time. The copper engraver, however, interrupted his work on my plate to accept other work, which caused my paper to be published only in January 1828 although the year 1827 appears on the title page. It probably reached Paris only about the end of January and the only answer I was given was the same "too late" that later was to be so fateful to the House of Orléans. In the beginning, the book indeed caused me more vexation than pleasure. I had intentionally chosen the title "De ovi mammalium et hominis genesi," so as to indicate in the very first line that not only had I searched also for the human ovum, but that the general description given was intended to apply to it as well. When I was about to send the title for the fair copy to the printer, I began to have second thoughts asking myself whether it would not be wiser to leave out "man". I would be ridiculed for this tautology, and asked whether I did not know or, indeed, whether I doubted the fact that man is a mammal too? But I had to answer myself, such a reproach would be much less hurtful than the spectacle of somebody boastfully announcing that he had found the preformed ovum, which you had seen only in animals, now in the human body as well. I therefore left the title as it was. But one cannot escape one's fate. The first printed evidence relative to my paper was the announcement by an anonymous reporter in a German journal, to the effect that now a Frenchman (I think it was Velpeau) had detected the ovum, found by me in animals, also in the ovaries of human females. How indeed could one expect a German reporter visiting Paris to be conversant with title pages published in Leipzig? What good did *homo* do, after all? Maybe I should have said *femina*.

Minister Altenstein, to whom—following an old custom—I had sent a copy, reacted by saying that he was glad I had rediscovered the mammalian ovum in the ovaries. My paper apparently carried no news for him. A heavy silence prevailed in the reviewing institutes during the whole of 1828. That did not really surprise me, as it is not unusual for an entire year to pass before a paper is somewhere announced, especially a paper by a still rather unknown man. Much more surprising was the fact that when I took part in a convention of natural scientists in Berlin in September of that year, not a single one of the anatomists with whom I became acquainted even so much as mentioned my paper. The paper had been made available to the public as early as the middle of January, and it was highly unlikely that no one had heard of it, especially as I had taken care to have it sent to some of them. Moreover, worrying that my letter to the Academy had been too concise, I had published a detailed commentary in Heusinger's *Zeitschrift für organische Physik*, Vol. II (January 1828). I was too proud or too vain to bring up the subject myself in Berlin. Was my work regarded as a joke or a gross mistake? Or was the subject matter itself of too minor an importance to bother about? I really and truly did not know. But from as early as 1821, the Göttingen Scientific Society had established a prize for the discovery of the site of origin of the mammalian ovum and, in 1824, had awarded that prize to a work by Hausmann according to whom the ovum coagulated from the fluid involved, and long after the mating act at that. Even though completely misrepresented, the subject appeared to be of interest after all. That the older men would not read my paper or, at least, would not let it shake their convictions, I could well imagine. But that the younger participants, also remained silent—that I found disturbing. Finally, on the very last day of the convention, Professor A. Retzius—a Swede, not a German!—asked me. "Could you not show us the mammalian ovum in the ovary?" "With pleasure," I replied, "if I can obtain a bitch." Such an animal was found by the janitor of the anatomical institute, and the demonstration set for the afternoon. A rather large number of anatomists turned up in addition to Retzius—Johannes Müller, Ernst Weber, Purkinje and other acquaintances, as well as strangers. Yet it almost appeared as if the perfidious fates wanted to play me a nasty trick. The janitor's bitch was so well nourished that it had put on masses of fat everywhere, even on the ovaries so the Graafian follicles were barely visible. Was it that mass of fat or a certain nervousness on my part? I was unable, at first, to discern a single ovum without dissection, something which had never happened to me before. Finally, I saw one shine through faintly and brought it happily under the microscope. As far as I could make out, everybody seemed convinced, although I am certain that they had been rather doubtful earlier. In any case, I must assume that none of them had ever tried to locate the yolk mass or the ovum, possibly because they had thought that the operation was too difficult, which it is not.

The first of the reviews which I saw in 1829 was written by Dr. Plagge (in *Heckers Annalen*, February 1829) who most emphatically ascribed the discovery of the mammalian ovum to himself. To substantiate these claims, he also soon published a treatise in *Meckels Archiv* (1829), including an illustration. The latter, however, clearly showed that he believed he had found the primitive ovum surrounded by three loosely fitting membranes in an open Graafian follicle in which the "yellow body" was fully developed. The "yellow body" however, forms only after the true ovum has been released. In this treatise Dr. Plagge challenged me to open the history book, to convince myself that Graaf had already found the true ovum where it was formed. He, Plagge, only regretted that he lacked the opportunity to check Graaf's work himself. I had been so diligent in acquiring earlier works on embryology that I happened to have Graaf's *Opera omnia* in duplicate, one of which I sent to Dr. Plagge, after I had underlined all places which clearly show that Graaf mistook the follicles, later named after himself, for the true ova, for which reason they were originally called *ovula Graafiana*. Primarily due to Haller's counterclaims, they were later reduced to mere *vesicles*. Still, these claims of Plagge's do constitute a recognition of the preformation of the ovum. Soon after that, other reviews were published, one by Purkinje in the *Jahrbücher für wissenschaftliche Kritik*, two by anonymous reviewers in the *Literatur-Zeitung* of Halle and of Leipzig, respectively, and still others at later dates, all of which admitted the discovery and more or less recognized its importance. Confirmations did not fail to materialize. In the sixteenth volume of the *Annales des sciences naturelles*, in 1829, Prévost described the ovum in the ovaries of the cow quite correctly as opaque, of from one-eighth to one-third millimeters in diameter, and as lying closely against the wall of the Graafian follicle. Neither did he doubt that it reached the uterus via the oviduct and that it absorbed moisture. He also did not fail to state that it was similar to what he had seen earlier in dogs. He only forgot to mention, however, that on that earlier occasion he had not regarded it as the ovum; that in dogs he had estimated its diameter to be about one millimeter; and that later it was found by somebody else who had recognized it for what it was, and also that even as late as 1827 his colleague Dumas had a liquid-filled vesicle leaving the ovary. *Article: Oeuf in dict. classique.* Generally speaking, however, I must no complain about France. Férussac's *Bulletin des sc. médicales*, as early as 1828 or 1829, carried a very emphatic report that the problem which had been pursued for centuries had only now found its solution. It was only recently that I have learned of this report. I also still remember recognition by Coste, but I have already forgotten the sequence of later declarations of recognition, and it would be a waste of time to try to reconstruct it. In Germany, in any case, when I left Königsberg, there were not many. Whatever doubts there were must have been very persistent, since Hausmann, the director of the veterinary school in Hanover, was able to expand his prize-winning treatise in which he denied preformation of the mammalian ovum and to publish it as late as 1840. By now he had found the ovum in the ovaries, also calling it *ovulum*, but he claimed that this was not the true ovum, as it dissolved. The true ovum was formed only after nineteen to twenty-three days, according to the type of animal, and came into being complete with all membranes, the embryo, as well as the blood vessels! This, as far as I know, was the last assault on the *ovulum praeformatum*.

As to objections and corrections, I will only remark that in the review mentioned, Purkinje had expressed his objection not to an observation as such, but to its interpretation. In the chicken egg, that is, as long as it is still in the ovary, Purkinje had noticed a small, completely transparent vesicle in the center of the whitish spot which is later replaced by the germinal disc. This vesicle disappears during the time the egg passes through the oviduct. It appears, however, to have an essential connection with the formation of the new individual, because of its location at the precise spot later occupied by the germ. I had investigated the immature eggs of animals lower than the mammals and found this vesicle everywhere at, or at least, very close to the surface, except in very young eggs. The same relationship applies to the mammalian ovum with respect to the rest of the Graafian follicles. I had therefore believed that the mammalian ovum, also surrounded by a circle of specific cells and pressed against the follicle wall, could be seen as originating in that germinal vesicle which, however, had taken on all properties of a complete ovum or, in other words, that the Graafian follicle produced a genuine ovum from its germinal vesicle. It was this comparison that Purkinje objected to in his review, as did other authors also, in fact, most of them. I admit that I am still unable to rid myself completely of this view, but would like to remark that it was meant to refer only to the process of formation. It should be quite clear from my paper and the commentary that, functionally, I regarded the mammalian ovulum as a true yolk mass which contains everything essential for fertilization. Expressed in the language of the cell theory, the following picture is obtained. The bird's egg, like the egg of most animals, is a cell containing a much smaller cell. Here, the yolk substance collects in the large maternal cell, since a large quantity of this substance is produced as the first nourishment of the embryo. Much less nourishment in the shape of yolk is produced in the mammalian ovum, since the maternal body continuously supplies new material. If one assumes that in this case the yolk is deposited in the inner cell, one at least preserves the original picture of the cell within a cell. The cell theory seeks out the remotest similarities, calling even the plainest of lumps which has neither a cavity nor a membrane by the name of cell. I obviously regarded my hypothesis only as an interpretation which helped me to understand generation. Without it I would have to regard the Graafian follicle with its fluid content as a newly created part not present in animals other than mammals. We uphold the principle that in other cases differences at a later stage can be traced back to original conformity. If so, why is application of this principle wrong in precisely this case? At a later date, I had occasion to do an experiment that seems at least to raise the possibility that the functions of these nested cells might switch. I had frequently performed fertilization experiments with the mature eggs of sea urchins, when I obtained a holothurian, the eggs of which, though still in the ovary, appeared to be quite mature. These eggs consisted of a large cell which contained a much smaller cell, both with quite transparent contents. Without further reflection, I took the small cell to be analogous to the germinal vesicle. To my great surprise it was precisely the small cell that divided, splitting very regularly into four parts. I could not follow the process any further, because the eggs soon spoiled. I do not want, however, to press my hypothesis. After all, it is indeed no more than a hypothesis, although, it appears to me, a quite natural one, which devalues the mammalian ovum as little as it is an offense to the human hand if one says that the last section of the bird's wing corresponds to the human hand. Also, some years after my paper, much was made of the discovery that a germinal vesicle or cell had been found in the mammalian ovum. This had not escaped me completely. In various places I mentioned a cavity in the yolk of these ova. Thus, in the *Commentary* (Heus. *Zeitschrift* II, p. 138) it says, "The ovum consists of an inner, dark, granular, spherical mass which appears to be solid but, upon closer investigation, reveals a small cavity." This is supplemented by a remark, "During the mating season, the cavity in the mature egg becomes very distinct." In the central Figure (IX) of the *Epistola*, the cavity is also clearly drawn. All this could, and indeed should, have been taken into account. That I have not called this cavity a cell is merely due to the fact that Schwann's cell theory only later came to light.

I refrained from any remonstrations or claims. It was all the more gratifying to me that later, sometime after 1840, such men as Reichert, Bischoff, Remak, and Kölliker, who spent much time and acumen on the study of the earliest stages of human development, and compared to their efforts my own work could only be regarded as a first building block, mentioned my work in such a spirit of friendliness and esteem, that I feel very much obliged and am all the readier to admit that I had had no more than the good fortune to have shot a flare into the darkness. To have given occasion for investigations of such subtlety and thoroughness is now, in my old age, rich compensation for having been ignored for some time. I am in no position to do full justice to all these works, nor is it my intention to make such an attempt. I will not here refrain, however, from taking the opportunity for an apology that was admittedly due twenty years ago. Professor Bischoff, who in many splendid monographs ("admirable" the English would say, who in their appreciation are accustomed to convey a more spirited language than we Germans) has followed the development of mammals starting from the preformed egg, had expressed his amazement at the fact that I apparently had failed to notice the division of the yolk during the earliest stages. Yet I had noticed it and rather frequently at that time but, in 1827, rather indistinctly only, as the yolk mass in the oviducts had a rather furrowed rim, probably because cleavage had already progressed a long way. After 1830, however, I observed division several times in the earliest stages and very clearly too, although not the first, but definitely the second division as well as another one in which I counted six division products, but where there might well have been eight. But I mistook all these eggs for spoiled or otherwise malformed, as I did when I poured away the artificially fertilized fish eggs, because I saw two large bulges, and soon four, on this surface, and regarded them as rotting, since unfertilized eggs also exhibited all sorts of bulges. That was, of course, an error on my part, but the blame must be borne by him who later gave proof of the division of the frog's yolk mass, publishing his findings in *Müllers Archiv* only in 1834. When eggs are seen in isolation and cannot be followed through the transformations, as with the earliest mammalian ova, such a process is very hard to guess at. If my memory does not fail me, this guilty person is, however, myself, because the furrows in the frog egg described and drawn, partly very wrongly, by Prévost and Dumas, did not permit such a conjecture. Bringing proof of the abovementioned yolk-mass division was almost my concluding work at Königsberg, to which I will return at a later point. Cleavage of the germinal layer only, without the rest of the yolk, as in fishes, was shown by others after me.

But enough now of the primordial ovum of the mammals and the conclusions directly following. Before dealing with the fate of my contributions to Burdach's *Physiology*, I should like to make brief mention of some other works on mammalian development published until 1839, as the promised contributions did not deal with this class of animal. Even prior to the publication of the *Epistola*, I had published an article: "On Viviparity, etc., in General as Such" (*Meckels Archiv*, 1827, pp. 556–568) and, at the same time, another: "On Gills and Branchial Vessels in Vertebrate Embryos," to be followed soon by another article in the same *Archiv* (1828, pp. 143–148), on "Mammalian Gills," which confirms Rathke's beautiful discovery of the transient gill slits of air-breathing vertebrates, supplements it with respect to vessel formation, and refers in particular to mammals, while using other classes for comparison only.

After the publication of the "Letter of Thanks," I combined the observations on the more developed mammalian ova, particularly with respect to the main differences of gross morphology and inner distribution of blood vessels, into a single treatise to be dedicated to the jubilee of Samuel Thomas von Sömmerring, a meritorious anatomist. The paper carried the title, "Investigation of the Vascular Connection between Mother and Fetus in Mammals. A Congratulatory Treatise on Occasion of the Jubilee of Samuel Thomas von Sömmerring" (Leipzig, Voss, 1828, Fol.). In fairly great detail and accurately, I believe, this treatise presents above all a description of the pig ovum, the outer membrane of which was until then taken to be smooth, but is really full of folds and villi containing manifold vascular networks. The history of the so-called *Diverticula*, which have no villi and contain only dead vessels, is given more completely and coherently than had been the case until then, as is proof of the fact that the vascular plexuses in the chorion appear to depend on a kind of attraction from the opposite surface of the uterus. Even with the unaided eye, I could clearly discern small openings in this inner uterine surface, the mouths of very long, twisted canals. As interpreted later by E. Weber, these were thought to be ducts of glands, on which I am not in a position to give an opinion, as I later had no opportunity of carrying out an investigation to clarify this point. At that time, I was inclined to assume that there was a direct connection with the vascular system of the placenta; as a result, the choice of a preliminary name for these vessels, "suction vessels," was unhappy. Although I could not establish it, I believed in their connection with the veins, because others had found quite sizable veins opening into the inner surface of the human placenta and because of my own experience, that if laying hens receive injections into the blood vessels, the injected fluid issues through preformed openings in the widened section of the so-called uterus. I have nowhere mentioned this occasional experience of mine, because I intended to perform some more detailed research which somehow never materialized. I hereby recommend this particular subject to younger scientists for further investigation.

I believe that the detailed observations I have made on blood and vascular formation in the chorion of the ova of ruminants have shown the existence in the younger villi of fetal cotyledons, of hollow spaces which filled up by injections via the chorionic vessels, and into which leads the outermost vascular network of the villi. Because these spaces are blood-filled in life, they have been named "blood lakes." These appeared to lack any kind of walls, so that these transient, small blood lakes in some way resemble the wall-less blood circuit of the hen's egg. Also new, as far as I know, was the observation of small chorionic villi in a stellate formation between the large fetal cotyledons.

I was most surprised, though, by the fact that as long as the fetal cotyledons are not completely formed, the extreme ends of the blood vessels pass from the placenta into the cotyledonal villi, but spread only over their surface, approaching the fetal blood network very closely, without ever fusing with it. This at least appears to be the conclusion to be drawn from the fact that, after a short maceration, the fetal villi had detached themselves from the uterine cotyledons in such a way that maternal blood was seen to have penetrated the outer layers. All of this seems to indicate that the maternal and the fetal circulatory systems attract one another but, having achieved proximity, again move away from each other, probably because an exchange of substances has indeed taken place. I therefore felt entitled to call the entire article, "Investigations of the Vascular Connection between Mother and Fetus." In a review, Carus has reproached me for this title, because there was no longer any doubt that the two circulatory systems were separate. But nowhere had the fact been remarked upon that the outermost branchings of the maternal vascular system indeed penetrate the topmost layers of the ovum and yet do not link up with its vascular system. Another reproach referred to my failure to draw for every artery the corresponding vein. This was accounted for by the fact that I had drawn no more than I could clearly perceive. In the case of the more mature ovum of the dog, however, it was quite impossible to reach the chorion without causing numerous tears. The same review calls the term "urinary sac" offensive and unsuitable, suggesting instead the term "respiratory bladder." That the umbilical vesicle, the erythrois, etc., of the mammals was in a way an analogue of the yolk sac of the birds had long been recognized, so it appeared appropriate to me to call the other membrane a sac as well, as it is also a pedicelate sac and communicates with the embryo via a canal. Now, since the contents of the sac are in fact a secretion of the embryo and contain uric acid, I did not hesitate to call it a urinary sac. The conventional term urinary bladder is hardly more elegant, but we take no offence, as we are used to it. What matters with a name is, therefore, habituation. On the other hand, giving a name has its difficulties and easily gives rise to objections. The name "respiratory bladder" is thus open to the objection that the allantois merely serves to raise the embryonal blood circulation up to the chorion, which is in fact where the respiratory function is performed, while in many ova the inner mucous layer of the allantois is completely separated from the vessels, standing well away from the chorion. Also, in hoofed animals, the allantois grows so rapidly that it breaks through the ovum at its ends, and has so little to do with respiration that whatever vessels it has carried along die off. What causes it to push along so rapidly is presumably its fluid content, which can hardly be ascribed to the small embryo alone, but to the ovum as a whole. As soon as the chorion has assumed its respiratory function, the excessive secretion of this fluid falls off. In birds, correspondingly, this secretion does not increase to such a degree because the shell membrane is soon filled with a ramified vascular system. Non-hoofed mammals appear to be midway between the birds and the hoofed animals.

Glancing once more through the article mentioned here, I find that, toward the end of paragraph nine and in the beginning of paragraph ten, the expression "placenta" was used instead of "embryonic membranes," which is liable to cause misunderstandings.

When in the winter of 1826–1827 I sat down to write the promised contributions for Burdach's *Physiology*, I keenly felt the limitations one takes upon oneself when one not only agrees to accommodate onself to the general plans of someone else, but also when one finds one has to fit a ready-made outline. The development of the chick and the frog was to be described in chronological sequence, which I felt as a constraint, since the interpretation of an observed process is often possible only at a later stage. I nevertheless agreed to comply, on the condition that the development of the frog was to be described only according to periods, as the rate of development varies first according to the amount of heat supplied and, later, according to the amount of nourishment available. Thus, the development of our common frog (*Rana temporaria*) at first usually proceeds faster indoors than in the open, where, in our latitudes, the water is rather cold at night. Subsequent stages, however, proceed faster in the open than indoors. What I found quite impossible, however, was to merely recount the observed happenings without developing some views and opinions of a more general nature. My very method of investigation and observation was permeated with general ideas and views which, in part, I had brought with me and, in part, formed in the course of the research. Indeed, I believe that without such speculations and hypotheses, which one expects to be either supported or refuted, one's work would resemble that of E. Home who, in 1822, in the *Philos. Transactions*, reported on the development of the chick in ten beautiful copper engravings, from which one learns not much more than the fact that the chick does indeed grow progressively larger. I therefore declared that I could not help interspersing remarks of a more general nature in my report, and this condition was accepted. My reports were delivered during the first months of 1827. There had been no intention to have detailed drawings, to supply which would have been difficult in any case. My own talents for drawing were minimal. The few figures which I had done for *Meckels Archiv* or others, were prepared with great effort and had undergone many changes until the lines had the proper shape, and even so they were not much more than sketches. A draftsman reasonably experienced in the preparation of natural history drawings could not be had for any amount of money. I therefore made some schematic longitudinal and cross sections of the embryo, because this seemed the only way to give a graphic explanation of the transformations of the first period. I also used different colors to bring out the formation of the gut from a part of the originally ventral surface of the rudimentary embryo, a surface which, at the same time, is also a part of the yolk sac. It was this last-mentioned formation which Oken had misunderstood in all other representations, because he had gotten used to the assumption, current at his time, that the gut grew out of the yolk sac. One of these schematic representations clearly shows this transformation to be essentially a pinching-off process. Although this sort of drawing did not demand excessive amounts of cleverness, I was still quite happy with its clarity. Later I learned that these drawings, as well as parts of the manuscript, had been sent to various people, particularly to Rathke of Danzig, to help him arrange his own representations, although Burdach never told me of this. Now I trust nobody will suspect me of regarding colored cross sections as an important invention, even if I was pleased with their clarity. Also, it would never have occurred to me to refuse them to Rathke, had he requested them, as we had excellent relations, regarding each other as colleagues working in the same field. But it was the secretiveness which galled me, being an indication of the fact that even prior to publication, Burdach regarded everything communicated to him as his private property, to be disposed of at will. In the second half of 1827, Burdach wrote to me proposing to transfer a number of paragraphs and also some whole sections of my presentations to other sections of the book, sections which I, however, had not yet even seen. This proposal, listing about thirty places, is still in my possession. But of the subsequent negotiations, which were partly in writing, I did not keep any record, not foreseeing that I would later have occasion to refer to them. It must have been these negotiations, however, to which Burdach referred in the remarks of his which I mentioned earlier. As far as I remember, I agreed to the deletion of entire sections, for instance, of what was later to become paragraph eight in the independent publication, but would not permit the transfer of single remarks to surroundings unknown to me. This matter remained unresolved where the second volume of the *Physiology* was already being printed. As I was unable to obtain the proof sheets supplied from time to time by the printers, as they appeared to be needed daily for checking errors, and as I also failed to obtain a second set of the proof sheets—thus not knowing at all what had become of my contributions—I decided in the spring of 1828 to publish these independently. This was to be a special work, including some general reflections appended to it under the title of *Scholia and Corollaries*, and for the preparation of which I needed no more than about one month. The book therefore, appeared as early as August 1828 under the title *On the Embryology of Animals, Observations and Reflections, Part I*. (Königsberg, Bornträger, in 4°.) A third plate was added to illustrate some typical details.

Earlier (p. 214), I mentioned the fact that, in his autobiography *Rückblick auf mein Leben* ("Recollections of My Life"), Burdach brought some accusations against me. Here they are (pp. 378–379):

"The advantage of being able to use and report to the public his (Baer's) investigations, I had to pay for, however, with many an annoyance. Baer often used to express his wishes quite unclearly and incomprehensibly, or even not at all and, subsequently, showed irritation and suspicion if one did not act according to what seemed to him clear demands." Such an accusation was what I might least have expected, as it was precisely Burdach who was regarded, by other members of the faculty, as a man whose opinion one had to divine because he used to keep silent whenever he felt hurt, but made his feelings known in other ways. We were indeed quite used to this. The following example will suffice to illustrate my point. Burdach had added to his *Literatur der Heilwissenschaft* (Literature of Medicine) a third volume, including the literature of 1811–1820, and gave it to me (1821), with the request that I look through it and let him know whether I had anything to add or comment upon—but he had to have it back on the very next day. Good-naturedly I undertook the task, sitting up half the night over it, but, having collected no titles for this purpose and there being no time for a more thorough search, I could add nothing, apart from some dissertations which I happened to have at home. Also, Burdach was known to be very painstaking in these compilations. I noticed, however, that the monographs on the salamander and on the proteus were mentioned under the category of "Sauria." Now it is true that Linnaeus had placed the salamander in the genus *Lacerta*, but once the new division into Batrachia and Sauria had been adopted, the salamander could no longer remain with the lizards. On the evening of the next day I went to see Burdach and brought him my modest contributions, as well as the above remark. Burdach did not say a word, but clearly conveyed that he had taken offense; yet I was left in doubt as to whether I had offended him by being late, although reading through the entire volume took me nearly twenty-four hours, or my additions were too few, or whether indeed it was my remarks concerning the salamander. As for the latter, I certainly could not have spoken arrogantly, as I could hardly have claimed any credit for this piece of knowledge which was already incorporated into all the textbooks. When this volume of the *Literature of Medicine* was published, however, I found the salamander and the proteus still with the Sauria, so I could only assume that the proposed transfer had not been welcomed. Has the book really profited by this? But to continue: "Altogether he (Baer, that is) has shown excessive irritability and complained with great vehemence"—in such moods one is usually quite explicit—"about my arbitrary method to obviate repeated consultations, wherever I had myself decided on changes concerning minor matters." I must have made myself understood, after all. We lived in the same town and saw each other frequently, in winter almost daily. It would not, therefore, have been too difficult to forward to me the displaced paragraphs in their new contexts, or to clear the matter with me orally, showing me the intended changes. What was I supposed to think, however, of changes which I had not seen, especially as Burdach later acknowledges the fact that I had demanded my contributions to appear as a small work in a major one. But let us continue and conclude the indictment, adding whatever comments I might like to offer as footnotes.

"He (i.e., always the defendant) was very much upset by the fact that I had not accepted his embryology of the chick embryo as an undivided whole but, following the plan of my work, had taken his general remarks which he had woven into the special history of development, and put them where these general relations were just referred to*. He had mentioned belly plates and back plates. Now, since the belly constitutes the lower part of the trunk, and the back constitutes the hind part of the chest, and since, on the other hand, these parts cannot be simply called fore and hind plates, as the article deals not only with man but also with animals, I selected the morphologically derived names of visceral and spinal plates, another act for which Baer could not forgive me**. Throughout the entire work I had made it a rule to trace

*For all that, these detached fragments will taste differently, depending on the dough they are baked with, and therefore one prefers to do one's own baking. As an example, let me refer to page 112 of the first volume. Talking about the oviducts of molluscs, Burdach in his manuscript had relied on Treviranus as his final authority. Now Treviranus, who for incomprehensible reasons does not admit the existence of the two outlet openings shown by Bojanus, assumes the oviducts to lead into the intestinal canal, specifically mentioning the Anodonta. To this I remarked that the openings shown by Bojanus were surely the outlets, and that, when the eggs had achieved a certain degree of maturity, I had been able, by applying pressure on the ovaries (foot), to force them through this duct and out of the openings, thereby confirming Bojanus' reliable observation. While retaining the quotation from Treviranus, Burdach added, "still, two tubes which serve as oviducts open between the foot and the inner gill". This is followed by my comment, in the usual parentheses. Now, Burdach having thus supplemented his own text, my remark not only becomes superfluous and contradictory, but the impression is almost created as if I wanted to appropriate Bojanus's observation. In some of the Anodonta, these openings are uncovered, with others they are hidden by the skin passing from foot to gill. It was such a species that Treviranus must have had before him, failing to cut through the covering skin.

**So it is the change of name which I could not forgive! Did we perchance exchange opinions on the subject? No, I learned of the changes only when the book was almost completely printed. During the preparatory stage nothing was mentioned. For months my contributions lay unprinted in Burdach's possession, during which period I could have made changes. It was this secretiveness, culminating in the withholding of the proof sheets, as opposed to my completely unqualified openness, that I could not stomach, and it is quite likely that I should have expressed my annoyance, although I do not remember having done so in this particular case. Had I been given the chance to discuss the matter, my terminology would not have appeared so ridiculous at all. I searched for expressions which would fit all animals, at least the vertebrates, which were always seen in the horizontal position, only man constituting an exception. Now, ever since Illiger, the lower side of a vertebrate—and of a bird in particular—is known as *Gastraeum*, belly side; in the words of Illiger, explaining his technical term, "the lower, or sternal side from the throat to the rectum." The opposite side Illiger called *Notaeum*, back side. It was therefore quite legitimate to speak of "Rücken-" (back) and "Bauchplatten" (belly plates), writing, as

(Contd.)

every new perception or discovery back to the first intimations or hints. When, in following this rule, I had mentioned two precursors of two of Baer's discoveries, he reacted as if I wanted to belittle his own findings*. These, and God knows what other misunderstandings, finally induced him to publish his work, including additions,** separately and without my foreknowledge† (*On the Embryology of Animals*, Königsberg, 1828, 4). In this book (page X), he also explains that his action was precipitated by my unwillingness to publish his contribution as a small work in a major one††. If I had wanted to answer that, I would have said that the opus happens to be a system, and not a collection of small works. However, I was conscious of the fact that I had dealt with him honestly and openly§ and kept silent§§."

I did, in German. It was more difficult to form suitable adjectives from the Latin term. And, by the way, since when is the "back" the posterior part of the chest? Do fish and frogs have no back? Especially in amphibians, where there is no separation between thoracic and abdominal cavity, in fishes where the thoracic organs are shifted below the head, the need arises for an expression for the entire upper and lower side of the trunk. To no lesser degree does this hold true for insects in which the abdomen is constituted by a more or less pedicled rear trunk with a belly and a back side.

*One of these discoveries is obviously the mammalian ovum. With regard to this, I should initially be stated, of course, that several authors had already seen it, that is, Prévost, Cruikshank, as well as Graaf, who saw it in the oviduct. As for seeing it in the ovaries, however, at best Prévost saw it without realizing what he saw. In any case he reported it as much larger than it is, thus giving grounds to doubt whether in fact he saw it at all. As to the second discovery referred to, I do not know what was meant. Was it perhaps the manner of development of the Arthropods which starts from the ventral side? Well, more about this below!

**This refers to the second half, comprising the *Scholia and Corollaries*, which are really given to general reflections. Whatever appeared in the reports as general remarks were only said here to elucidate the typical progress and could already be found in the original text.

†I do not remember how early I informed Burdach of my decision, but it certainly was before I sent off the manuscript. Be that as it may, I never intended to make a secret of my decision. The publisher was in Königsberg; the second half was written in Königsberg, where the third plate was also engraved. I still remember a letter written to Rathke in which I said that in the supplement I would go "through thick and thin," and that later we had laughed about this expression. And why the secret altogether? I saw only too clearly that I should have published on my own, before the second volume of the *Physiology* had appeared.

††Long before I delivered the material, in fact when I had started to write the article, I had done so on the understanding that I would be entitled to intersperse some general remarks. Can an intelligent report be written without saying that the plastic organs, too, are symmetrical, until the embryo turns on its side?

§Does that also apply to correspondence and other communications (to other parties) of which I was informed only by Rathke, and the extent of which I do not know even to this day? And was I supposed to show equanimity in face of this secretiveness?

§§The silence I can indeed attest to. As somebody's Aunt Sally said, "A misunderstanding arises when one person does not understand another." However, if one person keeps silent, the other will certainly fail to understand him, even if he should try.

But why bring up this accusation after twenty years, long after I had left and was now dealing with quite different subjects? When I independently published my description of the development of the chick, I also gave my reasons for doing so, despite the fact, which I also stated, that the later days of embryonic life had not yet been sufficiently investigated. I thought that the matter could have been left to rest at this point. But Burdach's intention perhaps becomes clearer in the following. In order to show that his difficulties with me had their root in my personality, he stressed the fact that his relations with Rathke had always been free of problems. This I do not mind, for Rathke was certainly a man of honor, but it should be remembered that Rathke did not live in Königsberg at that time, which precluded oral consultations, and that Rathke had always been in the habit of having his investigations published as soon as possible, while I, striving for general results which always require much comparative work, was in no hurry and had in any case reserved for the *Physiology* those parts that seemed verified beyond doubt. Burdach himself should have suggested to me to have my work first printed and then to prepare an abstract—if he could not accept the condition I had set, and which was known to him beforehand, of also giving general conclusions—or else he should have made this proposal after he had read the manuscript. In fact, however, he expressed great satisfaction with the latter and it was only several months later that I received, in writing, a list of the sections he wanted to place elsewhere. In the same section of his autobiography in which Rathke's qualities are appreciated, there is a paragraph which bears commenting upon: "He (Rathke) always told me openly whenever his views differed from mine and was quite tolerant when I advanced an opinion differing from his." Now this I believe I did also, even at the risk of encountering an expression of mute injury, as happened in the salamander affair. Burdach continues: "In the preface to his work on the development of river crayfish, he (Rathke) mentioned that I had drawn his attention to the position of the yolk in the spider embryo, and had asked him to see whether this situation, which deviates from that found in the vertebrates, also prevails in other invertebrates, namely in the Arthropoda. This quite unexpected mention was a very pleasant surprise, and I believe that I have shown myself worthy of it by exhibiting a similar literary scrupulousness." On this point I beg to report otherwise, or rather, I have already reported otherwise, including the dates concerned—and the contradiction revealed is quite pertinent to my argument. Having mentioned the typical similarity of the development of all vertebrates, the *Notes on Development of the Egg of Mammals and Human Development* (p. 24) goes on to state, word for word, "Indeed, with regard to invertebrates, I discovered with Burdach—even before Rathke's publications—and in 1824 in public lectures (as the students' lecture outlines will show) taught that their development proceeds in articulated animals from the belly to the back. Rathke was apprised of this by Burdach and at the beginning of the summer of 1825 he took issue with us in writing; but in the summer of the same year he made it his own public teaching (namely in *Isis*, 1825, p. 1098), instructed, to be sure, by his own very astute observations." To this is appended the following footnote: "With these matters now set forth publicly let there be peace between us after our slight vexation, which I felt for one reason only, that already at that time I might have published the distinction between vertebrates and invertebrates had it not been my hope that I might add this to my friend's observations; in this hope, I was relying on studies which, while indeed sketchy, were nevertheless adequate to show this distinction." All this was read by Burdach in the manuscript which I had shown to him before sending it to the printers, and I had asked him for his comment on the Latin expressions or anything else needing correction. On this advice, I changed the syntax of one sentence, to make it better understood. Otherwise he made no objections, nor did he comment on the above-cited sentences, which were occasioned by the following developments. Made aware of the problem by Herold's *Embryology of the Spiders*, I asked myself whether the development of the Arthropods did not proceed from the ventral toward the dorsal side. In trying to find an answer, I examined some crayfish eggs which, however, did not provide a clear-cut answer. But in eggs of our freshwater wood-lice I observed stages which did not leave any doubt. I saw a lower center line, bright but thickened, and at both sides darker rising masses which, according to my nomenclature, I called "plates," and which were still in a very undeveloped state, thicker at the ventral side, but thinning out and finally disappearing toward the back. There could be no doubt on that point, as I had observed the same phenomena in several types of eggs of other aquatic Arthropods, some of which I was even unable to classify. Later, Burdach asked me about this problem, possibly because he, too, had been made curious by Herold. I told him about my observations which left no doubt. The expression "I discovered with Burdach" is thus used as an illegitimate extension. At a later point Burdach told me that he had informed Rathke of my view and that Rathke had disagreed with it. Still, I stoodfast by my opinion and suggested that in so small an embryo as that of the crayfish, which I knew Rathke was working with, it would be more difficult to perceive the true conditions. At a later date, Rathke accepted my view and, at the end of 1825, published a preliminary report in *Isis* on his investigations of the crayfish, including a special section on the original line whence the development of the Articulates begins. I wrote a letter to Rathke in which I expressed some resentment (the above "vexation") seeing as how he had at first disagreed with my contention based on my research, that the development of the Arthropods began at the mid of the ventral side; but now, having changed his opinion, he proceeded to publish. Given our previous relationship, I had expected him to have informed me beforehand, to enable me to prepare a short report, as I had not yet begun any kind of continuous investigation of the development of the Arthropods. In reply he told me that e had known nothing about my own work, since the development of the Arthropods from the ventral toward the dorsal side was a hypothesis that Burdach had represented as his, Burdach's own. While Rathke had thus to be absolved completely, I intentionally mentioned the affair in the *De ovi mammalium genesi*, to stress the point that a person who has been busy for years with research on embryology, who had promised the results for a book to be edited (by somebody else), and who had not published anything of these results on his own, until that book had appeared—such a person deserved some consideration and regard in communications, both oral and written, to third parties. All this encouraged me in my decision to publish my work leading to the discovery of the mammalian ovum at the very earliest moment, and not to wait until the last detail had been worked out. I did not do so with other research which took much more of my time because I felt an obligation to accord priority to the *Physiology*. At that time I still believed in mutual sincerity, a belief which I had to abandon, however, when I heard of correspondence and communications concerning my work—from several sources except the one source which should have asked or at least informed me. Also, there were clear signs, after I had sent off the *Epistola*, that my contributions had been altogether too many. I thus decided on the separate publication which I had always had in mind, but which now had to be expedited. I had to reveal my reasons openly, but I think I did so with forbearance, to wit page X of the preface, etc. As far as I was concerned, the matter was now settled, and I thought I still deserved some gratitude for having unstintingly put the results of my research at the disposal of a work on physiology which ought to have begun with embryology. Of recognition there was indeed enough in the *Physiology* and the *Autobiography*, but the belated expression of gratitude cited above I could not leave without comment, as I found it impossible to agree with the adjectives "open and honest" which the other side appropriated for itself at least as far as it concerned me. Page 62 of the second volume of the *Physiology* presents a detailed polemic against a certain interpretation in my *Epistola*. Yet Burdach had been given the manuscript, and I would gladly have heard some objections, but there had been none. Now it can be argued that such objections could have crystallized at a later date. Hardly! After continued research, I myself changed and thoroughly discussed this interpretation in the "Commentary" (*Heusingers Zeitschrift*, Vol. II, p. 174), and this issue of the above journal had reached Königsberg in January 1828, at least at the same time as the printed *Epistola* did, if not earlier. It follows that the aforementioned objections were noted down after the perusal of either the manuscript or of the printed work, in which case my own rectifications had been ignored. And why were the most suitable terms "spinal" and "visceral" plates withheld from me? While the striving for perfection in the *Physiology* is most laudable, it is not served by the proliferation of nomenclature. Should I mention the various attempts of others to prove that they had seen what I saw, only earlier than I did, attempts that often were quite beside the point, such as the claim that Girgensohn had lifted a medullary membrane of the rhomboid fossa and had thus observed the original closing of the spinal cord. This is quite correct, but belongs to a much later period*.

But that would be too much of a digression. Rather, I must ask the kind reader to forgive me for this rather unpleasant discussion which I might have dispensed with in a scientific work on embryology, but could not in a biographical notice. It was admittedly my mistake to have tried to maintain for too long the relationship of the former student and, especially, to have exhibited it to an unconscionable degree in the *Epistola*. Now, at the age of seventy-three, I hold that Burdach, being the older man, should not at that time have accepted my prolonged restraint. Whether modest or immodest is quite besides the point here. He who consciously pursues his work always knows the real value of his findings, and who indeed would engage in exhausting investigations unless he was in search for something of value, even if it were only for his own enjoyment? The more conscious the search, the more of one's very self in the findings.

After such lengthy explanations, I shall say no more about this first volume of my *Embryology*, except that it appeared shortly before the meeting of Naturalists in Berlin (September 1828), and that I used the occasion of the meeting to hold a public lecture on the development of the chick and of the vertebrates in general. Also, that this volume was translated by Bréschet and that, in 1831, I was surprised to receive a medal from the Paris Academy. This medal was all the more welcome and unexpected, as I had had absolutely no hand in it, still remembering as I did the "trop tard," and as Alexander von Humboldt had taken it upon himself to inform me of the award, while Cuvier sat on the jury, of which he informed me later. In the citation by the Academy, mention was made of both works, the *Epistola de ovi mammalia genesi* and the *Embryology*.

*A few words only concerning Graaf, whom not only Plagge considered my precursor but whom Burdach also originally intended to represent as such. It was also Graaf to whom the ministerial "rediscovery" referred in all probability. I must presume that behind the minister, who could hardly be credited with this piece of literary verification, was my old friend and well-wisher Rudolphi, whom I had provided with intestinal worms. There must have been something in Graaf after all which caused people to see in him more than there actually was. That he called the follicles carrying his name "ova" is a fact beyond dispute. Had he not prepared drawings of a bovine ovum in the ovary, giving a diameter of one inch? But he had also seen ova in the tubes of rabbits, which he specifically described as considerably smaller than his presumed ovarian ova. Yet this did not convince him of his error. He explained the difference in size by the assumption that upon entering the tubes, the ovum leaves behind part of its substance. But what could have misled persons without repeated first-hand experience with this subject, is Figure IV of Plate XIV. There, a completely closed and developed "yellow body" (corpus luteum) represented as an ovum. This ovum, however, is nothing but a little lump of mucus literally a stop-gap.

I was even more flattered, however, when in 1855, more than a quarter of a century after the publication of the *Embryology*, the excellent Huxley sent me an English translation of the fifth *Scholium*, which he had incorporated into his journal, *Scientifical Memoirs*. Although I had long lost sight of the *Embryology*, to the first volume of which I had appended the *Scholia*, yet I remembered very well that, in writing the *Scholia*, I had intended to show that if one wanted to draw more general conclusions from the study of embryology, there was more to be said than was interspersed in the history of the chick. After apologizing in the preface for translating a somewhat less than recent work, Huxley goes on to say, "On the other hand, it seemed a pity that works which embody the deepest and soundest philosophy of zoology, and indeed of biology generally, which had yet been given to the world, should be longer unknown in this country," which is something that can be copied, but not told in the German language without some blushing. What is to follow cannot even be copied—with or without blushing—without raising some opposition.

13. An Interlude in St. Petersburg (1830)

When I composed the open letter to the Academy of St. Petersburg in July 1827, I had no inkling of the fact that Pander, who for several years now had been a member, had already announced his intention of resigning from the Academy. In fact, in the preface of the letter, I addressed him as "Member of the Academy." I was therefore not a little surprised when, soon after the manuscript had gone to the publisher in Leipzig, I received a letter from the botanist, Dr. Trinius, in which he enquired as to my readiness to accept a zoology professorship at the Academy of St. Petersburg, since Pander was soon leaving. Here I should explain that at this Institute one has to give notice half a year prior to one's intended departure. I had all but forgotten Russia, and was so engrossed in several research projects that I no longer even thought of moving, least of all to Russia, because when several years ago Vilna University had invited applications for the professorship of zoology which had become vacant due to the death of Bojanus, I had submitted my name and I did not even receive an answer. Still, the possibility of moving to Russia seemed to kindle my patriotic feelings, and the very curious coincidence of the letter from Dr. Trinius (written on June 24 [July 6, according to the New Calendar], and possibly delayed in St. Petersburg for a couple of days) arriving so soon after my letter to the Academy, signed on July 14, had been sent to print, excited my imagination. In the meantime, however, I had no idea of conditions at the Academy of St. Petersburg, especially those concerning scientific facilities. In his letter, Trinius had mentioned that there were grounds for hoping that salaries would be doubled. Since I knew that, due to the low rate of exchange, these salaries came to not much more than 700 Thalers, I replied that I did not see any possibility of coming until the new budget had been confirmed and, therefore, could not accept such an appointment. Still, I asked for information on the budget of the zoological collection, etc. These questions gave rise to a lengthy correspondence, some of the contents of which were much to my liking, some far less so. For instance, there was the fact that the zoological museum, and the other museums as well, had no budget of its own, its requirements being met from case to case by a general fund; or the fact that, prior to Pander's arrival, the zoological section of the library had been much neglected. Trinius fully justified my decision not to come to St. Petersburg as long as the budget had not been confirmed. This confirmation, however, was so long in coming, that I again lost interest in St. Petersburg. It was only the discord in 1828, discussed above, which again painted the East in a more favorable light. Wanting to fill the position of the zoologist as soon as possible, the Academy finally asked me whether I would accept the appointment if I were personally assured of the doubled salary, even if official confirmation for the general rise still did not arrive. In reply I stated that, to give a binding answer, I wanted to see the conditions at the site. I was worried by a possible lack of facilities to continue work I had begun. Also it is by no means agreeable to be the only one among colleagues enjoying better circumstances but, being by then a father of five, I would otherwise have found it impossible to exist in St. Petersburg.

At the end of 1828, I therefore obtained leave of absence for the purpose of a journey to St. Petersburg and was making the last arrangements for our departure, when my wife, much worried as she was by the whole idea, interpreted a totally coincidental incident during packing as a bad omen and became terribly upset, not to say desperate. I had no choice but to postpone the journey for the moment. As a result, I gave up the idea of an exploratory trip and declared that, provided I would be granted the conditions as promised, I was ready to accept the appointment. The call indeed came, and at the end of 1829 I left for St. Petersburg, although without family for the present, and without having formally resigned from the Prussian civil service. I had again become apprehensive about the possibility of continuing my research in St. Petersburg, without losing many years.

I arrived in St. Petersburg during the last days of 1829. The Academy regarded me at once as its effective member and altogether treated me with the greatest kindness. The men I found at the Academy were most interesting, and I soon became very friendly with several of them, among them the witty and lively Trinius; the humane and friendly secretary, Fuss; my former teacher, the noble Parrot senior; the obliging historian, Krug; the excellent orientalist, Frähn; and the venerable vice-president Storch. Beyond the walls of the Academy, too, I found many an old friend from my younger days, Pander as well as others. Yet some of the conditions I found were far less to my liking.

The zoological museum, installed in a couple of large halls of what was once known as the Art Cabinet, still bore the character of former curiosity cabinets. Large snakes and other creatures were nailed to the walls and the ceiling so that they appeared to crawl about on these surfaces, to excite the imagination of the spectators. The birds and chonchylia had been newly classified and ordered by Pander, the insects by Ménétriès, who right now was on the Caucasian mountains, together with Academician Lenz. Everything else was still waiting to be classified and was not arranged in orderly rows as one has become used to seeing today, but was partly on the floor, partly on raised stands, or in cupboards, as the limited space permitted. In particular some large, flat glass cases, fixed to columns and containing completely faded tropical butterflies, transposed one to the times of Seba. It was indeed Seba who had bought the bulk of this collection for Peter the Great's Art Cabinet, as he called his collection of curiosities according to the custom of that time. After Peter's death, this private "cabinet" became the possession of the newly founded Academy. Later scientific travels, especially by Pallas and his contemporaries, had added many additional exhibits. Nobody, however, had as yet dared to rearrange the entire collection. Some branches, though, had detached themselves, and henceforth made good progress: Frähn, actively supported by president Uvarov, had founded a large and rapidly growing oriental museum, while Trinius, with equal devotion, had laid out a large herbarium. Both collections put the stress on scientific usefulness rather than on spectacularity. My first thought upon inspection of the museum was: the zoological collection, too, must be removed from these halls in which the antique character was too deeply ingrained. My opinion was confirmed when I found that some of the systematic names of the free-standing mammals had been wrongly placed and were again similarly misplaced two days after I had put them where they rightfully belonged. This was done by a so-called guardian of the collection, who was a former servant of Pallas and knew something about taxidermy but nothing whatsoever about taxonomic clossification.

Indeed, the urgent need to dismantle the collections had been realized quite some time ago and a new impressive building, mostly still unoccupied, was ready in the immediate neighborhood of the old Art Cabinet. I therefore prepared a plan as to how the zoological collection should be distributed among the various rooms. Uvarov, the president of the Academy and the future minister, gave his tentative approval to the transfer as such, as well as to the new layout, but reserved his final decision until he could check the plans more thoroughly. Thus, nothing could be done at the moment, even the needed cupboards and repositories in the new building would have to wait.

Except for the welcome opportunity which arose for dissecting a young walrus, as well as some observations on artificially fertilized fish eggs, I did little zoological work, as there was no special room for this sort of work and no decision had yet been taken concerning the new building. I tried all the harder to acquaint myself with the library and the locally published literature, as far as it dealt with the natural sciences, and particularly zoology and anatomy. To this end, I listed most Russian journals which I found in the library, apart from the academic publications. I also had some shorter articles included in the Academy's publications (see *Writings*, III, a, 1 and b, 1).

I was particularly occupied, however, with a task which I had brought along from Königsberg and which I believed I should be able to dispose of within a few days, if not a few hours. Scientists abroad failed to understand why Pallas's *Zoographia Rosso-Asiatica* was practically unavailable. Rudolphi had acquired one copy from Pallas's estate and had spoken most highly of it. Since then, he had had to send it to different places because people wanted to have a look at the work. Some other men had obtained copies as gifts on occasion of their visits to St. Petersburg or following a special application to the Academy. It was the general opinion of the public that this work, which so many were eager to study, had not yet been made available to the book market. Thus, Cuvier, who certainly was familiar with the literature in his field, stated as late as 1830 in the *Table alphabétique des auteurs cités* ("Alphabetical Table of Authors Cited") appended to the second edition of his *Règne animal* ("The Animal Kingdom") Vol. III, p. 398: (Pallas's) *Zoographia Rosso-Asiatica*, three volumes in quarto, "a work which has still not been made available to the public because the engravings are lost. At least the Academy of Petersburg has been good enough to give the text to a few naturalists." That was roughly the general view. In St. Petersburg I was at once informed that the text of this work had been commercially available some years ago, that its availability had been announced in St. Petersburg's newspaper, and that the commissioner of the Academy, who resided at that time in Halle, was supposed to have made the appropriate announcement in Germany. As it turned out later, however, no such announcement had in effect been made, the title not having been included in the book-fair catalogues. This in turn was due to the fact that the title indicated the printing year of 1811, while the application for inclusion in the catalogue was submitted only in 1826! This incredible delay was caused by the inexplicable failure of the copper engraver, Geissler, to deliver more than a few of the copper plates, not even all those for the first volume. Geissler, who had accompanied Pallas on his travels to the south, had been strongly recommended by Pallas himself. The cause of this failure could not be established in St. Petersburg, although I was given access not only to the entire official correspondence with Pallas as long as the latter lived (he died in 1811) as well as later correspondence with Geissler, but also to all private letters on the subject. There was nobody to give answers, as all the persons involved had in the meantime either died or left St. Petersburg. Having most carefully gone over the entire collection of letters and documents myself, I was still far from understanding what had happened. It was very painful to read in these letters of Pallas, a sick man spending his last days in Berlin, how he entreats everyone to hurry up with the publication as he feels his end is near; how he complains that the copper engraver is not being paid, while the latter in fact does not demand payment from St. Petersburg before a certain number of plates, which he claims are ready, are delivered to the Russian consul in Leipzig; how all that is handed in are prints, but not the plates themselves, and how finally Herr Geissler offers to redraw all the plates of which subsequently a substantial number of copies are indeed delivered, but which postpones completion of the whole to an undetermined future. Concerning the contents of all these documents—112 in number—I submitted to the Academy a detailed report on March 3 (15), 1830, ending with propositions for an expeditious conclusion of this affair. One of my suggestions was for an authorized person, possibly the Russian consul in Leipzig, to find out what still existed of the material given directly by Pallas to Geissler, and to take it away from him; to inquire after the condition of the plates of which prints had been delivered, and, if possible, to redeem them, since information had been obtained that they had been pawned somewhere. Furthermore, inquiries were to be made as to the fate of Pallas's manuscript on insects and worms of the Russian Empire, which had not even been sent to the publishers and which ended up in private hands in Berlin after Pallas's death. The already printed volumes should be provided with new title pages, to facilitate their inclusion in the book-fair catalogues and to widely publicize their availability. Relations with Geissler should be completely cut off, as it had become clear to me even in St. Petersburg that he had for some reason intentionally put off completion of the plates during the last years.

The Academy accepted all my suggestions and decided to publish this report, as a service to the natural history public. I was personally charged with the investigation of the condition of the material delivered by Pallas and the causes of the past delays in Leipzig, and, in Berlin, of the fate of the manuscript for the entomological and helminthological volumes, as I was thoroughly familiar with the material.

I accomplished this mission to the best of my ability, out of reverence for the tragic fate of the scientific legacy of a man deserving so well of Russia and the natural sciences. In Leipzig, the cause of the delay became perfectly clear. I was sorry I had to report that it was Geissler, and that his only excuse was the very hard times brought upon Germany by the Napoleonic Wars. Warmly attached to Pallas as he was, he had taken on the work with great enthusiasm, but had very soon pawned part of the original drawings against a loan, revealing this circumstance neither to Pallas nor to the Academy. Obviously, he had already been in great financial straits when he accepted the work, which is easily explained by the fact that in the years 1805 to 1813 only very few natural history works with copper engravings appeared in Germany. Geissler obviously reasoned that preparing Pallas's plates from those drawings that he had retained, he would obtain enough money to redeem the others. Yet the political situation did not change, and in 1810 Geissler pawned most of the finished copper plates as well, sending only prints to St. Petersburg and promising the delivery of fifty plates, after the arrival of which he expected to be paid. These plates, however, never arrived, either at the consultate in Leipzig, or in St. Petersburg, and therefore no payment was made. At the same time, Geissler, pressed by Pallas, complained to the latter that the Academy would not pay. After Pallas had died, Geissler left Leipzig for good, without informing St. Petersburg of the fact. Tilesius therefore searched for him in vain, and it was only in 1817 that he was quite accidentally discovered in Nürnberg by another academician (Köhler). Being again pressed by the Academy, Geissler came up with the proposal to redraw all drawings, as some of them, he claimed, were very rough. This was indeed true of some drawings of the mammals;

others, on the other hand, were excellent. Agreeing to this proposal, the Academy had in effect made conclusion of the work impossible. After long negotiations I succeeded in redeeming all the drawings and copper plates. Some of the stuffed birds, which were to serve for Geissler's drawings and plates, had already been sold by Geissler to Professor Schwägrichen. Other natural history objects which Pallas had taken along to be used for the illustrations of fishes and insects, as well as the manuscripts for the insects and worms, had passed into private hands in Berlin, partly as gifts from Pallas himself while he was still alive, partly acquired from his estate. Their respective owners all promised to put them at the Academy's disposal if they were required for the completion of the work. The question now arose as to the additional texts to be printed. That the worms could not be published in the form in which they had been prepared—the manuscript consisted only of a bundle of disjointed notes—was beyond question. Pallas himself had declared that they were unsuited for printing without substantial additions by Tilesius. To this must be added that knowledge and taxonomic arrangement of the animals which Pallas, following Linnaeus, still called worms, had become completely transformed, so that to print the section as it was would make it appear like a ghost from the past century. As concerns the insects, I was more doubtful. The manuscripts were much more voluminous, the order of Coleoptera had been completely worked out, and details in other orders gave grounds for expectations, as Pallas had always had a preference for entomology. I thought it my duty to ask Klug, an experienced entomologist in whose hands was also part of the entomological legacy, for his scientific opinion. He counseled against publication, because taxonomy would be burdened with a large number of doubtful names, as Pallas did not at all take into account many of the newer criteria for classification. This explanation seemed acceptable to me, especially since we had no right to demand return of the insects. All I could do was to ask the owners of the manuscripts and the insects to put these at the disposal of whoever was going to work on the different branches of entomology.

These two reports, the first one on my investigations in St. Petersburg and the second one on the results of my journey, were printed in their entirety in 1831, to be appended to the *Zoographia Rosso-Asiatica*. I have nevertheless repeated the gist of these reports here since, due to the prolonged delay in the publication of this major work of Pallas, dark rumors have been spreading abroad and voices have become loud against the Academy, claiming that either academic rivalry or indifference were to blame for the delay. Of rivalry I have found not the slightest trace. I would have revealed it, had I found it, caring as I did more for posterity than for the Academy or in particular for any guilty individual in it. What I did find was merely keen interest and the desire to bring the matter to a successful conclusion although the Napoleonic invasion had reduced the rate of exchange and therefore the means of the Academy, to a minimum. Yet I must believe that the Academy would have preferred to let other works go unpublished. The only wrong for which the Academy could be reproached is its failure, immediately upon the death of Pallas, to send an authorized person to Berlin, and to take possession of that part of his scientific estate that he still had there; a few months after his death communication with Prussia was impossible because of Napoleon's invasion. It was also undoubtedly a mistake, although one made out of respect for Pallas's wishes, that the Academy agreed to Geissler's proposal to prepare new drawings. The money for these was a complete loss.

This entire investigation made a deep and painful impression upon me. I had already accused Geissler in St. Petersburg, and now I do so even more definitely. Yet, I felt regret, since he was a good-natured, diligent person who, because of his personal interest in Pallas, did not want Pallas's work which had been entrusted to him to be finished by other hands, and it was only thoughtlessness and false shame that caused him to sin against Pallas's scientific legacy. He was also quite destitute now and, moreover, terribly ashamed. After he had returned to me whatever he could still find, I could not help giving him a not inconsiderable sum of money as a gift, not knowing whether the Academy would reimburse me. When I later contacted the then secretary, Fuss junior, about this matter, he declared that the Academy would unquestioningly defray all expenses connected with the redeeming of the pawned drawings and plates, but could not pay Geissler anything, as any such payment would be construed as an admission of guilt. Actually, I have found no trace of the Academy's debt to Geissler; at the same time, I am putting on record Geissler's spurious complaints to Pallas concerning the Academy. In the matter of the gift I therefore refrained from taking any further steps, and I mention it here only so that, should the fact of this gift ever become public, it should be understood that it was no more than an expression of my personal pity for a man whose reputation must have suffered greatly through the involvement of consuls and court officers.

What remains, however, is the painful impression which the investigation left with me. Pallas, a man who, for erudition, power of observation, concern, and diligence, had very few equals; who in Russia, as everywhere else, had gained everyone's respect and love—this man felt compelled, in 1785, to leave the capital and to move to Crimea, then still settled by very few educated persons, because he found that his official position and the interferences characteristic of the large city did not permit him to work on his magnum opus—the *Fauna* of the great Russian Empire—which was to include the material he himself had collected and compiled since 1768, as well as that of his predecessors. Finally, in 1806, he concluded the first half, now published in two volumes and, in 1810, the second half, now forming the third volume. Despite the many great qualities of the work, however, the influence of his isolation from foreign literature was unmistakable. Soon, a prolonged delay occurred in the publication, caused by the author's lack of confidence in the domestic artists. In 1810 he moved to Germany, but was unable to shake off the paralyzing curse, and all that the old man managed to see before he died was a copy of the first volume, and the first sheet of the text of the second volume. Dying (1811), he still succeeded in distributing the natural history objects which he had brought along, clearly to permit their use elsewhere. Rudolphi, in the biography of Pallas (Rudolphi: *Beiträge zur Anthropologie*, etc., page 61) exclaims, "May this rich addition to natural history, this exquisite work, be soon completed!" adding, "Nothing will give better proof of the love of the Imperial Academy for its former revered colleague than the fulfilling of his dying wish, that the Academy take paternal care of the Fauna." This the Academy did as much as it could but, after eighteen years, the text, although finished long ago, was still relatively unknown everywhere and the illustrations in an inextricable tangle, so that one had to go to Leipzig to discover the origin of the delay. It is true that the Napoleonic campaigns shook Europe deeper than anything since the Thirty Years' War, and that the shocks followed one another in more rapid succession than the history of this continent had ever known. But all these interferences would not have had that destructive effect had Pallas remained in St. Petersburg, and had he personally supervised the preparation of the copper engravings.

My preoccupation with Pallas helped me reach another conclusion: He had taken too much upon himself and, in a manner of speaking, had drowned in the overabundance of his material. However prodigious his industry, to undertake a description of the flora and fauna of so large a country, and to undertake it with the thoroughness which he would not abandon, and at the same time publish works on physical geography, geology, and pre-historic animals, was simply too much. If Pallas had sat down to prepare his major work immediately after his return from his great journey, he would have been able to finish it while still in his best years, and could then have directed his attention to his *Botanica*. This, however, is the wisdom of hindsight. Who indeed can know what affected him! Probably, he began early enough. But soon the Crimea and the Nogaisk Steppe were incorporated into the Russian Empire, and when conditions had become normal, he followed his desire to travel there, too, up to the foot of the Caucasus.

In a public announcement on the occasion of the publication of the *Fauna* and the report on its fate (*Jahrbücher der Kritik*, 1834, December) I have elaborated on these reflections.

At this junction, I felt I had to take very serious counsel with myself to find out whether I had acted wisely and sensibly by accepting the call to St. Petersburg, and I could not but reach the conclusion that I had done a foolish thing. I had hoped to be able to continue my research in embryology. While the chair of anatomy was occupied by Herr Zagorsky, this circumstance would not have constituted an obstacle, as such continuity was generally thought rather desirable. Although there were no suitable premises for anatomical work, this too could have been arranged. However I found the procuring of suitable objects much more difficult than it had been in Königsberg, especially finding the mammalian fetuses which I most wanted, but also with regard to all other animals. With the coming of spring, I realized that I would have to find everything myself, and from far away at that, because the local bodies of water are very poor in lower animals, most probably because of the peaty ground rather than the northern location. I will be scarcely understood, whether in Germany or here, if I say that the naturally-occurring institution of street boys is completely missing here, and I will be still less understood if I add that I was most anxiously searching for them. The street boys of Königsberg had been my benefactors. I had drilled them to such perfection that for very small payments I could obtain anything they could lay their hands on, be it from the slaughterhouse or, since I lived very close to the city wall, from the surrounding countryside. In fact, my problem there was oversupply. Thus, in the spring, lizards arrived in such quantities that I tied their tails to pieces of string which I then hung from nails hammered into the edge of my working table. There were times when I had up to thirty such tassels swinging from my table. In Germany one will think: certainly there is no dearth of lower-class boys in St. Petersburg! Well, no, but in the central sections of the town, the children of the servant class were too well looked after and were not used to foraging for their upkeep and living. In the most remote districts, this might have been different. To this must be added the fact that everything here was handled wholesale by groups. An example will serve as illustration. When spring had progressed to the point where, according to my calculation, the perch were spawning, I looked up the fishermen at the borders of the town and promised them good payment if they would find nets of perch eggs and bring them to me promptly, keeping them in water. Two days later I was brought a bucket-full of roe with little water. The lower egg-masses in the heap were completely spoiled, only the uppermost were still usable. I explained to them that I could use only one or two egg-masses, and that they should be brought in a larger quantity of water. It was of no use. I was again brought a whole bucketful, because the fisherman's cooperative had assumed that for small quantities I would not pay as promised. Another time I succeeded in talking a young man into going to the slaughterhouse, promising him good payment for a cow or sheep fetus. He did not return. In his stead, a fellow from the slaughterhouse appeared on the next day, bringing along some offal, also including the uterus of a pregnant cow. He declared that these were the portions sold by the slaughterhouse as dog food, but that strangers had no right to look for business at the slaughterhouse. Neither did I succeed later, during my permanent stay, to lure boys from the neighboring villages into catching frogs for me. They were always brought in by some grown-up fellows, although I am certain that there is no frog-catchers' guild in existence. They were possibly worried lest I would not keep my promises to the boys, or else they found it altogether unfitting for the boys to make some money. Possibly the situation in smaller towns and villages is different. Thus I am told that the boys of Pavlovsk are now used to collecting fossils.

There was reason to hope that I would find more convenient suppliers in the course of time. I found much more disquieting the prospects that I would have to apply myself primarily to systematic zoology in St. Petersburg, something which I did in Königsberg only in reference to local animals or, at most, European animals. Zoology interested me more in its zootomic aspects. Would I be left with enough time to apply myself to embryology, especially when procuring objects was so time-consuming? The example of Pallas made me increasingly doubtful. The friendliness and complaisance with which I was welcomed in St. Petersburg exceeded my expectations and, indeed, was more than I justly deserved. The grander scale of everything at the Academy was much to my liking. I had also hoped that some arrangements which I considered necessary for continuous work could be realized. But that the proposals for the transfer of the zoological museum had remained undecided for several months, to be discussed in I know not which office, was truly disquieting, and I was even less able to acquiesce to the fact that the zoological museum had no annual budget, which made planned development, if not impossible, then at least uncertain.

In the meantime, still during my stay here, the Academy's new budget had been confirmed. It also included a yearly sum for the zoological museum.

What weighed more than all these doubts, however, was the fact, that when on my way to Germany via Königsberg I apprised my wife of the proposed move to St. Petersburg—with the rest of the family and all my possessions—she was not yet at all well disposed to the idea of this move.

Would it not be better to continue to travel along the previous, already level road than to face unknown difficulties in St. Petersburg and, on occasion of the transfer of the museum, go once again through the time-consuming routines of setting up and arranging? Perhaps it would be possible to obtain the means to continue research on the development of mammalians in Königsberg as well, and to find a solution to the absolute lack of a natural history draftsman and copper engraver.

14. My Third Stay in Königsberg (1830-1834)

Full of such thoughts and plans, I returned from Leipzig to Königsberg. I found the prejudice of my family against Russia undiminished. Finally, I told the minister that if Königsberg would put a special sum at my disposal for the continuation of the research on mammalian development and if a draftsman-cum-copper engraver were transferred to Königsberg, I would cancel my St. Petersburg appointment. Both were promised. With a heavy heart I then informed St. Petersburg that I would not return. They looked for another zoologist and found Dr. Brandt, my present-day colleague, a replacement which no doubt more than compensated them for losing me.

I had asked for the grant of a special sum because I intended to keep sheep and pigs, and in future other animals also, so that I could supervise their mating in order to examine them at definite intervals and to publish a well-illustrated work on the progress of development. This work, similar to Sömmerring's *Tabulae Embryonum*, should permit determination of the age of any fetus. In the first years of my research, I had borne most of the expenses myself, which did not go too well with my economic means and the growing needs of my family. From 1826, I defrayed larger expenses from the funds of the anatomical institute, but found myself limited there also, because Burdach had reserved for himself the right to enlarge the library. I could not, however, burden the anatomical institute with such a continuous expenditure as would be involved if my plan were to be realized.

The arrangement was set up with less difficulty than I had expected. A well-proven friend who had supported my research for years by providing me with shells and similar desiderata, Herr Jachmann, owner of Trutenau, a neighboring estate, had taken it upon himself to keep a number of sheep, as well as several pigs on the estate, the mating dates of which would be carefully recorded. Whenever I wanted a fetus of a certain age, an animal meeting that need would be brought to town by a farmhand, who would also slaughter it and take back meat and skin, which reduced costs. This arrangement worked to everyone's satisfaction.

Things went less well, in fact very badly, with the draftsman and copper engraver. Since the founding of the university, scientific activities had never completely ceased in Königsberg. It is true that Königsberg lagged in the newer branches when compared with Germany, but this lag was reduced in the manner earlier described, after the great wars. The visual arts, however, were

252

apparently never at home in Königsberg, and should any Königsbergers have excelled in this métier, they must have emigrated. I had already noticed this situation prior to 1828. A young man of my acquaintance who liked to dabble in watercolors and who felt a higher calling wanted to leave the juridical career which he had just begun and which did not suit him, and devote himself entirely to painting, provided he could obtain a scholarship at the Academy of Arts in Berlin. But in all of Königsberg, not a single man could be found whose reference attesting to the young man's artistic talents would carry any weight in Berlin, and the young man thus had to give up his hopes. I knew only one man in Königsberg who could paint in oil, but he was unable to develop whatever talent he had, as he was compelled to waste it on theater decorations and even lesser work in order to secure his existence. The lack of draftsmen for natural history objects and of copper engravers was felt still more by scientists. Since several natural history works had recently appeared in Königsberg, I thought I was quite justified in drawing the minister's attention to this matter and in expressing the hope that, if a young man who was both a draftsman and a copper engraver were brought to Königsberg, he would not only find full employment, but would also have the opportunity of spreading these arts.

The very idea of moving to Königsberg, however, appeared so terrible to Berlin artists that no one would voluntarily make such a decision. Eventually, a young man who had been raised from the lowest classes and had studied at the expense of the state was persuaded to accept the position, possibly not without application of some pressure. He arrived at the beginning of 1831 in a state which can only be described as total despondency. In those days, an involuntary posting from Berlin to Königsberg had the same connotations as did a compulsory move from St. Petersburg to Siberia. Königsbergers, on the other hand, regarded a transfer to St. Petersburg as banishment to the North Pole. My wife, for instance, had been assured by her friends that her children would undoubtedly freeze to death in St. Petersburg. At that time, people did not realize that, in the far north, we are apt to pamper both ourselves and our children as far as warmth is concerned. I have never been so badly frozen as I was during a December in Trieste. Today, thanks to the railroad and increased traffic, Königsberg has probably lost much of its Siberian overtones, even to Berliners. At that time, I suffered greatly from this attitude. I tried to cheer my draftsman with all sorts of friendly gestures, but to no avail. He seemed to have prepared himself for a speedy return to Berlin and thus had disregarded my request to bring along some copper plates, so that they had to be ordered anew. I had just begun to observe the so-called cleavage, in fact, the division of frog eggs immediately after fertilization, and wanted to have this drawn as long as frog eggs could still be found. On the second day however, the draftsman declared that his vision had become blurred and that he felt blinded. This was by no means an attempt at deception in order to rid himself the faster of the engagement, because he was a very modest and even timid man, but his very faintheartedness might have had that effect. I found him other work to do, trying first of all to fortify his self-confidence, but was not very successful. When I kept him in my company, he became excessively polite and uneasy. The best therapy for him, intercourse with other artists, I was of course unable to arrange. Then came the news that the cholera, rampant in Poland, was steadily closing in on Königsberg. Nobody listened more anxiously to all the news than my draftsman. He succeeded in obtaining the brochures prepared to help diagnose the illness and recommend the most effective prophylactic and therapeutic means, and as is often the case with such timid souls, he believed he could recognize all these symptoms in himself, even before the first person fell ill in Königsberg. Now he thought that he had cramps in the leg, now he felt that his blood was clotting, in which case he ran about in town to liquefy it again. This happened most often around midnight because it was when he was alone that his fears tortured him most. When the cholera eventually did invade the town and the general mood of fear spread, my man became quite useless. The sick were carried to the hospitals in baskets. Whenever he saw such a basket, he believed he could feel his blood clot. I tried to reassure him by publishing an extract in the newspaper from an article by an Indian doctor which I had just read and who positively denied that this disease was contagious. This article drew some attention here and there, but had little effect on the draftsman, since it was precisely on long-held assumptions of its being contagious that the severe quarantine measures had been based. He often did not show up when I expected him and then I had to accustom myself to hear about various symptoms and complaints. But when he once failed to appear for three days running, I became worried that, in his insuperable anxiety, he had really come down with the disease. I looked him up in his lodgings, but found the door locked and, having knocked and rattled at the door to no avail, was about to turn to the landlord to ask him to break open the door, as his lodger was probably dead, seeing that he had left the key in the lock and, therefore, could not have gone out. Thereupon a weak voice came from inside. My man lay deeply buried in his bed to reliquefy his blood which, he believed, had definitely clotted that night. He was too frightened to crawl out of his bed to open the door. From then on, I gave up all hope of ever getting him into a useful frame of mind and, so as not to take upon myself the responsibility in case he really fell ill and even died, I myself took a hand in expediting his return to Berlin where, as it turned out, he again had to go through the epidemic, which I hope he did with greater spiritual fortitude.

The experiment with the copper engraver was thus a total failure; my only reward was to be able to say he was the worst scaredy-cat I had ever met in my life.

The cholera also kept me busy in other ways. Although, with the exception of in my own home, I had completely given up practical medicine, the great wave of compassion which swept the doctors, and particularly the Medical Society, of which I still was a member, in face of the irresistibly advancing epidemic, also carried me along, inducing me to try to find out more about the fearful invader. When the first officially recognized case occurred in the city, all the schools were closed down, all lectures at the university stopped, and the medical practitioners organized a continuously manned station where one could apply for help at any time; I offered my services to investigate the likelihood that the first cases were brought in from outside. I therefore went to the localities where the first cases had occurred and made the fullest inquiries as to all circumstances. The results of my inquiries indicated that there was no trace of importation. The detailed report which I prepared for the Medical Society, and which was printed in the first volume of their proceedings as well as, I think, in the *Cholera Zeitung* (Cholera News), was regarded as a definite proof that cholera spread without transfer by persons or objects. Given the facts which were elicited without any prejudiced notions, I could have arrived at no other conclusions. Today, however, I can no longer accept those conclusions, since the premises on which they were based, namely that the cases investigated by me were indeed the first ones, have been severely shaken. The same doctors who had diagnosed some early cases as noncholeric which they had examined and found with some similarity to cholera, tended later to agree that these cases might have been cholera cases after all. Accordingly, then, the cases I had investigated were not the first cases at all, and the possibility of its importation was not disproved. Several weeks later a rumor spread, according to which a traveler staying in Pillau after coming from Königsberg had fallen ill with cholera and had died. The next person to die was the woman who had washed his body. The epidemic spread to Königsberg only after these two cases had occurred. As such pieces of information were very unreliable, depending on whether they originated with contagionists or with anticontagionists, I traveled to Pillau myself to make detailed inquiries, and I was convinced beyond doubt that the information was indeed correct, as was easily verified in the small town. This case seemed to tip the scales in favor of contagion, while later experience in France, where the disease did not spread from the northern to the southern provinces despite the absence of any quarantine measures, makes the disease appear to be totally dependent on external physical conditions. Altogether the whole cholera episode served to show how unclear our understanding is of contagion in its different forms, and how meaningless the word "miasma" is. My own effort showed me how difficult it is to establish the facts, and that inquiries by and through the police authorities yield false results almost of necessity, if only for the reason that the prescribed registration with the police of persons moving into and out of lodgings is almost never carried out in a regular manner.

Moreover, as was the situation with the cholera outbreak, the first cases of an epidemic usually occur in those classes of society that are in permanent opposition to the police authorities.

On my way back from one of the first infected localities, I landed right in the middle of a cholera riot which was just as impressive and spectacular as in other educated cities. People of all classes, with the exception of certain timid types, were furious at the quarantine measures already taken and at the decrees and publications by the government which soon followed them. Thus one evening, a decree was published according to which the bodies of those who had died of the cholera were not to be given a funeral, but were to be buried quietly and alone at a spot designated for that purpose. Then a respected citizen died and several other citizens joined together in planning to give him a proper funeral and to bury him in the churchyard the next morning using force if need be. Nobody interfered with the funeral procession, which proceeded from the churchyard to the market place as if to show off the appropriated rights. Wherever opposition is shown against the government, the rabble is quick to collect, full of pluck and flushed with victory. When reached the market place, it was already chock-full and the procession had grown tenfold. Trying to find out what was happening, I caught sight of an acquaintance, First Lieutenant von Auer, a man of a portly figure, who rode into the crowd, asking them, "Boys, what is it that you want?" "Now we'll have our cake and eat it, too!" was the answer shouted by a husky fellow of about twenty, who had joined this merrymaking without a jacket. The answer was quite clear, and Auer quietly turned his horse away from the crowd. Still the authorities tried to reason with the excited passions, and I was very much interested to follow the development of the riot, my experience in this field being limited to what I had read of Parisian mobs. First, however, I wanted to see whether everything was quiet at my home near the ramparts. It was although rumors of the riot had already reached this section of town. Returning to the market, I found that the riot had developed by leaps and bounds. When I had last seen them almost none of the rioters had been armed except for a few who had produced some sticks and had gone to look for the medical men who they supposed to have invented the cholera. Indeed, they managed to catch one, who succeeded in saving himself only after he had received a sound thrashing. Now, however, the more daring boys and women had equipped themselves with stones and a number of men were armed with cudgels. Stones were thrown at the windows of the police building until all the officials had cleared out. The mob then broke into the building, threw piles of documents through the windows, and burned them in the market place. At the same time, a heavily armored squadron of cuirassiers was waiting in a side street and let all this happen. This long hesitation was quite incomprehensible and appeared to me highly injudicious. In the meantime, the provost arrived accompanied by the students, who had armed themselves with various sorts of weapons, and a little melee developed between them and the rioters. It was only in the afternoon that the cuirassiers left their hiding place, advancing in close order to clear the market place. The victory-flushed mob received them with a hail of stones. Eventually, the cuirassiers had to use their firearms, with the result that several persons—I believe it was six—were badly wounded. Now the riot was over.

The delay seemed to me very unwise. A cavalry charge, carried out earlier, would no doubt have cleared the market place and saved the police building, without endangering human lives. Although it was said that the authorities acted as they did only to avoid a reproof from the King for using crass violence, yet it is a striking fact that, after all, violence could not be avoided after such delay. To my mind, a government which feels itself in the right must act promptly to suppress any open defiance. The prolonged avoidance of any decisive step in Königsberg created the impression that it was really not the local government that had taken all these troublesome measures, out of sheer caprice and against the King's wishes, and could not, therefore, now act with decisiveness. In actual fact, however, the opposite was true. All the measures taken had been dictated by Berlin, which wanted to keep the epidemic away from the capital at any price. In public, it was said that it was not so much the King, but Dr. Rust who hoped to attain that purpose by the severity of the measures taken. In Königsberg, however, where the difficulties involved were better understood, the local authorities were rather reluctant to implement the measures. On the very next day, Governor von Schön revoked the quarantine orders, and there was no lack of voices to claim that he had intentionally let the riot assume serious dimensions in order to justify this latest decision.

The end of the riot as soon as the authorities had shown some will to act, together with the removal of the quarantine arrangements, resulted in a sudden calming-down in Königsberg. The lower classes no longer felt hampered in their daily pursuits, and the propertied classes no longer feared for their property and seemed suddenly to regard the cholera like any other calamity, such as hail and thunderstorms, which, while not quite welcome, one had to live with. Even the disheartened made an effort to appear more courageous. In any case, life and daily routines seemed to move along more easily than before, when everybody had felt obliged to attest to either his patriotism or his fear of God by putting on as long a face as possible. Berlin, however, was very dissatisfied with the lifting of the quarantine, as its main aim was the protection of the capital. In Königsberg, on the other hand, the authorities tried to demonstrate the uselessness and, indeed, impracticability of all quarantine measures, in view of today's traffic. Newspapers, and in particular, the Königsberg *Cholera Zeitung*, supported the authorities in this respect, and such towns to the west as Elbing and Danzig soon agreed to the task assigned to them of holding off the evil invader. Rust, on the other hand, stuck steadfastly to his defensive system until the cholera penetrated the walls of Berlin. I was all the more against all quarantine measures because my investigations concerning the appearance of the cholera in Königsberg did not demonstrate any trace of its being imported. But even if its contagiousness were definitely established, a complete sealing-off is hardly possible in the Europe of today, unless one takes the responsibility right from the start of feeding entire populations, since the existence, or at least the comfortable life of each of us, has become so dependent upon others. It seems that there is no alternative except leaving the decision as to the degree a person wants or is able to isolate himself from others to the discretion of the individual. I became especially convinced of this after a study of the history of the plague, which had devastated East Prussia in the beginning of the eighteenth century. At that time, the authorities had enforced measures against the plague with even greater rigor and more brutality than our own government did against the cholera in the nineteenth century. They went so far as to erect a gallows near each town and near many villages, on which to hang anybody not staying at home. These measures notwithstanding, and possibly even favored by them, the plague killed off about a third of the population of the entire province; there is probably no other authenticated example like it in history. I had an article printed on the above, which I am unable to locate today, according it, as I did, very little importance not knowing that Herr von Altenstein—who was Minister not only of Education, but also of Medical Affairs—had entered my unassuming articles on the cholera, originally occasioned by my unhappy draftsman, in the "liabilities" column of my ledger.

Another matter which I believe I should mention, as it belongs to the realm of science, is the reorganization of the Economics Society of Königsberg. This society had originally been founded in Mohrungen and had later been transferred to Königsberg, where it flourished nicely for some time but, abandoning later its original basis, agriculture, it assumed a more scientific garb. Many members now called for more popular and practical lectures. In deference to their wishes, the mistake was sometimes made of offering the rostrum to persons who by right should have sat in the audience. The audiences shrank, and with them also the number of persons ready to prepare a lecture for only a few people. The last president, the public health officer Professor Hagen, had to call on all the respect and reverence he enjoyed to force lecturers to the hall and, in the end, audiences as well, especially during the summer.

I still remember a lecture on the cosmic system given by the then chief of police who had come upon Sommer's *Description of the Physical World*, or a similar book and, to his amazement, had found out that the sun was 1,400,000 times larger than the earth. This and other curiosities he disclosed to an audience of six, all of whom claimed to have possessed this knowledge since their school days. This was about the last straw. Soon after that President Hagen fell ill, and in 1829 he died. Apparently the society died with him

After the cholera had receded to make room for less dramatic illnesses, however, the son of the deceased, without my knowledge, called a meeting, after which he informed me that I had been elected president by acclamation. I had not the slightest reason to take upon myself still more duties, and within me felt neither the desire nor the skill to call upon and enlist lecturers or listeners. On the other hand, we had a large number of competent young lecturers at Königsberg who would certainly like to give lectures to a larger audience. Why are these lectures open only to members of the society? This exclusivity was merely an old habit lacking any good reason, I said to myself. Therefore, in a second meeting I proposed to announce the lectures to the public in the future, and to invite all educated persons in Königsberg. I am still amused when I remember the objections raised against such innovations. In fact, a formal opposition was developed which submitted a written protest in the subsequent session, formulated by a university professor, in which he remarked that we had not yet achieved the maturity required to give public lectures. I replied that there must have been time enough to attain such maturity. I stuck to my proposal: either admit the general public or elect another president since, if the public were excluded, all I could do was compose an epitaph commemorating a society which had died of senile decay. In the end, the majority opted for the public. Beginning from January 1832, public lectures were held and, in the inaugural address, I could not resist a few sarcastic remarks concerning the typically Germanic aversion to the spoken word, which went together with a lack of aversion to the written record. The lectures were more successful than I had hoped. Already by the third lecture, there were more guests than the large, densely-packed hall could accommodate, and there were more offers from lectures than could be accepted. Some of these lectures were excellent, and many later famous lecturers such as Dove, Moser, the elder Jacobi, and others, in fact started their careers here. Several of these lectures were later published in a small but rich collection under the title: *Lectures in the Natural Sciences and Economy Given at the Physical Society in Königsberg* (Königsberg, Unzer, 1834, in octavo). Bessel at that time refused his valued lectures, claiming that there was no need for science to be brought into a popular garb before the general public. He entirely tended toward the opposition in the beginning, but he appeared to change his views, and later published a collection of his lectures himself. He also made the proposal according to which the members of the society should assemble at a restaurant after every lecture, as the lecture meetings of the society were by now too large to permit discussion. At these informal meetings, the jovial and brilliant Bessel was always the life of the party and to those taking part in them, these evenings will remain among the pleasantest memories of Königsberg.

After my departure, the Economics Society published collections of the lectures under various titles, presently known as *Writings of the Royal Economics Society at Königsberg*, in quarto, including numerous illustrations and having mainly a scientific tendency, mostly reporting new observations.

At that time we lost two lecturers, through transfers, Herbart and Dove, and obtained others, such as Dulk, the elder Jacobi, and Rosenkranz, so that there was no dearth of scientific stimulation. Even closer to my heart was the news that the new home of the zoological museum, which I had pleaded for long ago, had now at long last been finished and could be moved into. I myself was given lodgings in the new building.

I now threw myself with all vigor into the resumption and continuation of my research on embryology of animals. The observation of an already completely hirsute calf which, on top of its hair, had a complete, fully coherent skin, induced me to publish a paper: "Observations on the Shedding of Skin of the Embryo, and Conclusions Drawn from the Same on Insect Metamorphosis" (*Frorieps Notiz*. Vol. 31, No. 10). Observations on the so-called renewal of the stomach in crayfish dealt with a related phenomenon, which turned out to be merely the shedding of the stomach lining (*Müllers Archiv*, 1834). The self-fertilization of a hermaphrodite snail was observed by chance (*Müllers Archiv*, 1835). Greater effort was expended on the study of the development of the tortoise, to understand the change taking place in the general vertebrate type, since in the fully formed animal the bones of the visceral half reach beyond the spinal column, and the entire muscular apparatus is attached only from the inner side. In this enterprise I did not succeed, however, as I could observe one single egg only (*Müllers Archiv* 1834). Better understanding was achieved later by Rathke.

Another object of intensive study was the spawn of fish. Of the many different egg types I eventually selected a Cyprinus species (*C. blicca*), in which to follow the entire process of metamorphosis. Only the cleavage of the germ which, in nature, already takes place during the night, remained unobserved, since I took the bulge formation, which I perceived during artificial fertilization, to be symptoms of decomposition. After embryo formation had been followed in considerable detail, I prepared a report under the title: "Research on the Embryology of Fishes, including an Appendix on the Air Bladder." The latter was of particular interest because of the manner of its development. After I had compared the shapes of the air bladder of as many adult fishes as Prussia could offer, it seemed to me that the prevailing concept of the air bladder being a rudimentary undeveloped lung had to be somewhat modified, as its function is more to constitute a hollow air-filled space in the trunk of the fish, rather than effect chemical changes in the blood. Relative to the trunk, the air bladder thus assumes roughly the same position as, in the higher animals, especially in mammals, the nasal sinuses with respect to the head. Later (in St. Petersburg) I have observed that in very small perch the air bladder communicates via a hollow duct with the esophagus, although in older specimens of this species the air bladder is completely closed. It seems to me that this does not alter the situation. If, as it appeared to me, development of this sac begins from the upper side of the alimentary canal—something which is hard to claim with certitude, as the first instant of formation has not yet been observed—the analogy with the sinuses becomes still more pronounced. Air bladders, which by their glandular structure point to a clearer change of the blood, or by their cellular and branched structure have greater morphological similarity with the lungs, must after all be regarded as rare exceptions.

I intended to publish the above work as an independent book, and since the text required only one copper plate and a few very simple woodcuts, and all I had demanded for myself was a few free copies, I had no doubts that Herr L. Voss would accept publication of the book. To my great surprise I obtained a definite refusal. It appears that the *Epistola* had not been selling too well. Since Herr Bornträger of Königsberg also found the task too specialized, I was obliged to look for a new publisher, unknown to me, after the copper plate had been engraved in Königsberg.

What I had worked for so hard and what had turned out such a failure, namely to have a skilled copper engraver settle in Königsberg, later found its own solution. Herr Lehmann, who had engraved the beautiful plates for Bojanus's work on the anatomy of the tortoise, could not find enough work in Vilna after the death of Bojanus and, in search for a new abode, had come first to Königsberg where he soon decided to settle down. My work was eventually accepted by Vogel's Publishing House, otherwise completely unknown to me, where it was left unprinted for so long that I had long left Königsberg and settled in St. Petersburg when I received a copy from Leipzig. I never received the ten other free copies agreed upon, which statement of fact should also serve to notify my scientific friends whom I have always supplied with my printed works.

In 1831 I had started on a closer examination of the apparent cleavage of the frog egg soon after fertilization. Having treated these progressive changes with acids, I could not have failed to notice that they were in fact genuine divisions, which only appeared to be furrows on the surface. In the common water frog (*Rana temporaria*) these divisions proceed with extreme regularity, so that the entire yolk mass divides into two halves, each quadrant of a sphere thus forming again into two halves and so on, until the whole at first has the appearance of a blackberry and, with continued division, the surface appears to be smooth again, because of the smallness of the products of division. With the grass frog (*Rana esculenta*), I found the process of division not as strictly regular; indeed the same principle cannot be mistaken although it is so sharply maintained. Only after these preparations for future developments are concluded does the typical vertebrate development set in: the rising of two ridges which, at the beginning, are so distant from each other that one hardly dares to see in them the two halves of the back, but which soon approach one another, attesting to what they in fact are. Even more discernible in the frog than in the chick is the originally open back structure; and the formation of the spinal cord and of the brain from two lateral halves detaching themselves from the back ridges. Altogether, the development of frogs and fishes differs from that of the rest of the amphibians, the birds and the mammals, in that with the former group, gill filaments are formed early and are soon covered up, in frogs they disappear gradually, while in fishes they are permanent, and these embryos soon swim freely about in the water. On the other hand, they do not grow an allantois, nor are they enclosed in an amnion.

It was not, however, these later transformations, already observed by me earlier, on which I now focused my attention, but on the preparatory phenomena preceding these transformations, on the self-effectuation of the substance by continuous cleavage. That this had indeed brought me into the innermost tabernacle of embryology was later borne out by the confluence of countless investigations. Not only is a similar division process observed in the most diverse animals as a result of fertilization, a process in which either the entire yolk mass divides, or only a small layer of it which I prefer to call the germ, but the very form of this cleavage is precisely that found in the lowest organisms, those in which growth and procreation are one and the same process, or in those that cannot grow without multiplying, and cannot multiply without having grown to this point by assimilation of matter from the external environment. There is always an inner part or nucleus, and a peripheral part. The nucleus is the dominant part. At first it has a round shape, but once it starts growing, it expands lengthwise with the midsection remaining at its widest only for a very short while as it soon constricts, giving the nucleus the appearance of a biscuit (dumbbell). The substance of the nucleus concentrates toward the two sides and soon separates into two round bodies. Immediately after this division of the nucleus, the surrounding mass, the yolk substance in the egg, divides equally, as if, in a manner of speaking, each of the rulers, newly created by the division, were now collecting about himself his share of the realm, in order, after a short rest, to split in a similar fashion, but in another direction. These divisions and the apportionment of the yolk mass are carried out with some effort, so that, with advanced division, one can see these individual cleavage products shift and push against each other until they come to rest. That it was the nuclei which triggered division I could not fully prove in the frog, as the frog egg is too dark and too large, and also because the nuclei dissolved in the acids I used to separate the cleavage products. At a much later date, however, I succeeded in giving full proof of the priority of the nucleus in the division process, using the eggs of the sea urchin that I observed in Trieste on the occasion of a journey undertaken from St. Petersburg (Report from Trieste, *Bulletin de la classe physico-mathématique*, Vol. V, No. 15). Mentioning these later observations, I should like to add that in these sea urchin eggs I also succeeded in clearly establishing—at least to my own satisfaction, that is—a condition which to this day is a subject of controversy.

In these small, if not transparent, then at least translucent eggs, I believed to have definitely observed that, at each cleavage, the cleavage products are without an outer membrane or covering of any kind, but that very soon, after a period of rest, a very thin outer layer is discernible, in other words, that a covering membrane appears to be present which again vanishes with each new cleavage. Scientists still argue whether or not a membrane exists, primarily because a cell would appear to need an outer wall, an original outer wall that is, not one subsequently created by coagulation. A quantity of organic matter that has no wall I would indeed hesitate to call a cell, but is it in fact necessary for every organic independent entity to be a cell? At that time, in Königsberg, my primary aim was merely to show that what Prévost and Dumas had described as cleavage only appeared as such on the outside, but was in fact a division. As far as I know, this view was not disputed even later, after many other classes of animals were studied. Still, the expression "cleavage process" has remained in use, even by men like Kölliker and Funke who know this cleavage process in its various forms so well. In cases in which it is only the germ that is divided (Reichert's "formative yolk"), the expression "cleavage" could conceivably be applied to the egg as a whole, although it does not describe the nature of the process which Kölliker has so fully proven for the cephalopod egg. Funke concludes from this lucid and thorough representation that "by its very nature, the cleavage process is a continuous process of cell division, the 'cleavage spheres,' from the first one constituted by the entire yolk, to the last, smallest one, are cells" (*Textbook of Physiology*, Third Edition, Vol. III, p. 182). Why then retain the expression "cleavage process" throughout the entire description, despite the fact that the priority of nuclear division is recognized? Does not the expression "cleavage spheres" contain an inner contradiction? Dividing a sphere, even if continued until there is total separation, can never produce further spheres. If, nevertheless, spherical shapes are produced, this in itself is proof that division is produced by forces acting from within. If, as is not hard in the sea urchin egg, it is possible to directly observe division of the nucleus, one has not even the impression of a cleaving, but of a tearing. The division products round up whenever, as in mammalian ova, the egg membranes permit them to do so, and they would behave similarly also in the frog egg, were there sufficient room. The tendency is, however, not clearly discernible in the various twitchings and quiverings observed during cleavage, but these soon disappear as the cleavage products become more densely packed and the apparent furrows—better splits—seem again to be narrow clefts. In the lowest forms of reproduction of independent organisms, as in such as many Infusoria, the division products even separate, because there is no solid integument to keep them together. There can be no doubt, however, that the process is the same.

The designation "cleavage process" is therefore based only on the external aspect of this process, especially in the frog egg. Can it be that I have become overly sensitive to the retention of this term, because Ruscomi [sic] had been very much angered by my remark that he as well as Prévost and Dumas had observed division only on the surface, hence their usage of the term "cleavage," an anger which he vented in *Müllers Archiv*, 1836, p. 205, etc., and which, when I made his personal acquaintance ten years later, I found still present. I always thought, however, that if I furrowed a lump of matter so deeply that it was cut, then the lump is not merely furrowed but split and, by splitting, divided. But when this lump now splits by itself and each split-off part even becomes rounded and, what is more, this cleavage process is initiated by, and starts from the nucleus, then the lump is really and truly divided and not cleaved. Cleavage is a process proceeding from the outside toward the inside.

I obviously did not say that what we had here was a cell division process, because the cell theory as well as the idea that animals, too, consisted of cells, was postulated by Schwann only in 1839, and the term "cell" for elements of animal structures was completely foreign to me*.

*I am not really obliged to discuss here my attitude to the cell theory as propounded by Schwann in 1839, because I had to give up whatever plans I might have had to continue these biographical notes and reflections beyond the year 1834. Since, however, Professor Valentin of Bern has felt called upon to describe or, rather, denounce me in public as an opponent of the cell theory without specifying to the scientific public his right to do so, I intend to provide the necessary explanations in a footnote. It is quite impossible to investigate animal embryos in their early stages of development without perceiving that they are not composed of the same elementary particles as in the later stages. One sees globules which consist either of an opaque substance or of a translucent one and which could be called vesicles. I hope I will be believed if I say that I have seen them. Although I worked mostly with low magnifications, sometimes higher ones had also to be used. These elementary particles I called "histiological (histological) elements," as opposed to "morphological elements" which constitute a larger organic apparatus. In the vertebrate brain, for instance, the morphological elements from which it is originally formed are always clearly discernible and it appears to me that a clear idea of the large vertebrate brain cannot be achieved unless one considers the many morphological elements making up its roof and its base. In a similar way, I thought, one would have to follow the histological elements through their transformation. I was unable to follow this transformation continuously, since I applied myself too much to the morphological aspect. Both expressions I used freely in lectures, but avoided them as far as possible in print, as I did not like the combination with "logos" although this use or misuse has long taken root, people speaking for instance of geological products and components. After my move to St. Petersburg I chose the expressions "morphogenetic and histiogenetic elements" because of their correct formation, and in spite of their unseemly length. The most correct expression would perhaps have been "morphic," but I balked at "histic" which appeared to have very little chance of being accepted. Even though I rarely followed the histiogenetic elements in their transformations, but only observed them as I happened to find them, I still perceived that the isolated masses of organic substances, the "histiogenetic elements," are without outer membranes, but often gradually acquire them, either by deposition of a secreted substance which hardens to form an epithelial layer, or by coagulation of the
(Contd.)

In fact, my observation of the processes taking place in the frog egg had a rather depressing effect on me at first. I had already gotten used to the idea

outer layer of the globular substance itself. This delimitation phenomenon appeared to occur with greater certainty the more heterogeneous the surrounding mass. Thus, when a hen's egg with all its albumen is poured into a bowl with cold water, no covering layer is observed at first. Such a layer, however, soon forms, and quickly and solidly, the colder the water. If an albumen layer including the outer membrane is now detached, a similar skin is also formed on the inner side of the detached layer. In the remaining albumen mass the same membrane formation takes place anew. In this way it is possible to separate a number of layers which were originally not distinct from each other. This phenomenon must have been perceived by every observer. Yet not everybody will have poured albumen into a flat watch glass, to observe the drying-out process microscopically. If the albumen obtained from the egg is quite pure, it will be found to be quite transparent at first. The moment it begins to dry, however, an outermost layer forms which contains very small granules. At a greater depth, these granules are not found, however, and here the substance remains transparent. When drying has progressed to the point where the entire mass cracks (if one must not also use the word "furrows" here), the fragments gradually detach themselves from the watch glass, starting from the edges. To see how these flat fragments, inasmuch as they are already detached, also become granular on their lower surface but stay totally transparent wherever they still adhere to the watch glass, until the central section, too, becomes detached and thereby assumes the same texture, is a pretty sight indeed. This genesis of an outermost layer is not to be regarded as a life induced phenomenon, but only as a physical process. As is known, a much more differentiated, continuous membrane is produced when albumen makes contact with fats. Also delimitation and the creation of integumental membranes with living animal elements often differ but little from purely physical processes. When the yolk divides, the separate products of this division are at first without their own membrane—even without the thinnest layer. Such a membrane is, however, formed by secretion, from the yolk mass, of a transparent substance and this coating turns into a delicate skin wherever it comes into contact with a heterogenous substance, that is, along the entire outer surface of the split yolk masses, where it meets the traces of liquid entrapped between the yolk membrane and the yolk mass. Yet no membrane is formed where this secreted substance meets itself—in the interstices of the yolk mass. That is, in the frog egg, the yolk cleavage products leave no gap between each other. While they are indeed separated, they are separated by no more than these interstices which contain no yolk mass and consist of the substance secreted by the yolk mass, the same substance that also forms the covering membrane whenever it meets something heterogeneous, yet becomes a connective mass where this does not happen. A similar case is that of the secretion from the dermis: it turns into an epidermis where there is nothing to connect, and into a connective mass where two pieces of dermis make contact without an epidermis. I had indeed had many occasions to encounter the genesis of an epidermis or a covering membrane. The gradual formation of the yolk membrane in the ovary I had followed frequently; every laying hen dissected affords an opportunity to observe several stages of this process. Some more hens must be sacrificed to follow the gradual covering of the yolk mass with albumen and the formation of the so-called shell membrane and of the shell itself. But I could not neglect verifying earlier hypotheses which indeed turned out to have described this process generally correctly.

I came closer to the aim of this footnote if I state that I had followed the last-mentioned as well as other gradual covering processes of animal elements when I read Schwann's work. On the one hand, the presence of discrete elements in animal embryos was

(Contd.)

that in all reproductive processes there preexisted an organized basis. Now, however, I saw a splitting of this organization to prepare the material for new formations. It took me some time to accommodate myself to the concept that

a concept quite familiar to me, and I did not hesitate to associate it in general with the different tissue elements of fully developed animals as well. I have had little opportunity to follow the great variety of these elements and I fully acknowledge the fact that, in his *Embryology*, Professor Valentin has had a great deal more to say about this subject, but the delimitation of these elements, which very frequently takes place at a later stage, I have observed quite often. When Schleiden's beautiful investigations on the early formation of vegetable cells recently became known, I did not hesitate to find that the vegetable and animal histiogenetic elements differed in that, in the former, the early and sharp distinction between solid wall and liquid contents or, if you will, the contrast between solid and liquid, appears essential, while in the latter, the histiogenetic elements consist of soft masses of an intimate interpenetration of solid and liquid substances which, secondarily, form their integument. The same difference is also revealed in their gross structure. A blade of grass, held between my fingers, stands stiffly upright, and so does almost any other outdoor plant, however small the diameter of its stem. A tapeworm of several centimeters wide, held in an identical manner, droops flaccidly over my finger. The entire body of the plant is rigid, that of the lower animals, soft. While aquatic plants are softer than grasses, their structure is still more rigid than that of the corresponding animals. It is true that among these animals there are some with integuments still harder than those of plants, the corals, sea urchins, and shell-encased snails for instance, but it is in fact secreted calcareous substances which, as covering or support, give them this strength. The living matter itself remains soft, while in plants the living cell tissue is rigid.

It was therefore my intention to establish the difference between the general types of animal and vegetable formative elements. It never occurred to me, however, to call both of them cells, as I understand the term "cell" to refer to a solid mass forming a cavity which may be empty or filled with a different substance. Without the wall and without a cavity created by an absence of the wall substance, I really cannot imagine a cell. Like Swammerdam, I would have called an animal formative element a "Klöschen" (little dumpling) or, to avoid culinary associations, any other word, if a designation was required for this form of basic element. That in the lowest Cryptogamia the form of these elements not infrequently approaches that of the animal element, I was well aware. Later I also observed that in some animal parts, particularly in those that become rigid and show little resemblance to living tissue, such as the integuments of the Ascidiacea, the histiogenetic elements come very close to those of plants.

When Schwann's work appeared, in which all histiogenetic elements were called cells and were regarded as essentially identical, while also claiming for them, as generally valid, Schleiden's description of the formation of the plant cell, I could hardly agree. Reading, for example, on p. 48, "The albumen membrane probably has the function of the cell membrane, the albumen constitutes the cell contents, and the yolk—a young cell," I must be forgiven for having burst out laughing. That the albumen membrane is formed only after the albumen has already been deposited and after secretion of albumen has ceased, is probably the oldest observation on the formation of a membrane and, at the same time, also the least disputed one. If, as is well-known, a hen's yolk is intercepted in the oviduct before it reaches the so-called "Lege," analogous to the uterus, it is seen to be already surrounded by albumen which, however, has no definite delimitation, being continually exuded from the folds of the oviduct, as long as the latter is not completely dead. There

(Contd.)

this division was no more than the formation of new elements that are still no more than parts and expressions of the dominant unity, since in typical embryonic development these elements are used as building blocks, but building

is carried along with the yolk also only a part of the albumen. Schwann also claims that, with animal (histiogenetic) elements, the cell membrane has priority and the nucleus is located near the rim of the cells. Both claims I must reject. The interior of an animal element I had almost always found to differ from its exterior, which is obviously also the case with every formative element of the fully developed animal. In the embryonic elements, however, as in the secreted fluids, etc., I found as a rule the interior (the nucleus) to occupy a central rather than a marginal position, and the secondariness of membrane formation I had discerned too often to be able to doubt it. The use of the term "cell" for both types of elements, "dumplings" as well as vesicles, I disliked all the more, as the term was justifiably used for the latter, yet, when applied to the animal elements, caused this forced comparison.

I first made these objections of mine public before an association of fellow scientists. Somewhat later I prepared an article for a journal to be published by the local Medico-Surgical Academy both in Russian and in German. The board of the Academy, my employer at that time, designated me as editor of the German edition. This appointment was not very much to my liking, but I thought that a semi-polemical article would be the most effective action to take against what appeared to be becoming the prevailing views. I therefore publicized my objections to Schwann's views in a lecture at the Academy of Sciences, but did not print the article, which I intended to reserve for the future journal of the other Academy. This is how our then secretary, Nicholas Fuss, made the acquaintance of the article, and it was he, not an expert, who, during his visit to Switzerland, probably told Professor Valentin of my deviating opinions. Negotiations connected with the publication of the German edition for the Medico-Surgical Academy were extremely protracted and, in the end, only a Russian journal was decided upon, the editorship of which was naturally given to someone else. In the meantime, however, Schwann's original theory had undergone substantial modifications, which made my article completely superfluous, particularly after the publication of Kölliker's excellent "Theory of the Animal Cell" in Schleiden's and Nägeli's journal.

Would I not agree, I could possibly be asked, that Schwann's Cell Theory has been epoch-making? I freely admit that, inasmuch as it has evoked great interest, thereby contributing to the development of histiology, or, as most still spell it, histology, Schwann's book has had a great effect. This continuing and fruitful effect, however, is primarily due to the fact that more attention was drawn to the histiogenetic elements than was the case so far, and that a certain degree of internal metamorphosis was perceived in these separate formations, although I hold that, by according too great an importance to the so-called life of the cell, for some time people went too far. If the cells, that is, the histiogenetic elements, were indeed to build the animal organism all on their own, they would have to possess a great deal of morphogenetic intelligence. It seems to me that the lower the organizational stage, the higher the ability of organic matter to shape itself into separate entities. In any case, the general designation of the term "cell" for all histiogenetic elements is to be deplored. This term is very appropriate for a certain form for which it has long been used, a form, that is, in which there is a sharp separation between solid wall and liquid content, even if later this content is filled with secondary insulation matter such as chlorophyll and amyl.

Generally speaking, my views have changed only to the extent that I am now less areprepd to separate the cells and "dumpling" shapes according to the organic kingdoms.

blocks that are still in a continual process of transformation. When the dorsal groove of the frog is still open, I could see it easily with the naked eye. Under the microscope, the two dorsal halves look like two embankments formed of cannon balls.

I encountered much more serious difficulties with the mammals. Because the chick embryo positions itself with its longitudinal axis at a right angle to the longitudinal axis of the egg, and because I observed a similar tendency in the more rounded ova of mammals, I was inclined to see in this phenomenon the expression of a profound necessity. As research on the so-called electro-magnetism was arousing lively interest at that time and was showing that an electrical current would cause magnetism to be deflected at a right angle, I sensed some connection, without, however, being able to put it more defi-nitely. The elongated ova of the hoofed animals, on the other hand, particularly of the pig, seemed to contradict this rule at first, in that I not infrequently found their embryos in a decidedly oblique position. Eventually I convinced myself that no contradiction was involved after all. After the ovum of this animal has become elongated and the first beginnings of the embryo are discernible, it is almost impossible to uncover the interior of the ovum with-out tearing the drawn-out, thin yolk sac. It is this tearing (produced by the detachment of the intervening placental folds) that causes this oblique position and, if reduced to a minimum by careful handling, the embryo will assume the transverse position. On this point I had no longer any doubts.

Another circumstance, however, one that no longer worries anybody today, upset me greatly: the apparently dissimilar development of sheep and pig ova in the early stages. As I could rely on the data provided by Herr Jachmann, and had one ovum drawn after the other, I had hoped to obtain a continuous series which, as I mentioned above (p. 252), would permit deter-mination of the age of the ova according to the drawings. As I had naturally chosen short time intervals for the first period following fertilization, I soon perceived that the series was by no means a continuous one, but that some later developments resembled earlier ones, or even appeared to precede them. It worried me less that the data for the early transformations which I had observed in dog ova agreed neither among themselves nor with those collected by myself. The long duration of estrus, combined with the unreliability of the data concerning the bitches brought to me, certainly reduced the importance of these differences. In ewes and sows, however, heat is very short and I could expect the reports as to the exact moment of mating to be trustworthy. Yet one was so much used to the idea, then prevailing, that individual life began with the act of mating that it took me a long time to rid myself of it. Even-tually I could not but assume that maturation of the ovum in the ovaries and, particularly, release of the ovum from the latter, were not directly dependent on the act of mating, a state of affairs later definitely verified by Bischoff and Pouchet. Another factor, too, seemed to me to cause the difference between ova of the same age. Particularly in the elongated ova of the hoofed animals, the size of the ovum did not appear to keep step with embryonic development, so that the same developmental stage of the embryo was sometimes associated with different sizes of the fetal membranes. I concluded that these differences had to be ascribed to different degrees of flexibility (flabbiness) of the uterus or to different secretional capabilities. The telescoping of pig ova at their ends is seen at later periods also in different circumstances, but appears to be due simply to differences in pressure.

I hesitated to express all this in public. On the whole, however, a despondency had taken hold of me, which was in part based on moral grounds, but in part doubtlessly on my physical state.

Not only had I not reckoned with the difficulties now posed by the mammals due to the irregularities in the progress of their development, but because of my particular mood, these irregularities affected me more than their real significance warranted, and prevented me from arriving at definite conclusions.

Apart from spiritual factors, it was, however, my physical condition which most affected this mood of dejection. I spent far too much time in the sitting position, bent over my desk, particularly from the time the returning warmth caused the snow to melt, and deep into the summer, this being the period of time into which, of necessity, all research on development had to be compressed. My digestion suffered greatly from this, all the more so as I had always been used to moving about in the open, particularly in the spring, ostensibly to welcome Flora's new children, but really because I definitely felt the benevolent effect of moving about out-of-doors. From a *Coureur des bois et des champs* I had turned into a hermit crab who, once it was chosen, never left the abode. As I was living in the zoological museum, and as in summer the lectures on zoology were my main official occupation, my visits to the nearby anatomical institute, which I regarded as my second home, were only few and far between. Of meetings in commissions or other official consultations in which, in St. Petersburg, one spends a considerable part of one's life, there were almost none in Königsberg. The academic senate assembled barely twice each semester and even so there was no great need to go there, as business was mostly transacted by people entrusted with it, and faculty business, apart from examinations, was mostly settled by written memoranda carried by messengers.

Thus, it came about that one year I had locked myself in my rooms far beyond winter and that when I walked to the city wall for the first time that year, a distance of a few hundred steps, I saw the rye in full ear, ready to ripen soon. This view shook me so deeply that I threw myself to the ground and reproached myself for the foolishness of my ways. "Nature's Laws of Formation will be discovered," I pleaded with myself in an Epicurean or Mephistophelean vein, "whether by you or by another, whether this year or the next is really of no importance and it is plain foolishness to sacrifice your own life's enjoyment which nobody will ever return to you." Yet, next year turned out the same. The consequences made themselves felt, indeed had done so long ago. My digestion was so bad that already several years before I moved to St. Petersburg I had been depending daily on artificial means to make my bowels move. I could or would not submit myself to regular medical treatment, as all such treatments began with the order to change my sedentary way of life. Unfortunately, I had as yet not overcome the sceptical attitude I had acquired earlier with regard to practical medicine. A secret remedy which somebody had recommended to me and which contained a not inconsiderable quantity of aloes brought daily relief to be sure, but which I now believe had unfavorable side effects due to excessive stimulation. Later I have had much better results with the use of pure rhubarb root, a fact which I should like to mention for the benefit of all those suffering from sluggish digestion. At that period I sometimes had to lie down in the afternoon, unable to do any mental work. When I sat down to the microscope or any other work right after the midday meal, I felt the blood shoot into my head. A regular nap taken after the noon meal, and the use of a saddle chair when writing, somewhat reduced these congestions which were much favored by my myopia and the resulting excessively bent-over posture when writing.

Yet, no thorough treatment was ever carried through, including avoidance of continuous sitting as a pathogenic factor. Such a course was prevented by the magnitude of my wishes or desires. The apparent simplicity of vertebrate development spurred me on to follow it in all directions, holding out hopes to be able to change traditional views. Thus, there was no doubt in my mind that the prevailing view, according to which twin-bodied monstrosities were produced by the actual growing together of two individuals, can only be explained by the fact that we have become so thoroughly used to the idea of the whole man or the whole animal, that the moment the question of twin bodies arises, this idea is bound to intrude, making us assume that they grow together, for which in fact no observational proof has ever been adduced. I equally had no doubt that botanists were using the wrong language when, at that time, they regarded the single-whorl perianth of the Monochlamideae as a fusing of corolla and calyx, or the single-petal corolla as a fusing of the multipetal corolla. It was quite obvious to me that the true situation was the opposite: in plants as in animals, developmental progress had to lie in separation and division, and it was only the conventional idea of the more developed double-whorl perianth that had distorted language. Thus every spring as soon as the sun had begun to pour down its rays, a seed box was prepared and sown with all sorts of plants, to observe their sprouting and later development, so that I might come out with a report.

Overall, however, I cannot but confess that I had bitten off more than I could chew and that the sheer impossibility of coping with everything upset me greatly. When I applied myself to frogs, which underwent transformation so rapidly, the plants shot up and I had not measured the internodal distances in order to report which had grown discernibly and which would grow no more—and these were after all only Phanerogamia; the Cryptogamia were still in the dark, as far as I was concerned. When I now remember the high hopes I had of being able to follow the development of animals at least in their major modifications, I cannot but smile. These hopes were inspired by the simplicity of the development of the vertebrates. But nature, if very simple in its operations which our imagination usually surpasses by far, is still infinitely varied. Thus I did not know the first thing about the alternation of generations, although Chamisso's observations on Salpa were known and mentioned yearly in my own lectures as an unintelligible curiosity. The description of the main types of development and subsequently of the main groups of organization, at least of the animal kingdom, I must admit, I saw as my life's task. Am I to regard it as enthusiasm for the subject, or as vanity or ambition if, as I must further confess, during those last years I always became agitated, not to say upset, when I found that others had contributed to embryology in fields which I had already touched upon, or at least mentally laid out as future lines of approach? This happened more often with the plant than with the animal kingdom. If I happened to read something of this kind shortly before going to bed, I could be certain to toss sleeplessly most of the night, with my thoughts whirling, either in disagreement with the author or elaborating his arguments. I therefore took something like the novels of Walter Scott for my nightly reading, with whom I was reasonably certain not to encounter echoes of embryology or of the systematics based on it. Yet, although the personal fates of his heroes and heroines sometimes kept me equally awake, I could not do without some sort of lightning rod for my imagination, as otherwise it would simply go on ruminating the latest stages of my investigations or other studies.

Reminiscences of this obsession with a scientific objective can be found in my speech on "The Development of Science." At that time (1836), I was already able to regard things objectively, a happy consequence of my move (to St. Petersburg).

I was really ill, my nervous system was too excited and my digestion worse than ever. This state of affairs I could no longer ignore, nor the fact that it was primarily caused by my sedentary mode of life. That the mammals had posed more problems than I had expected might have had an unfavorable effect, but that I had accorded excessive importance to the unexpected irregularities was no doubt already a result of my ill-humor. I had no doubt that a journey, preferably to the Adriatic, undertaken to follow the development of some Asteroidea, would shake me up and put me right again. But only now did I realize that all available financial means such as were not directly used for the needs of the family had been invested in the acquisition of books or used for anatomical research. What I had left would not even take me as far as Berlin, let alone farther away. I did not want to ask the ministry for support or for an advance, which in any case would probably have been in vain. But I did contemplate a radical change in my position, as I had despaired of ever being able to combine my present position with a more regular and diet-conscious mode of life. At present, everything was organized in such a way that, at least from the end of March to the end of July, I had more material for research than I could really handle. Not to have touched the material at all would have tormented me no less.

Although, as I feel it, such private reflections hardly belong in a biography, but should be buried along with ourselves, I believe I had to report them here, because, as I have learned only in recent years, the view had been spreading in Germany that I had left Königsberg for St. Petersburg either because I had been offended by not having been called to Berlin to succeed Rudolphi after the latter's death, or else because of a mere clerical error connected with the honoring of my demands for payment for the domestic animals delivered to me from Trutenau (p. 363). As the latter assertion is at least based on something that has really happened, I will report all the facts to the best of my knowledge. But first I would like to ask whether it is really so remarkable to exchange Königsberg for St. Petersburg, especially if one is Russian by birth? What is more, I shall presently give a rather tangible reason which turned up unexpectedly and must have been well-known in Königsberg, and which I also offered in my letter of resignation.

As regards the filling of Rudolphi's position, I can state in all sincerity that I had never aspired to it, that is, not to the position as it was at that time. Rudolphi lectured on anatomy and physiology and, in his last years, had become somewhat antiquated in both disciplines. In the capital, however, a new and younger lecturer could hardly start in the same manner in which Rudolphi had finished. As concerns anatomy, I had reason to believe that I was fully abreast of the science, and able to keep pace with future progress. Not so with physiology, where I could not fail to realize that I was well-informed only as far as embryology was concerned. It is true, though, that at that time physiology still lacked that rich underpinning of chemistry and physics which it enjoys now. It was quite clear to me that in the capital, the meeting place of young doctors from all the German universities, a new lecturer could not possibly present physiology from Haller's point of view, still held by Rudolphi. I might possibly have accepted a professorship in anatomy and physiology at any other German university, in the hope of being able to catch up soon with the progress of physiology, but dared not do so in the case of Berlin. Had I been offered Rudolphi's position, I could have accepted only anatomy and it is rather doubtful whether the university would have agreed to a division. Johannes Müller, whom I unhesitatingly regarded as the most competent successor to Rudolphi, still lectured on both sciences and their ramifications. Only after his early death were they separated.

I therefore did not undertake any steps to be called to Berlin, firstly because I knew that the ministry was averse to removing a lecturer from Königsberg, glad as it was when somebody had grown roots there, but more particularly because there were more and more signs that I had lost favor in the eyes of the minister, von Altenstein. My innocent and well-meant efforts during the cholera epidemic had in fact turned him choleric. This anger of his was—quite unintentionally—fanned by a faithful well-wisher of mine, Governor von Schön. Immediately after I had published my first article on the arguments of Indian doctors against the contagiousness of cholera, a high government official visited me early in the morning with a message from the governor who, so the message said, had enjoyed my article and wanted to encourage me to continue this work. I was not a little surprised, as all I had had in mind was my draftsman who was afraid of catching the disease by merely looking at one of the (casualty) baskets. That was still before the riots, but Herr von Schön, facing the almost insuperable difficulties involved in the enforcement of the measures ordered from Berlin, was already at that time looking for good reasons to call them off. I took good care not to follow von Schön's invitation, nor had I in that article declared myself against any of the governmental measures, although I found it unjust to spread fear through a surfeit of public announcements, without the slightest hint that contagiousness was in fact still in doubt. Laymen had thus accepted my article as a new revelation. When, after the riot and after the quarantine measures had been lifted, I had published my research on the first cases, I could not refrain from stating that the person who, according to the doctors, was the first to contract cholera and to die of it, had not left Königsberg for weeks, perhaps even months, and could not therefore have been infected through the agency of a contagium, unless one were to assume the agent to be a sparrow which had alighted on an infected object. That Berlin was extremely dissatisfied with the lifting of the quarantine and had sent an official to Königsberg to have it restored if possible, but that von Schön remained adamant, is beside the point here. I will not, however, hide the fact that, as we gradually learned, the minister was a decided contagionist not only in his official capacity, but also personally, although it was not quite clear whether it was he or Rust who practically terrorized the King and his Court with his views and measures against the importation of the cholera. I had known Rust since my Vienna days as a more than energetic man.

The governor spent the end of 1831 and the beginning of 1832 in Berlin. Upon returning he told me laughingly that apart from his official prerogative which gave him the right in urgent cases to cancel even a royal order, provided he could subsequently justify his actions, it was mostly I whom he had cited in support of his omissions and commissions. He also brought me a caricature which had appeared in Berlin, showing a sparrow with Rust's face, and carrying the heading "Passer rusticus, the common sparrow." Von Schön thought that this was the portrait of my hypothetical sparrow and appeared little satisfied with my remark that a far more plausible explanation was that Berlin humor had called Rust a *Sperling* (sparrow) because of the *Sperren* (quarantine), after the quarantine measures, hated also in Berlin, had been removed. On this occasion, I learned, however, that it was von Schön himself who had spread my sparrow hypothesis, telling also Rust himself. Now you are in hot water indeed, I said to myself, and proofs did not fail to materialize. A letter of mine, for instance, asking for payment for the animals delivered from Trutenau, was answered with the question as to the authority on which I based my claims. This sudden ignorance seemed so peculiar, that I could not impute it to the Königsberg board which was well disposed toward me, but to the minister personally. It was he with whom I had directly negotiated concerning the above-mentioned measures (p. 252) and of his decision, so I was later told, no complete copy had ever reached Königsberg. That may have been the case, but then several payments had been made in the past. How then had that happened? Be that as it may, it is completely erroneous to claim this as my reason for leaving Königsberg. While it is true that, because of the state of my health, I had longed for a change, I also had another motive, a very unexpected and painful one at that.

My older brother, Ludwig, who was childless, wanted to adopt one of my sons and intended to visit us at Christmas 1833, to make his choice. He never arrived. I learned that having completed his preparations for the journey, he fell ill and died. He had been the owner of the family estate. My brothers and sisters were now prevailing on me to take over the estate so that some day it would pass into the hands of one of my sons, thereby fulfilling the wish of my deceased brother who wanted to keep the estate in the family, bearing in mind the fact that my younger brother, then in military service, was unmarried and, as he suffered from gout, would probably remain unmarried. I promised to visit Reval during the spring vacation to have a closer look at the situation, and also invited my younger brother to be there. Since there he declared that although he intended to leave military service, he would not marry, and as I saw him with his feet so swollen that he could only remain lying down, it seemed obvious that for him to take over the estate was unwise and I declared my readiness to do so. The estate was heavily encumbered, also including the shares of the rest of us, and if all the interest was not paid on time, the estate was liable to be sold at auction. Although my own share in the estate was very small, amounting as it did to less than 3,000 rubles, I thought it well worth having a ready home for one of my sons, all the more so, as so far I had done precious little for their future. But to exercise my ownership rights from Königsberg was hardly advisable; to have me run the estate all by myself, even less so. I thus decided to inquire whether St. Petersburg would have me back and, having received a speedy answer, my future was settled.

It seems to me that these circumstances, which I have never made a secret of, were sufficient in themselves. I will only add that the journey in Russian coaches from Memel to Reval, in conjunction with the inevitably sparse diet, did wonders for my digestive apparatus, and as for the need for more movement—convincing proof of that was not only demonstrated before my very eyes, but shaken and jolted right into my bones.

Before dragging the gentle reader away from Königsberg, I ought to mention another local development which was not at all to my liking—a political tension within the educated classes. During the first years of my stay, soon after the Great War, Königsberg was characterized by an extensive concurrence of political views, which were patriotic, conservative, and loyal to the government, in particular, to the Royal House. Thus, when after the expulsion of the Bourbons in 1830, great agitation was felt in many German lands, Königsberg remained completely calm, including the easily roused world of the students. The ministry found it fitting to publish a special Letter of Commendation in which it expressed its appreciation of the fact that only at Königsberg University could no traces of revolutionary tendencies be found. Whether it was this laudatory statement that had had an effect quite opposite to that intended, or that the bold language used during the cholera period even by the most conservative to dissuade the government from continuing the quarantine system had simply caught on—people often seemed to continue in this vein, although the original cause had disappeared. The malcontents, of whom there had always been some, but who had never dared appear in public, now made themselves heard. Even before I had left Königsberg, society had split into progressives and conservatives. While public affairs had always been discussed openly, such discussions now became passionate, and partisan zeal made itself felt particularly by the fact that the members of one party regarded the adherents of the other not as merely narrow-minded, but as bad. This agitation must have increased further after I had left, at least it became more public. By 1848, the *Königsberger Zeitung*, which had always been regarded as the tamest of tame newspapers, had become the loudest of the loud. It was as if it had become ashamed of its servility in 1830.

Returning now to my own person, all I can say is that as far as the above-mentioned developments were concerned, the mutual recriminations of the parties made me feel very uneasy. Is it not possible to be of different opinions without hating and despising one another?

Having returned to Königsberg, I attempted to prepare a summary of the results of my previous research on the formation of the various mammalian ova, dispensing with the mass of individual illustrations and also drawing on other vertebrate classes, to demonstrate once more the general and typical in the vertebrate structure, this time in a more concentrated and, as I believed, clearer manner, using only a few woodcuts for illustration. Special treatment was to be accorded only to the very few investigations on the very early stages of the human ovum and embryo which I had had opportunity to observe, as most of the embryos had to be regarded as abnormally developed, probably spontaneously aborted for that reason. This work was intended to form the second volume of my work *On the Embryology of Animals, Observation and Reflection*, but before I could finish it, the news had spread that I had recently decided to leave Königsberg. The Prussian ministry now offered me a professorship at Halle, which I had to refuse with thanks. As it was I who had initiated the new engagement in St. Petersburg, I found it impossible to cancel it on my part. I thus submitted my resignation. At the end of the summer semester I handed over the zoological museum and the anatomical institute. My overgrown library as well as my other possessions had to be packed, and in the late fall we finally departed. We suffered from the bad roads, but since we were attacked neither by bears nor by highwaymen, my wife gradually found the country better than its reputation. It was no longer possible, however, to transport the library by boat that year and I received it only late the next year through the kind offices of Admiral Ricord. Unpacking could be undertaken only in the winter of 1835 to 1836. One consequence of this delay was my inability to realize my intention to work out the last section of the above-mentioned book, namely the report on my research on the human embryo, including comparison of related observations by other authors, which I had planned to do soon after my arrival in St. Petersburg, as here I could hardly find any of the pertinent literature. I simply could not do it without my own library.

This in turn caused my publishers, the Bornträger brothers of Königsberg, to finally lose patience and, in 1836, to print the manuscript which I had left with them as it was, with the added note that no more was to be expected.

*   .   *   *

Prior to my departure from Königsberg I had proposed as my successor Dr. C.Th. von Siebold, of whom great things could be expected in the field of natural sciences. Herr von Siebold had begun his fruitful investigations in a subordinate position in Danzig and aspired to greater activity. Orally and quietly I was told, however, that my proposal was unacceptable, as Siebold was a Catholic. Now it is true that Königsberg University was founded in 1544, at a time when the Jesuits were most actively trying to keep Poland obedient to the Holy See, and that the university was supposed to provide Protestantism with protection and patronage. But that fears were still harbored that Catholicism was apt to infiltrate via the study of animals in 1834 was indeed somewhat unexpected. Still, deep wisdom and foresight sometimes do reside with the fathers of the academic senate. Would a von Siebold have become *the* authority on comparative anatomy on the shores of the

Baltic? And who would have given proof of parthenogenesis in *Psyche Helix* and the queen bee, as the former does not occur that far to the north, and the latter did not have its Dzierzon?* It was, after all, a happy circumstance that Catholicism was still regarded as dangerous in the Königsberg of 1834.

*[Ed. note: Johannes Dzierzon, pastor and beekeeper who discovered that drones hatch from unfertilized eggs.]

5. Our Permanent Residence
in St. Petersburg
(1834-?)

At the end of 1834 I found myself in St. Petersburg, alone that is, as I had left my family with my people in Reval to help them to acclimatize and to follow me in spring.

If I wanted to report on my residence in St. Petersburg even in some detail, this book would assume a monstrous size, or become a brood of several volumes, and I would run the danger of spending the late autumn of my life, which possibly still has some beautiful days to offer, in the recapitulation of the gay spring and the hot summer. To register briefly the facts in a chronological summary may be useful as far as the history of states and rulers is concerned, because the historian has to organize his thoughts and research according to this framework. It is to this end that the historians have invented their registers, which are as thin and unlovely, but also as useful as architects' scaffolding. But the life of a man who has had no influence whatsoever on the waves of history, being only moved about by them, can be of interest only if he turns himself into a historical mirror, reporting how these movements affected him. This was also my initial plan. But I soon perceived that the field was too rich and too large to be thus harvested. What indeed has not changed within my lifetime! As a boy who had just begun to listen to the talk of adults, I heard them speak enthusiastically about the Egyptian campaign of Napoleon I, which had unexpectedly taken place at that time. This was also the occasion when whatever the fathers had retained from their school days about Alexander the Great would again float to the surface, hence probably the efforts of my uncle to portray the Macedonian hero as a shining example (p. 16). As a youth, I shared the fierce hatred which my surroundings felt toward the same Napoleon when he invaded Russia. The Great Alexander had become Attila, though more in our minds than in reality. Both invasions resembled each other in that they were started without a declaration of war and for no other reason than the reaping of *gloire* in other countries. But Egypt did not concern us; we did not care about the horrors of war there, we saw only the *gloire*. In Russia it was different. We felt the ravages of war, and instead of the glory we saw only the crime of the invader. *La gloire* was lost, however, and Napoleon atoned for this loss on the rock of St. Helena, as did Prometheus on the crag in the Caucasus. He regained sympathies lost, after Sir

Hudson Lowe had the courage to take over as his jailer, not in order to tear at his liver as did that brutal eagle, but to destroy him slowly, by calculated treatment, as do the burghers of Strassbourg with their geese, and as did the British government which, after the deaths of ward and warder, produced the *paté de foie gras* from the estate of the latter, to show how everything was bound to happen as it in fact did. It was only the German people who unshakably believed that magnanimity resided exclusively with the British—even with their government—if not always visibly so. And as to the Germans themselves—after the vast destruction they happily returned to their habitual political particularism, astonished that in the Grand Concert of Nations, Franz-Michel*, Fritz-Michel and Michel-Michel kept each other in check, causing their common voice to be lost. Only from time to time, when some great changes occur in Paris, does Michel shake himself in his several Procrustean beds, because the old dreams, according to which freedom is bound to come from Paris, apparently die hard. We Germans across the Narva, however, are told: You have no right to look to the West, you are no Michels, because you were subjugated by Peter the Great. You should look only toward the East. But of late, the East has begun shouting at us: Do not come too near to disturb our patriarchal quiet, because of what we have suffered at the hands of Biron. In vain does one search for a logical formula which would point to a causal connection between that court favorite, Duke Biron, from the first half of the previous century and the common German of the present day, for whom science is both walking stick and bread basket. In vain does one look for the connection, when there sounds that other threat: You want to stay separate over there! Woe to the vanquished! Not to cross the Narva river and not to stay behind it either, nor look beyond the Nieman! How to please everybody? Should one move backward across the Nieman river? Or should one strive toward the pellucid and tranquil regions of the light? The last choice will probably be the better one.

When the waves rise as high as they did up to the year 1815 and, after the storm, are still wildly dancing up and down in the Nachgewoge** (aftersurge), before they quiet down to a smooth surface, who is able to follow the individual droplet in its movements? It was, however, less the political movements that I intended to record, but the more tranquil progress in the regions of light which goes on and on, without anybody being able to tell how far. But

*[Ed. note: Michel—a name personifying the average, simple German.]

**During a storm, the wave crests are driven along by the wind, while the water itself travels very little. After a storm, small crests of water long continue to bob up and disappear at the same point, after which other crests nearby bob up and sink down. This phenomenon is most conspicuous in closed seas, such as the Caspian. This may be the reason for the fact that the Russian language has a special term for it, zyb', for which I tried to use the above expression. The waves of a storm are destructive, those of the zyb' merely a nuisance.

here, too, forces appeared too vast, too violent for me to grasp. Somewhere I happened to read, as a description of our age, "We let ourselves be pulled along by steam, that bastard born of fire and water, we draw with sunlight and write with lightning!" Who, however, could report on everything that had to pass before these mighty forces had been harnessed, who could tell all that without filling countless tomes! Certainly not one who already sees his repose being prepared and awaits the hour when deep sleep will finally beckon him. Until then he enjoys every new progress, consoling himself with the thought that the higher regions will go on to produce new light—and in the lower regions, on the other hand, the Law of Necessity will succeed in calming down the aftersurges of the storm.

Before bidding farewell I should like, however, to have a side glance at a limited field, the large number of popular journals in the German lands not conquered by Peter, which today chew up all natural history knowledge, to prepare it for the spoon-feeding of many classes of the population. The sciences must be popularized, they say. Indeed they must be, and I have always supported this idea. But now that this process is under way, and the fruits of the work of discoverers and inventors are being ground up in countless mills of which I know only the fewest, I am reminded of the bone mills in which the remains of living organisms are converted into an amorphous powder with which to fertilize the fields and to produce food for the people. This is certainly a worthy purpose, but it is also easily possible for adulterated and, therefore, unhealthy substances to slip into the powder, substances which are no longer recognizable, as all records of their antecedents have been lost. Whether he be Trojan or Latin, it will make no difference to me, says the miller and lets his mill grind away. I may be wrong, but it seems to me that this principle is beginning to also have an effect on the higher spheres of science, where one no longer takes as much care to distinguish between the observations and ideas of others and those of one's own, as was the rule in Germany, at least in my younger years. Beyond the Rhine, they were not too particular about it even then. Fortunately, there are still a few people around who are qualified to know the origins of the sources feeding the river of a particular science. Without these people, our literature was liable to assume the character of the Middle Ages, whose writings contained a great many claims of which nobody knows what they were based upon.

Looking back now on the expansion of knowledge within my lifetime, I find it immense. The inner structure of plants and animals has been bared, as well as the course of their development. Chemistry came to understand the rhythmic compounding of substances and followed their transformation through the process of life. Matter was seen as essential and dominant since, prior to the French Revolution, Lavoisier had shown that matter was indestructible, merely changing its form and compounds. But electricity was seen to produce magnetism, and light revealed as motion, having chemical effects and being able to produce images. Heat, too, appeared to be motion, and that it dominates chemistry has never been in doubt. All forces, though creations of our abstraction, have again come into their rights. They turn into each other, but the amount of motion remains the same, just as the amount of weight indicates the presence of substances in their different transformations. Thus, by observation, measurement and calculation, science steadily approaches the aim which, at the birth of the century, Schelling in youthful exuberance set out to reach in the *montgolfier* of the "intellectual ideology," to be at first admired and later ridiculed.

May others follow their respective egos in such vast movements, political and scientific! I have still another reason to expedite my exit. On the occasion of my jubilee, after I had already begun these confessions, a celebration was arranged in the best of friendly spirits and with the most excessive tributes, which to reduce to reasonable proportions would be a task of herculean dimensions, for which I am neither honest nor strong enough. I leave it therefore to the individual reader to perform those subtractions he deems suitable.

But I shall at least provide a description of my travels, as well as the most important events of my later years, for the enlightenment and benefit of the biographical lexica.

TRAVELS

I have moved about much in Russia, partly in recognition of the fact that the totally sedentary life which I had led in Königsberg for the last years had completely undermined my health, partly also because of my sincere wish to be of use to the fatherland. As far as I remember, I spent at least one month each year—the academic vacation—on travels which, during the first years, also included my visit to the estate (a distance of about 350 versts* from here) that my younger brother Andreas managed. Other journeys were undertaken in the interest of natural history or in an official capacity. The state of my health had decidedly changed for the better, and although throughout the entire time I was unable to dispense with the help of the *Rad. Rhei* (probably rhubarb root), the suspicion of an organic change in my digestive tract, which had been torturing me during the last period in Königsberg, proved to be entirely groundless. In retrospect, I can now say that, had I stayed on in Königsberg, I might have achieved more in the field of science, feeling right in the middle of the combatants in the scientific struggle there. I can equally say, however, that I would have jointed the invalids' corps, if not worse, far earlier.

The first longer trip I took was to Novaya Zemlya, in 1837. Zivolka, an officer from the Navigators' Corps, a man of many scientific interests who had

*[Ed. note: 1 verst=0.66288 miles.]

already participated in two expeditions to Novaya Zemlya under Pakhtussov, not only provided me with meteorological observations made during these expeditions, the results of which I have published (*Writings*, III, c, 8–11), but also told me much of this island, which he had come to like very much. He merely increased my interest which had already been aroused by the temperature conditions. I wanted to see for myself what nature could produce as far as life processes were concerned, given such meager means, and proposed to the Academy to send me there, at its expense. Had I been less eager, I would have undertaken the journey only the next year. As it was, I left the very moment I was informed that my travel allowance had been granted. First I went to Archangel and thence by a walrus-catcher to Novaya Zemlya. Herr Lehmann, a young naturalist from Dorpat, who had later visited Bokhara, accompanied me. Brief reports from this journey appeared in the Bulletin of the Academy (*Writings*, III, c, 14–20). The extraordinary sight of the change from the dark mountains to the mighty snow fields; of the colorful, extremely short-stemmed flowers, almost all of them found collected on the miniature lawns of the marginal shore; of the willows creeping along underground except for the uppermost shoots which protrude from clefts in the soil—all these belong to my most vivid memories. Yet the most sublime experience I can remember is the solemn stillness which prevails on the land when the air is quiet and the sun shining serenely, be it at noon or at midnight, a stillness broken neither by the hum of an insect nor by the swish of a blade of grass nor the rustle of shrubs, since whatever vegetation that there is closely hugs the ground.

As I was merely a passenger on a walrus-catcher which had retained its right to go about its business, I was unfortunately limited in my freedom of movement and could visit only four localities on the western shores and one on the shore of the Kara Sea. As we could stay in Novaya Zemlya no longer than six weeks before winter set in again, I felt a strong need for a second trip.

I did indeed undertake a second journey to the North in 1840 in the company of Herr von Middendorff and Herr Pankewitsch. This time the walrus-catcher was completely at our disposal. It was also planned, however, to visit the eastern and northern shores of Russian Lapland, as it is rarely possible to land on Novaya Zemlya earlier than the middle of July. We also visited many localities in Lapland. However, since the smacks of the Russian Arctic Ocean, being provided with one single, large sail, go reasonably fast only with full or nearly full wind, I intended to wait for a favorable wind, in the meantime visiting as many fishery stations as possible. This time, however, the wind was very unfavorable for us, as it was only on the sixth of August that it started blowing from the west, having earlier blown from the various eastern points of the compass, except for the very first days. Now we indeed could set sail for Novaya Zemlya. Since we had advanced rather far to the west by then, however, it would have taken us at least eight to nine days to reach Novaya Zemlya, getting us past the middle of August, and as one had to leave the island by the end of August at the latest, unless one wanted to risk being cut off by the ice, the crew most strongly expressed its opposition, claiming that they were not at all equipped to spend the winter on Novaya Zemlya. We managed to quiet them down by declaring that we, the scientists, were also not prepared for such an eventuality. At the same time we realized, however, that in the best of circumstances we would be able to remain on the island for only a very short time, while in the least favorable case we would have to spend the entire time at our disposal in the Arctic Ocean. We therefore had no choice but to give up the idea of visiting the island. It now seemed a better course to continue to the North Cape (of Norway) and to look at some more places on our way home. Setting out from Kola, Herr von Middendorff traveled to the Bay of Kandalaksha, making his way partly on foot and partly by boat. On this occasion he found that our maps were all wrong as far as this region was concerned, giving the wrong direction for the Kola river. I myself returned by sea. In the *Contributions to the Knowledge of the Russian Empire*, Vol. XI, pp. 139–183, Herr von Middendorff has published a detailed report on his separate journey. In the *Bulletin de la classe physico-mathématique*, Vol. XI, pp. 217–224, he also provided a detailed map including explanations, and in the above *Contributions*, Vol. VIII, pp. 187–258, he published the results of his ornithological observations. I gave summary reports in *Bull. sc.*, IX, pp. 298–300, and in the *Contributions to the Knowledge of the Russian Empire*, VIII, pp. 264–267, including maps.

Between these two journeys of 1837 and 1840 I undertook a journey through the south of Finland, for my own enlightenment and at my own expense, during which my attention was almost forcibly engaged by the abrasions and erosion marks found on the local rocks. With the sun very low, I saw a flat and low rock mound, from the mail coach, darkly striped like a zebra skin. Alighting from the coach to have a closer look, I saw parallel erosion marks several inches wide, that extended across the entire rock. These marks, then shaded, contrasted and alternated with the sunlit ridges. Apart from the often discussed fine abrasions, the surfaces of rocks in Finland show not only deeply etched grooves, but also more shallow abrasions from three inches to over one foot wide, which are themselves scored. When the sun is higher in the sky, they are less easily discerned, unless one puts a straight stick on the rock surface, in a direction perpendicular to the scoring marks. These marks were most distinct on the tops of flat rock ridges but, as I later saw in the highlands, also appear on sharper crests. After I had arrived in Helsingfors, Nordenskiöld, the renowned mineralogist, was kind enough to show me the great variety of those ancient diluvian movements found in the environs of this city.

This experience awakened my lasting interest in the subject and as I have found it difficult to accommodate myself to the daring and brilliant concept of a former glacial period as propounded by Agassiz, I have visited Finland repeatedly since this trip of 1838. In 1839, I traveled to the islands of the Gulf of Finland to obtain a first-hand impression of the frequency with which rock boulders to this very day are carried by ice floes. Although I was informed of larger boulders which had been sighted only recently, and although smaller boulders came along very frequently, so that in the course of a century individual islands had conspicuously grown by this accretionary process, the substantial and numerous heaps of large boulders that were found piled up in the sea itself tended to confirm the glacier theory. Much later (*Bull. de l'Acad.* VIII, pp. 195–216) I reported on these observations. These little-known and rarely visited islands are, however, of great interest also quite apart from these migrating stone boulders. The porphyry island Gogland offers a beautiful miniature mountain range where, during a morning's comfortable walk, one can reach picturesque rock faces, tumbled-down boulders, crevasses, and the like. Only glaciers are missing to create the illusion of Switzerland; instead, there is the sea all around. The other islands are flatter, but also attractive due to the patriarchal way of life of the inhabitants.

My first travels across southern Finland aroused my interest to such a degree that still more trips were to follow. On one of these, Professor Nordenskiöld was kind enough to accompany me as far as Yussari, to show me the old sea level marks on the coast. Another time I went to see Lake Suvando, located more to the east, which in 1818 had lowered its level and substantially reduced its size by breaking through to Lake Ladoga with which it communicates to this day, while being cut off from Lake Vuoxen with which it was connected until 1818.

When Herr von Middendorff was about to travel to Siberia, I took him on a special journey to Helsingfors, to show him the traces of the diluvial movements which abounded in this particular location. The commander of the port of Kronstadt, Admiral von Bellingshausen, was kind enough to put one of his own boats at our disposal to take us from place to place. In Siberia, Herr von Middendorff found neither diluvial scorings, nor any other abrasion or erosion marks, nor, as far as I know, have other travelers. As long as no good reason can be given why such marks should be absent in Siberia, the problem of the old Ice Age does not appear to have been completely solved. Even if one stresses the fact, as did Professor Tyndall recently, that an atmospheric precipitation in the Scandinavian mountains exceeding the yearly amount caused by the sun to melt and run off will produce a permanent snow and ice cap, it is still beyond my grasp how such a cap can have moved so far into the plains as to transport Finnish rock boulders to Moscow and beyond, while no such thing happened in Siberia. Although one might argue that Siberia is covered with a very recent rubble layer, traces of glaciers should be discernible on the northern mountain ranges. Such traces, however, are absent. Some essential facts apparently still elude us.

In 1845 I undertook a journey to the Adriatic where, in Trieste, I first observed the great diversity of the animal world in a southern sea. In summer, however, I found very little material for embryology, which still remained at the center of my attention. Such material became available mostly in the fall and afforded me many interesting observations. Particularly fascinating were fertilization experiments with ascidians and sea urchins. These experiments caused me to revisit Genoa and Trieste in the following year (*Bulletin de la classe physico-mathématique*, V, pp. 231–240).

In January 1851, the then Minister of Imperial Territories, Count Kisselev, declared that he had obtained the permission of His Imperial Highness to organize a scientific expedition, to be headed by a naturalist, with the aim of investigating fisheries in Lake Peipus and in the Baltic. The naturalist was to be selected by the minister of education. When this information reached the Academy of Sciences, I offered myself for the position, as I was interested in pursuing the application of natural sciences to a practical task. Another colleague had also applied and it was I whom the minister eventually appointed.

I now devised a more detailed plan according to which Lake Peipus was to be visited once during every season. In addition, the entire Baltic coast was to be inspected, from Narva down to Riga. As fishing in inland seas always needs more regulation than in the open sea, and as spring is definitely the most important fishing season in our latitudes, the spring season had to be devoted exclusively to Lake Peipus. The journey along the sea coast had to be timed for the summer season and was regarded more as an inspection tour to collect information related to yields and the most favorable sites. In addition to myself, the expedition also included an official of the Ministry of Territories, Herr Schultz, and a junior official from each of the three administrative districts of St. Petersburg, Pskov, and Livland. Together we made four different expeditions to Lake Peipus during different seasons, traveling the whole length of its shores, and visiting the fishing villages as well as the islands of Talapsk and Porka. Herr Schultz and I alone visited the Baltic coast in such a manner that he set out from Riga and traveled along the coast northwards, while I started from the mouth of the Luga, traveling south via Narva, the estates on the coast, Reval, Baltisch-Port, Hapsal, the island of Dagden and the estates at the Einwiek, to meet Schultz at Pernau, returning via Fellin, Dorpat, and Narva.

Reports on these travels and on their results as well as proposals for the regulation of fishing in Lake Peipus were printed in the first part of a volume published by the Ministry of Territories: *Issledovaniya o sostoyanii rybolovstva Rossii*, St. Petersburg, 1860, 4.

After completion of these investigations, I read in a journal that for the last year or two, the Swedish authorities had been working on a new set of fishing regulations. Whether or not these regulations had already been published I was unable to ascertain. Since fishing and fishes, the spawning period and so forth had been the subjects of scientific enquiry for over a century in Sweden, legislation making use of this body of knowledge was bound to be more specific than elsewhere. What is more, it was to be expected that Swedish experience would be directly applicable to conditions in Northern Russia. In particular, however, I hoped, that given their experience and extended attention to the problem, the Swedes would have taken steps to regulate the catching of small fish for bait. Small fish of little value are commonly used for bait in fresh-water fishing. The nets used for this purpose are of very narrow mesh. However, how does one prevent misuse of these narrow-mesh nets for the catching of the small fry of valuable fishes which should be left to grow larger? I found abuse of this kind to be deep-rooted in Northern Russia and, as I learned recently, a sensible peasant, Ivan Possoshkov, had complained about this pernicious practise as early as 1724. Of laws that limited and regulated the catching of bait fishes I had known only some local regulations in Germany, but none that had any general validity. I therefore proposed that the Ministry of Territories send me and Herr Schultz to Sweden to study the local fishing legislation and generally compare fishing in Sweden with that in Northern Russia and, in particular, in the Baltic provinces.

This proposal was accepted; however, we were rather late with our departure. We traveled on a steamship which landed at several places on the southern coast of Finland, affording us an opportunity to collect information on local fishing. From there we went via the Åland islands to Stockholm, where the fishing regulations had recently been made public. They did not, however, come up to my expectations, as they were only formulated in very general terms. All the same, they contained some important rules concerning fishing rights which I thought should be adopted by Russia. I profited more, however, from the opportunity to make the acquaintance of scientists who had carried out the official investigations into fishing, such as Professor Sunderwall, as well as of the writings of others whom I did not meet in person. Not less enlightening concerning an understanding of various aspects of large-scale deep-sea fishing was the continuation of our journey to Göteborg, thence to Marstrand and to Paster Eckström on the Island of Tshörn, who had made a name for himself as a writer on fishes and fishing. I was unfortunately unable to communicate with the man himself as I do not know any Swedish and none of the other languages I tried were of any avail, including Latin. It is to be regretted that this language, formerly the *lingua franca* of the literate world, is gradually losing its dominion. From the North Sea, I sent Herr Schultz straight home to carry out an experiment, suggested by me, of transferring salmon and similar fishes via Narva into Lake Peipus. I myself traveled by sea to Landskrona, thence by land to Lund where I unfortunately did not find Professor Nilsson, from whom I had expected to learn much. In Åhus I again embarked for Stockholm whence I traveled to the Åland islands to collect information on local fishing. After several days' stay I returned with the same steamship line to Helsingfors, further than which the line refused to take us because of the advanced season and the pitch-dark night. Fortunately, there appeared an old Swedish captain who offered to take us straight to St. Petersburg, at the expense of the company, which he succeeded n doing, a terrible thunderstorm notwithstanding. A description of this ourney is given in the sixth report of the above-mentioned first volume of the *Issledovaniya o sostoyanii rybolovstva Rossii*. I hope to be able to also publish a German edition of the results of these journeys undertaken to study fishing n the Baltic provinces and in Sweden.

The Ministry for Imperial Territories regarded these investigations only as preparations for enquiries into the large and economically important fisheries n the Caspian Sea. For a long time now, people had been complaining about he gradual decline of these fisheries. Several investigations had been arranged and many abuses discovered. As soon as corrective measures were announced, however, they were most vigorously opposed and little if anything was in fact achieved. I cannot explain here how complicated things had become due to he fact that some influential persons had secretly become owners of fisheries, while others had been given extensive fisheries as gifts by the government; then in 1802 Emperor Alexander declared that sea fishing could not be the private property of any single person, but had to be accessible to every citizen. Yet so far, the Imperial decree has remained a dead letter. It was therefore he task of whoever wanted to improve the situation to obtain a comprehensive picture of fishing in the Caspian Sea, to investigate complaints of decline and decay, and to propose protective measures.

I hope I may regard it as a positive comment on my services with the previous expedition that I was also entrusted with this one, as well as with the drawing-up of the plan for it. To make repeated visits to the most important fisheries and to look up the major points along the shores of the Caspian Sea would inevitably take several years. Three years were envisaged originally, but turned out to be too short a period to study natural conditions in the extended regions through which the rivers flowing into the Caspian Sea passed, as well as the different zones of the sea itself. As it was, the enterprise took almost four years. We selected Astrakhan as our headquarters. I myself, however, visited St. Petersburg three times in the winter to see how my family fared.

My traveling companions and assistants were Herr Schultz, who had shared my work with the fishing in Lake Peipus and on the Baltic, and Herr Danilevsky, a naturalist who later continued the investigations of the fisheries together with Herr Schultz. He has so far published three volumes of fishing in the Arctic Ocean and at the Pechora and is now engaged in a study of fishing in the Sea of Azov and in the Black Sea. Also with us were Herr Semenov, later replaced by Herr Weidemann, and Herr Nikitin, a draftsman who was also the laboratory assistant. In this description of these journeys I can only go into their history.

The first journey, begun only in June 1853, was primarily intended to provide some first-hand knowledge of the Volga and its fishing industry down to the (Caspian) sea. To start out, I sent Herr Schultz to Ostashkov on Lake Seliger, from which springs one of the northernmost tributaries of the Volga, to find out whether the spawning could be observed. Since it turned out that it was over by then, I traveled by railroad to Moscow and thence, after some preparations, to Nizhniy Novgorod, where I again met Schultz and Nikitin Here we rented a sailing boat built for the Caspian Sea, and slowly sailed down the Volga, frequently paying visits to villages on the river bank and suffering greatly from mosquitoes and the even more numerous small dipterans called *moshki.* Soon, however, our helmsman fell ill with cholera, and he died when we reached Kazan. We did not, however, take another boat, as being carried downstream by nothing faster than the flow of the river itself was in any case too slow a mode of travel, but traveled overland, still crossing the Volga several times. Thus, we set out on the left bank, going as far as the Kama where we looked up the old Bolgary, the mightiest tower of whose famous ruins, often described, we already found collapsed. We then crossed to the right bank at Tetyushi whence, traveling along that bank, we reached the picturesque Simbirsk, now regrettably burned down. We then went to Usoly in the Shigulinsk mountains and moved along these mountains as far as the great bend of the Volga, which we crossed to reach Samara, to meet Herr Danilevsky. From Samara we continued through the grass steppe inhabited by the Mordvins. This region without doubt formed the northern edge of the former Caspian basin and, by the lush growth of its grass, attests to the fact that, at that time, the water at the northern edge of this basin was totally or almost totally free of salt, just as it is completely potable in the present basin at a considerable distance from the mouth of the Volga. At Khvalynsk we again crossed over to the right, or mountainous, bank of the Volga, following it as far as Saratov, where we also had the opportunity of looking up some of the German settlements of this district. At Kamyshin we saw the two large ditches which were intended to connect the Ilavla, a tributary of the Don, via the Kamyshenka, with the Volga; the first of these was dug by the Turks in the sixteenth century, the other under Peter the Great, at the end of the seventeenth century. Neither has been completed and they appear to have been cut without the necessary circumspection. They should have been led much farther than the beginning of the Kamyshenka, which nowadays during the summer is so shallow, that it is unable to carry even small boats. In Kamyshin the expedition split up. One party traveled along the Volga down to Chernoy Yar. Another, which included me, crossed the Volga and traveled over the desolate salt steppe to the Elton salt lake where we were present during the mining of salt and saw about 614 million pounds stored in the form of long, roof-shaped piles. From there we went to the large Bogdo mountain and its salt lake, Beskunchatsk, which in summer is in fact a de pression covered with solid salt that is not, however, exploited today, being preserved for future millennia. Despite the aridity of the entire region and the salty soil, which, by the peculiar, almost leafless form of the plants and the absence of green vegetation makes a lasting impression upon the traveler, enough potable water has been found in deep wells to water 10,000 oxen which make their way from Kamyshyn to Lake Elton and back throughout the entire summer. When, on our way from the Bogdo to Chernoy Yar we passed the Volga islands, we came across a swarm of migratory locusts which was just moving along these verdant islands. The soil of all the Volga islands is free of salt and they are all covered with grass. The high banks at Chernoy Yar, the top edges of which are almost perpendicularly cut off, reveal a very distinct layer of Caspian shells, having a thickness of nearly three inches and clearly indicating that this was formerly the bottom of this sea. In Chernoy Yar the entire company embarked on two boats and sailed down the river to visit some of the large fisheries. Numerous cormorants and soon also pelicans, as well as the abundant yield of the fisheries, indicated the proximity of the sea. The region of the great fisheries in fact starts at Tsaritsin, where the Volga turns south-east.

On August twelfth we arrived in Astrakhan and were hospitably received at the home of Herr Saposhnikov. After we had made ourselves completely at home and had gotten properly organized, we visited several of the great fisheries on the Volga branches south of Astrakhan, reaching the mouths of the Volga. We also came upon a small water basin in which the magnificent *Nelumbium speciosum* was still flourishing. This plant is said to have been widely distributed throughout the delta of the Volga. However, since the Asiatics greatly relish the nuts of this plant, and, so it is claimed, even its roots, the plant will probably soon disappear altogether, all the more so as the marshy basin in which these plants still survive has become so filled with mud that even now it is hardly accessible in summer. A last journey was undertaken in the late fall and took us to the small fortress of Novo-Petrovsk located on the Mangyshlak peninsula on the eastern shores, where we were most cordially received by the commander and where we stayed for some time because of my right leg, which having become inflamed on one of the Peipus expeditions, had now suffered a relapse that persisted for some time. Returning after an absence of four weeks, we still managed to visit some of the fisheries before the Volga had frozen over. When winter finally arrived, I set out alone on a rather uncomfortable journey to St. Petersburg, because I deemed it necessary to see the minister on the question of the government's reaction to our proposal to unite all the fishery owners on the Caspian Sea into one large corporation. It was obvious that such an arrangement had the greatest chance of success in introducing the conservation measures for which the government had already made such sacrifices. It was equally obvious, however, that such an arrangement would lead to complaints by those who claimed that it was the small number of those holding fishing concessions, in fact a monopoly, which caused the fishery products of the Caspian Sea to be so unreasonably expensive, an argument generally heard in St. Petersburg. After my visit to the Caspian Sea I could see that this complaint was totally unfounded, as I had convinced myself that the individual owners were quite ready to undersell one another to find an outlet for their wares, but that it was the great distances, combined with the uncertainty and long duration of transport, which so greatly added to the price of the popular redfish salmon and, in particular, of caviar, while other fish, precisely because of the distances and costly transport, could get no further than Moscow, but certainly not to St. Petersburg. Yet, I could very well understand that, given the prevalent opinion as to the monopolistic nature of the fisheries, the government did not feel able to voice the question of a general corporation.

After a few weeks' stay I set out on the second journey by the most direct route and reached the Volga at Tsaritsyn, visited Sarepta and, on the lower Volga, observed winter fishing below the ice. Winter having passed, we first paid several visits to the fisheries on the branches of the Volga below Astrakhan. In May, we all traveled upstream to Sarepta, partly to see the catching of the local Alosa, still in progress north of Astrakhan, and partly to try and observe the spawning of the various types of sturgeon in Sarepta. As I could not obtain a steamboat, we had to spend three weeks in our open boat, during the period when the river is swollen and the current strong. In Sarepta we obtained a flat-bottomed barge in which holes had been made to allow the water to pass through. Into this barge we put some sturgeons in the hope that they would spawn. However, as the roe turned out to be still immature, Herr Danilewsky and I undertook another journey by land as far upstream on the Volga as Kamyshin, partly to observe the shape of the river banks, and partly to see two curious isolated heights consisting of a quartz-like rock showing leaf impressions from trees of the Neocene period. Having returned to Sarepta, we continued our experiments with the sturgeons and, in addition, traveled up the Sarpa and toward the Ergeni hills. On our maps, the Sarpa is still shown as a very long river interconnecting a large number of lakes situated at the foot of the Ergeni mountains. Today, however, it is only the two northernmost lakes—which, because of their shallow depth, should rather be called ponds—that are connected with the effluence known by the name of Sarpa. It is only in spring that a larger number of these ponds begin to communicate via a rivulet which has left substantial traces in the ground. If the Sarpa has ever had the length accorded to it by Pallas, this would certainly constitute proof of a gradual decrease of the water level in the steppe.

On our way back to Astrakhan we visited the Kalmuck temple, attended the service and paid our respects to Prince Tyumen, returning to Astrakhan only at the beginning of August. Since I was unable to take advantage of our last year's stay at the fortress of Novo-Petrovsk due to my inflamed leg, the entire company went there again. Herr Danilevsky and Herr Semenov were sent to the mouth of the Emba, to look into complaints about the alleged decline of local fishing. Herr Schultz and I busied ourselves near the fortress with a small anchor and also paid a visit to the curious islands Kulali and Morskoi, both consisting of sand and shells, and both probably created by the scraping and pushing action of ice floes, with the difference, however, that Kulali originated in a somewhat earlier period when the sea level was slightly higher, while Morskoi was created only in the course of the current century from a former sand bank. From the fortress Novo-Petrovsk on the Mangyshlak peninsula we went by steamship to Guryev, where I had the opportunity of seeing the delta of the Ural river without, however, penetrating deeper into the country. In September, after our return to Astrakhan, we set out in a small steamship to pay a visit to Chechen Island on the west side of the Caspian Sea, as well as to the large fishery, Chernoy Rynok, located on a northern effluent of the Terek and October found us traveling by land to the salt lakes of Astrakhan. In the winter I again returned to St. Petersburg.

The third journey, begun in 1855, was the most extensive, as it was designed to give us some knowledge about the southern half of the Caspian Sea, particularly about the important fisheries on the Kura. Relying on a public announcement that in the beginning of June, at the latest on the sixth of the month a steamship would travel down the Volga from Nizhniy Novgorod to Astrakhan, and hoping that this would be the fastest route to Astrakhan, as the high waters caused the Volga to flow swiftly in June, I hurriedly traveled from St. Petersburg to Nizhniy which as yet had no railroad connection. Upon arrival I was told, however, that while the steamship company had indeed promised such a trip, it had as yet done nothing toward its realization. This unreliability of steamship travel on the Volga was quite widespread at that time, as the companies were mainly interested in the shipping of goods, regarding passengers as only of minor importance. It was suggested that I wait for fourteen days, when the ship was likely to depart. As I could not accept this proposal, I had to leave at once for Astrakhan without further stay or rest to make up for the time lost, and, with the greatest of efforts, managed to reach the mail steamship a few hours before its departure. This ship brought me to Tarki, the Petrovsk Fortress, Derbent, and Baku, permitting me short stays in all these places. I disembarked at the mouth of the Kura River, where I took a boat that carried me upstream to the Boshiy Promysl fishery. This place, where my companions Danilevsky and Schultz were already waiting for me, has without doubt the richest catches of the various sturgeon types not only in the region of the Caspian, but probably in the whole world. We decided to stay here for a longer period of time. Partly in order to become acquainted with the Kura river, and partly to consult with Herr Danilevsky who had already left earlier for Shemakha where he wanted to study the Kura fishing archives from earlier years, I traveled with Herr Weidemann via Salyany and Shemakha to Mingechaur, where the Kura emerges from the last foothills of the Caucasus. I had the opportunity to travel down part of the Kura by the steamboat service which had recently been established. In this region the river is flanked by a narrow but beautiful and vigorous strip of forest, as far as the salt has been leached out of the soil by the river, while the banks are studded with many beautiful Tartar villages. Via Shemakha I returned to Boshiy Promysl, whence I traveled to Lenkoran, passing through the southernmost region of Russian fishing and the island of Sara. In Lenkoran I stayed for some time, to make excursions into the surroundings which were interesting in many respects. I had begun with Novaya Zemlya, the northernmost region of the Russian empire; now I intended to add the southernmost. One of these excursions brought us to the neighboring mountains, the northern foothills of the Persian Elburz, and as far as the Russian border river Shamba-Chai. The character of marginal mountains is particularly pronounced at these heights: the ascent from the Caspian side is uncommonly steep and covers a considerable height, while the descent toward the west has a much gentler slope and the height difference is also much smaller, indicating that the land on the west side must be much higher than the shores of the Caspian Sea. At the eastern foot of the mountains my aneroid barometer read 29.88", on the ridge 27.29", at the western foot 28.15", and close to the border river toward which the land is still sloping slightly, 28.35". Because of the abominable, short Tartar stirrups, the use of which calls for sharply bent knees, climbing the steep eastern slopes on horseback, and particularly descending, made such claims on my damaged right leg that it became inflamed again. In this invalid condition I and my companions traveled by the next steamboat to the Persian town of Enzeli, situated on the shore of the Caspian Sea whence, after a few days' stay, we crossed what is locally known as the bay, but which is in fact a fresh-water lake with an outlet into the sea, and went up a few versts on the Peribazar, a small river. The impressions from this journey belong to the most vivid ones I have retained from my travels. First I saw the aquatic plants which luxuriated in the warm water to a degree I have never seen before. We literally had to force our way through them. On the shores of the lake we were met by a majestic forest of huge trees of various kinds around which coiled creeping vines as heavy as a man's thigh and sometimes even as a man's body. Some of these vines reached even beyond the tree tops, forming long garlands floating in the air. This forest is particularly dense at the banks of the narrow river, so that from the river's mouth to the place where we disembarked, the boat traveled as in a dark tunnel. From this point my companions rode to the town of Rasht. As my leg did not permit me to ride, I had to be carried in a sedan chair, which afforded me an excellent opportunity to observe the unevenness of the ground, criss-crossed by many small water channels, since the carriers on one side not infrequently walked on much lower ground than those on the other, so much so that I was afraid of falling out of the chair. Still, Rasht had to be entered on horseback as, according to the Russian consul, such an entrance was *de rigueur* for an expedition organized by the government. The effects of the murderous climate of this humid, forest-covered strip of land below the high Persian plateau made themselves felt soon enough. Herr Schultz and our draftsman, Nikitin, whom we had sent here earlier, were already suffering from malaria when I arrived, the latter to such a degree that I hardly recognized him. Within a few days, Herr Danilevsky, a robust man, also came down with the disease and could scarcely move from weakness. I was the only one spared by this fever which an advanced age appears to escape more easily than a young one, but I was bed-ridden because of my leg, which required some rest. We thus turned the Consul's home into a veritable hospital. Only Herr Weidemann could ride to the Persian river Safid Rud, to study local fishing practices. When we were finally able to embark on the next steamship to travel to Ashur-Ade, the southeastern station of the Russian navy, the health of us all improved the moment we were at sea. From Ashur-Ade I wished to pay a visit to the neighboring shores of the Turkomans, to study the country and to see the underwater ruins of a submerged town or of a building. The otherwise most obliging commander of this station decidedly refused this request, however, as the Turkomans appeared to be in a state of agitation and we had therefore to be content with a journey across the Gulf of Astrabat to visit the pleasure palace built by Shah Abbas and the gardens of Ashraf, a vivid reminder of Persia's decline. From Ashur-Ade, I took the next steamship back to Lenkoran, whence I continued by land to the Akusha, the southern arm of the Kura, and went on to Boshiy Promyssl via Salyany where the river branches. From Boshiy Promyssl I traveled via Shemakha to Baku where the commander of the naval station, Captain Voyevodski, was kind enough to arrange for me to visit not only the neighboring islands of Nargen, Vulf, and Peshchaniy Ostrov, but also some of the more distant islands by steamship which had their origin in volcanic eruptions, such as Shiloi, Kurenskii Kamen, Duvannoi, Oblivnoi, Svinoi, Gorelaya Plita, and others. Accompanied by Commander von Hoven, we rode deeper into the country and, at Shikhovski, were duly caught in one of the violent storms occasionally plaguing this region. After we had also made several visits to the closest sights in the interesting surroundings of Baku and had seen the rich naphtha wells, the famous eternal fire, and the naphtha gusting forth from the sea, as well as the submerged caravansery, and after Herr Danilevsky had concluded his research in the archives at Shemakha, we, that is Herr Weidemann and myself, left for that town in September. Continuing our journey upstream on the Kura, we found that the Column of Shamkhor, still intact when Eichwald had drawn it, had fallen over in the meantime. We then turned left through the picturesque Delishan valley and toward the mighty mountain lake Gokchai which is surrounded by extinct volcanoes and is famous for its abundance of delicious fish. After we had stayed at this la ke for about three weeks, during which time we lived only on trout, we made a detour to Erivan (Jerevan) and thence to the Edshimiadsin monastery, saw Ararat in all its glory, but dared not to make a visit, as we were in a hurry to go to Tiflis, to be able to reach Astrakhan if possible before the onset of winter. This we were unable to realize, however, because although we arrived in Tiflis in the middle of October in the most beautiful weather, we had hardly begun to take a look at this interesting region and to study the fishing methods which here, in the torrential Kara River, differ completely from what we had seen elsewhere, when, unusually early, winter set in, a winter with very heavy snowfall. As early as November, an avalanche in the mountains had made them impassable—for some time even for the mail. Under different circumstances I would not have minded such an enforced stay, as I lived with an excellent friend of mine from the university, General Roth, the courageous defender of Achty, and as Tiflis offered many things of interest for every kind of study, and I found more educated men than I had expected. But I was most eager to reach Astrakhan, to conclude this expedition. I therefore started out on the twenty-ninth of December, as soon as it appeared that the way across the mountains had been made passable. I had two wheeled carriages at my disposal, as one can never expect snow on the other side of the mountains. The government had made all possible preparations to keep the way open across the mountains for larger wheeled carriages even in winter. On this I relied.

Yet, this particular journey was destined to become a most adventurous one, and I will interrupt my dry account of localities visited to relate some of the adventures one can have in the more remote regions of the Russian Empire. Even before we reached the mountains proper, when we passed through a region full of old Georgian ruins and even Roman structures from the times of Pompey, we were forced to stop frequently, since, due to the war, traffic was much heavier than usual, and Turkish prisoners of war, officers as well as common soldiers, were being moved from Kars into the interior of the country, which caused a shortage of horses. The carriage in which Herr Weidemann traveled collapsed even before we reached the foothills of the main mountain range and had to be left behind. It was now all the more necessary to preserve the other carriage, the one in which I traveled, and which was heavily loaded with various instruments, natural history objects and books. At Passanaur, the last station, I was told, however, that as the Kasbeck had put on its cap (i.e., was hidden in fog), a storm could be expected. The postmaster, a sensible and friendly man, although greatly harassed at the moment as all stations were choked with travelers who wanted to get on, advised me to take a sleigh and cross the mountains at a special pass reserved for the military. The carriage, which I could leave in the care of Weidemann's Kalmuck servant, would certainly be moved across the mountains, though not immediately. I accepted his advice and, taking a light sleigh, successfully negotiated the ridge, ascending a very steep rise and descending an equally steep drop, and reached an intermediate station likewise filled with travelers, but which I left at once, to arrive the very same day at Kasbeck, a station located at the foot of the huge mountain of the same name, yet still at a height of 6,360 feet. On the way we had observed that the Kasbeck's fog cap had increased during the first half of the day, then lifted, floated for some time above the mountain, but later dissolved, revealing a clear, starry sky. When we arrived it was uncomfortably cold, and as the temperature in the otherwise quite tolerable Kasbeck station was only thirty-nine degrees above zero (Fahrenheit), I at once ordered the stoves to be lit, but the temperature rose only slightly and was no more than forty-one degrees when night came. This was the last day of 1855. On the following New Year's morning we were given the less than comforting piece of news that the stock of firewood had been used up and that the wood for the new year had not yet been delivered, as authorization for its acquisition had arrived only one day earlier! A cheering prospect indeed to have to spend some January days without firewood at a height of almost 6,400 feet above sea level, since passing travelers informed us that the carriage which we expected had not even been sent off the previous day, as the contents of the broken-down carriage had not yet arrived at our previous night's quarters. This was the beginning of a longer stay of over eight days in this cold shelter which varied its permanent temperature of thirty-seven degrees only little, although, following the law of necessity, I had the fence of the station torn down for firewood, myself taking part in this spoliation of crown property in order to be able to heat the place. I later sent a report to Tiflis on this act of violence. There was no lack of entertainment. The surroundings invited small excursions to the extent the cold would permit; on New Year's Eve the local Ossets performed a ceremonial round dance around a bottle of brandy and, above all, there was a steady stream of passing travelers including, quite apart from the many officers and officials, also the Pasha who had endured the siege of Kars, and the English officers who had actually led the defense of the town and who were now being brought in as prisoners of war. The Pasha, who did not look much more intelligent than the common Turks, hundreds of whom I had seen in Tiflis as prisoners, had hardly entered the front room of the station when he turned toward a hard bench made of wooden planks and squatted down on it with his legs folded under him. Very curious indeed! For the journey he was given a comfortable carriage with an upholstered seat, but as this forced him to keep his knees bent at a right angle, he felt the need, at the first opportunity offered, to bend them at a more acute angle, folding his shanks under him. A European, on the other hand, who has made the difficult journey from Tiflis to Kasbeck in a carriage, sitting all the way, will want to straighten his knees and if he cannot lie down, will prefer the standing position for his rest. This was demonstrated on the next day when a Russian general passed through the station and ate the soup I had offered him standing up, to rest from the sitting position. Whether the habit of Asians to sit from early youth with their legs folded under them has caused the articular surfaces of the thigh bone to be pulled back more than in contemporary Europeans is something which I am not sure has ever been investigated. When Germans, Russians, Estonians, etc., working in the fields, or on a journey, have their meal at a spot where neither a stone nor a tree trunk can be found to serve as a seat, they will stretch out their legs, while the Asian will feel secure only if he can use his heels for a chair.

As far as food was concerned, while we were sentenced to freezing rather than starving, we did suffer from a certain monotony because during the entire eight days we spent here, we had nothing but the Russian national dish, a cabbage soup called Shchi, and bread. To be sure, a noncommissioned officer, who played the role of restaurateur, appeared every morning to ask us what we would like for dinner, but at noon he invariably brought only the cabbage soup, claiming that the other dishes had been eaten by hungry travelers passing through. Not that I ever complained about the monotonous fare at the Kasbeck station, as the Shchi was always excellently prepared, lending support to the good old rule which I had long distilled from my traveling experience, to the effect that, when abroad, one should always keep to the local national dishes which are always palatable, mostly even well prepared*. It was rather amusing, though, to watch the noncommissioned officer go through the motions of attending to the innkeeper able to offer a great variety of dishes.

When on the sixth day my carriage had still not arrived, although we had learned that it had left Passanaur several days ago, I dispatched Herr Weidemann on the regular highway to find out what had happened to it and to expedite it or at least its contents. Finally, on the ninth day, Herr Weidemann returned and soon after also the carriage, both in a defective state. Herr Weidemann had to travel back as far as Passanaur whence the carriage had been returned and, having had to cross the mountain ridges twice, contracted an acute inflammation of the throat. The carriage had indeed left Passanaur six days ago, but the Kasbeck having again "put on its cap," a violent snowstorm had set in, the carriage got stuck in the snow and overturned, spilling most of

---

*In Lenkoran I have lived for four weeks on a daily diet of pilaff, feeling very well, while in the Kalmuk Steppe I existed mainly on a soup made of goat broth. While eating this soup requires a strong act of the will, I soon found that it quenched the tormenting thirst better than water did.

I learned this reverence for national dishes on my first longer journey to Novaya Zemlya. We had lived for three days on the cold food taken along, when we arrived at the town of Vytegra. As I intended to stay for a while and as we found an inn with a distinguished name, I ordered beefsteaks to refresh ourselves by way of compensation. We were indeed served a black substance of which I am not sure to this day whether it consisted of a sort of meat or of roasted shoe soles, as it proved a match to the teeth of even the youngest among us. I returned from Novaya Zemlya a decided admirer of Russian kasha.

my things, many of which were never found again. I most regretted the loss of an open basket with eight partitions in which I kept glass jars filled with spirit to preserve whatever we found on our way. Of these jars, which already contained many and the most diverse objects, none turned up. Collecting the spilled articles, somebody probably discovered that the liquid in these jars was in fact the well-loved restorative and therefore decided on the spot to turn it to a better use, throwing away the rest of the jars' contents. The Kalmuck whom I had left with the carriage to keep an eye on it, having returned it to Passanaur, thoroughly searched it and, finding cigars and some victuals, declared all the former, and the animal products among the latter, as well-earned prize money, settled down comfortably in Passanaur, and waited to see how things would develop. Finally in the possession of the carriage, I hurried to leave the icy surroundings of the Kasbeck and, on the next day, traveled via the majestic Dariel pass where the Terek roaringly shoots down over and between rock fragments in a deep crevice. The road at first passes at a considerable height above the Terek, then gradually descends and crosses the river several times where it has slowed down to some degree, to continue on the other side which often has been hewn out of rock. For the first five or six versts, however, the romantic magnificence of the Dariel pass was not enjoyable to me, because the dangers were so formidable. The road was covered with smooth ice and as it was mostly inclined toward the Terek crevice, the carriage often had the tendency of sliding crosswise toward it, threatening to plunge into it. Five Ossets, who were escorting us, had to hold the carriage back, while I walked on foot behind it. Apart from the danger of dropping into the Terek, from which no more than a few fragments could have been salvaged, another hazard lurked wherever the slope of the road became steeper: the carriage started rolling down. Putting a chock first under one, and then under a second wheel was of little avail, as the chocks started sliding on the solid ice. But people here are prepared for such minor emergencies. A strong chain with heavy links had been taken along, which was slung around the wheels whenever the road sloped precipitously. The protruding corners of the chain dug themselves into the ice, plowing it up. After these agonizing and dangerous five to six versts had been overcome, my Osset escorts left me, assuring me that the danger was now conquered. The road had indeed become much more level, yet the day was not to end in tranquility and peace. Between the high Kasbeck station and the small town of Vladikavkaz, located at the foot of the mountains proper, there are three postal stations. When I arrived at the last station before Vladikavkaz, the officer in charge of this fortified station declared that I could not continue, as it would be dark before I could reach Vladikavkaz, which would put me in great danger because of the Lesghians who roamed about here to catch and hold for ransom travelers wanting to enter or leave the pass. He had already stopped some travelers before I arrived and read to me a sharp official reprimand which had been handed to him because he had been incautious enough to let some travelers continue their way in the dark without a military escort. All our remonstrations to the effect that, if he would let the travelers which he had stopped earlier go, we could form a convoy of three carriages between us and, counting the drivers, would be ten persons who could easily defend themselves against the Lesghians, were of no avail. Our plans for self-defense seemed ridiculous to him and he declared categorically that he would not send off the carriage. In any case, I would not be permitted to travel without a military escort, least of all at night. When I now presented a letter authorizing me to demand such an escort, I was given to understand that soldiers were not stationed here, but at two other locations, one four versts above, the other four versts below this point. I therefore should have shown my papers, and asked for an escort earlier, at the point we had already passed. Now I was very keen on still arriving at Vladikavkaz this particular night, as my watch had stopped several days ago and I was unable to make it go. It was Friday, and if I could not give the watch to a watchmaker early on Saturday, at the latest, I could expect to lose another day. Still, I would have resigned myself to this delay, as one always does when something goes awry with one's journey and when one unexpected delay follows another; but this officer's cold and dry objections and his refusals excited my blood and I therefore asked him rather defiantly whether he believed he also had the right to detain me personally? As he remained silent, somewhat disconcerted, I decided to take positive action and, summoning my servant, I now declared that we were about to set out on foot and demanded that the carriage be sent after me on the next day. With that we left. We had gone about five versts and it had become dark by then, when we heard behind us wild shouting and a loud commotion. When we turned round, the dying twilight clearly revealed the gleam of rifles. Had the Lesghians tracked us down after all? There was no sense now in trying to escape and my servant had already bravely drawn his Circassian dagger which he always carried with him. We just stood there, awaiting the attack. Yet it surprised me that I could hear no hoofbeats of horses. Had the Lesghians taken to carrying out their raids on foot? Well, as it turned out, the development was neither as dangerous nor as interesting. It appeared that the brave commander had become worried after all and had found a way to send half a company of soldiers after us, as well as to ready the carriage and have it follow us. I thus had my way and arrived at Vladikavkaz that very evening, but had to wait for two days until Herr Weidemann, who had stayed behind because of his throat infection, had caught up with me.

From here down to the steppe proper, where we could expect to advance without difficulty, the ground slopes only moderately. Yet there appears to be a law according to which, once something goes amiss with a journey, more and more mishaps are bound to follow. The unusually early winter had caught me in Tiflis and its avalanches had cut me off from the rest of the world. In Vladikavkaz, on the other hand, spring weather had set in the middle of January. During the first days, as long as the ground was still fairly sloping, we found the roads bad, yet we hardly knew how to judge the consequences of this development. But when, at Yekaterinograd, we reached the steppe proper and found its loamy soil softened to a great depth, so that the carriage could be dragged along only with the greatest of efforts, we began to understand why peace had to be concluded so soon in the Crimean War, in spite of the fact that Kars had been taken. To have to supply an army through the softened soil of the steppe spells the doom of all draft animals. I do not want to enlarge on our snail's progress along the bank of the Terek through the deep loam, but I must say a few words about Kislyar which, as far as the fathomlessness of its road mud is concerned, exceeds everything I had ever imagined. I wanted to get a letter to a nearby post office and asked Herr Weidemann to take care of the matter. Our innkeeper declared at once that this could be done only on horseback, as Herr Weidemann, while not necessarily in danger of being himself swallowed up by the mud, would inevitably lose his boots in it. The owner of the stable was in turn ready to provide a horse only if he could ride along on a second horse, to be at hand to help the first one, should it get stuck in the mud. I thus needed two horses, each costing me one and a half rubles, altogether three rubles, to have a simple letter brought to the post office from one part of the same small town to another. The commander had been kind enough to send a light carriage hitched to three strong horses to call for us to take us to his home. When on the next day I borrowed the same carriage to visit the fish market, its driver told me as we drove up closer that it was impossible to advance any further. It was only later that we discovered a negotiable approach from another direction. The next day we left Kislyar early at six in the morning, arriving at the next station only at six in the evening, as we only managed to advance at an extremely slow pace, although we had five horses to pull our carriage, as we had when traveling along the Terek. Gradually the ground became more solid and about halfway between Kislyar and Astrakhan a frost even set in, so that we covered the last stretches at a tolerably fast rate. In spite of that, the journey from Tiflis to Astrakhan, which is supposed to require no more than four, and at most five days, took us no less than thirty-one days.

Since I passed over other minor adventures, such as remaining behind all alone in the steppe during a violent Buràn (snowstorm), or being stranded on the shores of the Kara Sea without shelter and food and, because of a violent storm, without the possibility of building a fire, and my eventual rescue by a walrus-catcher from Kem, I thought that, to give some examples of the mishaps liable to happen to the traveler, I would mention our crossing of the Caucasus, although this story has taken up more space than originally intended. Back now to my summary.

Either the long stay in the cold and humid air, or perhaps another factor was involved, at any rate I was seized by a lingering fever after my return to Astrakhan which, within a few weeks, exhausted me to such a degree that I was hardly able to drag myself across the floor. As I had no distinct intermissions at all, I saw at first no sense in taking quinine as advised by the doctors. Eventually, however, I had to accept their counsel and it was indeed this medicine which broke the illness. This was, however, followed by a very slow convalescence. For complete recuperation in spring I decided to make a journey into the steppe as far as the Manych valley. As I could not, however, obtain authorization to go directly to the Manych valley, which would have necessitated a change of horses, and as I also wanted to observe the early spring migration of the Astrakhan shad upstream on the Volga, and to revisit the blubber-refining plants, I went at first as far as Sarepta together with Herr Weidemann, visiting some fishing sites on the way. From Sarepta we traveled on a new road across the Ergeni hills, to the Manych valley, crossing the Manych river which, at that point, already had very little water, and at its highest point further to the east was totally dry. We saw the large Lake Manych and followed the Manych valley for three days to the east, up to the mouth of the Kalaus. Somewhat to the west of the now pond-like Shara-Ulussun we crossed the Manych valley—completely dry at this point—to the north, following it for some distance eastward where we could see water as far as the eye reached. The valley thus still held water toward the west and toward the east, although it was now totally dry in the central sector, west of the mouth of the Kalaus, yet still showing clear traces of recent water flow. Here was no doubt the highest point of this mighty water furrow, that has an average breadth of one and a half versts. This knowledge was of particular importance to me, as it had been proposed to build a canal, a proposal which would have a chance of being considered only if the high point of the valley had been located much more to the west. What is more, former and still living members of the expedition of Monsieur Homaire de Hell assured me that this traveler had never bothered to take proper level measurements of the central sector of the Manych valley, having been satisfied with merely viewing it from the Ergeni hills. After this inspection, we hurried back to Astrakhan, making our way across the southeastern part of the Ergeni hills and the great steppe.

In the summer of 1856 I made another round trip on the Caspian Sea, this time with the military governor of Astrakhan, Admiral Vassiliev. In addition to some regions which I had visited earlier, I looked up the islands of Svyatoi and Chelekyan (the naphtha island) and saw the eastern coast of the Caspian Sea from the mouth of the Atrak to the Bay of Krasnovodsk, where we landed. We were also promised a trip to the Bay of Karabugaz, but nothing came of it. But this time I had an opportunity of visiting the Russian trading stations on Persian soil, as well as of performing several measurements in the deepest part of the southern basin of the Caspian Sea.

Fall and the early winter I spent in Astrakhan, writing reports on my travels so far.

In the same winter I joined Herr Ovsiannikov, who had been sent to Astrakhan to study fish poisons, on a trip to Chernoi Rynok, a large fishery on one arm of the Terek which I had visited once before. There was such a demand for horses along the mail road that some of the stations had none, so that on our way back we had to travel through the villages instead of by the mail road. We also learned that the stories about the hazards of travel in the steppe were based on more than mere rumors. Two days before we arrived at Chernoi Rynok, a higher Russian officer who carried some money had been attacked on the highway and shot to death together with his carriage driver. They were still looking for the attacking Lesghians who, as usual, had disappeared.

It was only in the beginning of 1857 that I could set out on my return journey to St. Petersburg, which became exceedingly vexatious, not only because of my foot, which had again become inflamed and compelled me to stay and rest at several places, but also because soon after Sarepta I had to leave my carriage due to the heavy snow. Several days later I had to acquire a new carriage, as all the snow had disappeared, yet once again I arrived in Moscow in a sleigh. This journey did not end until the fourteenth of March 1857.

Schultz and Nikitin had finished their business in Astrakhan before I did and had arrived in St. Petersburg much earlier than I. Herr Weidemann remained in Astrakhan, being employed there. When I left Tiflis in December 1855, Herr Danilevsky had stayed on to prepare extracts, from the archives, for the last eight years of fishery leases. He came to Astrakhan only in March 1856, whence he was sent to the Ural river of which we had briefly seen only the mouth. Danilevsky not only thoroughly investigated the delta of the Ural, but also traveled up the whole length the river as far as Orenburg.

I have reported on these journeys in the second volume of *Issledovaniya o sostoyanii rybolovstva v Rossii*, with two maps. In the third volume Herr Danilevsky reports in detail on the Ural fishing industry. On the technical aspects of this industry Herr Schultz reported in the fourth volume. Some parts of the journey and some investigations are reported in the *Caspian Studies* (*Writings* I, No. 15) and in several articles in the *Zapiski Imp. Russk. Geograf. Obshchestva*, as well as in the Bulletin of the Academy.

Having spent so much time traveling inside Russia, I felt the need for a visit abroad. In 1858 I therefore made a trip to Germany, visiting some German universities, especially Göttingen, as well as the meeting of natural scientists at Karlsruhe, and then I traveled in Switzerland. In the following year I set out on a second, longer journey that also included Copenhagen, Stockholm, Paris, and London, and which was dedicated primarily to matters of anthropological interest. A third trip in 1861, devoted to the same interest, aimed to bring together several mutually acquainted scientists in Göttingen, in order to work out and agree jointly on a way of describing the shape of the human skull. A great many skull shapes had been described and measured in recent times, but as measurements were performed according to very different principles, and not permitting direct comparison since these principles were often not even specified, it appeared desirable to attempt to agree on a common method. In 1861, Professor Wagner and I therefore invited some friends to a meeting in Göttingen. Those that came were Professor Vrolik of Amsterdam, Professor Lucae of Frankfurt, Professor Bergmann of Rostock, Professor Weber of Leipzig and the anatomists of Göttingen University. These deliberations were reported on (*Writings* I, No. 14).

As regards journeys within Russia, I undertook another one in 1860, upstream on the Narva, through Lake Peipus and as far as Dorpat, to make another attempt at transplanting salmon. A second trip during the same year brought me for my own interest to the Novgorod district, to see the large and beautiful institute of Herr Vraski for artificial fish breeding. In 1862 I traveled to the Sea of Azov on behalf of the Geographical Society, and in 1863 I was commissioned by Minister Golovnin to go to Kazan, an opportunity I used to travel on the Volga all the way from Tver (Kalinin) to Kazan. I found that, starting from the upper part of the Volga, it was primarily the right bank which was more eroded and, therefore, steeper, but that, here and there, the left bank was assuming this character, less frequently below Rybinsk than above. Somewhat above Nizhniy Novgorod, where there is now an extensive swamp, it seems that, at an earlier period, there existed a large lake which may have broken into the Volga lowlands and whose high southern shore I believe discerned at several points. From this spot on, the right bank of the Volga is uninterruptedly high, although the contemporary river bed runs sometimes at a distance of several versts from this bank, as is the case below Nizhniy Novgorod. In other regions, however, the river bed closely and persistently follows this high bank.

The journey to the Sea of Azov was occasioned by a curious set of circumstances. That this body of water is not at all deep was already known to the Greeks, who called it a swamp and left behind records of depth measurements. That the mouths of the Don are particularly shallow and that this shallowness extends as far as the roadstead of Taganrog was also known, as was the fact that sea level fluctuations in the eastern corner of the Bay of Taganrog are so large that, during persistent easterly winds, the water at Taganrog drains off of the sea floor, baring it for large stretches and causing ships in the roadstead fifteen to twenty versts away to ride on their keels. During recent years prior to my journey, however, strong complaints had been voiced, claiming that these conditions were only of recent origin, having been caused by the large, mainly foreign ships which were unlawfully dumping their ballast into the sea. A proposal had therefore been brought up not, as one might have expected, to rigidly enforce the long-existing ban on ballast dumping, or to deepen the mouths of the Don, but to prohibit entrance into the Sea of Azov to larger ships altogether, which would have to stay at Kerch to wait for supplies, while the Sea of Azov would be open only to coastal trade vessels. These proposals, which in fact originated not from the Sea of Azov, but in Kerch and Odessa, would probably have been ignored by the higher authorities had not the need to encourage coastal trade and thus commercial activities by the native population been presented as being in the patriotic interest. As it was, the proposal got as far as the Grand Duke Konstantin who, being the Commander in Chief of the navy, would have to present it to the highest government authorities. The Grand Duke declared that any measures would be premature before the reasons for the silting up had been investigated scientifically. He called for expert opinions from the navy, the Academy of Sciences and the Russian Geographical Society, all of which declared against the proposal, pointing out that, as far back as historical records existed, the sea had always been shallow, and particularly so the Taganrog roadstead. They also stressed the fact that the dumped ballast could not possibly reduce the depth of the entire sea as always claimed. The Grand Duke nevertheless ordered yet another investigation by the Academy and the Geographical Society. I offered my services for a preliminary investigation during the summer, which could be continued later by Herr Danilevsky, who in any case was commissioned to investigate the Sea of Azov and the Black Sea in the interest of the fisheries. The conclusions I was able to draw from my journey (1862) were as follows: Not only the Don, but also the crumbling of the shores, wherever they were not quite flat, caused more silt to reach the sea than was carried off via the Straits of Kerch, resulting in increased silting up close to the shores. The sandy spits of land protruding into the sea were also slowly built up by this process, but the claim that the shallowness of the large basin and of the roadstead of the Bay of Taganrog had increased compared to the past could not be substantiated (*Writings*, IV, d). The main reason for the proposal, however, I discovered, was that a coastal trading company had been secretly formed. Its proprietor, a certain Herr Dervitsky, in fact tried to talk me out of this journey. When I nevertheless showed up in Taganrog, he had disappeared.

CHANGES IN MY PUBLIC LIFE

Having been a full professor from the moment I joined the Academy of Sciences in St. Petersburg—first of zoology and, after Zagorski's death, of anatomy—I soon also became librarian of the foreign department of the academic library and also served for two years as Inspector of Private Boarding Houses, having been appointed to this office by Minister Uvarov. For several years I was also professor at the Medico-Surgical Academy, but resigned when, in 1853, I decided to travel to the Caspian Sea. Because of my advanced age, and in order not to stand in the way of younger members, I gave up my membership in the Academy in 1863, but was elected an honorary member by the latter with voting rights. Upon order of the present minister, Secretary of State Golovnin, I was also attached to the Ministry of Education.

During this period I rose on the customary ladder of advancement as high as Geheimrat (Privy Councillor) and was decorated with the St. Anne Order, 1st Class. His Majesty, the King of Sweden, honored me with the Order of the North Star, and Prussia thought me worthy of the highly regarded Peace Class of the Order *Pour le Mérite*.

Of the other local scientific societies which count me among their members I will mention only the Geographical Society, in the founding of which I had some part. If anybody should be interested in the names of other Russian and foreign societies which honored me by making me a member, he can find them in the description of the Doctor's Jubilee which was celebrated on the twenty-ninth of August, 1864, with the participation of many, and which was also instrumental in the genesis of this book.

As to my family—suffice it to say that I lost my first-born in Königsberg while he was still a boy, and my second son in Dorpat, where he had assiduously applied himself to the study of the natural sciences. A third son is an officer in the navy, at the present time serving in St. Petersburg as assistant to the port commander. The two younger sons are landowners in Estonia. My only daughter is married to Dr. Lingen, a local man.

My wife was taken from me on the fifteenth of March, 1864. When I shall follow her is for the biographers to append. I cannot say.

MY PRIVATE LIFE

I have no intention of trying to describe my private life, mindful as I am of the wise words a teacher once wrote into my memory book: "People as a rule are better than they appear to others, but not as good as they would like to appear themselves." It is indeed the height of naïveté to expect others to accept as true a picture of ourselves that which we present to them. Do we not grind away at the mirror our consciousness holds up before us, until our virtues are magnified and our vices reduced?

The only use I wish to make of the above heading is to pose here a question I have been asking myself recently. Without doubt I have pursued more scientific subjects than was good for me. There were even several efforts in measured rhyme, among them an epic in Estonian hexameters, which came easily. But I have never felt the slightest temptation to plan a short story, novelette or, still less, plan a novel or drama. Does this constitute proof of a lack of imagination? Yet in my younger years I was very much drawn to the literary creations of others, be it poetry or prose. I was less attracted by the *Dii minorum gentium* (lesser gods), than by Shakespeare, Lessing, Schiller, Goethe, Herder, Jean Paul, Sterne, Swift and also Walter Scott, in fact more by Englishmen and Germans than by Frenchmen of whom, after I had grown out of my childhood, I found only Molière to my liking. Altogether I may say that during my life I have cause to believe that I suffered from hyperactivity rather than from sluggishness of the imagination. Yet what I lacked was what Goethe called "Lust am Fabulieren" (the delight in spinning a yarn). I also remember well that, concerning versification, it was the difficulty involved in rhyming and in keeping to a certain meter that I saw as a challenge. But to take something swiftly shaped by the imagination, to hold it fast, slowly elaborate on it, dress it in choice words which then have to be consigned to the paper in an endless sequence of letters—this has alwaos seemed to me the most frightful slavery; that is, unless one intends to present a scientifically conceived opinion in a spirited, graphic and convincing manner. This is why I was always a ready speaker, relying as I did on the right of the speaker to be persuasive. But how anyone could decide to spread out a short story over several sheets of paper, or even to stretch a novel over several volumes, has remained beyond my grasp, and I would be inclined to regard it as plainly impossible, were it not a daily occurrence. I must indeed have lacked this "Lust am Fabulieren" to help me overcome the wearisomeness of writing. In my younger years I could honestly write to my friends that, "walking up and down, I have composed the most interesting letters to you, but was unfortunately unable to write them down." In later years I have tried to use this peculiarity of mine as an excuse to myself whenever I felt badly about my negligence in dealing with my correspondence. How much self-deception has sneaked into this argument I am unable to judge. I should like, however, to take this opportunity to most earnestly and contritely ask forgiveness of all those to whom I wrote only a few words, or who in vain waited for letters from me. Had my personality not been of such limited interest to begin with, this dearth of readable letters alone would save me from the objectionable practise, nowadays spreading in literature, and in German literature in particular, of burdening the dead with all sorts of eulogies, letters and other scraps of paper.

Another flaw of mine is unfortunately so much in evidence in this book that I need not bother to point it out. Although an old hand at writing, I am still unable to determine the structure of a book beforehand. The old saying: "all beginnings are hard," does not fit me as far as being an author is concerned. I always found the beginning to be easy, but the end difficult, and often unattainable. When I started to write this book, I honestly believed I had to recall every incident from my childhood, as otherwise I was liable to run out of material—yet soon I was swamped by material. Whatever I wrote about my school days and early education should be regarded as of purely local interest and skipped over as superfluous by whoever lacks this interest.

Ich bin schon alt, es mahnt der Zeiten Lauf
Mich oft an längst geschehene Geschichten,
Und die erzähl' ich, horcht auch niemand drauf.

Chamisso

(I have grown old; the drift of time brings back
More often the tales of deeds long passed;
'Tis these I tell, though none, perhaps, may listen.)

Writings

Since the occasion and purpose of many works to be named here are discussed in the Autobiography, partly even in great detail, I shall refer to such places (by: *Life*, p. . . .) and only give notes concerning some others.

Though I occasionally cite translations, excerpts and reviews, completeness in this respect is not at all intended. I cite what I found in the Writers' Lexicon of the provinces of Livonia, Estonia, and Courland, and in Carus and Engelmann's *Bibliotheca Zoologica*, and aside from that, whatever I happened to remember. To want to search beyond that would be in bad taste.

B.

I. Independently Published Works

1. *Dissertatio inaug. medica de morbis inter Esthones endemicis, quam cons. amplissimo medicorum ordine pro gradu doctoris medicinae l.c. die XXIV. Aug. public. def. Car. Ernst. Baer. Dorp.* 1814, 8°. 88 pages.
   Life, p. 104. It is also noted there why the disputation did not take place on the day named in the title. Page 105. Announced in Merkel's *Zuschauer*, in Crichton, Rehmann, and Burdach's *Russische Sammlung für Naturwissenschaft und Heilkunst*. Vol. I, pp. 321–337.

2. *Zwei Worte über den jetzigen Zustand der Naturgeschichte. Vorträge bei Gelegenheit der Errichtung eines zoolog. Museums in Königsberg. Königsberg, Gebrüder Bornträger.* 1821. 4°. 48 pages.
   Life, p. 178.

3. *Begleiter durch das Königl. zoologische Museum zu Königsberg.* (Sold for the museum's benefit.) Königsberg, 1822. 8°. 64 pages.
   Life, p. 176.

4. *De fossilibus mammalium reliquiis in Prussia repertis dissertatio. Sectio prima, pro loco in ord. medic. in Acad. Albert. obtinendo d. XV Sept. 1823 h.l.c. publice defend. Sectio secunda pro receptione in facultatem, d. XVI Sept. 1823 h.l.c. publice defend. Regiomontii, typis Hartungianis,* 4°. 40 pages.
   Life, p. 178. Several copies were sold by the book trade without section headings. In the appended theses the studies that had been already begun discussed embryology, e.g., *Legem a naturae scrutatoribus proclamatam, evolutionem, quam prima aetate quodque subit animal evolutioni quam in animalium serie observandam putant, respondere a natura alienam esse contendo.*

5. *Vorlesungen über Anthropologie, für den Selbstunterricht bearbeitet.* First part. 8°. XXVI and 525 pp. with eleven copperplates in broadside folio. Königsberg, Gebrüder Bornträger. 1824.
   Life, pp. 203–205. Announced in Oken's *Isis*, 1826, pp. 937 and 938 and elsewhere.

6. *Ad instaurationem solemnium, qnibus ante 50 hos annos summos honores in facultate medica auspicatus est Carolus Godofredus Hagen, med. et chirurg. doctor, artis chemicae et physicae prof. p. ord. cet. cet. in audit max. die XXVIII Sept. celebrandum indicat ordo medicorum. Adjecta est Mytili novi descriptio. Regiom.* 1825. 4°, 14 pages.
   The fiftieth anniversary of the distinguished Professor Hagen senior's doctorate should have been celebrated publicly by the medical faculty at

Königsberg on the day indicated in the title. As dean of this faculty at that time I wrote the invitation program and named a mussel, which I considered new, after the guest of honor, *Mytilus Hagenii* since it belongs to the family Mytilacea, and I wished to retain the names of species in the wider sense, as far as I could, although I saw clearly that the mantle in this mussel differed in structure from that of *Myt. edulis*, which I expressly pointed out. However, this mussel, which lived abundantly in the Gulf of Riga, had never been described before, being identical with Pallas's *Mytilus polymorphus*. I did not know of a good picture of this mussel since we did not have the eleventh volume of Martini's *Conchylien-Cabinet*. But even if I had been able to compare the picture in this volume, I might have considered the species occurring in Prussia different because the diagnosis by Pallas is completely wrong. *Cavum commune testae versus nates obsolete quinqueloculare dissepimentis brevissimis*, says Pallas (*Reise*, I, p. 478). I had to consider this information in particular as substantial. I thus stated at the end of my description that externally *Myt. Hagenii* is very similar to *Myt. polymorphus*, but that there are no dissepiments except two small rudimentary muscles at the hinge. Later on I had the opportunity on the Volga and in the northern part of the Caspian Sea to see many thousands of this kind of mussel, and I examined hundreds of them with regard to shell formation, but in none of them did I see anything else except the two small muscle rudiments; thus I do not know at all what is meant by *dissepimentis* since, even with regard to these rudiments for the hinge muscle, the shell could at the most be called triple. That Pallas's diagnosis prevented any understanding shows in the fact that Spengler and Chemnitz also thought that the mussel they had obtained from the Volga, which is described in Martini's work, Vol. XI, on p. 256 and illustrated in Figure 2028 is not the one described by Pallas. Pallas himself did not provide an illustration. Under these circumstances the name *Mytilus Hagenii* should have become the current one, for if the diagnosis is necessarily misleading, what is there to give the name its meaning? But since the mantle is more closed than in *Mytilus edulis* and in similar mussels, this species was raised to a special genus and called *Tichogonia* Rossm., *Dreissena* v. Beneden, and still other names. Since the same mussel also occurs in Holland, it is more probable that the Prussian is descended from the Dutch than from the Caspian. I also wish to point out that I had sent the mussel to Baron Férussac, asking him whether he knew it, but I did not receive a reply. He did not give an opinion until the work had appeared.

7. *De ovi mammalium et hominis genesi. Epistola ad Acad. Imp. scientiarum Petropolitanam. Cum tab. aenea (colorat.). Lipsiae, sumptib. Leopoldi Vossii.* 1827. 4°. 40 pages.

Life, pp. 215–229, where the first reviews are also cited. Translated by Breschet under the title: *Lettre sur la formation de l'oeuf dans l'espèce humaine et dans les mammifères.* Paris, printed by Duverger, 1829. 4°. 84 pages.

312

I know of this translation only from Engelmann's *Bibliotheca historiae naturalis*. Vol. I, p. 247.

8. *Ueber Entwickelungsgeschichte der Thiere. Beobachtung und Reflexion. Erster Theil, mit 3 col. Kupfertafeln.* Königsberg, Gebr. Bornträger. 1828. 4°. XXII and 271 pages.

Life, pp. 208–211 and 232–240. This contains a detailed report stating that this first volume consists of two halves, the first a reprint of the embryology of the chicken in the egg prepared for Burdach's *Physiology*, the second consisting of appended general considerations under the name "Scholien und Corollarien." Soon after publication of this work a review by Oken appeared in his *Isis* (1829, pp. 206–212) which I found very entertaining. Regardless of much friendly appreciation, he nevertheless became very lively and biting as soon as a statement deviated from his own view. Thus the report on the formation of the intestine, which according to him has to grow from the yolk sac toward the embryo. In the appendices particularly I corrected the view, prevalent at the time, that the more highly developed animals in their formation gradually pass through the organization of the lower animals, to the effect that rather the previous conditions are undeveloped intermediate conditions from which all the peculiarities of the different classes, families, genera, and species gradually emerge. The previous view had been elaborated particularly by Meckel and Oken. The examples and expressions that I chose for describing them had been taken from Meckel, without mentioning his name. Oken believed that he had been directly attacked and defended his view manfully by simply making statements. For instance, I had remarked that the Myriapoda, Acarida, and Hydrachnidae were originally hexapod, and only later became polypod, whereas conversely many insects which metamorphose (e.g., butterflies) begin by being polypod and end up by being hexapodal. To this Oken replied: "Does the author not know that these animals (Myriapoda, etc.) are lifelong embryos?" But that is precisely what I disputed and declared to be wrong. I did not notice other reviews from this initial period or at least I do not remember them now, except one in the October issue of the Halle *Lit.-Zeitung* for 1829. Later references were all the friendlier. As already mentioned in the biography, Breschet translated this volume, as far as I remember, without the scholia and corollaria; as late as 1853, Huxley translated the fifth scholium, the keystone of the previous ones, which he published in his *Scientifical Memoirs* with great praise as *Fragments Relating to Philosophical Zoology*, whereas in France the whole appendix may have seemed superfluous and bothersome.

Second part of the same work. With four copper plates, Königsberg 1837, published by Bornträger. 4°. 315 pages.

Life, pp. 232–240. There remains quite a lot to be said.

In writing the report on the gradual development of the chick I felt very much restricted by the fact that, like a piece of a mosaic, it had to be fitted into a prescribed space. It was to discuss only the embryo, not the development of the egg. It was to be kept in the style of a narration and I found that one cannot narrate with certainty if one does not report how the type gradually develops. What had been taken up of that kind was eliminated and gave rise to disorder. It seemed to me that one could and should delve into the matter even more deeply; thus the appendix originated. Some important parts of the appendix should really have been incorporated in the presentation in order to make it more lucid. Moreover, my views also underwent some changes. It was only with reluctance and inner contradiction that I called that which lies between the upper and the lower layer of the germ the "vessel layer" following Pander. This name seemed very suitable for the layer which, attached to the intestine, covers it and the yolk sac and furthermore is the future mesentery; besides that, the entire mass of the body develops from the original middle layer, and this layer can therefore be called the flesh layer. Thus one is led to the first obviously expressed separation, the separation of a vegetative layer from an animal layer through which the formation of the abdominal cavity occurs. I myself was not always very successful no matter how hard I tried to be consistent in new names. For instance, I later came to disapprove of the word "Dorsal cord, *Chorda dorsalis*" since I have always considered this cord to be specifically the central trunk, and whatever is formed above it to belong to the dorsal side, whatever is under it, to the abdominal side. I therefore would have preferred the word "Vertebral cord, *Chorda vertebralis*" since I was unable to create a convenient name from the word *rhachis*. I would really have liked to work all of it through again. Since in the meantime I had also studied the development of the other animal classes and toward the end of my stay had given a course on embryology for medical and non-medical people, among whom there were also several university lecturers, the new edition was planned in accordance with these lectures. I began, in these lectures, with the description of the development of the egg and the embryo of the chicken because here one can show almost everything; then I passed on to the reptiles, whose eggs develop outside the water, and finally to the mammals, whose course of development was explained by comparison with the chick. Thereafter followed the Batrachians and fishes, that develop still differently, and finally, all that I had to say about the development of insects, worms, molluscs, and protozoa. In preparing these lectures, delivered without notes, I had not yet finished the embryology of the invertebrates when the season of the year forced me to leave Königsberg, and various matters connected with this forced me to break off the work. Moreover, there was not much I could report on the basis of my own observations. But I was sorry that, in the hope of filling this gap while in St. Petersburg, I did not submit an entirely different paper for print, dealing with more complete research into the early stages of human ova. I reported in my *Life*, p. 276, that I was unable to fill the gap while in St. Petersburg. My entire presentation, in both the above-mentioned volumes, has been reproached for being too mechanical. I admit that I accepted this reproach as a compliment, for one stands more firmly on a board than on ether or the sky at dawn. To speak only of what has been seen and to derive thoughts only from observations, but not to arrange what has been observed according to the different thoughts, corresponded perhaps to a natural inclination, but I had adopted it as my principle on the basis of my experience. It was natural that even in the beginning of my research, I endeavored to find out what previous times had known of these processes and thought about them. Aristotle, Harvey, Malpighi, Swammerdam were compared with pleasure, but Fabricius ab Aquapendente repelled me with his tedious controversies so that I did not manage more than one or two pages about these. In order to force myself to a complete review of the growth of knowledge of embryology, I announced a lecture on the history of this study to the Medical Society at Königsberg for September or October 1821. Now Fabricius ab Aquapendente, too, had to be read thoroughly. But I was astounded by the emptiness of this book which had such a great reputation in its own time, although now hardly anybody knows what it contains. Much reasoning in order to present even the most foolish thing as necessary and natural! The author reports on much that occurs invisibly in the egg, but very little and wrongly about that which is visible. I still have the manuscript of the lecture and I quote from it only the following paragraph. "In the egg an embryo appears which grows up, consequently three activities (*actiones*) must take effect, namely production, growth, and nutrition. Each activity is served by two forces (*facultates*), production by *fac. immutatrix* and *fac. formatrix*, growth and nutrition by *facultas attractrix* and *retentrix*, *f. concoctrix* and *expultrix*. Thus Fabricius believed that he knew the exact forces acting in the egg, but he was unlucky when he made observations although he can very definitely declare why his opinion is the correct one. He says rightly that every activity must result from within a substance. Well, the yolk and the white in the egg serve to provide nutrition and growth. Which substance is effective in the generation of the embryo? This must be brought about by the chalazae, for the so-called tread is only the scar which remains after the egg becomes detached from its stalk. Thus the twisted cords, which are called chalazae, and which occur in unfertilized eggs equally developed as in fertilized ones, are the real procreative parts—only after fertilization, however. Of them, however, the chalaza at the blunt end is the predominantly effective one. Fabricius overflows with reasons why this must be so; these I will spare you, but everything depends on the blunt end of the egg being in front when the egg is laid. As in this statement, Fabricius is generally unlucky as soon as observation is involved. The embryo, which at first appears midway in the length of the egg, turns toward the blunt end after the first few days, and as soon as the chalazae lose their support upon the disappearance of the yolk membrane, it lies very decidedly at the blunt end. Fabricius was of the opinion that this always had to be the case, and actually represented it like that pictorially from the third day onward. When he opened the egg at the blunt end and inspected it on the second day, he could not see anything of the embryo. On the third day, however, he shows it in the picture at the blunt end; this could have become possible only through the strong rotation of the yolk. This wrong opinion was the real reason why the chalaza of the blunt end had to be procreative, and the tread a mere scar, a designation which it has even retained."

The study of Fabricius was an excellent tonic for me in healing philosophical views which did not drive directly from observation. Thus I did not want to give explanations of the process but only accurate observations of them and their consequences. I believe I mentioned here and there that I realized that all processes are the necessary consequences of effects exerted by that which exists. I believe I said it now and again in concluding sentences, e.g., in the conclusion to the preface to the first volume, where I expressed the conviction that the cradle has not been made yet, nay, that even the tree from which the wood for the cradle is to be taken has probably not been planted yet, for the man who will, in the future, recognize the forces acting in the egg with absolute conviction. But I wished to conceive the processes in a positive manner and to describe them simply and comprehensibly. I wish it could always have been done very mechanically. I also believe that I have greatly facilitated understanding by using simple terms, such as turning inside out and outside in, sprouting, etc., that can be easily associated with development, growth, etc., but that are more definite, and also by using schematic illustrations. Now, expression can be more concise, since even the designations introduced by Wolff are superfluous for transient opinions. It was also my intention to publish, at a later date, a shorter and more fluent book which would not bear the traces of being plowed up. However, the study of embryology is like climbing an Alpine peak. One always expects to reach the peak soon, and all the time new and unexpected slopes open up. But Professor Valentin reached the goal before me, and the alternation of generations set me back altogether—not to mention parthenogenesis and pedogenesis, which cannot be absorbed in the alternation of generations. In my youth I thought I was being modest when I did not want to recognize forces, like Fabricius, but only their effects and quite thoroughly at that. In my old age I have had to learn that such modesty is really very immodest.

9. *Untersuchungen über die Gefässverbindung zwischen Mutter und Frucht. Ein Glückwunsch zur Jubelfeier von Samuel Thomas von Sömmerring.* Leipzig, L. Voss, 1828. Folio 30 pages.

Life, pp. 230–232. Congratulatory publication addressed to S. Th. Sömmerring in the name of the Medico-Physical Society at Königsberg.

10. *Berichte über die Zoographia Rosso Asiatica von P.S. Pallas, abgestattet an die Kaiserl. Akademie der Wissenschaften zu St. Petersburg.* Königsberg 1831, 4°. 36 pages.

Life, pp. 244–248. The academy had these reports printed at my suggestion, omitting only the indication of the individual steps that had to be taken in Leipzig in order to redeem the pawned original drawings, copper plates, etc. The original documents, to which the first report in particular refers, are stapled together for storage. I cannot refrain from emphasizing here that my proposal was to publish only a selection of the plates accompanying Pallas's work (cf. the last page of the report), but that after my departure this decision was changed and the Academy had the entire series of the redeemed but mostly bad and antiquated plates printed, in order to publish them in the *Icon. ad Zoogr. Ross.-Asiat.*

11. *Untersuchungen über die Entwickelung der Fische, nebst einem Anhange über die Schwimmblase.* With one copper plate and several woodcuts. Leipzig, Vogel, large 4°, IV and 52 pages.

Life, pp. 260–261.

12. *Predlozhenie o razvedeniyu Kvinoi v severnykh oblastyakh Rossiiskoi Imperii.* Soch. Akademika Bera. St. Petersburg, 1839. 8°.

In a number of northern provinces of the Russian Empire, especially in northern Finland and in the provinces of Olonets and Archangel, the grain harvest fails fairly frequently. This causes great distress because transport to the inner parts of these provinces is difficult. At such times it is usual to use pine bark mixed with a little bread flour as food. I therefore promised to try the cultivation of quinoa (*Chenop. Quinoa*) whose seeds are ground into flour and eaten like bread on the mountain plateaus of the Andes where barley no longer thrives. Unfortunately, only very few attempts have been made, and as far as I know, none in the regions concerned. I informed State Counselor von Engelhardt of this article; he was then editor of the *Zemlyad. Gazeta*. The proposition was supposed to be tried again.

13. *Instruction für diejenigen Personen, welche über Raupenfrass auf den Feldern zu berichten haben.* 1839. 8°.

A short article that I wrote according to the wish of my colleague von Köppen, which was also distributed in the Russian language.

14. *Bericht über die Zusammenkunft einiger Anthropologen im September 1861 in Göttingen, zum Zweck gemeinsamer Besprechungen.* Reported by K.E. von Baer and Rud. Wagner, with one lithograph plate. Leipzig, Voss, 1861. 4°. 84 pages.

Life, pp. 301–302. This publication, which is a report on the meeting held for the purpose of discussing some anthropological tasks, especially those containing measurements, I can list as written by myself, except for the specifically marked insertions and the conclusion. In view of the distance of the printing works some printing errors have occurred. I would beg the reader to read the name Severtsov at least twice on p. 37 instead of Seventsov and the Island of Marken instead of Marsen on p. 9.

15. *Kaspische Studien.* Nos. I–VIII.

These are reprints of the individual articles on the Caspian Sea and its environs which I published in the Bulletin of the Academy. Since a number of the reprints of this collection are being sold in book-shops, I was of the opinion that I could not omit them here. The first seven numbers form the first volume and are provided with a special title. The eighth is to be followed by others, health permitting.

16. *Reden, gehalten in wissenschaftlichen Versammlungen und kleinere Aufsätze vermischten Inhalts.* First Volume: Reden. St. Petersburg, Schmitzdorff, 1864. 8°. VI and 296 pages.

This collection is intended primarily to assemble lectures previously delivered and printed in widely varied places, and one lecture not yet printed; in the second volume, which I hope to publish in the course of this year, there are some other short articles, mostly dealing with natural science in the widest sense of the word, which have not been published at all, or at least not in the German language.

17. *Nachrichten über Leben und Schriften des Geheimrathes Dr. Karl Ernst von Baer, mitgetheilt von ihm selbst. Veröffentlicht bei Gelegenheit seines fünfzigjährigen Doctor-Jubiläums, am 29. August 1864, von der Ritterschaft Ehstlands.* St. Petersburg, large 8°.

The present book. It originated when the Knights of Estonia requested me to give an account of my life and as complete a list of my writings as possible, which the Knighthood intended to publish on August 29, 1864. However, I was not able to finish the book until later. It is not intended for commercial purposes.

A new impression is also intended for the commercial book trade.

II. Articles and Brief Communications in Journals of Natural History and Medicine

[for addition of the Publications of the Academy of Sciences in St. Petersburg, see Section III]

a. *Nova acta physico-medica Academiae Caesareae Leopoldino-Carolinae naturae curiosorum.*

1. Beiträge zur Kenntniss der neidern Thiere. With 6 copper plates. (Written 1824–1826.) *Nova act. Acad. C.L.C. n.c.* Vol. XIII, part 2, pp. 525–762. (Published in 1827.)

These contributions consist of seven separate treatises of which the first six are intended to discuss, anatomically and zoologically, some animal forms of low organization, partly new and partly lesser-known ones, in order to make a judgment in the seventh treatise of the kinship of lower animals, especially in order to prove that intestinal worms do not form a class of their own but belong to different classes, and that the organizational types of Cuvier's three great groups of invertebrates are also to be investigated through the lower developmental stages, and that altogether the type of organization (arrangement of organs) is to be distinguished from the organizational stage (differentiation). The individual treatises have the following titles:

1. *Aspidogaster conchicola,* ein Schmarotzer der Süsswassermuscheln, pp. 527–557. Along with plate XXVIII.

2. *Distoma duplicatum, Bucephalus polymorphus* und andere Schmarotzer der Süsswassermuscheln, pp. 558–604. Along with plate XXIX, Figs. 1–19 and plate XXX.

3. Ueber Zercarien, ihren Wohnsitz und ihre Bildungsgeschichte, so wie über einige andere Schmarotzer der Schnecken. Pages 605–639. Along with plate XXIX, Figs. 20–27 and plate XXXI.

4. *Nitzschia elegans.* pp. 660–678. Along with plate XXXII, Figs. 1–6.

5. Beiträge zur Kenntniss des *Polystoma integerrimum,* pp. 679–689.

6. Ueber Planarien, pp. 690–730, Plate XXXIII. Excerpt in the *Annal. des scienc. nat.* Vol. XV, 183–187.

7. Ueber die Verwandtschaftsverhältnisse der niedern Thierformen, pp. 731–762.

Fragments of this last treatise were translated into English almost thirty years after being written and appeared as "Fragments referring to Philosophical Zoology" in *Scientifical Memoirs, Natur. History* by Arth. Henfrey and Th. H. Huxley, Vol. I, part 2, p. 176, together with excerpts from the *Embryology*. Cf. *Writings*, I, 8.

On the other hand, a subordinate section was later corrected in a way which I am not prepared to accept as it stands but which, in my opinion, I must set right, the opportunity now not only presenting, but forcing itself on me. In the second of the above-listed treatises, after discussing *Bucephalus polymorphus* and other parasites of freshwater mussels, I had reported in a special section headed "Chaotic Swarming in the Interior of Mussels" on cases where the interior of mussels, and especially of certain parts, were completely filled with an enormous mass of moving organisms. Professor K. Th. E. von Siebold in his article "Parasites" in Wagner's *Manual of Physiology* (Volume II, 1844) wrote an appendix "On Pseudoparasites," and he concludes the appendix by listing *Leucophra fluxa M.* and others, which are supposed to be only fragments of a mussel covered with scintillating ciliated organs; he adds: such scintillating ciliated mussel fragments were formerly confused with infusoria-like parasites (in *Isis*) and used by the adherents of the *generatio aequivoca* to prove the existence of an original creation. Then follows the note:

Baer ("Beiträge zur Kenntniss der niedern Thiere") in *Nov. act. Acad. N.C.* Vol. XIII, page 594, Table XXX, Fig. 28. Cf. Raspail (*Histoire naturelle de l'Alcionelle fluviatile*) in *Mém. de la soc. nat. de Paris*, 1828, p. 145, who knew the scintillating cilia in lower animals fairly well. Cf. also the dispute between Baer and Raspail (1828, p. 671 and 1829, p. 556) in which Baer greatly resented Raspail's reproach that he has taken "all tatters, nothing but tatters" for animals. (*Handwörterbuch der Physiologie*, II, p. 692.)

I have received many and important corrections from Herr von Siebold and I am quite prepared to receive future ones—but this I cannot accept.

First of all, as regards the dispute with Raspail: this does not at all refer to the section quoted by von Siebold, which did not then exist. The "Beiträge zur Kenntniss der niedern Thiere" had not even been printed when Raspail disputed it. The matter was as follows. I had sent part of the "Beiträge" to Bonn in 1824 and part in 1825, and some additions even in 1826. Since the printing took a long time, I sent a very brief announcement of the contents to Férussac, without heading and written on a single sheet. Férussac included the announcement in his *Bulletin des sciences naturelles*, T. IX, pp. 125–126. Raspail knew only the announcement of the contents, for the "Contributions" had then not been published, not even in separate printings, when he made his report on his investigations of *Alcyonella* to three different societies in Paris. It is probably the same which later appeared in the *Bulletin des sc. nat.* T. XII, pp. 190–196. I had read reports on it in all kinds of journals even before then. Raspail, who knows the cilia on the skin of the mussel fairly well, as von Siebold rightly notes, declares that everything movable, which has been found in the bodies of mussels—spermatozoa, Bauer's animalcules, etc., also in particular *Aspidogaster conchicola*, which I described and of which I said expressly that it has the formation of the mouth, the digestive apparatus and the hermaphroditism of the trematodes, but has an elongated abdominal plate—represent pieces of skin, and to make the report more piquant, he adds that I order the Aspidogaster "dans la classe des gastéropodes," (in the class of the gastropods). If this is not impertinence I would like to be shown what impertinence is. It is almost forty years since I rejected this censure (*Schriften* II, e. 7) and even now I find that I had the right tone. This is also confirmed by Raspail's reply (*Isis*, 1829, pp. 526–564) in which he now admits that the Aspidogaster is an animal, and although he distinguishes quotations by spacing, he leaves out the most important point, e.g., attribution of the above-named animal to the trematodes, and states that I changed the second Treatise during proofreading, after I had taken note of his work. Well, Mr. R. should have calmed down; Königsberg is not a suburb of Bonn. Professor Müller, who was then in Bonn, saw to the proofreading of the text, and I was sent only the lithograph plates. I am said to have written him a letter in a diffidently polite tone. I have never been diffident before such majesty! The tone of the letter may have been polite, after all, I had not then seen in print that everything that moves in the mussel body consists only of separated pieces of skin.

Meanwhile, Raspail has been dead for a long time and I would not have mentioned him at all if Herr von Siebold had not disapprovingly mentioned my opposition to Raspail. After all, Raspail did not know the section dealing with the chaotic swarming in the interior of the mussels of which von Siebold was thinking. I have to mention a little more about this section, especially since I want to describe, belatedly, under what circumstances I saw the great swarming, and how I view the matter now. I am far removed from writing a definite conclusion to this section. I still believe that it is wrong to declare all movement as scintillating ciliated parts of the body. Though the scintillating ciliary movement had not become quite clear to me, what I call "points" is obviously that which was later called cilia. The paper by Purkinje and Valentin on ciliary movement appeared almost ten years later. However, its traces may be recognized in my description, e.g., when I maintain that some masses begin their motion after they are torn off, which Treviranus had already seen earlier. But I gladly admit that the entire presentation suffers from a lack of definiteness and expresses a feeling of astonishment. Both are due to the fact that I would have preferred to view the smooth-walled, completely isolated bodies as infusoria which had penetrated from outside, as I hinted in a note to page 597. But at that time there seemed conviction so firmly rooted that entozoa cannot maintain themselves outside living animals any more than animals free-living in water can continue living inside, that I only said: "It is not impossible that these animals, so similar to infusoria living free in water, have penetrated into the mussel body from outside since this is riddled by canals which open freely at the edge of the foot and which suck in water." I have found this great mobility only three times, under special circumstances, in mussels which were near death and which were completely soaked by water. If one keeps a number of mussels in a vessel with water, one soon finds that the body swells up and becomes somewhat more transparent. If the mussels are taken out of the water, they immediately and quickly press the water out and close the valves. Later, when life becomes weaker, the pressing out of the water, the reduction in body size, and the closing of the valves proceed much more slowly. Later still they cannot reduce the body size at all any more nor can they close the valves. But some of them remain in this state for a very long time without any signs of decay. Such were the mussels in which I observed what I call the swarming three times. Some had been in the vessel with water for three weeks without dying, after the others had died off. All of them, those that died early and those that lasted for a long time, were from the Trutenau pond where the mussels and snails had more parasites of all kinds than I ever obtained from any other body of water. In the same water there was also a great wealth of animals which I believed I had to refer to as infusoria although among them there may have been ova and embryos of parasites. The water poured in daily for replenishing was, to be sure, from elsewhere. But since a little of the water that was poured out always remained, clinging to the bodies and shells of the mussels, I believe now that these animals procreated all the time and that their eggs, embryos, and the mature animals were sucked up with the water and probably also penetrated into the slack sex openings, and that eventually they were present in very large numbers. Later on I tried here to arrive at the same amount in dying mussels, but in vain. Even the special entozoa which I described were not to be found here. But I do not doubt that the Trutenau pond can still provide the so-called swarming. I am prepared to believe that the smallest particles are moved only by the whirl of the cilia of other animals or parts, but I cannot concede that everything movable proceeds only from isolated tatters.

2. Schädel- und Kopfmangel an Embryonen von Schweinen, aus der frühesten Zeit der Entwickelung beobachtet. *Nova acta Acad. C.L.C. n.c.* Vol. XIV, pp. 827–837. With one plate.

One embryo at the first stage of development, still without visible trace of extremities, was also without any rudiment of a head, and could be proof that acephalia can exist as a result of originally defective predisposition without previous destruction of the head.

3. Ueber das Gefässystem des Braunfisches. (Submitted 1834.) *Nova acta Acad. C.L.C. nat. cur.* Vol. XVII, pp. 395–408. With one plate.

That a large number of arteries and veins break up very early into networks in the porpoise, Illustrated: a large network of veins on the psoas, a weaker one in the peritoneum, and an incipient sacral and hypogastric venous network.

b. *Deutsches Archiv für die Physiologie*. Published by J.F. Meckel jointly with a society of scientists. Halle, Vols. I–VIII (1815–1823), 8°. Later published under the title; *Archiv für Anatomie und Physiologie*. Published by J.F. Meckel jointly with several scientists and listed according to years of publication.

1. Beitrag zur Kenntniss vom Bau des dreizehigen Faulthieres, mit Abbildung (1823). *Meckels Arch*. Bd. VIII, pp. 354–369.

2. Ueber *Med. aurita*. With one copper plate (1823). *Meck. Arch*. Bd. VIII, pp. 369–391.

3. Ueber das äussere und innere Skelet. Sendschreiben and Herrn Prof. Heusinger. With one copper plate. *Meck. Arch. für Anat. und Ph*. 1826, pp. 327–376.

Life, p. 199. Exoskeleton and endoskeleton in general; simple ring shape for the former, double for the latter in individual vertebrae. Cartilaginous skull of many fishes, especially of the sturgeon and the type of skull bones in the exoskeleton.

4. Ueber den Seitenkanal des Störs. With illustration (In year 1827). *Meck. Arch. f. Anat. und Ph*. p. 367.

The lateral line is surrounded by cartilaginous rings and passes through the lateral shields. The illustration was not included in this year of publication owing to an oversight; it was published in the following year. (Plate VII, Figure 2.)

5. Ueber die Kiemen und Kiemengefässe in den Embryonen der Wirbelthiers. *Meck. Archiv für Anatomie und Ph*. 1827, pp. 556–568. Translated in *Annal. des sc. natur*. T. XV, pp. 264–280.

Generalization of Rathke's discovery of the gill clefts and the appertaining vascular arches.

6. Noch eine Bemerkung über die Zweifel, welche man gegen die Milchdrüse des *Ornithorhynchus* erhoben hat, und Betrachtungen über das Eierlegen und Lebendiggebären. *Meck. Arch. f. Anat. und Ph*. 1827, pp. 568–576.

All kinds of unfounded doubts were raised concerning Meckel's discovery of the milk gland of *Ornithorhynchus* because it does not look like the usual conglomerated glands. May I point out here that the mammalian gland of the *Delph. Phocaena* does not look like them either; it consists of ramified but widely separated canals and spreads over a large part of the abdominal surface. I found it thus in animals which were not pregnant. I do not know how it came about that I was later reproached for having stated that this gland consists also of non-ramified tubes. After all, I sent a drawing to J. Müller which was rough, and had been made directly according to the animal, and it was as clearly branched as possible.

7. Ueber einen Doppel-Embryo des Huhns aus dem dritten Tage der Bebrütung. With illustration: *Meck. Arch. für Anat. und Ph.* 1827, pp. 578–586. Primarily intended to prove that the double formation is primitive.

8. Ueber die Kiemenspalten der Säugethier-Embryonen. *Meck. Arch. f. Anat. und Ph.* 1828, pp. 143–148. Translated in *Annal. des sc. natur.* T. XV, p. 282.

Supplement to Treatise 5. In mammalian embryos there are four gill clefts and five vascular arches surrounding them.

9. Ueber den Weg, den die Eier unsrer Süsswassermuscheln nehmen, um in die Kiemen zu gelangen, nebst allgemeinen Bemerkungen über den Bau der Muscheln. With one copper plate. *Meck. Arch. f. Anat. und Ph.* 1830, pp. 313–352.

The outlets of the ovaries, though demonstrated by several observers with certainty, were not found by others and their existence was denied or supposed to be in entirely different regions. I show here that in some species of freshwater mussels the outlets are more hidden, but that the entire path of the eggs is very analogous not only in these, but also in other Acephala.

10. Bemerkungen über die Erzeugung der Perlen. *Meck. Arch. f. Anat. und Ph.* 1830, pp. 352–357.

Mainly directed against Home, who declared that pearls are coverings for mussel eggs. In reality they are pathological products. I have found them only in the mantle. According to later observations, dead parasites often give rise to the formation of pearls. That is very believable.

c. *Zeitschrift für organische Physik.* Published by Dr. C. Friedr. Heusinger. 8°. 3 Vols. 1827–1828.

1. Commentar zu der Schrift: De ovi mammalium et hominis generi. Epistola ad Acad. Petrop. *Heus. Zeitschr. f. org. Phys.* II. pp. 125–193.

Life, p. 225. The content of the above Latin work is rendered in German and in a somewhat changed arrangement.

2. Noch ein Wort über den After der Distomea. *Heus. Zeitschr. f. org. Phys.* II. pp. 197–198.

Since the organ through which residues of nutriment are excreted by the Distomum opens from a trunk which is formed by the uniting of ramified channels, the outlet opening should not be called anus.

3. Ueber *Furia infernalis. Heus. Zeitschr. f. org. Phys.* II. p. 361.

This brief note bears my name and was written by me. I did not submit it but it was selected by the editor from one of my communications in *Frorieps Notizen* (II, f. 4).

4. An die Physiologen Deutschlands und die nächste Versammlung der deutschen Naturforscher. Unterzeichnet: *Quidam. Heus. Zeitschr. f. org. Phys.* II. pp. 362–370.

This appeal appeared without mentioning my name because I was unable, if for no other reason than because of being far away from Germany, to take a substantial part in the proceedings. For it was not rare that scientific tasks, which a short time before had been elaborated thoroughly in Germany were undertaken anew by Frenchmen who completely ignored their German predecessors. When protests were made, they professed ignorance. Serres's *Anatomie comparée du cerveau* was still vividly remembered; in it Germans recognized Carus and Tiedemann. It was strikingly clear that the German scientific world was at a great disadvantage compared to the French in that the latter had in its Academy an organ through which its voice was heard all over the world whereas the Germans had none. The reports on scientific achievements in Germany were not concentrated anywhere. It was therefore not at all easy for the French, or almost impossible for them to find out what had been achieved in any particular subject in Germany in recent times. For the same reason, however, it was also very tempting to pretend ignorance if a work of this kind was discovered, assuming that it would not be generally known in France. Furthermore, knowledge of German was rare in France. Since a young editor had now started a new journal of physiology in Germany (Heusinger), I proposed that the journal should endeavor to report on all German works on anatomy and physiology. Strangely enough, *Meckels Deutsches Archiv für Physiologie* (German Archive for Physiology) contained many translations from French and English; German papers were never mentioned, unless they had been sent to his *Archiv* for publication. I believed the need for such a reviewing archive would be felt so keenly that I hoped the authors of major works would become used to submitting notices containing their main contents; thus it would only be necessary for those who would be interested to devote time and effort for several years to obtain those authors' abstracts. The abstracts could then be trimmed down at will by an editor if they were too wordy. From this half-joking, half-serious proposition I expected at least some effect, even if not a great one. But no matter how cosmopolitan German thought is, prefacing a history of Oldenburg or of Jever with the invasion of the Aryans, if not with the Stone Age, in his actions the German is in favor of separatism and defends it staunchly. Therefore the publisher raised objections: not that the required collaborators could not be found at a small university, but that the journal would have to have double its size. At the next meeting of natural scientists in Berlin in 1828, which I attended, the proposal was not mentioned at all any more. I was quite aware, of course, that the person submitting a proposal of general interest has to be the one to press it and implement it. But in this case it seemed impossible to me. Yet, within a few years, the obvious need had nevertheless exerted its influence to such an extent that J. Müller in his *Archiv für Anatomie, Physiologie*, etc., published reports on the progress of the anatomical and physiological science from 1834 onward and Wiegmann in his *Archiv für Naturgeschichte* did the same for zoology and botany from 1835 onward. But both were of cosmopolitan dimensions. The increasing need has now brought into being several reports of this kind, but always for polyglot matter. Should the German learn all the languages from Lisbon to Constantinople in order to speak only of German books after all? That he probably will not do.

d. *Archiv für Anatomie, Physiologie und wissenschaftliche Medizin*, published by Dr. Johannes Müller jointly with several scientists. Berlin, 8°. (From 1834 onward.)

1. Die Metamorphose des Eies der Batrachier vor der Erscheinung des Embryo und Folgerungen aus ihr für die Theorie der Erzeugung. *Müllers Arch*. 1834, pp. 481–509. With one plate.

The cleavage of the yolk after fertilization is reported. Cf. *Life*, pp. 261–268.

2. Ueber die sogenannte Erneuerung des Magens der Krebse und die Bedeutung der Krebssteine. *Müllers Arch*. 1834, pp. 510–527. With illustration.

This so-called restoration is molting, and the crabstones may be viewed as salivary concretions.

3. Beitrag zur Entwickelungsgeschichte der Schildkröten. With illustration. *Müllers Arch*. 1834, pp. 645–650.

The earliest development of turtles was completely unknown. I personally have set eyes only on one single egg. The consequences which I derived from that are partly unfounded and disproved by Rathke's beautiful investigations.

4. Selbstbefruchtung, an einer hermaphroditischen Schnecke beobachtet. *Müll. Arch*. 1835, p. 224.

5. Doppelter Muttermund des einfachen Fruchthälters vom Ameisenfresser. *Müll. Arch*. 1836, p. 384.

Very brief note that, as in the sloth, the simple uterus in the ant-eater also has a double orifice into the vagina.

e. *Isis* oder *encyclopädische Zeitung* by Oken. Jena, later Leipzig, 4°. (From 1817 onward.)

1. Ueber eine Süsswasser-Miessmuschel. *Isis*, 1826, pp. 525–527.

2. Ueber den Braunfisch (Delphinus Phocaena). With one copper plate. *Isis*, 1826, pp. 807–811.

I maintain that, among other details, the duodenum was wrongly considered a fourth stomach; Fr. Cuvier reacted very angrily to this but it was later nevertheless confirmed.

3. Die Nase der Cetaceen, erläutert durch Untersuchung der Nase des Braunfisches. *Isis*, 1826, pp. 811–847.

Life, p. 199.

4. Ueber den Bau der *Medusa aurita* in Bezug auf Rosenthals Darstellung. *Isis*, 1826, pp. 847–849.

5. Nachträgliche Bemerkung über die Riechnerven des Braunfisches. *Isis*, 1826, p. 944.

6. Noch ein Wort über das Blasen der Cetaceen. *Isis*, 1828, pp. 927–931.

In the description of the nose of the porpoise, quoted above under No. 3, I had declared that the anatomical structure proves that the cetaceans do not eject swallowed water through the spouts. Faber, the zoologist, contradicted this assertion in *Isis*, to which I reply in this article.

7. Die Zurechtweisung einer noch nicht bekannt gemachten Untersuchung wird zurückgewiesen. *Isis*, 1828, pp. 671–678.

Against Raspail, whose description of *Aspidogaster conchicola* was not yet published, and his idea that all independently moving bodies seen in mussels are mere pieces of skin, because they are moved by means of the cilia. Also against his assertion that all *Alcyonella* and *Plumatella* form only one genus. Cf. above, II, a. 1.

8. Aufforderung ein Paar Riesenschlangen betreffend. *Isis*, 1828, pp. 923–924.

The larger of two giant snakes kept in a cage, *Python Tigris fem.*, has laid fertilized eggs. I enquired whether the other snake, which was much smaller, lighter in color and had a reddish line along the forehead, belonged to another species or was a male of the same species. Professor Wiegmann declared the snake the male of the same species.

9. Verwüstung des Leins im J. 1828 in Ostpreussen durch die Gamma-Eule und die Grasraupe. *Isis*, 1831, pp. 593–604.

f. *Notizen aus dem Gebiete der Natur- und Heilkunde*, gesammelt und mitgetheilt von L.F. Froriep. 4°. From 1822 onward. *Neue Notizen*. From 1837 onward. Third series by M.J. Schleiden and Rob. Froriep, beginning in 1847.

1. Ornithologische Fragmente. *Fror. Notizen*, Vol. X, No. 17 and 18.

2. Nachtr. zu den Ornithol. Fragmenten. *Fror. Not.* Vol. XI, No. 13.

3. Bemerkungen über die Entwickelungsgeschichte der Muscheln und über ein System von Wassergefässen in diesen Thieren. *Fror. Not.*, Vol. XIII, No. 1.

4. *Furia infernalis* in Liefland. *Fror. Not.*, Vol. XX, No. 2, pp. 23–30.

Not for, but against the legend of the *Furia infernalis*. The legend had been at rest for a long time and completely banished into the realm of the fable, when a report appeared which was repeated in many newspapers: this hellworm had actually been observed in Livonia, in the parish of Ecks. I opposed this and pointed to anthrax in animals, and the black and blue pox in man. (A printing error reads "Catten" instead of "Letten".)

5. Wassergefässe in den niedern Thieren. *Fror. Not.*, Vol. XX, No. 3.

6. Beobachtungen über die Häutungen des Embryos und Anwendung derselben auf die Erkenntniss der Insecten-Metamorphose. *Fror. Not.*, Vol. XXXI, No. 10, col. 146-154.

Translated with supplements and corrections by Breschet. *Annales des sc. natur.*, Vol. XXVIII, pp. 5-31.

7. Ueber die Entwickelungsweise der Schwimmblase der Fische. *Fror. Not.*, Vol. XXXIX, No. 12, pp. 177-180.

8. Neue Untersuchungen über die Entwickelung der Thiere. *Fror. Neue Not.*, Vol. XXXIX (1846), No. 839, col. 38-40.

Identical with III, d, 14, but with a postscript by the publisher.

9. Ueber Herrn Steenstrup's Untersuchungen betreffend das Vorkommen des Hermaphroditismus in der Natur. *Fror. Notizen.* Third series, Vol. I, col. 129-135.

g. *Verhandlungen der Gesellschaft naturforschender Freunde in Berlin.* Berlin, from 1829 onward. 4°.

Ueber Linné's im Wasser gefundene Bandwürmer. *Verh. d. nat. Freunde in B.* Vol. I. (1829), pp. 338-390.

Tape worms (*Bothr. solidus*) from *Gasterost. pungitius* several times found alive in a bay of the Gulf of Riga; they were reminiscent of the tape worms found by Linné in water.

h. *Bulletin des sciences naturelles et de géologie* (second section of the *Bulletin des sciences et de l'industrie*) published under the editorship of M. le Baron de Férussac. 8° (1824-1831).

Sur les Entozoaires ou Vers intestinaux. (1826). *Fer. Bull. des sc. nat.*, Vol. IX, p. 123.

Announcement of the content of the "Beiträge zur Kenntniss der niedern Thiere", title by Férussac.

i. *Vorträge aus dem Gebiete der Naturwissenschaften und der Oekonomie gehalten in der ökon.-physikalischen Gesellschaft in Königsberg. Kön.* 1834, 8°.

In this collection which I edited, I myself wrote:

1. Preface, pp. III-XII.
Life, pp. 258-260.

2. Das allgemeine Gesetz der Entwickelung in der Natur. Pp. 1-32.
This lecture is included in the *Reden* (with very slight changes) (*Writings* I, No. 16).

3. Ueber die *Chinchilla.* Pp. 265-268.

k. *Naturalist. Vestnik estestvennykh nauk i sel'skogo khozyaistva.* The first year (1864) supplement to the journal: "Uchitel' "; the last year (1865) independent. D. Mikhailovym.

1. Deistvitel 'no li kity vybrasyvayut vodyanye stolby? Esli ne vybrasyvayut, to otkuda vzyalos' takoe mnenie? *Naturalist,* 1864, pp. 173–182.

2. Mesto cheloveka v prirode: 1) Razlichie mezhdu chelovekom i drugimi zhivotnymi v telesnom otnoshenii. *Nat.* 1865, Nos. 2, 3, 4, 5.

l. *Horae societ. entomologicae Rossiae.* Vols. 1 and 2. Petrop. 1861 and 1862. 8°.
Also under the title: *Trudy Russk. Entomologicheskogo Obshchestva.*

1. Welche Auffassung der lebenden Natur ist die richtige? und wie ist diese Auffassung auf die Entomologie anzuwenden. *Horae soc. ent. Ross.,* Fasc. 1, pp. 1–43 (1861). Russian as *Zapiski Russk. Entom. Obshchestva,* No. 1.

Newly reprinted and published with my consent as a separate brochure by the Entomological Society in Berlin (Publishing House of Ascher). Later included by me in the book: *Reden und kleine Aufsätze,* Vol. I. (*Writings* I, No. 16).

2. Ueber die Beobachtungen der schädlichen Insecten und über die Mittel gegen dieselben. *Horae soc. ent. Ross.,* Fasc. 1, pp. 139–158.

m. *Beiträge zur Kunde Preussens* of Hagen.

Vergleichung des Schädels vom Auer mit dem Schädel des gemeinen Ochsen. *Hag. Beitr. z. K. Preuss.* II. pp. 235–237 (1819).
Life, pp. 165–166.

n. *Flora oder Botanische Zeitung.*

Botanische Wanderung an der Küste von Samland. (1820). *Flora,* 1821, No. 26.

o. *Verhandlungen der physik.-medicinischen Gesellschaft in Königsberg über die Cholera.* Volume I. 1832, 8°.

According to the *Schriftsteller-Lexicon für Livland, Ehstland und Kurland* (*Nachträge*) the following, written by me, are contained in it:

1. Bericht über den Ausbruch der Cholera in Königsberg und Pillau.

2. Geschichte der Cholera in Königsberg.

I do not own this book so I cannot look at it. But I do remember that I made two such reports for the [*sic.* The sentence stops short in the original book. Ed.]

p. *Cholerazeitung*, which was published in Königsberg (1831) by the town's physicians; it was the first one of this name.

This cholera journal published other small essays of mine, e.g.:

3. Ein Bericht über die Pest in Ostpreussen im Anfange des 18ten Jahrhunderts.

4. Ermunterung für Besorgliche. *Cholera-Zeitung*. P. 40.

5. Fernere Ermunterung für Besorgliche. *Chol.-Zeit*. P. 46.

6. Kleine Expectorationen, signed *Moutarde*.

q. *Journal für Geburtshülfe, Frauenzimmer- und Kinderkrankheiten* of Dr. A.E. von Siebold.

Later also under the title: *Neues Journal für Geburtshülfe u.s.w.* of Dr. Casp. Jacob v. Siebold.

Beobachtungen aus der Entwickelungsgeschichte des Menschen. With one lithograph plate. *Siebolds Journ. für Geburtsh*. Vol. XIV, No. 3 (or *Neues Journ*. Vol. VII, pp. 401–407, 1835).

Since I could not manage to elaborate in detail my observations on the early embryonic stages of man while in Königsberg, and before this section, fragments about the development of invertebrates, were supposed to be published, I sent several selected pieces to Professor Casp. von Siebold at Göttingen. *Life*, pp. 275–276.

III. Publications of the Academy of Sciences in St. Petersburg

a. *Recueils des actes des séances publiques de l'Acad. Imp. de St. Péters-bourg.* 4°.

From 1827 to 1848 the Academy annually published a collection of lectures and public notices which had been presented at the end of the previous year at the annual session on December twenty-ninth. The following of my lectures are contained in these *Recueils*:

1. Blicke auf die Entwickelung der Wissenschaft. Dazu ein Anhang. *Rec. des actes de la séanc. publ. tenue le 29 Déc.* 1835, pp. 51–128.

This lecture was later (1864) printed in my book : *Reden* (Lectures), as the second lecture.

Translated into Russian under the title : "Vzglyad na razvitie nauk. Rech Akad. Bera" and printed in *Zhurnal Ministerstva Narodnogo Prosveshcheniya,* May, 1836.

2. "Ueber die Verbreitung des organischen Lebens." *Rec. des actes de la séanc. publ. tenue le 29 Déc.* 1838, pp. 143–193.

Printed again in the *Lectures,* as the third lecture.

b. *Mémoires de l'Academie de St. Pétersbourg.*

The memoirs of the Academy of Sciences in St. Petersburg, formerly edited in Latin and called *Commentarii* and *Novi Comment., Acta* and *Nova acta,* received in 1803 the general title of *Mémoires,* in French. Since the former collections were included in the count, the first series of the *Mémoires* became the fifth "Série" (series). In 1830 the sixth series was started; in this the historico-philological treatises were separated from the natural sciences and the latter continued in separately numbered volumes under the title: *Sciences mathématiques, physiques et naturelles.* A short *Bulletin* was append-ed to the first volumes, which I am pointing out especially because my name appears in it. However, another division was carried out, from the third volume onward; the works on natural history were in a special series as *Sciences naturelles,* separated from the *Sciences mathématiques et physiques,* which unfortunately led to some difficulties in the designation. The treatises submitted by scientists from abroad formed a separate series under the name:

Mémoires présentés à l'Académie Impériale des sciences de St. Pétersbourg.
In order to avoid this variety in designations, all treatises were at last united again in 1859 under the title : *Mémoires de l'Acad. des sc. de St. Pétersbourg, 7, Série,* and it was arranged at the same time that each treatise could be purchased separately.

1. Note sur un Mammouth fossile semblable à l'Eléphant actuel d'Afrique. *Mém. de l'Acad. Imp. des sc. de St.–Pétersb.,* VIme sér. *Sciences math., phys. et nat.* Vol. I (1831). *Bullet. scientif.,* pp. XVI–XVIII.

The Königsberg zoological museum received a tooth, similar to that of the African elephant, which was said to have been found in the Rombinus Mountain near Memel. Since the tooth still bore traces of soft parts, I could not consider it fossilized. (*De fossil. Mamm. reliquiis in Prussia repertis.*) Thereupon Nitzsch wrote to me saying that he really had seen an excavated tooth of this kind and had described it. I found a similar one among the stock of fossil bones in St. Petersburg (in 1830).

2. Ueber die Geflechte, in welche sich einige grösser Schlagadern der Säugethiere früh auflösen. Mit einer coll. Steindrucktafel, das arterielle Armgeflecht am Wallrosse, dem Manati und Braunfische darstellend. (Submitted 1833). *Mémoires présentés à l'Acad. de St.-Pétersb. par divers savans.* Volume II, pp. 199–211.

3. Ueber doppelleibige Missgeburten. *Mém. de l'Acad. Imp. des sc. de St.-Pétersb.,* VIme série. *Sciences mathém. et phys.* Volume III. First part: *Sc. math. et phys. Bulletin,* No. 2 (1835).

Two perch embryos (*Perca fluv.*), of which one had a double head and the other a double upper body, which were examined less than a day after fertilization, gave occasion to prove that the organic doubling was present from the beginning. The fact that this brief communication found its way into the mathematical-physical class, instead of the class of natural history, shows the state of confusion to which the complicated title of the memoirs led.

4. Anatomische und zoologische Untersuchungen über das Wallross (Trichechus Rosmarus) und Vergleichung dieses Thiers mit andern See-Säugethieren. 1. Zoologische Abtheilung. With a map of the distribution. Submitted, 1835. *Mémoires de l'Acad. Imp. des sciences de St.-Pétersb.* VIme series. *Sciences mathém., phys. et naturelles.* Volume IV. Second part: *Sciences naturelles,* Volume II (1838).

5. Untersuchungen über die ehemalige Verbreitung und gänzliche Vertilgung der von Steller beobachteten nordischen Seekuh (Rytina Ill.). *Mémoires de l'Acad. Imp. de St.-Pétersbourg.* VIme série. *Sciences mathém., phys. et natur.* Vol. V. Second part (or) *Sciences naturelles.* Vol. III, pp. 58–80 (1840).

6. Ueber doppelleibige Missgeburten oder organische Verdoppelungen in Wirbelthieren (1844), mit 10 Tafeln. *Mém. de l'Acad. de St.-Pétersb.* VIme série. Vol. VI. *Sc. naturelles, Anat. et. physiol.* Vol. IV, pp. 79–194.

Partial and complete duplicities, in man as well as in animals. The small fishes mentioned under III, b. 3, were also illustrated here.

7. Crania selecta ex thesauris anthropologicis Acad. Imp. Petropolitanae. With lithograph plate XVI. (1859.) *Mém. de l'Acad. Imp. des sc. de St.-Pétersb.* VIme série. *Sciences mathém., phys. et naturelles.* Vol. X. Second part (or) *Sciences naturelles.* Vol. VIII, pp. 241–268.

8. Ueber Papuas und Alfuren. Ein Commentar zu den beiden ersten Abschnitten der Abhandlung: Crania selecta ex thesaur. etc. *Ibid.*, pp. 269–346.

9. Die Makrokephalen im Boden der Krym und Oesterreichs verglichen mit der Bildungs-Abweichung, welche Blumenbach *Macrocephalus* genannt hat. With three plates. 80 pages. 4°. *Mém. de l'Acad. des sc. de St. - Pétersb.* VIIme *sér.* Vol. II. No. 6.

The cranial shape which Blumenbach presented pictorially as *Macrocephalus* is a natural malformation based on the original unity or at least very early growing together of the parietal bones, for which I proposed the name *Scaphocephalus.* The excavated ones are from antiquity; they are based on artificial malformation and are undoubtedly identical with the Macrocephali of Hippocrates.

c.—f. *Bulletin de l'Acad. des sc. de St. Pétersbourg.*

Instead of appending to the individual volumes of the *Mémoires* brief notices under the heading *"Bulletin,"* as had been done in the past, the Academy in St. Petersburg published, beginning in 1835, a separate collection of short essays, tables of contents of larger works, etc. Since this *Bulletin* ensured quicker printing than the *Mémoires,* it soon became the custom to submit larger essays, too, to the *Bulletin,* sometimes even divided into parts.

Unfortunately the *Bulletin* also changed its title and arrangement. At first it appeared undivided under the title: *Bulletin scientifique, publié par l'Académie Imp. des sciences de St. Pétersbourg et rédigé par le secrétaire perpétuel. St. Pétersb.* 4°. Volume I (1836)–Vol. X (1842).

Then it was divided into a *Bulletin de la classe physico-mathématique de l'Acad. I. de St. Pétersbourg,* of which seventeen volumes appeared between 1843 and 1859, and a *Bulletin de la classe historico-philologique,* of which sixteen volumes appeared during that time.

After that both *Bulletins* merged again, a merger effected like that of the *Mémoires;* unfortunately, however, not as a new series or in some other way distinguished from the first series, but as *Bulletin de l'Académie Impér. des sciences de St. Pétersbourg,* with new numbering of the volumes, so that particular care has to be taken to spot the elimination of the word 'scientifiques' in order to distinguish the last series from the first one. In this series eight volume have been published so far.

c. *Bulletin scientifique publié par l'Académie Imp. des sciences de St. Péters-bourg et rédigé par le sécretaire perpétuel. St. Pétersb.* 4°. Volume I (1836)–Volume X (1842).

1. Entwickelungsgeschichte der ungeschwänzten Batrachier. (1835). *Bull. sc. I*, No. 1, pp. 4–6; No. 2, pp. 9–10.

A summary notice of lengthy investigations regarding the general results of the embryology. However, I took back the detailed presentation with its numerous illustrations which I had submitted in order to complete it.

2. Beobachtung über die Entstehung der Schwimmblasen ohne Ausführungsgang. (1836). *Bull. sc. I*, No. 2, pp. 15, 16.

Brief excerpt in Wiegmann's *Archiv für Naturgesch.* of 1837. Translated in *Institute*, IV, 1836, No. 187.

3. Delphini Phocaena anatomes sectio prima. (1836). *Bull. sc. I*, No. 4, pp. 26–28.

Some general results of continued dissections.

4. Sur le prétendu passage de l'eau par les évents des Cetacés. (1836). *Bull. sc. I*, No. 5, pp. 37–40.

After I had questioned Russian sailors, I denied even more emphatically than I had previously in *Isis* that the water ingested through the mouth is ejected.

5. Bericht über eine ausgewachsene Missgeburt. *Bull. sc. I*, No. 16, p. 128.

Adult cow, with incomplete twin formation on the shoulders. Described in detail, after dissection, in the treatise: Doppelleibige Missgeburten. (Above III, b. 6.)

6. Note sur une peau d'Aurochs (*Bos Urus*) envoyé du Caucase. (1836). *Bull. sc. I*, No. 20, pp. 153–155.

6 [*sic*]. Seconde note sur le Zoubre ou Aurochs. (1836.) *Bull. sc. I*, No. 20, pp. 155–156.

The second note contains general remarks on the Zubr or aurochs of the Recent and other Asiatic horned cattle. Both notes are jointly translated under the title: Ueber den Zubr oder Auerochsen des Kaukasus, in Wiegmann's *Archiv für die Naturg.* 1837, pp. 269–273.

7. Sur quelques mémoires relatives aux colonies russes en Amérique par Mr. le Baron (Admiral) Wrangell. *Bull. sc. I*, No. 19, pp. 151 and 152.

Report on the treatises which appeared in the first volume of the *Beiträge ur Kenntniss von Russland*.

8. Berichte über die neuesten Entdeckungen an der Küste von Nowaja Semlja. [*sic*]. (1837.) *Bull. sc.*

Fairly complete excerpt in *Athenaeum*, 1836, No. 535, pp. 57–59.

From there passed on to the *Magazin für Literatur des Auslandes*, with unfounded variations.

9. Ueber das Klima von Nowaja Semlja und die mittlere Temperatur insbesondere. (1837). *Bull. sc. II*, No. 15, pp. 223–238.

10. Ueber den jährlichen Gang der Temperatur in Nowaja Semlja. (1837). *Bull. sc. II*, No. 16 and 17, pp. 242–254.

11. Ueber den täglichen Gang der Temperatur in Nowaja Semlja. (1837).

12. Expédition de M. le professeur Nordmann, sur la côte orientale de la Mer Noire. (1837.) *Bull. sc. II*, No. 6, pp. 91–95.
From letters from Professor Nordmann to Baer and Fuss, written by the former.

13. Zwei Beispiele von fortgewanderten Felsblöcken, an der Südküste von Finnland beobachtet. (1837.) *Bull. sc. II*, pp. 124–126.

14–20. Baer's Expeditions to Lapland and Novaya Semlja.

14. Erster Bericht (Baer's) über seine Reise nach Nowaja Semlja. (From Archangel 1837.) *Bull. sc. II*, No. 20, pp. 315–319.

15. Historischer Bericht von der fernern Reise. *Bull. sc. III*, pp. 96–107.

16. Physisches Gemälde von Nowaja. Semlja. *Bull. sc. III*, pp. 132–144.

17. Geognostische Constitution (by Lehmann). *Bull. sc. III*, pp. 151–159.

18. Vegetation und Klima. *Bull. sc. III*, pp. 171–192.

19. Thierisches Leben. *Bull. sc. III*, pp. 33–352.
Included in Wiegmann's *Archiv für Nat.*, 1839, pp. 160–170.

20. Ziwolka's Messung einiger Berge von Nowaja Semlja. *Bull. sc. III*, p. 374.

Excerpt from Nos. 14–20 in *Athenaeum* 1838, No. 560, pp. 606–608. Transferred from there to the *Mag. für die Literatur des Auslandes*, 1839.

21. Untersuchungen über die ehemalige Verbreitung und die gänzliche Vertilgung der von Steller beobachteten nordischen Seekuh (*Rytina* Illig.) (1838). *Bull. sc. III*, pp. 355–359.

(Excerpt from the detailed treatise in the *Mémoires*. (Above III, b, 5.)

22. Ueber das Skelet der Nawaga, welches in einem grossen Theile seiner Länge hohle Luftsäcke aufnehmende Räume enthält. (1838.) *Bull. sc. III*, pp. 359–360.

23. Nochmalige Untersuchung der Frage: Ob in Europa in historischer Zeit zwei Arten von wilden Stieren lebten? (1838.) *Bull. sc. IV*, pp. 112–128.
Printed in Wiegmann's *Archiv für Naturg*. Vol. V. (1839), pp. 62–78. Mr. Pusch published a very fervent article of more than ninety pages in Wiegmann's *Archiv*, 1840, pp. 47–137 against this essay, which tends to prove, contrary to Pusch, that the aurochs and the bison of the ancient Germans were really two separate species of horned cattle, which were preserved in some regions in Europe up to the Middle Ages. Aurochs and bison, tur and zubr (in Russian) had always meant the same species. In his triumphal joy he even goes so far as to undertake to prove, from the well-known verses of the *Nibelungenlied*, that aurochs is the male and bison is the female of the same

species, just as Schelch and Elch (elk in German) are the two sexes of one species of red deer; but in his zeal he fails to notice that both elk and bison are applied to males. One receives a lively impression of this zeal if one substitutes—in the following verses, which I copy literally from the original text (Holtzmann and Lachmann are the same on this)—cow for bison and hind for elk.

"Dar nâch sluoc er schiere einen Wisent und einen Elch.
Starker ûre viere und einen grimmen Schelch."

He fights equally fervently against the opinion that the Germans, having arrived at the Vistula, applied the name aurochs, which was current, to another animal which they had previously named bison. He maintains that the Germans would not have forgotten which animal had previously been designated by this name. However, the history of zoology is full of such confusions. I was reluctant to reply because of this zeal. Since, soon after, I received the picture of the skeleton of an aurochs bull, in which a vertebra had been pierced by a stone arrow, which was even found next to the skeleton, I gave up a reply altogether. There are now so many proofs from lake dwellings, etc., that in the past man lived together in Europe with two species of wild horned cattle that no doubt can exist about that any more. Nor can it be doubted that in some regions a few individuals survived for a long time, and thus the positive testimony of Herberstain, that he saw both species in Poland, cannot really be doubted.

24. Ueber das Klima von Sitcha und den Russischen Besitzungen und der Nordwestküste von Nordamerika überhaupt, nebst Untersuchung der Frage, welche Gegenstände des Landbaues in diesen Gegenden gedeihen können. *Bull. sc. V*, pp. 129–141 and 146–153.

(A letter from Ikak [Labrador] from the missionary Henn addressed to the Resident Minister v. Struve was inserted into my article on the climate of Sitcha by an oversight, which now seems utterly incomprehensible to me. The notes to this letter are written by me. The letter was probably sent to me by Struve and may have been delivered by me, but I do not remember any more. But it cannot have been my intention that the letter should be inserted into my article.)

Reputedly printed in Berghaus's *Annalen der Erd- und Völkerkunde*, VII, pp. 458–471. Also contained in the first volume of *Beiträge zur Kenntniss des Russischen Reiches*. Excerpt in *Athenaeum* 1839.

25. Nachricht von der Wanderung eines sehr grossen Felsblockes über den Finnischen Meerbusen nach Hochland. *Bull. sc. V*, pp. 154–157.

Reprinted in Berghaus's *Annalen der Erd- und Völkerkunde*, VII, pp. 544–548.

26. Sur la fréquence des orages dans les régions arctiques. *Bull. sc. VI*, pp. 66–73.

Translated in Poggendorf's *Annalen der Ph.* Vol. XCVIII, pp. 601–611.

27. Ueber die Knochen- und Schilderreste im Boden Lieflands. Nach einem Briefe des Hrn. Dr. Asmuss. *Bull. sc. VI*, pp. 220–223.

28. Petite note sur les observations de température faites pendant l'hiver 1839–1840 dans la steppe des Kirghises par MM. Tchihatcheff et Dahl. *Bull. sc. VII*, p. 66.

In greater detail in the *St. Petersburger Zeitung* (below, IV).

29. Die neuesten Entdeckungen in Nowaja Semlja, aus den Jahren 1838 und 1839. (1840) *Bull. sc. VII*, pp. 133–134.

Investigations when I was no longer present.

30. Sur les dégâts occasionnés par des insectes nuisibles. *Bull. sc. VII*, pp. 178, 179.

Short note on various damage by insects.

31. Temperatur-Beobachtungen, die an der Westküste von Nowaja Semlja unter dem 74° n. Br. angestellt sind. (1840.) *Bull. sc. VII*, pp. 229–248.

32. Rapport sur un ancien dessin représentant les ruines de Madjar. *Bull. sc. VII*, p. 197.

Brief note about an old drawing of the ruined town of Madahar. This drawing was later published in the article on Madahar in the fourth volume of the *Beiträge*.

33. Revision des täglichen Ganges der Temperatur in Boothia. (1841.) *Bull. sc. IX*, pp. 3–9.

34. Nachricht von der Erlegung eines Eisfuchses an der Südküste des Finnischen Meerbusens, nicht weit von St. Petersburg, und daran geknüpfte Untersuchung über die Verbreitung dieser Thierart. *Bull. sc. IX*, pp. 89–107.

The killing of an arctic fox in the Province of St. Petersburg provided the occasion to prove that the distribution range of this animal extended beyond the boundary of the forests, and to undertake a few more outings into the forest region.

35. Bericht über Marken, die der Capt. Reinecke bei Gelegenheit der Aufnahme des Finnischen Meerbusens zur Bezeichnung des Wasserspiegels hat machen lassen. *Bull. sc. IX*, pp. 144–146.

According to a communication by Capt. Reinecke, but several misunderstandings are said to have crept in.

36. Proposition pour le voyage de Mr. de Middendorff en Sibérie. Cette proposition est signée aussi par MM. Brandt, Lenz, Sjögren et Meyer. *Bull. sc. IX*, pp. 276–282.

37. Ueber Herrn v. Middendorff's Karte von seinem Wege durch das Russische Lappland. *Bull. sc. IX*, pp. 298–300.

38. Ueber das Werkchen: *Descriptio ac delineatio geographica detectionis freti sive transitus ad occasum supra terras Americanas in Chinam atque Japonem ducturi. Amstel. ex officina* Hesseli Gerardi 1613. 4°—und das Interesse, welches dasselbe für Russland gewährt. (1842.) *Bull. sc. X*, pp. 267–271.

d. *Bulletin de la classe physico-mathématique de l'Académie Impériale des sciences de St. Pétersbourg.* St. Petersb. Vols. I–XVII. 1843–1859. 4°.

1. Bericht über kleine Reisen im Finnischen Meerbusen in Bezug auf Diluvial-Schrammen und verwandte Erscheinungen. *Bull. physico-math.*, I, No. 7, pp. 108–112.

2. Instructionen für den Dr. v. Middendorff zu seiner Reise nach Sibirien, by Baer, Brandt, Lenz und Meyer (edited by the first). *Bull. physico-math.*, I, No. 12, pp. 177–185.

3. Neue Belege für die Auswanderung von Eisfüchsen. *Bull. physico-math.*, Vol. II, No. 2 and 3, pp. 47 and 48.

In 1842 several specimens of arctic foxes were killed in Finland, one in the Province of St. Petersburg, in addition to the one previously mentioned, and one in Courtland, on the Lithuanian border.

4. Bericht über die Reise des Herrn v. Middendorff. *Bull. physico-math.*, Vol. II, pp. 140–160.

Consists mostly of the original descriptions by the traveler with a few additions by me based on the traveler's private letters.

5. Os d'homme gigantesques. *Bull. physico-math.*, Vol. II, No. 17, pp. 266–268.

The local medical-surgical academy received bones of the thigh and shank of a man of quite extraordinary size which, had the bodily proportions been normal, would lead to the conclusion that the living person was almost nine English feet tall. I later learned that this giant lived in Tiflis and was one of General Yermolov's runners, without being more than of moderate giant size. I even found his remaining bones in Tiflis in 1856. It turned out that the entire skeleton was strangely enlarged in its lower parts. The head did not strikingly exceed medium size, nor did the uppermost vertebrae. But the following vertebrae increased much more than usual in size, so that the last lumbar vertebrae were already very striking. Even more enlarged in all dimensions were the bones of the thigh and the shank, and most of all the bones of the foot [Ed. note: Classical description of the skeleton of an acromegalic].

6. Neuer Fall von Zwillingen, die an den Stirnen verwachsen sind, mit ähnlichen Formen verglichen. With one plate. *Bull. physico-math.*, Vol. III, No. 8, pp. 113–128.

A duplicity of human embryos joined at the foreheads, described from academic collections and with comparison of similar cases that have become known, illustrated on the accompanying plate.

7. Vergleichung eines von Herrn Obrist Hofmann mitgebrachten (alten) Karagassen-Schädels mit dem von Herrn Dr. Ruprecht mitgebrachten Samojeden-Schädel. *Bull. physico-math.*, Vol. III, No. 12, pp. 177–187.

8. Rapport adressé à la classe par la commission chargée de diriger les travaux de l'expédition de Sibérie. *Bull. physico-math.*, Vol. III, No. 4, pp. 56–60.

A proposal of the Commission for the Siberian Expedition to extend the expedition up to the coast of the northern part of the Pacific Ocean, to Okhotsk òr Udskoi, in order to make continued meteorological observations there.

9. Nachträgliche Instruction für Herrn Magister Castren. *Bull. physicomath.*, Vol. III, No. 5, pp. 79 and 80.

Master (of Arts) Castrén is requested to collect material for physical anthropology on his journey.

10. Antrag der Sibirischen Commission zu einigen nachträglichen Beobachtungen auf der Expedition des Herrn von Middendorff. *Bull. physicomath.*, Vol. IV, pp. 251–253.

11. Ueber das Klima des Taimyr-Landes nach des Beobachtungen der Middendorff'-schen Expedition. *Bull. physico-math.*, Vol. IV, pp. 315–336.

12. Ueber den literärischen Nachlass von Caspar Friedrich Wolff. First report. *Bull. physico-math.*, Vol. V, Nos. 9 and 10, pp. 129–160.

13. Ueber mehrfache Formen von Spermatozoen in demselben Thiere. *Bull. physico-math.*, Vol. V, No. 15, p. 230.

Short note which was published without my knowledge and consent.

14. Auszug aus einem Berichte des Akad. v Baer aus Triest. *Bull. physicomath.*, Vol. V, No. 15, pp. 231–240.

The cleavages of the egg of Echinus species after fertilization are discussed and the fact that it is the nuclei from which the cleavages of the yolk start. Printed in *Frorieps Notizen* (above II, f. 6).

15. Zusatz zu Dr. J. F. Weisse's Aufsatz: "Ueber die Vermehrungsweise des *Chlorogonium euchlorum* Ehrenb." *Bull. physico-math.*, Vol. VI, No. 20, pp. 315–317.

The manner of procreation of the *Chlorogonium* is not so much viviparity as it is multiple spontaneous cleavage, since the body of the mother is completely distributed, into the brood and nothing is left of it except the covering.

16. Bericht über Herrn Dr. v. Mercklin's anatomisch-physiologische Untersuchungen über die Kranken und gesunden Kartoffeln. *Bull. physicomath.*, Vol. VI, No. 24, pp. 381–383.

17. Ueber nothwendig scheinende Ergänzungen der Beobachtungen über die Boden-Temperatur in Sibirien. *Bull. physico-math.*, Vol. VIII, No. 14, pp. 209–224.

From the observations carried out by von Middendorff and several persons selected by him in the mine shaft near Yakutsk and in some adjacent boreholes, it seems to follow that the shaft wall had cooled down in the course of the work and therefore this shaft does not indicate the true value of the soil temperature of this region, but too low a temperature. The new boreholes, which all indicate a higher temperature, are to be considered closer to the truth. It follows furthermore that the soil temperature is higher than the mean air temperature, as has also been observed in other northern regions. The causes of the difference are given. A new investigation is thought desirable.

18. Bericht über einige ichthyologische Nebenbeschäftigungen auf der Reise an den Peipus, vom Ende Aprils bis Anfang Junis. *Bull. physico-math.*, Vol. IX, No. 23, pp. 359–362.

Some material on the nutrition of fish and the size ratios of different parts of the body at different ages.

19. Materialien zu einer Geschichte des Fischfanges in Russland und den angränzenden Meeren. *Bull. physico-math.*, Vol. XI, Nos. 15, 16, pp. 225–254, Nos. 17, 18, pp. 237–288.

Reports on the history of fishing and legislation concerning fishing in Russia and adjacent countries, with a discussion of the principles on which the fishery policy should be based. Russian in *Uchen. Zapiski Imp. Akad. Nauk.*, Vol. 2.

20. Ueber das Wasser des Kaspischen Meeres und sein Verhältniss zur Mollusken fauna. Sendschreiben an Herrn Akad. v. Middendorff. (*Kaspische Studien* No. I) *Bull. physico-math.*, Vol. XIII, pp. 193–210.

21. Das Niveau des Kaspischen Meeres ist nicht allmälig (langsam) gesunken, sondern rasch.—Documente, die dafür sprechen.—Die Bugors. (*Kaspische Studien* No. II.) *Bull. physico-math.*, Vol. XIII, pp. 305–332.

22. Nimmt das Kaspische Meer fortwährend an Salzgehalt zu? Salzlagunen und Salzseen, die sich auf Kosten des Meeres bilden. Hommaire de Hell. With one map. (*Kaspische Studien* No. III.) *Bull. physico-math.*, Vol. XIV, pp. 1–34.

23. Notice sur un monstre double vivant. *Bull. physico-math.*, Vol. XIV, No. 3, p. 34.

A double child, joined at the crown of the head; the bodies are opposed at a 90° angle, as in cases hitherto observed, so that one individual lies on his side while the other rests on his back. Unfortunately I could not wait for the death of the children, who had been born here and brought to the hospital, because I had to leave for the Caspian Sea. In spite of my wish the dissection was not assigned to me.

24. Bericht über die Versuche, den Astrachanischen Häring (*Clupea caspica* Eichw.) im eingesalsenen Zustande in den Gebrauch zu bringen. *Bull. physico-math.*, Vol. XIV, pp. 316–318.

25. Abschätzung von Gewinn und Verlust an Salzgehalt im jetzigen Kaspischen Meerbecken. Zufluss salzhaltigen Wassers aus der Wolga-Uralischen Steppe, aus der Pontisch-Kaspischen Steppe, aus dem Felsboden der Mangischlackschen Halbinsel, aus dem Transkaukasischen Salzboden. Abgang derselben durch Bildung von Salzseen und durch Anreicherung von abgesonerten Buchten. (*Kaspische Studien* No. IV.) *Bull. physico-math.*, Vol. XV, pp. 53–59; 65–80.

26. Das Mantysch-Thal und der Mantysch-Fluss. (*Kaspische Studien* No. V.) *Bull. physico-math.*, Vol. XV, pp. 81–112.

27. Besuch an der Ostküste (des Kaspischen Meeres). Der Chiwasche Busen und Kolodkin's Atlas des Kasp. Meeres. Tschelekän oder die Naphtha-Insel. Temperatur des Kasp. Wassers in der Tiefe von 300 Faden. (*Kasp. Studien* No. VI.) *Bull. physico-math.*, Vol. XV, pp. 177–202.

28. Noch ein Wort über den *Neft-deghil* in Bezug auf S. 269 der Nr. 17 des XV. Bandes vom Bulletin de la classe physico-mathématique. *Bull. physico-math.*, Vol. XVI, pp. 118, 119.

29. Der Astrachanische Häring oder die Alse (*Alosa*) des Kaspischen Meeres. *Bull. physico-math.*, Vol. XVI, No. 21, pp. 327–332.

Continuation of the report in III, d. 24.

30. Ueber das Vorkommen von Kropf und Cretenismus im Russischen Reiche. *Bull. physico-math.*, Vol. XVI, No. 23, pp. 357–367.

31. Nachrichten über die ethnographisch-craniologische Sammlung der Kaiserlichen Akademie der Wissenschaften zu St. Petersburg. *Bull. physico-math.*, Vol. XVII, Nos. 12–14, pp. 177–211.

32. Dattel-Palmen an den Ufern des Kaspischen Meeres, sonst und jetzt. *Bull. physico-math.*, Vol. XVII, No. 27, pp. 417–431.

33. Zum Andenken an Alexander von Humboldt. Ansprache an die mathematisch-physikalische Classe am 13. Mai 1859. *Bull. physico-math.*, Vol. XVII, No. 34, pp. 529–534.

Included in the book: *Reden*, etc.

e. *Bulletin de la classe historico-philologique de l'Acad. des sc. de St.-Pétersb.* Volumes I–XVI. 1844–1859. 4°.

1. Ueber labyrinthförmige Steinsetzungen im Russischen Norden. With one plate. *Bull. hist.-phil.*, Vol. I, pp. 70–79.

2. Ueber Reguly's Reise zu den Finnischen Völkern des Ural. *Bull. hist.-phil.*, Vol. I, pp. 297, 298.

3. Fernere Nachrichten über die Reise des Herrn v. Reguly. *Bull. hist.-phil.*, Vol. I, pp. 298–300.

4. Neuere Nachrichten von Reguly über die Wogulen. *Bull. hist.-phil.*, Vol. I, pp. 349–351.

5. Neueste Nachricht über Reguly's Reise. *Bull. hist.-phil.*, Vol. II, pp. 122–126. *Bull. hist.-phil.*, Vol. II, pp. 205, 206.

6. Bericht über eine typographische Seltenheit, die in der Bibliothek der Akademie der Wissenschaften gesucht wird. Von dem Akad. v. Baer als Bibliothekar der ausl. Section der Akad. Bibliothek. *Bull. hist.-phil.*, Vol. VI, pp. 37–54.

Completely reprinted with an addendum by Weigel in Dr. R. Naumann's *Serapeum, Zeitschr. für Bibliothekwissenschaft, Handschriftenkunde u. älterer Literatur*, 1849, Nos. 14 and 15. Frequent enquiries were received from Holland whether the library of the academy had the work known under the title of *Speculum salvationis humanae*; the work is provided with woodcuts of biblical texts and legends printed in movable type, and the Dutch view that type-printing was carried out in Haarlem earlier than in Mainz is based on this. The reply was that this work is not in our possession and I myself gave one of these replies in 1844 to an enquiry from the librarian Noordziek. Quoting the reply in a printed work, a Mr. Sartorius stated in a Dutch journal that the book being sought, and even the complete specimen of the Dutch edition, which had once been in the possession of P. Scriverius and particularly on which the Dutch sought to base their claims, had been bought by Peter the Great during his sojourn in Holland. It was said to be in the library of the academy, where Bacmeister described it under the false title, *Historia Jesu Christi per imagines*; Professor J. Beckmann was supposed to have seen it there. Herr Noordziek then approached the Russian ambassador in the Hague again and asked for another investigation. "It is extremely important for the supporters of Haarlem and Coster to know the exact truth in this matter," he wrote (in French), and asked that this *Histoire de Jesus-Christ* be described in detail. It is strange that Herr Noordziek did not at all look at Bacmeister's "Essai sur la bibliothèque ... de l'Académie des sciences." A detailed reply had to be given to all this: 1) that Bacmeister had given a detailed description of another book which was and is often being confused with *Spec. salvationis hum.*; this book, however, was not printed in movable type but in full plates and is called *Biblia pauperum* or *Historia Jesu Christi per imagines*; Beckmann saw this book on which, to be sure, the name Scriverius is inscribed; 2) that this book was brought to the library of the Academy after Peter's death by his valet; 3) that this, then, was the book bought by Peter I in Holland; 4) that it was a simple question and not even a probable assumption by Meermann, whether the long-missed specimen of *Spec. salv. hum.* had been bought by Peter I, and 5) that this, the last-named book, has never been in our library. I wish that these eternally recurring enquiries could be answered once and for all. It seemed remarkable to me that with all this stubborn determination to seek the justification for the Haarlem claims in Russia, Herr Noordziek did not react at all to my request to check which book is named in the *Boeksal*, where the purchase by Peter I is mentioned for the first time. Perhaps the *Biblia pauperum* is already mentioned there?

7. Der alte Lauf des Armenichen Araxes. With 2 maps. *Bull. hist.-phil.*, Vol. XIV, pp. 305–349. (*Kaspische Studien* No. VII.)

It seems that the Araxes, once separate from the Kura, formerly emptied into the Caspian Sea.

f. *Bulletin de l'Académie Impériale des sciences de St. Pétersbourg.* St. Pétersbourg, Volumes I–VIII. St. Pétersbourg 1860–1864. 4°.

1. Ergänzende Nachrichten über Dattelpalmen am Kaspischen Meere und in Persien. (Cf. III, d. 32.) *Bull. de l'Acad. I* (1860), pp. 35–37.

The existence of a large date palm near the village of Sari was confirmed by the Khanykov expedition, which sent a leaf. The existence of a low palm with runners on the Potemkin Peninsula was also testified to by a member of the expedition, Capt. Lieutenant Restori, who saw it. The next place where the travelers saw isolated date palms, and with ripe fruit at that, was Tebbes.

2. Ueber den Schädelbau der Rhätischen Romanen. *Bull. de l'Acad.*, Vol. I, pp. 37–60.

The Neo-Latin peoples, pushed back into the highest mountain valleys from which the Rhine and the Inn rise, seem to be a remnant of the ancient Rhaetians and are strikingly brachycephalic.

3. Bericht über die neuesten Acquisitionen der craniologischen Sammlung (der Akad. d. W.). *Bull. de l'Acad.*, Vol. I, pp. 339–346.

4. Uber ein allgemeines Gesetz in der Gestaltung der Flussbetten. (*Kaspische Studien* No. VIII.) *Bull. de l'Acad.*, Vol. II, pp. 1–49, 218, 256, 353–382.

The right bank of rivers, especially those flowing meridionally, is steeper in the Northern Hemisphere than the left bank because of the stronger pressure of the water toward this side in consequence of the earth's rotation. The relationship is reversed for the same reason in the Southern Hemisphere.

I had treated this subject twice in the Russian language, first in my official reports on the travels along the Caspian Sea at the end of 1854, published in *Zhurn. ministerstva gosudarstv. imushchestv* 1855; from there in *Vestnik estestvennykh nauk* 1856, pp. 220–224; after that revised in August 1856, first in the *Astrachanische Zeitung* under IV, m; and then in *Morsk. sbornik* (IV, e, 1). I am inclined to believe that this last essay (of 1856, published in January 1857) became known in Paris, since at the time that I wrote the above-named and more detailed essay in German (September 1859 to February 1860), the influence of the rotation of the earth on flowing water was mentioned several times at the Academy in Paris, whereas previously it had never been mentioned.

Revised and in Russian, the content of the article appeared in *Morskoi sbornik* in 1858, but very much abridged since it was treated only as a supplement to the previous article, published the preceding year.

The view concerning the pressure of flowing water on the right bank is also confirmed from Vienna, the Danube being given as proof by Professor Süss (*Der Boden der Stadt Wein*, 1862) and by Professor Klun (*Schriften der Geogr. Gesellschaft zu Wien*). I found later on that this question was treated in various popular writings.

5. Baer and Schiefner: Proposition pour l'organisation du musée ethnographique de l'académie des sc. et de faire voyager Mr. Radloff à Stockholm et Copenhague (extract). *Bull. de l'Acad.*, Vol. II, p. 191.

6. Ueber das Aussterben der Thierarten in physiologischer und nicht physiologischer Hinsicht überhaupt, und den Untergang von Arten, die mit

dem Menschen zusammen gelebt haben, insbesondere. First half. *Bull. de l'Acad.*, Vol. III, pp. 369–396. Second half. First part (with one plate). *Bull. de l'Acad.*, Vol. VI, pp. 514–576. (Steenstrup's *Unters. über Alca impennis.*)

7. Ueber ein neues Project, Austern-Bänke an der Russischen Ostsee-Küste anzulegen, und über den Salz-Gehalt der Ostsee in verschiedenen Gegenden. (With one map of the salt content of individual regions of the Baltic Sea.) *Bull. de l'Acad.*, Vol. IV, pp. 17–47 and 119–149.

Investigation of the salt content of sea water which is necessary for the thriving of oysters, and the salt content of the sea water in different sections of the Baltic Sea.

8. Ein Wort über einen blinden Fisch als Bildungs-Hemmung. *Bull. de l'Acad.*, Vol. IV, pp. 215–220.

9. (Baer und Schiefner.) Ankündigung einer Ausgabe des Werkes von Prof. Worsaae, *Nordiske Oldsager* (Nordische Alterthümer) mit Russischem Texte. *Bull. de l'Acad.*, Vol. IV, pp. 89–96.

10. Nachträge zu dem Aufsatze: Ueber ein neues Project, Austern-Bänke an der Russischen Ostseeküste anzulegen. *Bull. de l'Acad.*, Vol. V, pp. 61–67.

After a visit to the Schleswig oyster banks.

11. Bericht über die craniologische Sammlung der Akademie in den Jahren 1860 u. 1861. *Bull. de l'Acad.*, Vol. V, pp. 67–71.

12. Ueber das behauptete Seichterwerden des Asowschen Meeres. Bericht einer Commission aus den Herren Lenz, Helmersen, Wesselowski, Stephani, Kunik, Baer (Berichterstatter) and die Akademie der Wissenschaften. (With one map.) *Bull. de l'Acad.*, Vol. V, pp. 72–105.

Translated in the work "Azovskoe more" which appeared as a supplement to *Morskoi sbornik* and contains the opinion of the navy. Cf. *Life*, pp. 302–303.

13. Prix Rklitzki. *Bull. de l'Acad.*, Vol. V, pp. 106 and 107.

Drafts of statutes which were submitted to the Academy for examination.

14. Vorläufige Nachricht von den Sammlungen, die der Lieutenant Ulski im Kaspischen Meere gemacht hat, v. Baer, Weisse und Mag. Goebel. *Bull. de l'Acad.*, Vol. V, pp. 265–267. Russian: *Zap. Imp. Ak. Nauk*, Vol. II, p. 121.

Lieutenant Ulski, a member of the expedition of Captain Ivashintsov for the investigation of the Caspian Sea, had collected soil samples, snails, crayfish, worms, water samples, etc., from the Caspian Sea and handed them over to the Academy for identification.

15. Bericht über eine neue von Professor Wagner in Kasan an Dipteren beobachtete abweichende Propagationsform. *Bull. de l'Acad.*, Vol. VI, pp. 239–241.

Paedogenesis or production of Diptera larvae from larvae of the same species.

16. Rapport sur l'ouvrage de Mr. le Professeur Margó: Ueber die Endigungen der Nerven in den quergestreiften Muskeln. *Bull. de l'Acad.*, Vol. VI, p. 132.

344

17. Zusatz zu des Grafen Keyserling: 'Notiz zur Erklärung des erratischen Phaenomens. (With one map). *Bull. de l'Acad.*, Vol. VI, pp. 195–207.

18. Ueber einen alten Schädel aus Mecklenburg, der als von einem dortigen Wenden oder Obotriten stammend betrachtet wird, und seine Aehnlichkeit mit Schädeln der nordischen Bronzeperiode. (With one plate.) *Bull. de l'Acad.*, Vol. VI, pp. 346–363. Russian: *Zap. Imp. Ak. Nauk,* Vol. II. The shape of the skulls of several Slav races is discussed.

19. Vorschlag zur Ausrüstung von archaeologisch-ethnographischen Expeditionen innerhalb des Russischen Reiches. *Bull. de l'Acad.*, Vol. VII, pp. 288–295.

20. Neuer Nachtrag zu Nr. VIII der *Kaspischen Studien:* Ueber ein allgemeines Gesetz in der Gestaltung der Flussbetten. *Bull. de l'Acad.*, Vol. VII, pp. 311–320.

21. Noch ein Wort über das Blasen der Cetaceen, mit bildlichen Darstellungen. *Bull. de l'Acad.*, Vol. VII, pp. 334–341.

IV. Historical, Geographical, Agricultural and Provincial Journals, Including Political Daily Newspapers

a. *Historische und literärische Abhandlungen der Königl. Deutschen Gesellschaft zu Königsberg.* Edited by Schubert. Königsb. 8°.

Ueber das Verhältniss des Preussischen Staats zur Entwickelungsgeschichte der Menschheit. Lecture given on January 19, 1834, at the Royal German Society. *Hist. u. lit. Abh. der D. Gesellsch.* Third Collection (1834), pp. 237–248.

b. *The Journal of the Royal Geographical Society of London.* 8°.

1. On the ground ice or frozen soil of Siberia. *Journ. of the Geogr. Soc.,* Vol. VIII. pp. 210–213 and *Athenaeum* 1838, No. 540, p. 169.

2. Recent intelligence of the frozen ground in Siberia. *Journ. of the Geogr. Soc.,* Vol. VIII, pp. 401–406, Athenaeum, No. 565, p. 509.

In the second letter to the R.G.S. I had included as many reports as I could find on the extent of permanently frozen ground in Siberia, since the academy was about to equip an expedition which was primarily to investigate the thickness and extent of this icy ground, and I requested the Society to carry out similar investigations in North America, at least concerning the horizontal extent. The society readily fulfilled the request, and Dr. Richardson drafted an instruction for this purpose (*Journ. of the R.G.S.,* Vol. IX, pp. 117–120), and various reports have been received.

c. *Beiträge zur Kenntniss des Russischen Reiches und der angränzenden Länder Asiens, auf Kosten der Kaiserl. Akad. der Wissenschaften, herausgegeben von K.E. v. Baer und G.v. Helmersen.* St. Petersb. 8°. From 1839 onward.

This collection is the property of the Academy since it was published at its expense. Since the two editors decided on the inclusion of individual contribution, however, it did not seem suitable to list them under section III.

Of my own writings this collection contains:

1. Preface to the first volume (concerning the Russian-American colonies). Vol. I, pp. V–XXXVII.

2. Compilation of American writings concerning the nations on the north-west coast of America, and those given in the present book. Vol. I, pp. 275–289.

3. Ueber das Klima von Sitcha. Resultate aus den meteorologischen Tagebüchern des Adm. v Wrangell und Beleuchtung der Frage, welche Gegenstände des Feld- und Gartenbaues in Sitcha und den Russ. Kolonien überhaupt gedeihen können. Vol. I, pp. 290–320.

4. Short articles (concerning the North American colonies). Vol. I, pp. 321–328.

5. Foreword to the fourth volume. Vol. IV, pp. III–XI.

6. Eine alte Abbildung der Ruinen von Madshar erläutert. Vol. IV, pp. 53–96.

7. Foreword to von Köppen's essay: Ueber Wald-und Wasservorrath im Gebiete der obern und mittlern Wolga. Vol. IV, pp. 163–193. It deals with the devastation of forests and the original lack of forests in the Russian steppe.

8. Neueste Nachrichten über die nördlichste Gegend von Sibirien, zwischen den Flüssen Piassida und Chatanga. Vol. IV, pp. 269–300.

News from Siberia. Vol. VII, pp. 41–272.

9. Kornbau bei der Stadt Jakutsk, pp. 45–55.

10. Auszug aus dem Verwaltungsberichte über das Gouvernement Irkutsk und die Provinz Jakutsk für das Jahr 1839. (According to *Zhurn. Min. Vnutr. Del.* 1840.) pp. 55–68.

11. Zunahme der eingeborenen Bevölkerung, pp. 89–117.

12. Uebersicht des Jagderwerbes in Sibirien, besonders im östlichen. pp. 117–204.

13. Hereto the following appendixes: Fur trade. Different qualities and different prices of sables. Occurrence of beavers in Siberia and in the European part of the Russian Empire. Yield of the hunt in different regions. Age of the sable trade. pp. 204–272.

14. Nachtrag zu Middendorff's Bericht über die ornithologischen Ergebnisse der naturhistorischen Reise nach Lappland während des Sommers 1840. Vol. VIII, pp. 259–272. On the course of the Lapland journey.

15. Kurzer Bericht über wissenschaftliche Arbeiten und Reisen, welche zur nähern Kenntniss des Russischen Reiches in der letzten Zeit unternommen sind. Vol. IX, Div. 1, pp. 1–336 and Div. 2 up to p. 725. The rest (containing the report on geological trips) is by von Helmersen.

16. Foreword to the eleventh volume (translation of Pogodin's *Nestor*).

17. Foreword to Bode's *Verbreitungsgränzen der wichtigsten Holzarten des Europäischen Russlands*. Vol. XVIII, pp. 3–10.

18. Die uralte Waldlosigkeit der Südrussischen Steppe. Vol. XIX, pp. 109–117.

d. Publications of the Russian Geographical Society.

This society (Russian Geographical Society) has published, in addition to several independent works, a collection of essays on general geography under the title: *Karmannaya knizhka* (Handbook), and journals of which I have quoted *Zapiski* (Memoirs) and *Geograficheskiya Izvestiya* (Geographic Journal). In *Vestnik Geograf. Obshchestva* there are several essays of mine, but they are only translations from the *Bulletin*, as well as my first annual report on the Caspian travels, which has also been published in the *Zhurnal Min. Gos. Imushchestv* and is quoted below.

1. O vliyanii vneshnei prirody na sotsial 'nye otnosheniya (otdel 'nykh) narodov v istorii chelovechestva. *Karmannaya knizhka dlya lyubitelei zemlevedeniya*, published by the Russian Geographical Society. 1848. 22, pp. 159–235.

2. Ob etnograficheskikh mzeledovaniyakh voobshche i v Rossii v osobennosti. *Zap. R. Geogr. Obshch.*, Vol. I, second edition, pp. 64–81.

The reprint in this second edition is not as complete as in the first. One of the ministers—not the Minister of National Education—disliked a passage which was therefore omitted.

This article is translated from the first printing in the *Denkschriften der Russischen geographischen Gesellschaft zu St. Petersburg*, Vol. I, pp. 60–92.

3. Zaslugi Petra Velikogo po chasti rasprostraneniya geograficheskikh poznanii. First article. *Zap. R. Geogr. Obshch.*, Vol. III, pp. 217–253.

4. Second article. Te zhe Zapiski., Vol. IV, pp. 260–283.

5. O drevneishikh obitatelyakh Evropy. Read at a session of the society on October 10, 1859. *Zap. Geogr. Obshch.*, 1863, No. I, pp. 1–20.

6. Neskol'ko slov o proekte soedinit' Chernoe more s Kaspiiskim posredstvom kanala. *Ibid.*, pp. 21–32.

With slight changes in German under the title: Ein Wort über das Project, den Manytsch zu kanalisieren, und die öffentlichen Streitigkeiten darüber, in Petermann's *Mittheilungen*, 1862, pp. 446–451.

7. Otchet o puteshestvii na Azovskoe more. Historical introduction. *Zap. R. Geogr. Obshch.*, 1864, Vol. 2, pp. 87–118.

This essay contains a history of the knowledge of the Sea of Azov and of the commerce traversing it (unavoidably taking into account the Black Sea). The important results of my journey concerning the supposed decrease of water depth—the subject of complaints—were previously published in a report written in German in *Otchet I. Russ. Geogr. Obshchestva*, 1862, pp. 25–33.

8. Ob ustroistve pri Obshchestva "Sobraniya Etnograficheskikh Predmetov." *Geograficheskiya izvestiya* published by R.G.O. 1848, pp. 35–43.

9. A letter in French regarding the attack of a certain Monsieur Trémaux on the report of Lieutenant Kowalewski concerning his trip in Africa. *Geograficheskiya izvestiya*, pub. R.G.O. 1850, pp. 640–642.

10. Otchet o puteshestvii na Manych. *Vestnik Geogr. Obshch.*, 1856. Vol. 6, pp. 231–254.

e. *Morskoi Sbornik.*

1. Pochemu u nashikh rek, tekushchikh na sever ili na yug, pravyi bereg vysok i levyi nizmen? *Morskoi Sbornik*, 1857, p. 110.

2. "Dopolnenie k stat'e: Pochemu u nashikh rek, tekushchikh na sever ili na yug, pravyi bereg vysok i levyi nizmen." *Morskoi Sbornik*, 1858, No. 5.

f. *Zhurnal Ministerstva Gosudarstvennykh Imushchestv.*

Since the expeditions for the investigation of fisheries, with which I was charged, were initiated and equipped by the Ministry of Imperial Domains, my reports were initially sent to this ministry. Most of them were printed, some complete and some with omissions. It is incomprehensible to me why some of the reports, especially the final ones which summed up the results, were not printed. As opposed to this, other brief essays, which I had published in Astrakhan mostly in the local government newspapers, are included in the Journal of the Ministry of Imperial Domains.

1. Issledovaniya dlya razresheniya voprosa: Umen'shaetsya li kolichestvo ryby v Chudskom ozere? *Zh. M. Gos. I.*, No. XLIII, pp. 248–302.

From five of my reports concerning the state of fishery in Lake Peipus and on the Baltic coast, without the concluding report and the measures based on it.

2. Rybolovstvo u Alandskikh ostrovov i u beregov Shvetsii. *Zh. M. Gos. Im.*, No. LI, Section 2, pp. 75–94.

3. O Kaspiiskom rybolovstve. Extract from Baer's account in 1853. *Zh. M. Gos. I.*, No. L. Section 2, pp. 37–56.

4. Izvlechenie iz otcheta . . . za 1854 god. *Zh. M. Gos. I.*, No. LV, Section 2, pp. 6–92 and 137–182.

5. Dopolnitel'nyya issledovaniya nad rybolovstvom i nekotorye obshchie voprosy, kasayushchiesya Kaspiiskogo morya. *Zh. M. Gos. I.*, No. LVII. Section 2, pp. 147–164.

6. O Kaspiiskom rybolovstve. Article IV. *Zh. M. Gos. I.*, No. LVIII, pp. 1–28.

7. Ob uchrezhdenii estestvenno-istoricheskago muzeuma v Astrakhani. *Zh. M. Gos. Im.*, No. LXI (1856), pp. 269–275, from the *Astr. Gubernskiya Vedomosti.*

A museum of natural history was really founded at Astrakhan, to which this region is particularly conducive because it contains much that is peculiar; however, after the departure of Civil Governor Struve, who favored its foundation, the wise town fathers dissolved it again.

8. Ob upotreblenii l'da na yuzhnykh beregakh Kaspiiskago morya i o vvedenii torgovli im. In *Zh. M. Gos. I.*, No. XLI (1856), pp. 276–280, from the *Astr. Gubernsk. Vedom.*

9. Ob upotreblenii Astrakhanskoi seledki. *Zh. M. Gos. I.*, No. LXII (1857), pp. 255–270. Ibid.

g. *Zhurnal Ministerstva Narodnago Prosveshcheniya.*

1. Izvlechenie iz doneseniya Ministru Narodnago Prosveshcheniya Akademika Bera o poseshchenii letom 1863 goda Kazanskago Universiteta. *Zhurn. Min. Narodn. Prosveshcheniya,* 1863, No. 119, Section 2, pp. 516–521.

2. Zamechaniya na ustav universitetov i drugikh uchebnykh zavedenii. *Zhurn. Min. N. Prosv.*, 1863. No. 120, Section 3, pp. 1–24.

h. *Zemledel'cheskaya gazeta,* founded by E.A. Engel 'gartom.

Mnenie o pol 'ze i vozmozhnosti razvedeniya Kvinoi na severe Rossii, iz pis 'ma ak. Bera. *Zeml. gazeta.*, 1839.

My article on quinoa had already been published in this newspaper.

There follow two essays on the botfly larvae in the frontal sinuses of sheep, but I am unable to find them at the moment because this journal lacks any kind of index.

i. *Preussische Provinzialblätter.* Königsberg. 8°. From 1829 onward.

1. Nachträgliche Bemerkungen über den Raupenfrass, der sich im Jahre 1828 im Lein in Preussen gezeigt hat, nebst Vorschlägen zur möglichsten Vermeidung eines ähnlichen Schadens. *Preuss. Prov. Blätt.*, Vol. II (1829), pp. 574–600.

2. Einige Bemerkungen über die Indianischen Vogelnester und den Chinesischen Handel. *Preuss. Prov. Blätt.*, Vol. IX (1833), pp. 720–725.

3. Glossen zu dem Aufsatze über Benutzung der Knochen. *Preuss. Prov. Blätt.*, Vol. IX (1833), p. 764.

Reply to this. Vol. X (1833), p. 348.

4. Antwort auf die im Juni-Hefte dieses Jahres in den Preussischen Provinzial-blättern in Betreff der Töchterschulen aufgeworfene Frage. *Preuss. Prov. Blätt.*, Vol. X (1833), pp. 114–115 (signed *"Putus"* because the enquiry had come from *"Purus"*).

5. Bitte an die Freunde vaterländischer Naturgeschichte (um Einsendung fossiler Knochenreste). *Preuss. Prov. Blätt.*, Vol. X (1833), p. 522.

6. Ansiedelung eines Kupferstechers in Preussen. *Ibid.*, p. 523.

7. Anfrage wegen der wilden Schwäne. *Preuss. Prov. Blätter.*, Vol. X (1833), p. 770.

Reply by Pastor Löffler in the same journal. Vol. XI (1834), pp. 131–139.

8. Bemerkungen zu diesem Aufsatze. *Ibid.* pp. 139–142.

Remarks concerning the essay by Pastor Löffler. *Preuss. Prov. Blätt.*, Vol. XI, pp. 422–424.

9. Erwiderung. *Ibid.*, pp. 425–429.

Reply to the reply. *Preuss. Prov. Blätt.*, Vol. XII, pp. 475–585; 598–610.

10. Notiz über das Brüten der Schwäne. *Preuss. Prov. Blätt.*, Vol. XI, pp. 429–430.

11. Ueber die in Preussen vorkommenden Gänse und Enten. *Preuss. Prov. Blatt.*, Vol. XI (1834), pp. 24–27.

12. Empfehlung zoologischer Werke für Schulen und für das Selbst-Studium. *Preuss. Prov. Blätter.* Vol. XI (1834), pp. 113–130.

13. Ueber die Wanderungen der Zugvögel, veranlasst durch mehre in dieser Beziehung in der Schweiz, in England und Schweden angestellte Beobachtungen, mit Zusätzen von Prof. Baer. *Preuss. Prov. Blätt.*, Vol. XI (1834), pp. 256–284, 339–342, 431–435, 521–524, 592–596; Vol. XII (1834), pp. 32–36, 165–168, 244–248, 361–363.

It is predominantly the tables which had been printed in Poggendorff's *Annalen*, 1833, and to which I wanted to add some more. I cannot say whether this was really achieved, since the printing had been delayed at the time of my departure, and I do not have the continuation of this journal.

14. Anzeige von Lorek's *Fauna Prussica*. *Preuss. Prov. Blätter.*, Vol. XII (1834), pp. 417–418.

k. (*Königsberger*) *Staats-, Kriegs-* and *Friedens-Zeitung*, edited by Hartung, usually called *Königsberger-Zeitung* by Hartung.

Although, according to page 309 of the foreword, I modeled myself upon the painstaking completeness of the *Schriftsteller-Lexicon für Livland, Ehstland und Kurland* by Recke and Napiersky, there was no doubt in my mind that not all my articles, which appeared frequently especially in Königsberg, should be quoted.

The fact that I corresponded publicly with all the contributors and other patrons of the newly founded zoological museum in the newspapers, addressing myself "To the friends of natural history in Prussia," thanked them by name for their contributions, is really part of my autobiography and is mentioned there (*Life*, p. 177). This not only facilitated private correspondence, it was also intended to encourage emulation. The menageries and other natural sights which were exhibited in Königsberg were a second subject of public discussion. I endeavored to identify the animals in the menageries taxonomically and added natural historic notes from the best-known works, which caused not only an increase in the number of visitors, but also an influx of menagerie owners as well as of persons who came of their own accord. These exhibitions also inspired a number of essays which, judging by their titles, seemed to be special treatises but referred to such exhibitions as those on albinos, Brazilian Indians, New Zealanders, the so-called bear-like sloth, crocodiles, giant snakes, the cobra, monsters, etc. I viewed each such exhibition as a stimulus to learn something about the objects and to reproduce the knowledge thus acquired.

Occasionally foreign reports were quoted as curiosities for the entertainment of the public. There were also small articles in the newspapers themselves, e.g., that two young whales had been caught in the Elbe but, according to the accompanying data, they seemed to be a species of dolphin; there was another newspaper report to the effect that anthrax had been observed in wheat and how it should be treated, which was greeted with a *"non plus ultra* of journalistic license."* I barely replied, at least not sharply. On the other hand, the anonymous article:

1. Zur Neujahrsfeier (*Hartungs Königsb. Zeitung*, 1822, No. 156), which demanded the organization of private charity, excited passionate opposition (*Life*, p. 189) which was voiced by the authorities in No. 6 of 1823, and required an address from me.

2. An Unbefangene (*Hart. Zeit.*, 1823, No. . . .), and

3. Noch eine Replik (*Hart. Zeit.*, 1823, No. 20) and led to the foundation of private charity societies. (*Life*, p. 190 f.)

The following should also be cited:

4. Biographische Skizze über Herrn Prof. Eysenhardt. *Hart. Zeit.*, 1825, No. 156.

5. Nekrolog des Prof. Dr. Karl Gottfried Hagen. *Hart. Zeit.*, 1829, No. 29.

1. *St. Petersburgische Zeitung.* In addition to the reprint of a number of my articles that had appeared elsewhere, I find the following separate communications in this newspaper:

1. Ueber eine Aeusserung der Preussischen Staatszeitung in Bezug auf den gefrornen Boden in Jakutsk. *St. Petersb. Ztg.* 1838, No. 91.

2. Lösung des in Nr. 112 der Preussischen Staats-Ztg. befindlichen Räthsels. *St. Petersb. Ztg.* 1838, No. 94.

Admiral Krusenstern had sent one of my articles dealing with permanent ground ice in Siberia to the Geographical Society in London. There appeared an article in the *Preussische Staatszeitung* with a London dateline, stating that my reports induced great doubt in the Geographical Society and Professor Erman therefore sent his own observations there. Since the term permanent ground ice (Boden-Eis) was criticized at the same time, beeause one should say frozen soil (gefrorner Boden) it was easy to recognize that this London was in Berlin, and that Erman had sponsored the article directly or indirectly. But for the sake of Admiral Krusenstern, to whom the public censure seemed to be of great importance, I had to write the above reply in which I gave a detailed explanation, stating that it is not the rock which freezes, and not even the soil, but the water in the soil; that frozen water is called ice in German and that therefore permanently frozen water in the soil may be called permanent ground ice. Erman probably envisaged only continuous masses of ice in connection with the expression ground ice. Besides, in an article which also appeared in the *Journal of the Geographical Society*, Vol. VIII, he placed great emphasis on the fact that according to his observations, carried out at the Yakutsk mine at a depth of fifty feet, the ground ice or the frozen soil had to reach to a depth of 600 feet. Later observations place the boundary less deeply, and I believe that my article, quoted under III, d. 17, will convince the reader that this boundary was at a depth of less than 400 feet.

3. Feier der funfzigjährigen Dienstzeit des Vice-Admirals von Krusenstern. *St. Petersb. Ztg.* 1839, Nos. 28–37.

4. Ausführliche Ankündigung der "Beiträge zur Kenntniss des Russischen Reiches und der angränzenden Länder." *St. Petersb. Ztg.*, 1840, No. 19.

5. Ueber des Klima der Kirgisen-Steppe, mit vorangeschickten allgemeinen Bemerkungen über Meteorologie überhaupt. *St. Petersb. Ztg.*, 1840, Nos. 66–70.

According to observations made by Chikhachev and Dahl during Perovskii's expedition.

6. Würmer, welche die Bienen vertilgen. *St. Petersb. Ztg.*, 1840, No. 202.

7. Erinnerung an einen Zug der Uralischen Kosaken gegen Chiwa, im Anfange des 17. Jahrhunderts. *St. Petersb. Ztg.*, 1840, No. 249.

On the occasion of the unsuccessful expedition of General Perovskii, I related that, according to Müller, more than 200 years earlier a handful of Ural Cossacks had conquered Khiva because they came suddenly in early spring and only with light cavalry.

8. Czoma de Körös und Reguly Antal, Ungarn, die nach den Sitzen ihrer Väter forschten. *St. Petersb. Ztg.*, 1842, Nos. 233 and 236.

9. Sendschreiben des Herrn Dr. . . . an den Akademiker Brandt. Mit Anmerkungen des Ak. Baer.

A kind of defensive article which I thought it necessary to write because a man, who had my full recognition as a scientific traveler, considered it national jealousy that I had proposed to the Academy the provision of a moderate sum on the occasion of his travel through a Russian province; this sum was to be available at all times, so as to able to arrange an immediate journey to a given place in case of an important natural phenomenon. It must be mentioned that according to its statutes the Academy is obliged to arrange such prompt investigations, but that it does not have the required means at its disposal to implement this purpose; it has to request the financial means from the state treasury, and thus funds are not always available or at least not easily accessible; furthermore, two years prior to this journey the Academy itself had planned an expedition for the investigation of a great natural phenomenon but the plan did not reach a further stage—perhaps because it had been devised too grandly. Therefore, an available, albeit much smaller sum! A similar proposal was made later by von Middendorff for a special purpose.

He requested that arrangements be made for the Academy to be notified speedily if a mammoth with remains of fleshy parts is found again in the frozen soil of the far north; a sum of money should be kept in readiness so that someone could be sent out immediately in order for the fleshy parts of this animal to become known at last.

10. Dichtung und Wahrheit. *St. Petersb. Ztg.*, 1844, No. 113.

The stimulus to the slight unburdening of the heart to which I have given the above striking heading is much stranger than for the previous one. For in the *Haude- und Spener'sche Zeitung* of May 9, 1844, and embellished and flowery in the *Hamburger Correspondent* of May 17 of the same year, the following communication, ostensibly originating in Pressburg, appeared:

"The journey, undertaken by a Herr Reguly at the suggestion of the Hungarian Academy, in order to trace the trail from St. Petersburg, or rather the historic footprints of the Magyars, is causing an extraordinary stir here. Since he had no financial means whatsoever, he was promised support by the Royal Academy by Herr v. Baer in St. Petersburg if he promised to send faithful reports on the results of his journey to the Academy. Reguly refused this, solely because the offer was made by a Russian. He refused, equally decisively, the proposal of a highly placed man, and in the meantime found means which enabled him to travel to the Urals."

A very remarkable little example of national jealousy and national boastfulness. For these statements contain so much that is false that the real truth could be found if each sentence were turned to mean the exact opposite. At that time I only endeavored to weaken as much as possible the bad impression which this twaddle was bound to make on all those who had supported Reguly out of scientific and human interest. He himself could not be reached by mail because he was traveling along the Urals to the farthest north, having enjoyed free board and lodging as well as other benefits on the estate of the Vsevoloshskii family in the Urals for almost a year. I knew that Reguly, who had the practical but not the boastful support of Swedes, Russians, Poles, and Germans here, remembered this well and could not have inspired the newspaper article. It would have been extremely disagreeable to him, too.

I related the beginnings of Reguly's undertaking in the *Beiträge zur Kenntniss des Russ. Reiches*, Vol. IX, pp. 220–269, and reported about its continuation in several articles mentioned above in the *Bulletin*, but I deliberately left out some things which might have caused damage in his country. I would like to review Reguly's activities again here in order to show how unsuitable such boastings by ultrapatriots are and what harm they can cause.

Reguly, who was born in 1819 in the Westprim Comitat, undertook a journey across Germany in 1839 which was intended to take four months. In the north of Germany he conceived a lively interest in the history of antiquity which, it seems, had not been supported in his previous studies. He went to Copenhagen, where Scandinavian antiquities were already being assiduously collected and where Reguly was completely captivated by the study of antiquity; this, however, also powerfully aroused his Magyarism. He then went to Stockholm via Gothenburg and stayed there for several months, not only in order to study Scandinavian antiquity but also to prepare for the study of the Finnish language. He first had to learn Swedish for this purpose, for all the books containing information concerning Finnish were written in Swedish. Thus he came to Finland where he spent ten months at the remote dwelling of a Finnish peasant. Now completely captivated by Finnish as by primeval Magyar interests, he traveled throughout Finland as far up as Lapland, where he studied the Lapp language; he got as far as Archangel Province. He also visited the capital, Helsingfors, because of the literary aids, and Magister Gottlund was the first to report to the literary world on this scientifically captivated, or rather possessed, man. For Reguly constantly permitted himself to go off into new scientific ramifications of his task, which was growing beyond all bounds. For instance, from Helsingfors he made a side trip through Estonia as far as Dorpat, in order to study also the Estonians, who belong to the Finnish race as well, and from Dorpat he came to St. Petersburg, having on the way studied a special branch of the Finns residing near Narva. In Petersburg he threw himself with fervor into the study of comparative linguistics. I made his acquaintance because he had been recommended to me by Dorpat, but his pleasing appearance, his childishly hearty as well as fine and seemly behavior, and his indefatigable interest in the task of which he was so full were an even better recommendation. I came to like him very much. He really aroused my admiration when he spoke Estonian. Though he spoke slowly and seemed to ponder the words and inflections, he spoke grammatically correctly and his pronunciation was that of a born and bred Estonian, although he lived among the Estonians only for a few weeks. According to Gottlund he had likewise aroused general attention and admiration in Helsingfors because of the ease with which he expressed himself in Swedish and Finnish, and even more because of his pure and faultless pronunciation. He had doubtlessly a very decided talent for learning languages by using them. He began the study of general linguistics only here and continued it assiduously. But many individual languages had to be tackled to find the nearest relations of the Hungarians. First he had to become fluent in the Russian language in order to be able to study the aids written in this language and to travel successfully in the country; he then obtained a preliminary knowledge of the East Finnish and Tartar languages. As far as I know, Reguly approached the Magyar Academy from here and expressed his wish to visit East Finnish tribes and to obtain the financial means necessary for that. The family had had to cover the expenses of his travels until then. However, since these subsidies arrived at a slower rate than Reguly needed them, he left debts behind here and there which, as far as I know, have all since been repaid; nevertheless, they had remained unpaid for some time, and perhaps did him more harm than he realized. At that time, at Stieglitz's, the banker, I frequently saw a member of the Austrian Embassy, and I thought that, by an assault on the latter, I could achieve the speeding up of the support from public funds. I was, however, repulsed firmly and with diplomatic coldness with reference to the debts, whereas it seemed to me that this circumstance in particular indicated the necessity of financial help, especially if Reguly's ability was not in doubt. Reguly needed very little for his living, but he was utterly incapable of giving up the scientific interest, which had gripped him, for economic reasons. I have never, before or since, met a man who was so completely captivated by a scientific task. Yet he was not at all inclined to preconceived opinions and hypotheses. On the contrary, he always found that he had to increase his knowledge which was held together by his good memory. He had not expressed assurance to the Magyar Academy that he would find the original residence of the Hungarians in the Urals, but he had said that he had recognized so much that was related to Hungarian in the East Finnish languages that complete investigations on the spot seemed necessary to him. The Magyar Academy at first charged him with several scientific tasks in St. Petersburg and held out prospects of future support. When these tasks had been fulfilled satisfactorily, an especially selected commission submitted a report at a plenary session of the Magyar Academy on May 4, 1842; this report was circumspect and comprehensive dealing with Reguly's achievements and the hopes he raised, and emphasis was rightly placed on his very level-headed and cautious views, particularly in view of his age. The commission followed this up with an emphatic proposal of support by considerable financial resources, since such a favorable opportunity of furthering the scientific national interest would not be found as easily again; furthermore, Reguly was already in the field, which was very promising but where much still remained to be done. Regardless of this proposal, submitted by seven members and approved by all, the financial resources were not approved, with the proven saying which covers a multitude of sins: There are no funds.

I never tried to find out from which side the obstacles arose, I only saw that the commission of the Magyar Academy had referred to certain funds. But I wrote the following which also appeared in the same work on page 242: "We must not arrogate the right to pronounce judgment on conditions which are too remote from us. Nevertheless, there is something basically wrong here. Is there no money for national interests when national feeling has been proclaimed so loudly in the Diets! Has Hungary no Rumyantsev of blessed memory? Or is one led to believe that Hungary's magnates have no interest in scientific research? Perhaps they have been neglected or even insulted? We do not know—but we hope that Reguly, like his famous fellow-countryman (Csoma de Körös), will succeed in pursuing his goal. If this has to be done with sacrifices, and even with great sacrifices, the task itself, of course, will not gain by that."

That is what happened, although Reguly had no opportunity of refusing an offer by the Academy here, since none had been made. Least of all could anything have been done through me—the Russian!—as that newspaper drivel stated, since Reguly wanted to carry out linguistic investigations and I had no voice at all in this sphere which belongs to the historical-philological class. Later, I do not know whether it was in 1842 or 1843, another small contribution toward the travel expenses (200 florins in coin) arrived from the Academy in Pest, but this was insufficient for the journey to the Urals and had been more than used up by the lengthy wait in expensive St. Petersburg. A substantial subsidy had indeed been promised by His Majesty the Emperor of Austria, but this was a long time in coming and it was to be feared that even before the money arrived, a substantial part of it would have been consumed again. A Hungarian highly placed in the Russian civil service, Privy Counselor Bol, advised Reguly very urgently to give up all his plans and to return to Hungary. Reguly decidedly refused; he endeavored to obtain such employment in the Russian civil service as would enable him to be sent to the Urals. This undertaking seemed very risky to me, for all such promises, no matter how sincerely meant, usually turn out to be void as soon as the chief is replaced. I told our worthy Frähn of my concern. "Should we not subsidize his travels privately?" asked Frähn. "I shall give as much·as . . . " I promised the same sum on my part. Several others joined with their contributions. The sum was not a large one but I cannot name it, for it is not usual to keep accounts of such things here. But it was sufficient to enable him to reach the Voguls and spend some time with them. It was our idea that Reguly should first of all carry out the intention, publicly announced, of traveling to the Eastern Finns in order to prove to his country the seriousness of his undertaking and his persistence, but that he should then return, before pursuing new tasks, and that he would do well to first study comparative linguistics somewhere in Germany, if the means could be found, and that he should choose new tasks only then. According to the judgment of experts, his decided talent for languages and his ardent zeal lacked thorough training. Provided with these means Reguly left late in the fall of 1843 and spent the winter with the Voguls. At first he was very cheerful, but later became depressed worrying about the future (pp. 244–250 of the *Contributions*). Then suddenly in 1844 he received 1,000 florins in cash from the Emperor of Austria, and this put an end to his worries. However, the disagreeable impression of seeing Reguly consuming himself in expectations may be imagined, especially on reading in the *Allg. Zeitung* in 1843 that Reguly was engaged in travels to the Urals with the support of the Magyar Academy, and when, in the following year, the above-mentioned article on Magyar arrogance provided the somber background to an exquisite hatred of the Russians. I cannot understand what such drivel can achieve. Nothing good, for certain. May I be permitted to relate two more small intermezzos in order to make it clear that not all Russians are cannibals—nor were they toward Reguly. The year was 1842, when I had not seen the Hungarian traveler for some weeks, whereas he used to visit me frequently. When I made enquiries, I heard that he had moved and there was a rumor that he was gravely ill. I had to visit him to see whether he needed help. But I only found out to which district of the town he had moved, not the house and not even the street. I drove to the district and there the search had to begin. I examined the coach drivers whom I saw in their hackney-coaches, and when I found one whose heavily bearded face expressed much honesty, I chose him as an assistant, counting on the compassion which the Russian always has for the needy. "Listen, little brother," I addressed him, "I have to visit a young gentleman from Hungary who was recommended to me. He is said to be gravely ill, but his mother does not know anything about it. He might die and we would then not even be able to say that we had tried to help him. We must go to him, though I only know that he lives in this neighborhood but do not know in which house. Would you like to drive me and help me search; you are better at talking than I am. You ask in the shacks while I seek out the Dvorniki (house managers). I shall pay you for the loss of time." My long speech was answered by a single word: "Naidem!" but said in a tone which turned the word into a whole sentence, and meant approximately: "We shall find him, what is there to talk about!" Thus we started our search, not an easy thing in St. Petersburg because the lower-class Russians know people solely by their first names and patronymics and do not bother about surnames. I did not know Reguly's patronymic. We therefore had to look according to the description of the person, and we found him eventually after a three hours' search. Reguly was still on his sick-bed, his illness probably due to excessive mental strain. When the coach driver saw the patient from the doorway, and the slowness of his movements when he tried to get up, he refused to accept payment—for an act of kindness. I actually had to argue with him and explain that he had to be compensated for the loss of his time, and that it was certainly not shameful to accept such compensation. As soon as Reguly obtained the necessary funds for traveling to the Urals, provision had to be made for his sojourn there. There are neither hotels nor furnished rooms in northern Siberia, but there is another institution, which is called Russian hospitality. Reguly had found out that the Voguls, the sirens whose song had lured him, lived on the estate of the Vsevoloshskii family. But this estate was in trusteeship; this was an adverse circumstance, for such an administration is under obligation to economize as much as possible and I did not know who were the members of the trusteeship. I went to the office, with scant hope of success. When I arrived, I found the entire board of trustees assembled—all of them completely unknown to me! I explained my request in rather halting Russian: whether a foreigner—a Hungarian who wanted to study the Vogul language—could obtain lodging for some months in the Siberian administration. I must have made myself understood, for, though it may have seemed

strange to the gentlemen that a sensible man should travel from Hungary to
the far north in order to learn Vogul, a sheet of paper was asked for and a
directive to the local administration was drafted right in my presence request-
ing that Reguly be given board and lodging. The following morning a fair
copy of the document was sent to my house. When Reguly came to Siberia,
the office there was so obliging that they had two Voguls come, one of whom
Reguly kept with him for several months. Herr von Demidov, who was here
at the time that our Hungarian departed, ordered the most Slavic hospitality
to be offered to him if he should need it in Nizhne-Tagilsk, without ever having seen him. I do not see any cannibalism in all this, nor do I see cause to
reject with scorn the friendliness and kindness. It might have been better for
Reguly if people here had been less obliging, for he unfortunately forfeited
his health in Siberia and was buried young, without ever publishing the results
of his travels—but this could not have been foreseen. Apart from this, we
really had no intention of turning him against his own country. As mentioned
before, the plan arranged with my good friend Frähn was that Reguly should
go to the nearest Voguls and return from there. But upon receipt of the Emper-
or's money he found new tasks. When he informed me that he intended to
travel to the farthest North in order to see the entire region inhabited by this
nation, I sent him a very blunt letter regarding these endless roamings, and I
hoped that the tone of my letter would make him stop. I still have his somewhat desperate and testy reply, but he would not be deterred. He felt he was a
rich man who now had much to do.

One may ask whether such a stupid newspaper item deserves such a
thorough discussion. This newspaper article certainly does not. But at the time
I answered only briefly, in the article cited, in our newspaper: It is not unknown to us that there is a rather lively aversion to the Russians in some
quarters; but it is complete news that the aversion includes even Russian
money, and this news may be very welcome to some people here. That even
the occasion of Reguly's journey should give cause to sing the same tune is
especially pleasing, etc.

However, I have good reason to discuss the matter here once again and in
even more detail, since it is one of my life's experiences and was touched upon
jokingly and in passing on p. 279. This is a fitting opportunity to talk about
it in all seriousness. For it has become the custom in recent times for many
Russian journals to scold (not to say revile) the Germans; this newspaper
article still treats them as being identical with the Russians. Sometimes these
articles are just stupid. For instance, someone complained that the production
of the "Messiah" by Händel bored him terribly; this person was of the opinion that only Germans could invent and stand something so boring. Now
whose fault is it that this good man goes to hear on oratorio and expects polka
music or something similar? Others who scold are somewhat less narrowly
stupid. But what is the purpose of all this? Do they believe that patriotism,

and a really national one, can thus be proved and reinforced? The proof would be very unconvincing. True patriotism presupposes self-respect and therefore does not need to proclaim it, nor does it need to put down others in order to lift itself up, for it is aware of its own worth and presupposes that others are aware of it too; because he does not doubt himself at all, a true patriot can appreciate others. Of all the important nations, the English probably have the most resolute patriotic and national feeling. Is it not generally known that a wrong or a favor done to an Englishman even in the remotest corner of the earth causes each of his compatriots who hears of it to sympathize? However, this strong national feeling does not prevent the English from appreciating foreign worth. At least in scientific matters, no nation expresses its recognition as forcefully as the English; in practical matters it probably is no different. Patriotism cannot be enhanced by self-praise or by the degradation of others; on the contrary, this can only enhance vanity. Patriotism is enhanced by exemplary deeds which inspire emulation.

The consequences of self-praise and abasement of others are obvious. First of all there is mutual ill will which cannot produce anything positive, and furthermore, suspicious investigations of causes come into being. If we meet a person in ordinary life who endeavors to be above others or constantly abases them, we assume that this person has some defect to hide and, once our suspicions are aroused, we discover the cause all the more easily. The small instance of Reguly is a striking example. He had traveled to Siberia— and it was self-evident that he had received the required means from his family or otherwise from Hungary; nobody would have thought to ask. Nor did anybody here think of writing in a newspaper that the support from Hungary had been too scant. When the first article appeared in the *Augsburger Zeitung*, a newspaper widely read here, I had to give a more detailed account of the occurrences since I was intent on maintaining the local readiness to be of help. This was done in the *Contributions*. After this report was completed and done with and the article referred to another journey, I read in another article that Reguly had repelled my seduction and had traveled at the behest of the Magyar Academy. I am far from believing that the Magyar Academy commissioned these articles. However, if they were written by an unauthorized person, this person had to receive his information from a member of the Academy, for only thus or through a letter from Reguly could my name have gotten into the newspaper article. And what ends did this article serve, even if it came from someone utterly unauthorized? Only to bring to light the participation of the Magyar Academy. This was a matter of course anyway. The deficiency, however, which was thus among others to be covered up, was that the Academy, in spite of all interest in the matter, did not have the financial means at its disposal; the cause might also have been that a person with a definite talent for languages combined with a great inclination to the relevant historic investigations did not find any opportunity in Hungary to obtain the required training or even to show his inclination—whereas in foreign countries this was awakened and broke through almost forcibly. There would no doubt have been an opportunity for such development in Vienna, but at that time the Magyars began to lock themselves into their borders. I hope this enterprising and persevering nation, which I have come to like through Reguly, will forgive me for not being able to suppress the fear that, by this separatism, they may have lost in Reguly a man of whom the nation could have been proud; I further hope they will forgive me if I add my conviction that all this separatism strikes me as antiquated views from the Middle Ages or of even earlier times.—The natives of North America are divided into tribes which hate each other and endeavor to exterminate each other. This has always been viewed as proof of barbarism, for civilization unites and joins people and nations.—In the latest attacks on Germans here too, I see only an endeavor to stifle and cover disagreeable feelings of complacency; below, under No. 15, I shall give another proof of this. For what other purpose could they serve? There is an abundance of fools everywhere, but the fact that the papers lend themselves as their mouthpiece raises the fear that the editorial offices have not fully realized yet that they should serve civilization, and that, if they do not do this, they do more harm than good.

11. Neuere Nachrichten über die Expedition des Herrn von Middendorff. *St. Petersb. Ztg.*, 1844, Nos. 13–16.

In addition to the reports by von Middendorff on his fate in the far north, there are also excerpts from private letters written from there to his relatives.

12. Feier zu Ehren des Herrn v. Middendorff (bei Gelegenheit seiner Rückkehr von der Reise durch einen grossen Theil von Sibirien). *St. Petersb. Ztg.*, 1845, No. 82.

Friends and admirers arranged a joyful welcoming feast when von Middendorff returned hale and hearty from his great journey. I recognize only the addresses which are printed under my name. The trimmings probably stem from the editor—certainly not from me.

13. Schluss-Nachrichten über Reguly's Reise. *St. Petersb. Ztg.*, 1845, No. 88.

14. Der Ehrenhaftigkeit ihr Recht. *St. Petersb. Ztg.*, 1848, No. 68.

A censure of the dishonesty of the daily press, which has begun to come to the surface with colossal audacity. The person attacked by utterly ignorant and therefore unauthorized people was Pirogov, thus this time not a German but a national Russian for whom a Nemets (German) entered the lists.

15. Bering und Tschirikow. *St. Petersb. Ztg.*, 1849, Nos. 114, 115, 116.

This is also of a polemic nature. At that time a tendency began in the form of individual attacks with the aim to belittle the deserts of German persons concerned with Russia or science and to exaggerate those of national Russians, a tendency which later turned into a full torrent and found everything German antiquated and rotten, in contradistinction to the fresh vitality which people believed they felt in themselves. A Navy lieutenant by the name of Sokolov, who was quite honest in searching the Admiralty archives for old reports on ocean travels and had several of them printed, was one of the skirmishers who initiated the incursions at that time. However, instead of complaining that the Admiralty had left untouched such reports which were some of them more than a hundred years old, he attacked people who did not even know the suppressed reports. My paper on the merits of Peter the Great with regard to geography (above: IV, d, 3) was read; it concluded with the tragic fate of Bering who, after solving the great question of the continuity or separation of Asia and America, was more or less buried alive between the two continents on a desolate island now named after him, namely in the earthern cave which had been prepared for him, the ceiling of which collapsed on his feet and buried them, and although there was still life in the upper part of Bering's body, his feet remained buried. When this lecture was delivered, even before it was printed, an accusation by Lieutenant Sokolov appeared, charging that there was continuous talk only of Germans (to whom the Dane Bering belonged), and none of Russians, and that especially Bering's associate Chirikov, who was unjustly ignored, was a much abler seaman than Bering, etc.

Bering's character is also under attack. Bering is said not to have reached America proper at all, but to have landed on Kodiak Island, etc. Well, I had read not only all the printed reports, but also many hand-written ones about Bering's travels, and I accorded his perseverance and devotion the greatest recognition. I therefore felt qualified to defend him against those attacks whose source I well knew.

But as to the accusation that Chirikov is always being neglected, this can only be the Admiralty's fault since it has not published anything about him. The historiographer Müller wrote the history of Bering's expedition and there he said but little about Chirikov. Nor had I ignored him, but I had mentioned him only in passing for he did not fit at all into the framework of my task. Bering had been chosen by Peter for the first expedition, which proved the separation of America, although his result met with little credence in Russia, and it was first acknowledged by Cook. Chirikov was a member of the second expedition, and more detailed information concerning him was made known from the Archives of the Admiralty by Sokolov. Whatever was known before Sokolov's time of the side expeditions of the two Laptevs, Malgins, etc., had also been made public almost exclusively by Germans. The Russians, who had done little for the recognition of the first seafarers for over a century, complained when the century had passed that they were not being sufficiently appreciated!

m. *Astrakhanskiya gubernskiya vedomosti.*

I remember two articles in addition to those quoted above from the *Zh. M. Gos. Imushchestv* (under IV, f) about the founding of a museum of natural history in Astrakhan and the proposal to salt the local herring.

1. An explanation of the cause why the right bank is steeper not only on the Volga, but also on all other large Russian rivers, was given by me in the Astrakhan newspaper in the form of a letter in August 1856, printed in No. 40 of that year.

2. An appeal to use the warm climate of Astrakhan more for cultivating silk and similar industrial branches, and to use part of the soil, which is annually flooded by the Volga and therefore without salt content, for the planting of trees. I cannot quote the number. It was probably one of the last of 1856.

Since the people of Astrakhan are firmly set against any innovation, just as they declared initially that the salting of herring was not feasible, there now also appeared a reply to this suggestion, maintaining that the daily wage is far too high for people to be hired for silk cultivation. It was not at all my opinion that silk cultivation should be undertaken by hired people, but that the working class, which in Astrakhan yearns only for fishing and if need be for hunting, should raise silk-worms as a side-line; this applied especially to women. While the people of Astrakhan almost completely neglected silk cultivation, the German colonists in the Yekaterinoslav Province earned more than a million rubles annually from silk under less favorable conditions. Just as in the diamond districts of Brazil great indolence and poverty are said to hold sway, because everyone wishes and hopes to become rich by a lucky find of diamonds, fishery in Astrakhan has the same effect, since it enriches some individuals but leaves most of the people poor. But every member of the working class dreams his dreams. Even the growing of vegetables, which the Russians otherwise like and know well, is not done by Russians in Astrakhan. It is left completely to the Tartars, at least as far as market vegetables are concerned.

Even in the

n. Taganrog newspaper whose name I do not even know any more, I have let myself be led astray in my seventy-first year and allowed an article to be inserted. The temptation was of course great and concerned my earlier assignment there. While I was at Taganrog, a Navy officer from Kerch poured out a veritable stream of crocodile tears in the Odessa newspapers about the increasing shallowness of the Sea of Azov, due to ballast thrown overboard. Since he believed himself able to give the quantity of the ballast involved, he calculated by how much the soil of an area of one square verst was raised by this ballast, but he was unfortunate enough in his calculation to assume that a square verst has only 500 square sazhenes, whereas in reality 500 sazhenes in length placed end to end amount to one verst. I could not but still his tears in the Taganrog newspaper and explained that he had exaggerated only 500-fold and, if he took into account the whole sea, many thousand times. However, there is a more serious side to this matter. I do not believe for an instant that a Navy officer can make such a great mistake in regard to relationships of area, as seems to have happened here, not even out of overhaste. It does happen frequently though, that when an authority has certain intentions, as was the case with the chief of Kerch at the time, who wanted the exclusive marketing right of the Sea of Azov for his town, other persons support them with their articles, even against their own conviction. Cf. concerning the journey to the Sea of Azov: *Life*, pp. 302–303.

o. The newspaper of Tiflis, whose name I do not know any more either, also accepted one of my articles in 1855 in which I first spoke about the change in the course of the Armenian Araxes.

* * *

It would be absurd to give so much space to mere newspaper articles, if one is concerned only with a list of scientific achievements, especially if among them there is a substantial number of slight value, but the former have a closer connection with life than most of the latter. I therefore believed I could not overlook them in an appendix to my biography. They are to be regarded only as noted events. Besides, old age has the prerogative, or at least the reputation of being garrulous, and in the second half of my life I have made so little use of this prerogative!

V. My Contributions to Non-periodical Publications of Others, and Works of Others, Inspired, Introduced, or Edited by Me

1. Berichte von der königl. anat. Anstalt zu Königsberg. Zweiter Bericht von K.F. Burdach. Mit Bemerkungen aus dem zootomischen Tagebuche des Dr. v. Baer, Prof. extr. 1819, 8°.

These notes from pp. 13–48 predominantly concern sturgeon; in addition the seal, the porpoise, and the cat. Discussed in *Life*, p. 165.

2. C.L. Ebel. *Ornithologisches Taschenbuch für Preussen*. 1823. 8°.

I induced the conservator Ebel to compile this handbook according to the bird species appearing in our country and according to the books available in our country because of the repeated request of the head forester in Prussia, my patron and the benefactor of the zoological museums, to provide him with a usable and cheap handbook for identifying birds. I supplied only a brief preface and an appendix of desiderata.

3. F.O. Lietzau. *Alphabetisches und systematisches Register zu Cuviers Vorlesungen über vergleichende Anatomie*. Leipzig 1834. 8°. 141 pages and ten tables of systematic surveys.

Index volume to Meckel's translation of Cuvier's *Lecons*. This index was prepared not only at my instigation but under my special direction, while Dr. Lietzau was living in my house. Since I noticed several mistakes after the printing of the index, I entered into an unpleasant correspondence with the publisher, reproaching him for not providing sufficiently accurate proofreading. He tried to maintain that the mistakes must have been in the manuscript. But Dr. Lietzau was very accurate and wrote an excellently legible hand. As regards the proofreader, it will be noticed even in the first sentence of my foreword, with half or even less attention, that the word "als" has been omitted. If it had been missing in the manuscript, it would undoubtedly have had to have been inserted.

4. *Die Physiologie als Erfahrungswissenschaft* by K.F. Burdach. Vol. I, 1826, Vol. II, 1828, 8°.

In the first volume there are individual scattered small contributions or notes, but in the second volume there are larger sections by me, about which reports can be found in *Life*, pp. 213–241 (with interruptions).

5. *Das alphabetische Register zu Pallas Zoographia Rosso-astatica*, CXXV pages. 4°.

I sent this work, which is smallish and is appended to the third volume, from Königsberg after my return there. I thought that my name appeared in it but I now see that this is not so. Possibly I myself forbade the mention of my name, for I still remember very clearly that I noticed a large number of printing errors in the text during the compilation of the systematic names and synonyms from printed works, so that I had a horror of the second index, that of popular names, because I thought that this would only add new errors. Besides, there was no zoologist in St. Petersburg who could have checked the printing. I have just discovered Haliactus instead of Heliaetus in the first column.

6. *Russkaya fauna ili opisanie . . . Sostavl. Yu. Simashko*. Vol. I. 8°.

The first volume of Simashko's *Russian Fauna*—of anatomical and physiological content, was also to contain the so-called natural history of man. The author of this work requested me repeatedly and very insistently to take over the division of the human species into main races and sub-divisions. But since these cannot be stated as something finished and generally valid, the reasons as to why something is grouped thus and not differently must be developed and I decided to write the whole article on man myself instead. Thus a fairly bulky work originated dealing with this subject which received a separate title in the Russian translation but is not on sale separately, only as a section of the above work:

Chelovek v estestvenno-istoricheskom otnoshenii, Akademika K. Bera. S. Peterb. 1851. 8°. 235 pages with 17 plates of national representations and their skulls.

Both translation and printing are insufficiently scrupulous, therefore I did not provide book trade with separate printings, as had been my original intention.

7. *Dr. A. Th. v. Middendorff's Reise in den äussersten Norden und Osten Sibiriens während der Jahre 1843 und 1844*. Vol. I, Part 1. 1848. 4°.

I cannot claim to have worked out special treatises for this classical work but the first volume contains:

1) As a history of the origin of the journey, pp. I–XXVIII of the introduction, a substantial part of my report on this memorable journey in Volume IX of the *Beiträge zur Kenntniss des Russ. Reiches*, Section 2, which had not been published then.

2) This also contains the latest reports on the northernmost regions of Siberia. From the *Beiträge z. K. d. Russ. R.*, Vol. IV (cf. above IV, c, 8).

3) Furthermore there is in the text, pp. 53–65, my article "Ueber das Klima des Taimyrlandes" (above III, d, 11) newly checked with the original observations by W. von Middendorff.

8. *Izsledovaniya o sostoyaniya rybolovstva v Rossii*. published by the Ministry of Imperial Domains. SPb. 1860, 4°.

After I had finished the travels on and around the Caspian Sea and had written the last general reports, I requested the Ministry of Imperial Domains to put a sum at my disposal for having the drawings of fishing gear, which had been made during the journey and had been executed very accurately by the draftsman Nikitin, engraved in stone; the sum was also to suffice for publishing several maps, which I had received of river courses, lakes, etc., with various communications, pictures and descriptions of fishes and other not as yet completely elaborated material. The Ministry of Imperial Domains, which at the time of my travels had passed from General Count Kiselev to General N. Murav'ev, preferred to arrange the publication not only of my past investigations of fisheries, but also of the future ones, in its own name. Without a reply to my request, I learned from the newspapers that the Emperor had granted a much larger sum than I had requested, and I was asked by word of mouth what else I could provide. I could not agree to this since, for one thing, I had to have money at my disposal, e.g., to combine several maps and have them changed to the same scale, to have drawings made, etc.; on the other hand the material could not be elaborated at such speed because I had resumed my function at the Academy. Besides, editions that do not bear the author's name but are published by an authority are never secure from arbitrary changes or additions. After his return from Sitka, Admiral Wrangel had to suppress the edition of his report on the journey to the Arctic Ocean, which the Admiralty had already begun, because he found changes; he therefore entrusted the Russian original of his work to a publisher. The Minister naturally charges an official with the editing, but his name does not appear anywhere and he is thus undiscoverable. Any changes, therefore, depend solely on the opinion of such an editor. Thus I found in the first volume of this edition, which contains reports on the journeys to Lake Peipus and the Baltic coast, quite a wrong explanation of the shape of a net. I had chosen to give local names everywhere in order to promote understanding at the places most immediately concerned, and thus I also used the word "Kleshchitsy" on occasion; this I found explained as follows "t.e. bol'shie zimie nevoda" (i.e., large winter seines). This is completely wrong. Kleshchitsy are fixed nets, three-sided ones, with not very large mesh in the slack middle panel and much larger mesh in the front and rear net. When a large fish endeavors to pass through this three-sided net it pushes part of the central slack net through the last taut net in the shape of a bag, whereupon it can move neither forward nor backward. However, nevod is a seine. The Russian language makes an exact distinction between fixed nets and seines. Furthermore, I saw the Kleshchitsy used in summer only. Since the Kleshchitsy are described correctly in a later section of the same book, on p. 73, it made me look as though I did not know what they are. I wrote my reports from Lake Peipus, like the later ones, in German, but the translation of the first report was made by one of my companions whose knowledge of the Russian language was not very good at that time. It was therefore natural that the reports were subjected to language revision. But it seems to me that this revision should have been carried out under my instruction and control. The corrector of the terms thought, however, that he had to explain some things which were incomprehensible to him. It is always dangerous to attempt to explain what one does not understand! The reports from the Caspian Sea were translated by Herr Danilevskii, who is completely fluent in both languages and who also knows fisheries very well. I did not find any changes or additions in this translation.

The following reports written by me are contained in the quoted work:

In the first volume (Vol. I) there are six, mostly brief reports concerning fishing in Lake Peipus and on the coasts of the Baltic Sea. A seventh report deals with the journey to the Åland Islands and Sweden. *Life*, pp. 285–287. Then there follows a project of the police regulation of the Peipus fishery, with an earlier reasoning in favor of the proposals. Then follow articles not written by me. A map shows the district through which I traveled and the location of the places mentioned in the report.

The second, larger volume consists, with the exception of three appendices, exclusively of my reports on fishery in the Caspian Sea. Two maps are included: one of the fishing districts on the lower Volga and the adjacent regions of the sea; the other shows the Russian fishing districts in the southern half of the Caspian Sea and in the Kura.

The reproductions of the fishing gear are published separately in broadside folio under the title:

Risunki k izsledovaniyu Kaspiiskago rybolovstva, published by the Ministry of Imperial Domains, 1861.

The map contains eighty-six very cleanly executed sheets. I intended to publish this collection of illustrations with a continuous comparison of the only similar work by Duhamel du Monceau as commentary. However, since the Ministry of Imperial Domains undertook to publish it independently, I could not interfere.

9. *Description ethnographique des peuples de la Russie par T. de Pauly. Publié a l'occasion du jubilé millenaire de l'Empire de Russie.* St.-Pétersb. 1862. Royal folio with sixty-two colored plates.

Monsieur de Pauly had prepared the above-mentioned magnificent work, written in French, for the jubilee with which the thousand years of existence of the Russian Empire were to be and were celebrated in 1862. When I heard about the work and saw the many elegantly executed illustrations, I took part in it all the more, since I had several times proposed a new ethnographic investigation of the various nations of the Russian Empire. The illustrations were made partly from material which had been unused and was kept at the Geographical Society, partly from new drawings made for this purpose, and partly from older drawings. I received the offer to make a complete revision of the text which had been predominantly prepared by Herr von Erckert. But

I was too occupied by other work at the time to be able to study all the available material, as this would certainly have taken longer than a year. I was able to read only a very small part but it seemed to me that not a little effort had been expended. Although a complete representation of this kind would require a lifetime's work, and would require additional travels in order to represent the current state of affairs correctly, the whole work seemed to fulfill an urgent requirement and could serve as the basis for future presentations. I thus did not object to writing a foreword as introduction, which dealt in particular with previous undertakings of this kind by way of comparison. I suggested to the author, who is also the editor and publisher, that he make a special reprinting in octavo without the costly colored illustrations. The book, which is very expensive in its royal folio edition, could then be taken, or even parts of it could, by any travelers on their journeys, and additions or possibly necessary corrections could thus be made. However, this proposition was not accepted. It still seems to me, even now, that the Imperial Russian Geographic Society would do well to arrange for such a printing, and to come to an agreement on this matter with the author. I also contributed to the work with a selection of characteristic skull shapes of the peoples of the Russian Empire. It is so well-executed from photographs that I regret that it will be little known to anthropologists due to the high price of the work.

10. Eine Anrede an die Universität Dorpat, bei Gelegenheit ihrer 50 jährigen Jubelfeier im Jahre 1852, im Namen der Akademie der Wissenschaften gesprochen, is contained in the work: *Das zweite Jubelfest der Kaiserl. Universität Dorpat*. 1852. 4°, pp. X and XI.

11. An article by me: Ueber die frühesten Zustände des Menschen in Europa, 39 Seiten mit einigen Polytypagen, is contained in the (St. Petersburgischer) *Kalender* for the year 1864. 8°.

This was also translated into Russian in the Russian edition of the same Calendar under the title:

O pervonachal'nom sostoyanii cheloveka v Evrope.

The purpose of directing attention in Russia to the oldest remains of human industry, and thus to arouse interest in mankind's earliest conditions, seems to have been achieved better with this article than with the articles in the publications of the Academy. But many years will still pass before participation will be general enough for every find to be used scientifically. The working class does not lack interest in antiquity, but when digging up old grave mounds, the workers look first of all for treasures which can be converted to cash. If every stone tool and every piece of bronze were paid for, stored, and mainly, if the places of the finds were thoroughly investigated, Russia's soil could still yield important knowledge concerning the earliest migrations.

12. I edited:

1. *Vorträge aus dem Gebiete der Naturwissenschaften und der Oekonomie, gehaltten in der physikalisch-ökonomischen Gesellschaft in Königsberg*. First

volume with lectures by Argelander, Baer, Bujack, Dr. Dulk, M.H. Jacobi, Ernst Meyer, C. Moser. Kön. 1834. 8°.

For what is written by me and contained in this work, cf. above under II, i.

Jointly with M. von Helmersen:

2. *Beiträge zur Kenntniss des Russischen Reiches und der angränzenden Länder Asiens*, of which twenty-three volumes have appeared but Vol. XVI is still unpublished.

Whatever was written by me in this collection is quoted in detail above under IV, c. The later volumes were almost exclusively edited by v. Helmersen and much was written by him.

I also arranged the editing of fascicles 3–5 of the *Icones ad Faunam Rossico-Asiaticum aut*. P.S. Pallas. But these contain no text. It was assumed that every owner of the text would be able to insert the illustrations in the appropriate place.

VI. Critical Reviews

a. Unofficial reviews.

The reviews of the following books belong among them:

1. *Lühhikenne Oeppetus Estima Tallorahwa Aemmadelle.* Tallinnas 1812. IV and 96 pages in 8°. (Short instructions for the midwives of the Estonian country people.) Published anonymously in 1814 in: *Russische Sammlung für Naturwissenschaft und Heilkunde,* edited by Dr. A. Crichton, Dr. J. Rehmann and Dr. R.F. Burdach, Vol. I, No. 1.

Burdach requested this review. I did not otherwise suffer from the temptations of premature reviews. *Life,* p. 104.

2. Dr. F.A.L. Thienemann: *Naturhistorische Bemerkungen, gesammelt auf einer Reise im Norden von Europa. 1. Abtheilung. Säugethiere, mit 22 illuminirten und schwarzen Kupfertafeln. Jen. Lit. Zeit.* 1824, No. 186.

3. Friedr. Tiedemann: *Tabulae nervorum uteri. Jen. Lit. Zeit.* 1824, No. 188.

4. Goldfuss: *Naturhistorischer Atlas.* Royal-Folio (without year). Same author: *Ausführliche Erläuterungen des naturhistorischen Atlasses.* 1824. 4°. *Jen. Lit. Zeit.* 1825, No. 28.

5. Meissner: *Systematisches Verzeichnis der Vögel, welche im Museum der Stadt Bern aufgestellt sind. Jen. Lit. Zeit.* 1825, No. 115.

6. Baron And. de Férussac: *Histoire naturelle et particulaire des mollusques terrestres et fluviatiles.* Books 1–21. Folio *Jen. Lit. Zeit.* 1825, No. 139.

7. Ch. Ludw. Brehm: *Lehrbuch der Naturgeschichte aller Europäischen Vögel.* Two Parts. 1823 and 1824. 8°. *Jen. Lit. Zeit.* 1825, No. 184.

8. Joh. Friedr. Naumann: *Ueber den Haushalt der nordischen Seevögel Europas, mit 2 colorirten Ansichten.* Broadside folio. *Jen. Lit. Zeit.* 1826, No. 43.

9. William Scoresby's des *Jüngern Tagebuch einer Reise auf den Wallfischfang,* bound with *Untersuchungen und Entdeckungen an der Ostküste von Grönland.* Translated from English by Kries. 1825, 8°. 414 pp. *Jen. Lit. Zeit.* 1827, No. 237.

All reviews in the *Jen. Lit. Zeitung* are signed *r, but the subsequent ones in the yearbooks for scientific reviews are signed with full name, according to the regulations of this institute.

10. Serres: *Anatomie comparée du cerveau dans les quatre classes des animaux vertébrés, appliquée à la physiologie et à la pathologie du système*

nerveux. Two volumes. 4°. With sixteen plates. Paris 1824 and 1826. *Jahrb. für wissenschaftliche Kritik*. 1828. pp. 621–648.

11. Pallas: *Zoographia Rosso-Asiatica*.

Reports on the *Zoographia Rosso-Asiatica* by Pallas, provided to the Imperial Academy of Sciences. *Jahrb. für wissensch. Kritik*. Dec. 1834. Nos. 111, 112 and 113 of the second volume.

b. Official reviews.

A member of the St. Petersburg Academy often has occasion to write official reviews. In doing that, one loses the inclination for other reviews; as I noticed in my own case, the voluntary reviews cease as soon as one enters the Academy.

Of the official reviews the clearly disapproving ones are not printed. It is usually left to the secretary of the Academy to decide which of the partly or decidedly favorable ones are to be printed. However, it has been the custom since 1832 that all the reviews of works presented for the contests of the Demidov Award are printed annually, collected in a small volume, if they won a prize or even only a public commendation. Therefore, the decidedly disapproving reviews are excluded here, too. These volumes have the title: *Prisuzhdeniya uchrezhdennykh P. N. Demidovym nagrad*; they are numbered according to the number of the contests as 1-oe, 2-oe, etc. I cite them as *Dem. nagrady* with the year of the prize award, but the prize award is based on the competition of the previous year.

I find the following of these reviews printed and signed by me; however, they were not all written by me:

1. Zur Fauna der Krym: a contribution of Dr. H. Rathke. With Brandt. *Bull. sc*. I, No. 2, p. 16.

2. Uebersicht des Katunnischen Gebirges, by Herr Privy Councilor Gebler. With Brandt. *Bull. sc*. I, No. 13, pp. 102–104; No. 14, pp. 110–111.

3. Die Forstinsecten, oder Abbildung und Beschreibung der in den Wäldern Preussens und der Nachbarstaaten als schädlich oder nützlich bekannt gewordenen Insecten, by J. Ch. Th. Ratzeburg. *Bull. sc*. III, pp. 244–247.

4. *Anatomia chirurgica truncorum arteriarum atque fasciarum fibrosarum*, by Nicolao Pirogoff, professor at Dorpat. Reval, 1839 with 51 plates. With Zagorski and Brandt. *Bull. sc*., Vol. IX. Suppl. I, p. 3.

5. Prof. Nordmanns Monographie des *Tergipus Edwardsii*. With Brandt. *Bull. physico-math*., Vol. III, pp. 269–272.

6. Anatomie und Physiologie des Fischnervensystems by Dr. O.S.C. Girgensohn with 15 plates. With Brandt. *Bull. physico-math*., Vol. III, pp. 347–349.

7. Nicol. Pirogoff: *Anatome topographica sectionibus per corpus huma-*

num congelatum triplici directione ductis illustrata. Petrop. 1859, Vol. 8. With lithographed plates in large folio. *Bull. de l'Acad.*, Vol. II, pp. 396–404. Also Dem. nagrady. 1860.

8. Ueber das handschriftliche Werk des Herrn Dr. Knoch über den *Bothriocephalus latus. Bull. de l'Acad.*, Vol. III, pp. 521 and 522.

9. Faldermann: *Additamenta ad faunam Rossicam.* Vol. I, 4°. With Brandt Demid. nagr. 1837.

10. Göbel: *Reisen in die Steppen des südlichen Russlands.* 2 Vols. 4°. With Hess, Lenz und Bongard. Demid. nagr. 1838.

11. Faldermann: *Additamenta ad faunam Rossicam.* Vols. 2 and 3. (Also under the title *Fauna entomologica Transcaucasica.*) With Brandt. Demid. nagr. 1839.

12. Stuckenberg: *Beschreibung aller im Russischen Reiche gegrabenen schiff- und flossbaren Canäle.* With Koeppen. Demid. nagr. 1841.

13. *Fiziologiya,* published as a guide for the students by Aleks. Filomaoitskim. Moskv. 3 parts. 8°. With Brandt. Dem. Nagr. 1841.

14. Kratkaya zootomiya ili rukovodstvo k poznaniyu stroeniya tela domashnykh zhivotnykh. Works of Kikina. With Brandt. Dem. Nagr. 1841.

15. Kruse: *Necrolivonica.* 4°. A small appendix to the complete critique by Napiersky. Dem. Nagr. 1842.

16. *Puteshestvie po severnym beregam Sibiri i po Ledovitomu Moryu. Works of Rear Admiral Wrangell.* Dem. Nagr. 1842.

17. Stuckenberg: *Hydrographie des Russischen Reiches.* Vols. 1 and 2. 8°. A special critique along with that of Koeppen. Dem. Nagr. 1843.

18. *Polnoi kurs prikladnoi anatomii chelovecheskago tela.* N. Pirogov. With Brandt. Dem. Nagr. 1844.

19. Adelung: *Kritisch-literärische Uebersicht aller Reisen der Ausländer in Russland bis zum Jahre 1700.* Dem. Nagr. 1845.

20. *Antropologiya ili kratkoe rukovodstvo k poznaniyu zhizennykh otpravlenii chelovecheskago organizma.* Works of Dokt. Bredov. 8°. With Brandt. Dem. Nagr. 1846.

21. Anatole de Démidoff: *Voyage dans la Russie méridionale et la Crimée.* 4°. Vol. 8. With atlas. With Brandt, Helmersen and Middendorff. Dem. Nagr. 1847.

22. *Patologicheskaya anatomiya aziatskoi kholery* N. Pirogov. 8°. With atlas. 1849 and 1850. In addition to a detailed review by Professor von Samson. Dem. Nagr. 1851.

23. *Gidrograficheskoe opisanie severnago berega Rossii* by Lieutenant-Captain Reineke. 4°. In addition to special expert opinion by W. Struve. Dem. Nagr. 1851.

24. *Kratkii ocherk fiziologii cheloveka i drugikh zhivotnykh.* Works of Zholkevicha. Special vote. Dem. Nagr. 1851.

25. *Monografiya vrachebnykh piyavok Voskresenskago.* Dem. Nagr. 1860.

26. Prof. Dr. Schmidt: *Die Wasserversorgung Dorpats, eine hydrologische Untersuchung.* With Helmersen. Dem. Nagr. 1864.

27. *Samoproizvol'noe razmnozhenie gusenits u nasekomikh,* Professor Wagner. Kazan'. Folio with Brandt and Owsiannikow. Dem. Nagr. 1864.

VII. Occasional Printed Works, not Intended for General Distribution

It may seem doubtful whether these works should be cited here at all. However, since one or the other my happen to fall into the hands of a bibliographer, and their number is not large, I quote them here:

1. *Fragen über das Vorkommen einiger Thiere in Preussen und in dem Regierungsbezirke Posen.* Folio. One sheet. 1826.

These questions (*Fragen*) were distributed among the head foresters and other friends of natural history in Prussia. Many replies were received.

2. *Ordo systematicus bibliothecae Academiae Imp. scientiarum Petropolitanae.* (1838.) 8°.

Provided with a new title in 1843. Review of the systematic classification according to which I rearranged the books. Intended only for the use of the library and members of the Academy.

3. *Materialien zur Kenntniss des unvergänglichen Boden-Eises in Sibirien,* collected by K.E. von Baer.

When Herr von Middendorff was to travel to Siberia, I collected all the reports I could find on the permanent or at least long-lasting soil ice in Siberia and adjacent countries, as well as in North America; however, I lost myself in this activity to such an extent that, although 218 pages of the work were already printed, which were to serve von Middendorff as a guideline, those concerning relevant places were not prepared and there was no end in sight when von Middendorff prepared for his departure. I gave the traveler what had been printed, but I did not feel like continuing because the article, destined for the fourth volume of the *Contributions*, was too bulky and seemed to me to have entirely too little content. For there were no really special data to be found in all the observations. The general treatment could be expected from Middendorff's travel works, and that was sufficient.

4. *Praelectiones histiologicae.* 4°.

For my students at the Medico-Surgical Academy in 1847 or 1848 I had a compressed review of histology in Latin printed in four sheets in quarto at my expense, and I added several lithograph plates. They were not for sale because they contained little that was original. But the expression histological elements instead of "cells" was retained for histological peculiarities and an attempt was made to give the reasons.

VIII. Articles Intended for Publication but Not Printed

I really cannot say whether the previous section should be in a bibliographical list, but I know well enough that this last section does not belong in it. However, it contains some contributions to the biography, albeit not particularly important ones. Now, since I remembered various things while inspecting papers and printed works which I have kept, I have collected the following notes about intended but not realized publications that I do not wish to keep back now, partly to relate some small occurrences, partly to heap blame upon myself.

1. For instance, I find four printed sheets of a work on the artificial and natural classification of plants and animals; I undertook as early as 1819, i.e., in the second year of my employment, to publish the work at my own expense since I could not find a publisher, but I was soon convinced that such an undertaking was beyond my financial powers. The next impetus for this was the small work by Professor Goldfuss: *Ueber die Entwickelungsstufen des Thiers*, accompanied by an illustration in which the relationships between animals were compressed into the shape of an egg. Such regularly schematized representations were not at all to my taste and seemed to me to be trifling. Oken also had aroused my opposition in this manner with his regular four-stage classification. I showed that there is really an Arthropod in the egg shell, for the side groups are in relation to the center group but not to the subsequent side groups. In general, however, I endeavored to emphasize the principles of a natural classification individually and to give reasons for it. Thus separate sections deal with the implementation of the following propositions: 1) The relationship between animals can be judged only by the overall structure, not by individual organs of the body or individual manifestations of life. 2) It cannot be expressed by constructing a simple straight line. 3) A natural zoological system cannot assume a completely regular form, etc. On the whole there was an intimation of the difference between the positioning of the parts (type of organization) and the degree of organic development, which I tried to make clear in the last section of the "Beiträge zur Kenntniss der niedern Thiere." But it is all rather more of a soliloquy than the result of final views, and it thus became an economically palpable lesson that one must not publish too soon, least of all at one's own expense, and especially if one has a prosector's salary of 300 Thalers and half that in other income—and thus I broke it off. *Life*, p. 209.

2. I had progressed farther and was engrossed in the most assiduous study of Zoology, when, in 1824, the Landes-Industrie-Comptoir in Weimar announced a *Dictionary of Natural History, Suited to the Present State of Mineralogy, Botany and Zoology.* There was no lack of praise, which partly preceded and partly followed immediately after the publication of the first part. I remember having read that this work would show what German industriousness can achieve. I therefore fell voraciously upon the first half of the first volume when it came to Königsberg, and there I awaited the fruit of the joint labor of many German scientists. But how disappointed I was! I found mostly translations from the *Dictionnaire classique,* often also wrong and hasty ones, so that sometimes the exact opposite of what should have been said was said, even about the best-known subjects. Under *Ancylodon,* after the teeth at the tip of the upper jaw have been discussed, it states, for instance, that "the other parts of the pharynx are provided with teeth as in the narwhal," whereas the entry should have read "are, as in the narwhal, not provided with teeth." This could have been a printing error, but it was certainly no printing error that the article *"Animal"* stated that the dictionary was based on Schweigger's arrangement of the lower animal classes. Since I was very well acquainted with Schweigger's works, I immediately looked up *"Acetabularia"* and found that this article, too, was translated from the *Dict. classique,* and it stated with certainty the existence of polyps, although Schweigger, who had found the *Acetabularia* to be green, had declared it to be a plant. Thus I found everywhere that the *Dict. classique* had been closely followed even if an article was merely mentioned. But I was really amazed when I noticed that the translator, through an error which I find completely incomprehensible, reduced French measurement everywhere to one-tenth of its real size and that he did not even notice that he moved exclusively among pygmies. For instance, it states about the *Adeona,* which is illustrated life size in Schweigger's *"Untersuchungen"*: "it attains the size of several inches," because the *Dict. classique* says it has "deux à trois décimètres." This happened not only here but in all the other articles about corals. In really moral indignation over such contempt for the public, I wrote an acid review. As soon as I had written it, however, it seemed to be ignoble of me to attack in such a way a book of which much had been expected. Perhaps Froriep, who was very busy, did not even look through it and could perhaps be prevailed upon to suppress the first part and replace it with a better edition. I therefore sent my remarks to Froriep. He thanked me, saying how sad it was that one was often so badly served in spite of the greatest goodwill; he added that this undertaking had already cost him thousands, but he did not suppress the first batch; he only had a large number of correction sheets printed. He may have changed the editor, but I did not even want to look at the subsequent parts. The entire undertaking advanced only just to over half the alphabet, and it probably did the entrepreneur as much damage as the customers. If I had printed my review as

I wrote it and as it still lies here, I might have held back at least a few customers. But the reviewer, named or unnamed, would nevertheless have been considered a malicious person. In reality no harm would have been done.

3. Another review, written nine years later, did not reach the public either. However, it consisted only of six to nine lines and was directed against Merten's contributions on the knowledge of the fetal membranes in the bird egg; this was published in *Meckels Archiv*, 1830. According to this article there is the greatest analogy in both layers of the yolk membrane with the transient membrane, and they are really named decidua externa and interna, although the embryo with the amnion lies between them! There was not a trace of the investigations by C.F. Wolff or Pander. I remarked that Meckel should either write a denial himself or let someone else write it to save his honor. He preferred to terminate the *Archiv* with the incomplete volume for 1832, leaving out the year 1831.

4. I now sincerely regret that a large volume of a work of mine, the anatomy of the *Delphinus Phocaena*, remained unprinted. The pictures had all been made, the observations especially written down, partly edited and ready for the fair copy, when I began to have doubts; the observations from different years coincided in general but they did not coincide for individual sections of the musculature and the special vascular distribution, or even with regard to the breast bone. Now I consider these doubts too scrupulous; however, by now the work is too obsolete. My regrets here are toward myself, not with regard to science. Science continues to grow, even if we are not there, and is stopped from growing only when great discoveries escape it, as happened, for instance, when the realization of the mechanical equivalent of heat was delayed by several decades. As regards the matter of the porpoise, there life itself has its say, too.

5. The last-mentioned suppression was brought on by myself. The memory of another one, of which I was innocent, has always been very amusing to me because it shows how easily conservative thinking leads to infallibility, and no more was lost in the process than a few hours vainly spent at the desk. A few days after my transfer to St. Petersburg there appeared in the *Supplément* to the *Journal de St. Pétersbourg* an article on the aurochs which was extremely antiquated. The Lithuanian aurochs was still the stock race of domestic cattle, etc. Since I had just busied myself with this subject, I expressed astonishment to the secretary of the Academy, P. Fuss, at the fact that articles of this kind, written by persons not conversant with the subject in question, are accepted by the better journals. Fuss asked me to draft an article on the subject in the spirit of the latest knowledge acquired. He would arrange its acceptance. I drafted such an article without any polemics, but it did not appear, nor was it returned to me and thus there was nothing to prevent it from appearing elsewhere. The *Journal de St. Pétersbourg* receives official communications in which, of course, nothing must be altered. Now it

had also declared itself infallible in its own creations. Later I made the acquaintance of the editor of the *Supplément* and found him to be a witty man, very well versed in matters of political science; he knew nothing whatever about natural sciences but now and then had to enter this field, and on such occasions he became infallible.

6. Finally I should mention the article, mentioned in the note on p. 267, dealing with the cell theory; having been kept too long in order to be printed in a special place, it became antiquated in view of the development of this theory. At the time of its birth it would have been timely.

With this I take my leave of the friendly reader; for if I wanted to add a section on the printed articles which could have remained unprinted, the undertaking would lead us too far afield. It is time to conclude.

Name Index

Editor's Note: The original work did not contain a name or subject index. These indices have been added to the translation. The indexer experienced some difficulties in establishing them, stemming from the lack of a systematic basis in the original text.

Subject Index

388